Respectfully dedicated to all University of Notre Dame athletes past, present and future

Rockne of Ages

Jeffrey G. Harrell

Rockne materials and photos compiled by:
John Davenport

Rochelle Day / Layout & Design
Georges Toumayan / Webmaster

Richard T. Ryan / Editor
Dr. Len Clark / Editor
Courtney McDermott / Editor

Published in the United States by Mato Enterprises, LLC,
of South Bend, Indiana.
spiritofknute.com
Rockne of Ages and spiritofknute.com are registered trademarks of
Mato Enterprises, LLC.

All photography has been credited in the Photo Index at the end of the book.

*Library of Congress Cataloging-in-Publication Data is available upon request.
ISBN 978-1-194-2500-704

PRINTED IN THE UNITED STATES OF AMERICA
Book design by Rochelle Day
Jacket design by Rochelle Day & Georges Toumayan
Jacket Photograph: Portrait of Knute Rockne, 1930 (Davenport Collection)

First Edition: May 2020

CONTENTS

Just as in Rockne's time ...

Author Introduction

Knute Rockne was an amazing man.

Knute (Ka-noot) Rockne, the Norwegian immigrant and part-time chemistry professor who shaped the game of football as a player and a coach at the University of Notre Dame in the early 20th century like no other coach in sports history.

In fact, let's declare November 1, 1913 as the birthday of modern football.

On that day, at The Plain at West Point, N.Y., the passing combination of Gus Dorais-to-Knute Rockne led Notre Dame to a thorough thrashing of powerful Army, 35-13. Never before had a crowd been left slack-jawed and giddy over the freshness of watching a football being tossed up and down the field with such thrilling flair.

Rockne had few peers, if any, as a coach. An .881 all-time winning percentage in 13 seasons sets Rockne atop college football history. Modern strategies, tactics and organizational approaches to conducting practices still bear Rockne's indelible coaching imprint.

He wrote three books — "Coaching," a widely-distributed manual; "Four Winners," a novel; and "Coaching Problems." Rockne also penned a syndicated column for the Notre Dame publication "Campus Comment," and he turned out numerous articles for "Collier's" and other prominent magazines. Some of his articles were reproduced in the "Autobiography of Knute Rockne" that his widow, Bonnie Skiles Rockne, published not long after his death.

Those articles lay scattered and forgotten for decades. Today, the Notre Dame faithful may see his statue outside the North Gate and absorb the immortal spirit of the coach who built

9

Notre Dame Stadium, but most passersby see only a statue. Too many biographical attempts to bring Rockne up to date over the years has petrified into the same life story with a different author's name.

No one has bothered to explore Rockne's death.

"Rockne of Ages" picks up less than a year before Knute Rockne's extraordinary life ended in a Kansas pasture at about 10:45 a.m. on March 31, 1931.

Pieced together from a treasure trove of time-period references, including more than 100 time-period newspaper articles and the U.S. Department of Commerce's official crash investigation report, "Rockne of Ages" shines a long overdue light on the story of Notre Dame priest Father John Reynolds.

This book's mission is to uncover the long-lost details that surrounded the epic Rockne plane crash before history swept it under the rug as a tragic accident. Our aim is to present the story through documented and tape-recorded eyewitness accounts, such as Father Reynolds — whose voice is heard on tape saying he gave his plane ticket to Rockne.

Our hope is to resurrect the spirit of Knute Rockne by leaving his life story to the one person who knows better than anybody: Knute Rockne. The section "Rockne on Rockne" lets Rockne breathe in a posthumous autobiography that is directed toward every coach on every level to read, explore, analyze and use as a textbook to revisit the game's fundamental foundation. That's the voice of Rockne in "Rockne on Rockne," no rehashed biographer's version necessary.

The game of college football shaped so significantly by Knute Rockne enjoys unprecedented popularity and success in our time. Just as in Rockne's time, it also faces serious challenges and criticisms — from health and safety questions to controversy over the role of the student-athlete, an issue that Rockne addresses directly in Chapter 25.

We hope this full presentation of Rockne's voice will enrich our appreciation of the game's past, deepen our enjoyment of how it is played now, and contribute to our consideration of how it should advance into the future.

Jeffrey G. Harrell, South Bend, Indiana

INTRODUCTION

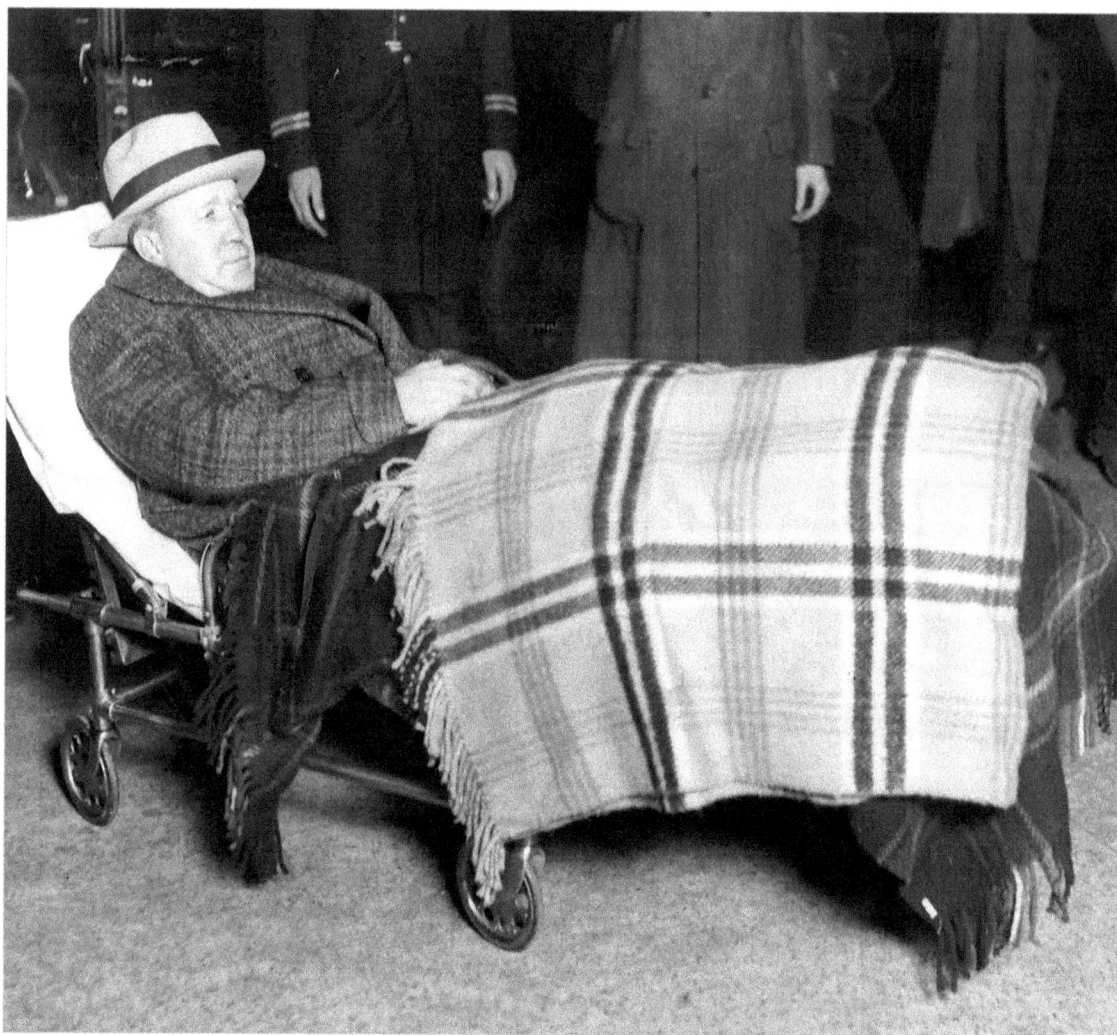

"Why do you think I'm taking a chance like this? To see you lose?"

Prologue

Knute Rockne was beat up.

Going into the 1930 season, his 13th as head coach of the University of Notre Dame, Rockne's worn-out body moved delicately on a pair of wobbly legs nearly crippled by phlebitis.

Twelve grueling years racing non-stop around the clock coaching the best college football team in the land had finally caught up with the legend in his own time. No coach, not Glenn "Pop" Warner, not Amos Alonzo Stagg, not even Walter Camp, who was widely considered to be the most important figure in the earliest development of American football, worked as tirelessly as Rockne to build the game for the future.

It was Rockne who had perfected the forward pass. It was Rockne who had devised the pre-snap shift. It was Rockne who had installed the first complex passing system to complement the running game. It was Rockne who not only shaped the modern ball, but designed it with laces and a valve to regulate air pressure so it fit comfortably in the quarterback's hand for passing.

Rockne built the Notre Dame Fighting Irish football team into a national institution and singlehandedly sold the college football game to an entire nation. Rockne designed and built the 54,000-seat football mecca known as Notre Dame Stadium, a college football hub that has since been expanded several times and now holds more than 80,000 fans.

There was Babe Ruth...and there was Knute Rockne.

All the other superstars of the '20s — Red Grange, Jack Dempsey, even presidents Warren

At practice, Rockne sat in the backseat of a car and shouted out instructions over a public address system.

G. Harding and Herbert Hoover — paled in their larger-than-life shadows. And not even the mighty Ruth could match the visionary intellect of Rockne.

There weren't enough hours in the year to keep up with Rockne's grueling schedule. He oversaw the business end of his own line of sporting goods, including his new streamlined football, which was sold nationally through Wilson Sporting Goods. He was the face of the Studebaker Corp., traveling relentlessly to cities across the country, motivating the South Bend-based automobile manufacturer's sales forces with the same charismatic flair he used to fire up his teams.

The pay from Studebaker, $10,000, far outweighed the $125-per-20-minute-talk fee Rockne had received from the Leigh-Emmerich lecture firm in New York. But with the higher salary came a relentless travel schedule that took Rockne from coast to coast all winter long from 1928 into 1929, and stretched into football season.

When the National Association of Finance Companies contacted Rockne to address its annual convention in 1929, Rockne did not respond, prompting the NAFC to ask Studebaker President Albert Erskine to intercede and persuade the Notre Dame coach to appear. Erskine also headed up Notre Dame's lay board of trustees and was a prominent patron of the university — and to its' head football coach.

Erskine forwarded the association's letter to Rockne with an appended note: "Dear Rock. It's worth $300 if you want it." Rockne took the money and made the trip to Chicago to speak to the convention.

PROLOGUE

In addition to a relentless lecture circuit, Rockne also entertained frequent offers to work in Hollywood on movies. At 42, however, Rockne's health had deteriorated severely; the Notre Dame football coach was in danger of dropping dead on the spot.

The previous season had been hell on Rockne. Having all four wisdom teeth pulled at the same time exacerbated a series of nagging ailments. Then, immediately after the Fighting Irish shut down Indiana 14-0 in the 1929 opener, Rockne was forced to his bed with a serious illness that threatened to keep him from traveling with the team to Baltimore for an important matchup against rival Navy.

That week Rockne lay in bed perusing the book "Gray's Anatomy," it hit him what might have knocked him down. "Doc," Rockne said in a phone call to his personal physician Dr. C.J. Barborka, "I think I have phlebitis."

Only Rockne could have diagnosed himself with such a complicated and debilitating attack on his body. Graduating from Notre Dame in 1914, Rockne had every intention of moving to St. Louis to study medicine and pay his way through St. Louis University Medical School coaching football on the side. But when St. Louis Medical School administrators insisted his plate would be filled with a med student's curriculum that would leave little time for extra hours to coach football, Rockne decided his best interests would be served by remaining in South Bend.

Dr. Barborka agreed with Rockne's assessment. Thrombophlebitis, an inflammation of the veins in his legs, would keep Rockne bedridden. The doctor also advised Rockne to rest quietly and stay calm. Excitement could cause a blood clot in his legs to dislodge and launch into his blood stream, creating the potential for a fatal heart attack or stroke.

But the Norway-born Rockne was the legendary "Rock," tough as leather, fiercely competitive, the unequivocal Viking of college football coaches. "Can't" was not in his vocabulary. Not even a life-threatening condition could keep him away for the game against Carnegie Tech, a middle-of-the-road group that had embarrassed Rockne's Fighting Irish the previous year in Notre Dame's final game at old Cartier Field — the only loss the Fighting Irish suffered in the 23-year history of Cartier Field.

In the locker room under Pittsburgh's Forbes Field before the game, the door flew open and interim coach Tom Lieb burst in to stun Rockne's Ramblers with Rockne in his arms. Team physician Dr. Maurice Kelly stood awestruck and shocked in a corner.

"If he lets go," Dr. Kelly said to a man next to him, "and that clot dislodges to his heart or to his brain, he's got an even-chance of never leaving this dressing room alive."

Rockne stood in the middle of the locker room surrounded by his team. As he began to speak to his players in a quiet, determined tone, his voice grew louder and clearer as if each word were a sail catching the tail wind of an ocean squall.

"A lot of water has gone under the bridge since I first came to Notre Dame, but I don't know if I've ever wanted to win a game as badly as this one," Rockne pleaded in his demanding metallic, nasal call to arms that could drive a group of men into a fiery inferno with no thought other than coming out wet with victory.

"I don't care what happens after today. Why do you think I'm taking a chance like this? To see you lose? They'll be primed. They'll be tough. They think they have your number. Are you going to let it happen again?"

Each member of the team hung on every word as if it were Rockne's last.

"We will probably win the toss. I want you in run down the field and tackle them and go on the defensive. Stop them dead and take the heart out of them! You men in the backfield, be alert, heads up, smart; look for that ball when they throw a pass, and when they do, go in and get the ball.

"I want you to block as you never blocked before; I want you to do as well, as hard, as me-chanically perfect as you can think of. And the quarterback thinks clearly and calls the right play. And you men, all eleven of you dig those cleats in deep, get your jaws set and when you start for that goal line, drive, drive, drive!

"Go out there and crack 'em. Crack 'em. Crack 'em. Fight to live. Fight to win. Fight to live. Fight to win... win... WIN!"

They did win, in a dogfight that ended 7-0. After the game, the battered team and their ailing coach returned to South Bend.

Rockne's condition refused to subside just as stubbornly as his fierce nature refused to give in to bed rest. The rest of the season, Rockne attended the games, and coached, from a wheel-chair, traveling to other schools to play "home games" while the new Notre Dame Stadium that Rockne had fought bitterly with the school's ruling Holy Cross fathers to build was under construction.

At practice, Rockne sat in the backseat of a car and shouted out instructions over a public address system designed specifically for his weakened voice by Lou Burroughs and Albert R. Kahn, a pair of audio manufacturers whose company, Radio Engineers, serviced radio receivers in the basement of the Century Tire and Rubber Company in South Bend. Rockne dubbed the system his "electric voice," a moniker that inspired the name of the company that continues to produce microphones and PA systems today — "Electro-Voice."

Frank Leahy had dislocated his elbow during the Navy game. With family coming to the game against the University of Southern California at Soldier Field in Chicago, Leahy badly wanted to play. Besides, Leahy reasoned, "If (Rockne) could risk his life, why couldn't I play football with a dislocated elbow?"

Doctors removed Leahy's cast on orders not to do anything foolish. When he came off the practice field, Rockne got out of the car and approached Leahy with the question: "How's the elbow?"

"Couldn't be better," Leahy replied.

"In that case, let's see you flex it," Rockne commanded.

Realizing that Rockne had not been at the Navy game, Leahy figured Rockne did not know that he had injured his right elbow. He produced his left arm, moved it up and down, made motions like a baseball pitcher stretching, and won Rockne's green light to order interim Head Coach Tom Lieb to use Leahy at right tackle. Rockne probably wouldn't be at the Southern California game, anyway, Leahy assumed.

He assumed wrong.

... one of his favorite leisure activities: golf.

Leahy, predictably, re-injured his elbow during the first half of the Southern California game. He was lying on the training table at halftime when the door swung open and Rockne appeared, pale and frightfully frail in a wheelchair. Rockne tried to stand, but his legs couldn't hold him and he fell backwards. Leahy leaped off the table and stood in the doorway to watch as Rockne held up his chin as high as he could, and, in a weakened voice that barely resembled his usually-powerful staccato, launched into a speech that made the Gipper rally cry sound like idle chit-chat.

"Boys, get out there and play them hard the first five minutes," Rockne beckoned. "They'll hate it, but play them hard. Rock will be upstairs watching you. Go ahead now. Hit them hard. Win! Win! Win! That's the only reason for playing. Crack 'em! Crack 'em! I'll be watching!"

It took a trainer to hold Leahy back from jumping in line with the rest of his teammates to hit the field for the second half. When it was over, Notre Dame had beaten Southern California for its seventh straight victory of the year.

Later in the week after the Southern California game, Curly Lambeau, the founder of the Green Bay Packers who had played at Notre Dame in 1918 during Rockne's first year as head coach, approached his former mentor to see how he was doing.

"What kind of team you got?" Lambeau asked.

"Best damn team I ever had," Rockne answered. "But I can't tell them that."

"Why?" Lambeau inquired.

"They might believe me," Rockne replied.

The end of the 1929 season saw the Fighting Irish finish 9-0, their fifth undefeated season under his lead. Rockne was a national championship coach for the second time, the first one coming in 1924.

When January 1930 rolled in, Rockne flew to Florida to take a welcomed family vacation in Miami with his wife, Bonnie, and his four kids — Knute Jr., Bill, Mary Jeanne, and the youngest, Jackie.

His health, particularly his legs, remained shaky. He planned a visit with one of his former players — Charlie Bachman, who was head coach at the University of Florida — during a stopover in Jacksonville on his way to Miami. But Rockne wrote Bachman a letter saying the visit had to be delayed.

"Did not wire you to meet me at Jacksonville as I could not get out of the berth anyway," Rockne wrote. "Is there any chance for you to drop down here? We have a great plan for me to sort of vegetate. Will drive up in our car just as soon as I can travel. Have lots of football I have to go over with you..."

The Florida vacation agreed with Rockne. He returned home to South Bend before catching a flight in March to the West Coast to conduct business for Studebaker in Los Angeles. He also took time to travel to Seattle, Washington, to partake in one of his favorite leisure activities: golf.

Football would remain on hiatus when he returned to South Bend. Again, Rockne was forced to summon Dr. Barborka, who diagnosed the coach with a severe case of bronchitis. Rockne laid low for a few weeks, then caught a train to Rochester, Minnesota, where he wound up being admitted to the Mayo Clinic.

By mid-May, Rockne was back home on Notre Dame's campus. His faltering health prompted letters to Bachman and a handful of other coaching pals informing them that he needed to meet and get their advice. The meeting, he wrote, would be held at 1 p.m. on May 31, "... to discuss the problem which affects all of us very vitally."

Rockne was not only ill in May, 1930, he was too exhausted to catch his breath from a vacation. The coach was only 42 years old, but hidden underneath that rugged bald head and pug-nose prizefighter's mug was the body of a worn-out 72-year-old.

The meeting with his closest coaching confidants called for a heartfelt discussion over whether Rockne would be able to lead the Notre Dame Fighting Irish for a 13th season.

Nine days after that May 31, 1930 meeting at Notre Dame, Rockne traveled to Chicago to attend the Ninth Annual Collegiate Track and Field Championships at the University of Chicago's Stagg Field.

The field's namesake, Amos Alonzo Stagg, had served as a mentor to Rockne since the landmark Chicago football and track coach had recognized the teenager as one of the kids sucking wind under the stands after ducking out of a marathon race early. It was a good day for Rockne to take in the collegiate track championships with the coach who had served as a beloved father figure — and to discuss his health and coaching plans with one of his most revered advisors.

Just a few short miles north of the South 57th Street stadium up Lake Shore Drive, a series of events began swirling around the corner of Randolph Street and Michigan Avenue in downtown Chicago that would determine the fate of Knute Kenneth Rockne.

SECTION 1
THE HIT

... Lingle unwrapped one of the cigars he had purchased from the Sherman Hotel's kiosk ...

1

A TAIL ON JAKE LINGLE

T he loud blast of a car horn startled pedestrians in their tracks as they strolled along Randolph Street under a clear blue downtown Chicago sky during the early afternoon of June 9, 1930.

Jake Lingle left his plush residential suite at the Stevens Hotel around noon and walked a mile-and-a-half to the Tribune Tower to meet with the city editor at The Chicago Tribune. The Tribune's top street reporter was on the trail of a story surrounding a murdered body found a couple of days ago and needed to discuss rumors of a brewing gangland riff with his boss.

With business for the day concluded and now on his way to catch the 1:30 p.m. train to the horse track, Lingle unwrapped one of the cigars he had purchased from the Sherman Hotel's kiosk. He buried his head in the Daily Racing Form he had picked up from the newsstand in front of the public library and made his way south across Wacker Drive toward the suburban station of the Illinois Central Railroad at the corner of Randolph Street and Michigan Avenue.

The deafening blast of the horn about 50 feet way away startled Lingle.

"Play Hy Schneider in the third!", a booming voice shouted through the open window of a car that had rolled up on the south side of Randolph. Lingle caught the eyes of two men sitting in a roadster.

"I've got him," Lingle replied with a grin and a slight wave.

Two other men on foot suddenly appeared from the shadows of a back alley and flanked

Lingle from behind. One was tall, decked out in a gray suit with light hair showing from the bottom edge of a straw boater: He had just emerged from a public restroom where he had taken a hit of a powdery drug to relax his shaky nerves. The other was a shorter, stocky figure with black glossy hair slicked back on his head.

Lingle was oblivious. His eyes scoured the racing form for the day's potential winners. He walked four blocks to Michigan Avenue, then continued toward the subway station, head buried in the racing form. Entering the station, Lingle proceeded downstairs to the underground walkway leading to the Illinois Central suburban electric railroad in Grant Park.

The two men tailed Lingle step-for-step, hiding in plain sight. The subway station was too packed with afternoon shoppers and office workers for anyone to stand out. The two men were fixated on Lingle. They didn't as much as peek away from their target when the screeching brakes of an arriving train filled with passengers from South Bend reverberated loudly throughout the station.

Former Chicago Coroner's Physician Dr. Joseph Springer spotted his longtime friend Lingle walking a short distance away. Lingle didn't look up from his racing form. Springer saw two men walking suspiciously close to Lingle as he made his way into the underground subway station, but the doctor figured they were part of the afternoon rush.

Lingle came to a halt about 25 feet from the east exit. The dark-haired man slowed, took a few steps back, then paused at the sight of a priest stepping off the train. The priest walked toward Lingle and both men on the train platform.

Lingle looked up and spotted the priest's white collar. He smiled and waved. His eyes were hopeful a return wave from the priest would bless him with good luck later at the track.

The priest returned the nod. Lingle took it as a sign from above that it was going to be his lucky day.

It was a good day for Rockne to take in the collegiate track championships with ... a beloved father figure ...

"Jake was a dear friend of mine." — Al Capone

2
PATH OF A MOB REPORTER

Nobody ever confused Alfred "Jake" Lingle with Ernie Pyle, Grantland Rice, or even a janitor sweeping the newsroom at the Chicago Tribune.

Solidly built of medium height with curly black hair and a prominent cleft on the bottom of a moony face that emitted a self-satisfied smirk of cynical boyish charm, Lingle married his childhood sweetheart, Helen Sullivan, and the couple raised two children born a year apart, Alfred Jr. and Dolores. Lingle held true to his marriage vows. He was a faithful husband who limited his drinking to a glass or two of beer, largely because of a stomach ulcer.

The streets of Chicago were Lingle's office. A bona fide "legman" reporter with a grade school education who started at the Chicago Tribune as a 20-year-old office boy in 1912, Lingle never staked claim to a byline. He wasn't illiterate, but he had no interest in culture, and he probably never read more than a half-dozen books. When it came to writing simple English, he couldn't, which was why Lingle's name was virtually unknown to Tribune readers.

Lingle earned $65 a week working under the title of "reporter" at the Tribune, although he never typed a word, had no interest in reading writers who wrote them, and only stepped inside the building that housed the prominent Chicago Tribune newspaper to meet with an editor or collect his paycheck.

Lingle's gift was an uncanny ability to blend into the streets and back alleys of Chicago's toughest core and dig up stories from the underground whispers of a wide spectrum of sources. Everybody knew Lingle, and Lingle knew everybody — from hotel clerks, bookies, gambling

Lingle's tight bonds with Chicago police and Capone ...

house owners and bootleggers to the highest order of Chicago's power elite on both sides of the law, spanning police ranks, judges, lawyers, prosecutors and politicians, including the city's two high lords of crime, Al Capone and George "Bugs" Moran.

Instead of writing, Lingle relentlessly plied his trade on the phone. Story after story, scoop after scoop was called into the Tribune's city editor's desk then turned over to the paper's rewrite men. Jake Lingle was the Tribune's house crime expert, the paper's

golden goose, the bridge between the streets and the actual writers who turned the deepest, darkest secrets of Chicago's underworld into the light that shined from front-page headlines on the crime story of the day.

The $65-a-week Lingle pulled from the Tribune was chump change, a legitimate paycheck that kept the eyes of the IRS off the massive flow of cash he piled up moonlighting as a bagman on the payroll of Al Capone. Along with gathering street chatter to phone in to the Tribune's city editors, Lingle delivered

Lingle ... became close personal friends with Chicago Police Commissioner William Russell.

payments from Capone's Cicero headquarters to crooked politicians and judges to the tune of an estimated $60,000 a year.

Balancing enormous press clout with gangland street influence gave Lingle money to burn. He owned a Lincoln car with a chauffeur. He plunged on the stock market. He hit the horse track daily during the season in pursuit of his lone vice, gambling, sometimes laying as much as $1,000 down on a horse race but never betting less than $100.

Lingle took care of his wife and two children handsomely by providing them with a lavish apartment on Chicago's West Side. When he worked the streets, Lingle resided at the best hotels, most notably a suite of apartments at the plush Stevens Hotel on Michigan Avenue where the switchboard

One of Lingle's favorite gifts ...

Then there was Al Capone.

Lingle stood in high favor with Capone, and neither made an attempt to conceal the friendship in public. It was not unusual for Lingle to be seen hanging out at Capone's headquarters at the Hawthorne Inn in Cicero. Nor was Capone shy about welcoming Lingle into his home near Miami on several occasions. One of Lingle's favorite gifts to flaunt was a belt with a diamond-studded buckle given to him by Capone.

"A Christmas present," Capone admitted. "Jake was a dear friend of mine."

Lingle's tight relationship with Capone afforded him an open understanding to work Chicago's streets on both sides of the law — and both sides of town between Capone's South Side and Moran's North Side operations. He once bragged that his friendship with Capone had allowed him to "fix the price of beer" in Chicago.

His personal finances were top secret, however. A secret account Lingle kept with the Lake Shore Trust and Savings Bank lined his pockets with a perpetual wad of cash. Collaborating on an investment partnership with his pal, Police Commissioner William Russell — a joint securities account opened in November 1928 with a $20,000 deposit — remained as hushed as an FBI investigation.

Not that Lingle possessed keen financial vision. Had Lingle liquidated his securities at the height of a bull market in September 1929, he would have turned a profit of $85,000. Instead, he held on, and a month later Black Thursday rang in the Great Depression. Lingle's and Russell's profits evaporated, along with an additional $75,000.

Lingle showed losses of more than $200,000 on paper. But rather than lower his standard of living, the river of cash

operator had orders never to disturb him unless the caller's name appeared on the list Lingle had provided.

When he needed to get away from the city, Lingle stayed at a posh $25,000 Lake Michigan-front summer home he owned on the "Michigan Riviera" at Long Beach, Indiana. Winter vacations were spent a month at a time in Havana, Cuba, where Lingle made sure every bookmaker at the race track and every dealer at the gambling tables knew when he was in town.

He hobnobbed with millionaires. Dined at the most expensive restaurants. Smoked 50-cent cigars. Rubbed elbows with the governor of Illinois, the state's attorney general, judges, and county and city officials of Chicago's political machine. Lingle golfed, vacationed, and became close personal friends with Chicago Police Commissioner William P. Russell.

flowing in daily from his underworld business connections afforded Lingle the luxury of elevating his lifestyle with a slew of deposits into Lake Shore Trust and Savings, totaling nearly $64,000 between the end of 1929 and the spring of 1930.

The deposits, and Lingle's lavish lifestyle, were not lost on his bosses and colleagues at the Chicago Tribune, although none of his Tribune associates viewed Lingle's gangland relationships as anything other than the good cultivation of news sources. Lingle lied that his father had bequeathed him $11,000 when in fact his father left only $500 in a will. He also fibbed about the value of some of his stocks tripling during the bull market. In fact, Lingle and Russell had been wiped out. None of Lingle's Tribune colleagues was aware that he was brazenly taking loans from gamblers, politicians, businessmen, mobsters, anybody who would pay him to curry a favor using his enormous press clout.

Lingle always took the money. Rarely, if ever, did he pay anybody back.

Lingle borrowed $2,000 from Jimmy Mondi, a Capone gambling operator in Cicero and downtown in the Loop — a loan that was never repaid. Another $5,000 borrowed from Alderman Berthold A. Cronson was never paid back. Loans of $2,500 from Carlos Ames, president of the Civil Service Commission; $300 from police Lt. Thomas McFarland; $20,000 from roadhouse and gambling parlor operator Sam Hare — all suffered the same fate.

Yet Lingle continued to survive with his knees and limbs intact. His good health was much more valuable to Chicago's underworld and the city's political machine because his citywide influence generated money. Stories were "planted" in the Tribune on Capone's

Moran was the prime target ... then drove away.

behalf. Law enforcement connections were engaged to tip off Capone about impending police raids on the gangster's bootlegging and other illegal activities. Lingle could easily "put the fix in" for gamblers, bootleggers and anyone else who was having a problem with law enforcement.

Once, Lingle negotiated his position as Tribune reporter to spy for Capone on rival Bugs Moran's North Side Gang. That effort helped Capone and his crew block Moran's efforts to muscle in on Capone's territory.

Lingle's tight bonds with Chicago police and Capone put him on the right side of perhaps gangland's most prolific power play, the St. Valentine's Day Massacre.

At 10:30 a.m. on Feb. 14, 1929, seven members and associates of Moran's North Side Gang were lined up against a wall inside a garage at 2122 North Clark Street and

31

mowed down in a heavy blaze of Thompson submachine gun fire.

The four executioners were never identified. But the suspects were rumored to be former members of the Egan's Rats, a notorious organized crime gang in St. Louis named for mobster Tom Egan who co-formed what became feared as the city's worst political terrorists. All four hitmen were working on the orders of Capone with inside help from members of the Chicago Police Department avenging the killing of a police officer's son. Two of the shooters wore suits, ties, overcoats and hats, while the other two were dressed as uniformed policemen.

Moran was the prime target. Capone's main rival avoided the slaughter when he showed up at the garage early, saw nobody there, then drove away. Afterwards, Capone allowed Moran to live and continue to operate his business on the North Side as long as Capone got his cut of the action. It became crystal clear to everyone on the streets that there was only one crime boss calling the shots in Chicago.

By 1930, the protective wall put up around Lingle by Capone began to crumble. Too many loans taken in return for favors that weren't paid back were piling up on Lingle's tab. His street cred on both sides of the law suffered when he got too deeply involved in the struggle for money and power in the city's gambling syndicate. Lingle may have been the resident "gangologist" at the Tribune, but out on the street he was a "favor seller" whose word was getting cheaper by the day.

Lingle took one step closer to the morgue the day he was given $50,000 by Capone to secure protection for a West Side dog track. As he had done so many times before with loans, Lingle failed to follow through and kept the money. Except this wasn't some low-level street gambler trying to buy favor through Lingle's press influence ... this was Al Capone.

The noose tightened when Lingle got involved with the re-opening of the Sheridan Wave Tournament Club, an elegant society gambling parlor on Waveland Avenue under the protection of Moran's North Siders before it shut down in the wake of the St. Valentine's Day Massacre. In its heyday, the club was the ritziest casino in the city and perhaps the entire country, a social hub for the city's fashionable clientele who enjoyed food, drink, women and whatever else they wanted on the house, and enriched the owners by tens of thousands of dollars each night.

Moran took 25 percent of the gross from the Sheridan Wave Tournament Club. Lingle's cut was 10 percent.

Moran worked for 18 months trying to persuade sympathetic city officials to help him reopen the Sheridan Wave Tournament Club. With city approvals in hand, Moran brought in Joe Josephs and Julian "Potatoes" Kaufman, an old friend of Lingle's, to manage the club. Kaufman approached Lingle and asked if he could use his influence with the police department to get the club reopened.

"You'll be satisfied, of course," Kaufman pitched with a rhetorical question, "with the 10 percent cut you got before?"

"Not by a damned sight," Lingle shot back. "I want 50 percent this time."

"But we have to pay Bugs Moran 25 percent," Kaufman reasoned.

"To hell with Bugs Moran," Lingle huffed.

"Well," Kaufman insisted, "Bugs is the boss of the North Side. You know that. We couldn't do business unless he said the word."

Fully aware that nobody did underworld business in Chicago without Capone's word,

Lingle puffed his chest out and refused to back down.

"Moran cuts no ice with the police nowadays. He's on the blacklist," Lingle said. "Give him the air and put me on your payroll for his cut. I'll do the protecting, and I want 50 percent for doing it."

Kaufman couldn't believe his ears. He bumped his offer up to 15 percent.

"Fifty percent or you don't run," Lingle replied.

Kaufman's tone flared angrily.

"Say, Lingle, who do you think you are? A mob all by yourself? You're getting the swell-head. You can't put any such stuff over on me.

I'm no sucker. There'll be nothing doing on any 50 percent for you. And I'll open, too. You can bet your shirt on that."

Lingle remained cocky.

"Come through with my 50 percent," he fired back. "Or on opening night you'll see more squad cars full of coppers at your door than you ever saw before in your life."

Under the cloud of Lingle's threat, the club was set to reopen on June 9. But Kaufman couldn't bring Lingle in. The doors would stay shut.

Moran was furious.

Lingle's buddy, Capone, was livid.

... a frantic scene of people pouring from the station.

3

KILLERS IN A SUBWAY

The night before the scheduled reopening of the Sheridan Wave Tournament Club, Lingle made his way over to Randolph Street in the Loop to meet with one of his most knowledgeable sources, attorney Louis B. Piquett.

Piquett, a former bartender who studied law in night school, landed his first job as chief clerk to the city prosecutor of Chicago largely because of his prolific activism in Chicago Democratic politics. Political networking didn't keep Piquett from being indicted on corruption charges in 1923 — not long after he had been appointed city prosecutor by Mayor William Hale Thompson. After the charges were dropped, Piquett left the prosecutor's office and entered private practice in 1923. He had carved out a lucrative law business defending Chicago's underworld by being the first set of ears to hear every truth behind every dead body found on the streets of Chicago.

Piquett, one of the Lingle's most valuable sources, had information on a murder victim, Red McLaughlin, a known mob acquaintance whose body had been found in a canal.

As Lingle stood on the sidewalk discussing the murder with Piquett, a blue sedan with two men inside pulled up and stopped at the curb. Lingle spotted the car out of the corner of his eye. He cut the conversation off in mid-sentence, told Piquett goodbye, then abruptly ducked into a nearby store.

The next morning, Lingle walked to the Tribune offices and met briefly with the city editor over rumors of a gang beef that had caused McLaughlin to wind up with a bullet in his head.

With an hour to spare before the 1:30 p.m. train left for Washington Park horse track in Homewood, Lingle stopped in at the Sherman Hotel's coffee shop for a bite to eat. Standing at the counter when he walked in was his friend, police Sgt. Tom Alcock of the Detective Bureau.

"I'm being tailed." Lingle's nonchalance in recounting the shadowy encounter with Piquett the night before gave Alcock reason to shrug the claim off as idle chatter.

A few minutes later while walking on Randolph Street toward the subway, Lingle heard the call, "Play Hy Schneider in the third!" coming from a car carrying two men that had pulled up within earshot on the south side of the street.

"I've got him," Lingle called back.

Lingle was oblivious to the fact that he had just been fingered for two hitmen on foot.

Before reaching the subway, Lingle stopped about 25 feet from the east exit. The dark-haired man slowed and took a few cautionary steps back. Lingle had noticed a priest walking from the train platform.

He smiled and waved at the priest.

The priest returned Lingle's wave with a nod that took his eyes directly into the stark gaze of a dark-haired figure looking to see who Lingle was waving to.

In clear view of the priest, the man in the hat stepped directly behind Lingle. He pulled a snub-nosed .38 Colt from his waistband, but his drugged nerves got the better of him and he clumsily fumbled the gun.

The dark-haired man quickly snatched the weapon from his accomplice. The priest stood motionless; his eyes fixed on the surreal sequence of events happening directly in front of him.

The gunman lifted the barrel of the .38 to the back of Lingle's head. The gun exploded with a single blast that echoed through the subway station.

The bullet powered upward into Lingle's brain and exited through his forehead. Lingle lurched forward, still clutching the racing form in his hands. The train that would've taken the Tribune reporter to the horse track pulled into the subway station right on time, but Lingle lied on the ground bleeding profusely. A cigar remained tightly clenched in his teeth.

Stunned passengers poured out of the train and scattered over the chaotic platform. The gunman tossed the gun to the side and ran into the crowd to blend in before police could reach the fallen victim.

Bystander Patrick Campbell noticed the dark-haired gunman hurrying away and took off in pursuit.

The priest moved swiftly toward the dying body. He knelt next to the gravely injured Lingle to administer last rites. Lingle whispered into the priest's ear.

He took one final breath...

Jake Lingle died with his head cradled in the priest's arms.

The blond suspect unwittingly doubled back past Lingle's body and ran up the staircase. Reaching the top of the stairs, he jumped a fence, but altered his direction and took off running west on Randolph Street. With police in full pursuit with guns drawn, the suspect tossed off a left-handed silk glove and scampered onto Wabash Avenue. He disappeared into the dense sidewalk crowd of downtown Chicago.

The priest released Lingle. He stood, started to run off but bumped into Campbell, obstructing the path Campbell was clearing in his attempt to run down the dark-haired gunman, who by now had disappeared into the crowd.

"Somebody has been shot, I'm getting upstairs to see what is going on!" the priest shouted to Campbell. Chicago Police Lt. William Cusack of the Detective Bureau heard the exchange.

"He was no priest," the police lieutenant barked as the priest fled in another direction. "A priest would never do that. He would have gone to the side of the stricken person."

The detective never saw the priest stop to administer last rites to the dying Lingle.

... one relative in town was equipped to deal with Johnnie ... Father Edward Reynolds was kind, patient, and tough as nails ...

4

FATHER REYNOLDS

John Joseph Reynolds came into this world in Brooklyn, New York, in 1894, the son of Thomas Reynolds, an engineer on the ferry boat that connected New York City and New Jersey, and Elizabeth Reynolds, the mother he would lose at the age of 6 to brain cancer.

Unable to raise three young boys and a girl on his own, Thomas Reynolds sent his children to an orphanage in Brooklyn. When details were worked out with the orphanage, the siblings found homes with family members in Bellows Falls, Vermont, a small village in the town of Rockingham that served as home to the Boston & Maine Railroad.

Johnnie had difficulty with losing his mother at such a young age and being farmed out to an orphanage by his father. At the orphanage Johnnie was constantly getting into fights over anything that triggered his temper, even when somebody made fun of his Brooklyn accent. He was the last of his siblings to find a home with a relative because he was too hard to handle

Only one relative in town was equipped to deal with Johnnie and raise the mad-as-hell child with a hair-trigger temper and quicker fists as a son: The Rev. Edward Reynolds, C.S.C., pulled Johnnie out of the orphanage and took him into the home where he served as parish priest of Bellows Falls.

Father Edward Reynolds was kind, patient and tough as nails, which earned him the respect of the local townsfolk. Bellows Falls was home to the railroad and a paper mill, both of which were rife with union activities. Father Edward was counted on to act as the town's tough-minded peace-keeper whenever the threat of a union strike surfaced, a community service that won him

Friends came easier as his athletic prowess began to shine brightly.

significant influence with the hierarchy of the paper mill.

But Johnnie was a handful. Despite his small wiry size, he could be a dynamite-stick blast even for Father Edward. Johnnie took on any kid in the neighborhood. Any adult. Any time. Any place. Anywhere. Johnnie's fragile rage didn't need a reason. Once, when he was 12, a teacher attempted to dish out a dose of discipline with a ruler. Every time the teacher hit him, Johnnie fought for the ruler and tried to hit her back.

"I licked every kid in town because they made fun of my Brooklyn accent," Johnnie Reynolds would boast.

By the time Johnnie entered Bellows Falls High School, teenage maturity had mellowed him into the makings of a popular student. He excelled in the classroom. Friends came easier as his athletic prowess began to shine brightly.

Johnnie developed into a prolific runner, a star on the track team who specialized in the 2-mile run.

But there was still the occasional fight. A friend, Owen Murphy, punched Johnnie in the nose during horseplay one afternoon. Murphy was left with a broken thumb from the fight. Johnnie took a shot to the nose that left him with a deviated septum and severe sinus problems that would plague him the rest of his life.

Although located halfway across the country from South Bend, Bellows Falls was a mere six degrees of separation from Notre Dame. Owen Murphy's family was related to the O'Conner family, which produced Paul "Bucky" O'Conner, a star Bellows Falls High School athlete who would go on to play running back at Notre Dame under Knute Rockne in the coach's last national championship season.

The angry youngster from Bellows Falls had grown into a respected Notre Dame priest ...

By the time Johnnie Reynolds graduated from Bellows Falls High School in 1912, he was practically running the parish for his uncle. Father Edward offered to help his 19-year-old nephew get a good job in the office at the local paper mill where his union peacekeeping efforts had earned him enormous influence.

"Or," Father Edward suggested, "if you want to be a priest, I'll send you to Notre Dame. They have a good English course there."

Johnnie had to get out of Bellows Falls. Notre Dame offered the perfect landing spot where he could study for the priesthood at Holy Cross seminary. With his uncle's blessing, Johnnie headed to South Bend to enter the seminary and study English.

He also planned to join the track team; a squad coached by 27-year-old Knute Rockne.

Rockne's coaching career at Notre Dame would be bookended by a pair of Bellows Falls High School students — Johnnie Reynolds, a Notre Dame track star who set a national record for the 2-mile run in 1916; and Paul "Bucky" O'Connor, a third-string running back who would rush for 142 yards and lead the Fighting Irish to Rockne's last championship during the final game of the 1930 season against Southern California.

Johnnie Reynolds ran track, studied English and history, and became fast friends and drinking buddies with his track coach. Rockne liked tough kids and Johnnie was as tough as anybody on the track team. Despite sinus problems from all the punches he took growing up, Johnnie Reynolds picked up a prolific smoking habit.

Johnnie Reynolds had come full circle. The angry youngster from Bellows Falls had grown into a respected Notre Dame priest and intellectual professor of American history. But Father Reynolds wasn't about to shed Johnnie from his mindset.

"They bothered me, but I kept on smoking," Reynolds said of his chronic sinuses. "I had more fun smoking than I had trouble with the sinuses."

Johnnie Reynolds graduated with an A.B. degree from Notre Dame in 1916 and planned to go right into Holy Cross Seminary to pursue his studies for the priesthood. Upon graduation, the words written under his photo in the Notre Dame yearbook described a mature Johnnie Reynolds that few, back in Bellows Falls, would have recognized.

"This year his thirst for knowledge and for the things beyond directed him to enter Holy Cross Seminary. He is a conscientious student and Father Oswald says that he is a professional acrobat in Greek and Latin. His quiet unpretentious manner and good nature cause him to part, in June, with a host of classmates who regard him as a scholarly gentleman and true friend."

John Joseph Reynolds was ordained a priest in 1922. The Rev. John J. Reynolds, C.S.C., briefly taught American History at Notre Dame, then moved to Portland, Oregon, where he was appointed administrator at Portland Prep School. Under Father Reynolds' leadership, Portland Prep School evolved into Portland Junior College, an evolution that would eventually expand into a full-fledged university, the University of Portland.

In 1927, Father Reynolds left Portland and returned to the University of Notre Dame to teach American history. His residence was at Morrissey Hall, and he was the assigned rector at St. Edward's Hall, supervising several members of the football team among the student residents.

While Father Reynolds was out west, his pal Knute Rockne spent seven years singlehandedly turning Notre Dame into a household name and selling the school's football program to a mass audience from coast to coast. A national schedule stretched from Army in the East to the University of Southern California on the West Coast. Upon Father Reynolds' return to South Bend, he quickly reunited with his old track coach "Rock" — now the most famous football coach in America — over beers, cigars and stories.

Johnnie Reynolds had come full circle. The angry youngster from Bellows Falls had grown into a respected Notre Dame priest and intellectual professor of American history. But Father Reynolds wasn't about to shed Johnnie from his mindset. Even the priest maintained an unbridled streak of character that wasn't afraid to experience life on its own terms.

On his off days, Father Reynolds caught the South Shore train to Chicago, sometimes to see his doctor for his sinus problems, sometimes to hit the horse tracks, sometimes to visit his two brothers — Edward and Thomas — both of whom lived in the city. Thomas Reynolds worked at the luxurious Edgewater Beach Hotel on the North Side near Wrigley Field, the site of the infamous shooting of baseball player Eddie Waitkus in

1949 by a 19-year-old female fan that would serve as the inspiration for the book and later the movie, "The Natural."

Johnnie Reynolds embraced Chicago. He was small in stature, 5-feet-6 maybe, but walked around with a natural street sense that came out through a quick-witted tone that often emphasized his words with a conclusive, "see." The white-collar Father Reynolds wore as a Catholic priest did not prevent Johnnie Reynolds from straying into the occasional backroom card game. Nor did the Notre Dame priest shy from getting up close and personal with the ins and outs of the horse track.

Only Father Reynolds knew the words the fallen victim had whispered.

5

AS GOD'S WITNESS

Seeing the victim lying on the ground bleeding profusely from the head, Father Reynolds hurried to the mortally wounded man just in time to attempt to administer last rites. The man was barely able to whisper in the priest's ear before he took his final breath.

Only Father Reynolds knew the words the fallen victim had whispered. He got up, left the man dead in a pool of blood on the platform, and started to make his way out with the crowd when he bumped into a large man with a big stomach.

"Somebody has been killed, I'm getting upstairs to see what is going on," Father Reynolds said to Patrick Campbell.

The priest hurried up the stairway out to the street. Upon exiting the tunnel onto Michigan Avenue, he peered around the street corner and saw a frantic scene of people pouring out from the station. Father Reynolds was stunned to spot the light-haired accomplice standing on the corner.

The man appeared to be waiting for a pickup. Nobody stopped, so he ducked into a nearby store and asked to use the toilet. The suspect disappeared into the restroom, unwrapped a small piece of paper containing white powder, snorted the powder and left the paper behind in a stall for police to recover later. He walked hurriedly out of the store and disappeared down State Street.

Back inside the subway station, the dark-haired gunman had tossed the murder weapon on the cement and was now lost in a crowd of bedlam.

Father Reynolds had bolted from the scene without stopping to talk to police. He skipped

his doctor's appointment and, instead, decided to get out of Chicago as quickly as possible and catch the next train back to South Bend.

By the time he returned to Notre Dame, news of the murder of Chicago Tribune reporter Jake Lingle had spread like a wildfire.

Father Reynolds immediately tracked down his superiors at Notre Dame and told them what he witnessed.

Their collective order was direct: "Stay quiet, and don't get involved."

The Lingle shooting — Chicago's 11th

Not until the hit on Jake Lingle had a newspaper reporter been gunned down in such a sensational public mob execution.

murder in 10 days — dominated headlines in the city and across the country. The Tribune editorialized that Lingle was killed because "... his killers either thought he was close to information dangerous to them or intended the murder as notice to the newspapers that crime was ruler in Chicago..."

Gangsters getting whacked in Chicago's most violent wave of gangland murders to date was everyday news. But the murder of this Chicago Tribune reporter initially appeared to be unprecedented — that is, until St. Louis

Star reporter Harry T. Brundidge took it upon himself to investigate the case and shed light on the true story behind the Chicago crime reporter's murder.

Brundidge was one of the nation's premiere newspaper scribes, a superstar newshound who traveled to scenes of the biggest stories across the country and scooped the locals as prolifically as he ruled the presses in St. Louis. When it came to tapping underworld sources in Chicago to unravel the full story on the Lingle murder and shed light on the residual shock waves that reverberated through every newspaper that covered organized crime, Brundidge had no equal.

"Up here, where a gent is apt to get 'knocked off' for sending his shirt to the wrong laundry, a house of cards was built," Brundidge wrote in his piece on Lingle that appeared in the St. Louis Star two weeks after the murder on June 26, 1930. "Its foundation was beer, booze, graft, and all forms of racketeering and the architects were a lot of comic strip politicians, itchy-palmed coppers and some money-hungry newspapermen. They made a lotta promises and a lotta dough, and kept some of the former."

Brundidge keenly pointed out that Lingle was not the first newspaper reporter to get whacked after crossing the mob. Chicago Daily News tipster Julius Rosenheim was also gunned down for blackmailing bootleggers, gamblers and brothelkeepers, and threatening to expose criminal operations in the Daily News. And there were others, all of whom, like Rosenheim, may as well have died quietly behind the scenes from natural causes. Not until the hit on Jake Lingle had a newspaper reporter been gunned down in such a sensational public mob execution.

The news of Lingle getting rubbed out came as little surprise to the veteran newspaper reporter. After all, Lingle's lavish lifestyle outside the Chicago Tribune — symbolized by the personalized diamond-studded belt buckle with the initials "A.J.L." gifted by Al Capone — had been common knowledge around Chicago's newsrooms, a fact spelled out succinctly during Brundidge's interview with Tribune publisher Col. Robert McCormick.

"I'm not asserting that Lingle was an honest man," McCormick said. "Neither am I denying that perhaps he was honest. But at the same time, I'll tell you he didn't have enough money to be as big a man in the underworld as he's said to have been, if the pay-off in that underworld is as big as it's supposed to be."

Reporters who mirrored Lingle's brazen style further fueled Brundidge's exploitation of a newspaper industry that had been compromised by the greed of more and more newspapermen who were doubling as mob accomplices.

Brundidge quickly flipped the switch on the initial false perception around Chicago that Lingle was killed because he had exposed the mob in unflattering crime stories. Calling the victim out as a reporter who profited handsomely by using his newspaper clout to work both sides of the law had stirred the suspicions of editors in newsrooms everywhere.

"(Lingle) wouldn't go to a ball game or a race track with anybody bearing a title lower than a deputy commissioner of police, and he became the only reporter in newspaper history who could bet $500 or $1,000 'across the board' on a horse race without having goose pimples while the ponies were running around the track," Brundidge wrote.

"Jake had paper profits in the stock

market that made him think he was financially independent. Bright young men on other newspapers who emulated Jake's business methods moved out of little $90-a-month apartments and exchanged their Chevrolets for Cadillacs. The guy who didn't have a racket in Chicago was just a poor dumb wit. Jake... KNEW he had to be SEEN before a guy with any kind of a racket could make a move. Jake was giving $10 tips for two-bit service and spending a lot of time in Florida with 'Scarface' and other unnamed gents, and with these friends he also visited Cuban race tracks. His imitators among the newspaper fraternity were doing well, too. Some went to Europe on salaries that ordinarily wouldn't rate a vacation in an Ozark fishing camp.

"But..." Brundidge emphasized in his St. Louis Star column, "... all of this isn't telling readers of The Star why Jake Lingle was murdered or why a phone may ring at any moment now, bringing the news that another reporter got a ticket to the hot place where his 'past the fire lines' badge won't help him out a bit."

Police suspected the Aiellos, a crew of henchmen working for Bugs Moran on the North Side, but Brundidge scoffed at the cops' shallow perception. Capone had called all the shots in Chicago since the St. Valentine's Day Massacre. If anybody knew who had shot Jake Lingle, it was Capone.

Brundidge set out to visit Capone at his Miami Beach estate, where he had been lying low since his release from prison a few months earlier in March. At 8:15 p.m. on July 17, Brundidge arrived unannounced, got off the train in Miami and checked in at the Pancoast Hotel in Miami. He hired a car service that drove him straight to Capone's plush estate on Palm Island. When he pulled up to the iron gates at the entranceway to the palatial residence, a guard said Capone was off somewhere with his attorney.

"When will he return?" Brundidge asked.

The guard shrugged. Brundidge took a seat on the ground and waited for Capone to return. At 10 p.m. sharp, a long limousine stopped in front of the gates. Brundidge noticed immediately that only Capone's younger brother was in the limo.

A few minutes later, a black sedan pulled up. The door opened. Capone himself stepped out flanked by two armed guards and another man.

Brundidge stuck out his hand and introduced himself. Capone recognized the reporter from the stories he had been reading in the papers about the Lingle murder.

"This is a surprise," Capone replied. "Come on in."

Brundidge had struck gold where no other newspaper man had dared to pan. He took a seat next to "Scarface Al" on a divan on the sun porch of Capone's magnificent home.

"You seemed to have raised merry hell in Chicago," Capone remarked. "What brings you here?"

Brundidge didn't mince words. "I thought I would ask you, who killed Lingle?"

"Why ask me?" Capone shot back. "The Chicago police know who killed him."

"Was Jake your friend?" Brundidge inquired.

"Yes, up to the day he died."

It was clear to Capone that Brundidge had done his homework. When Brundidge brought up rumors of "a row" between Capone and Lingle that had spread on the streets, Capone emphatically denied any riff by saying, "Absolutely not."

"It is said you fell out with him because

49

Capone appeared to be caught off guard when Brundidge asked if he had refused to see Lingle ...

he failed to split profits from handbooks," Brundidge pressed.

"Bunk," Capone snapped. "The handbook racket hasn't been really organized in Chicago for more than two years and anyone who says it is doesn't know Chicago."

The reporter noticed that Capone's tone grew shorter with each question. Capone appeared to be caught off guard when Brundidge asked if he had refused to see Lingle after his release from a correctional workhouse in Philadelphia.

"Who said I didn't see him?" Capone replied.

"The Chicago newspapers, the files of which, including his own paper, the 'Trib,' set forth the fact."

"Well," Capone responded, "if Jake failed to say I saw him, then I didn't see him."

Brundidge's inquisition shifted to the diamond-studded belt buckle Capone gave to Lingle as a gift. "Do you mind stating what it cost?"

"Two hundred fifty dollars," Capone said.

"Why did you give it to him?"

"He was my friend," Capone replied.

"How many rackets was he engaged in?" Brundidge quizzed.

Capone slightly bristled at the question with a shrug of his shoulders and a smirky grin. Brundidge sensed he was on the verge of getting more answers than this notorious gangster realized he would be giving up. The astute reporter dug in with his heels.

"What was the matter with Lingle, the horse races?" Brundidge asked. "How many other Lingles are there in Chicago in the newspaper racket?"

"Phooey, don't ask," Capone hissed.

"Seriously," Brundidge pushed, "what do you think of newspaper men who turn their profession into a racket?"

"I think this," Capone replied in a circumspect tone. "Newspapers and newspaper men should be busy suppressing rackets and not supporting them. It does not become me, of all persons, to say that, but I believe it."

Brundidge saw his opening to go straight for the jugular. "How many newspaper men have you had on your payroll?"

Capone paused. Brundidge knew he had struck a sensitive nerve with the hardline question. Capone's black sociopathic eyes darkened even deeper as he submitted to an answer with a shrug.

"Plenty," Capone replied.

"Have you had any telephone calls from newspaper men in Chicago since publication in the St. Louis Star that Lingle was not the only one in his profession in Chicago with a racket?"

"Plenty," Capone repeated.

Capone leaned over. He put his arm around Brundidge's shoulders and squeezed a conciliatory squeeze that stirred up a bees' nest of anxiety in the reporter's stomach. Brundidge's line of questioning dug deep, perhaps too deep for Public Enemy No. 1's comfort zone. Capone answered every question, but Brundidge had toed a contentious line with the mob boss — a line that, if crossed, could result in the same tragic consequences for anybody who stuck their nose too deep into gangland business that had struck Jake Lingle.

"Listen, Harry, I like your face," Capone said. "Let me give you a hot tip. Lay off Chicago and the money hungry reporters. You're right... because you're right, you're wrong. You can't buck it, not even with the back of your newspaper, because it is too big a proposition. No one man will ever realize just how big it is, so lay off."

"You mean?" Brundidge pressed.

"I mean, they'll make a monkey out of you before you get through," Capone cautioned. "No matter what dope you have to give that grand jury, the boys will prove you're a liar and a faker. You'll get a trimming."

"I'm going to quote you as saying that," Brundidge declared.

Capone laughed off the mild admonishment. "If you do," he replied, "I'll deny it."

Tired of the questioning, Capone got up to show off his palatial property. They walked around the grounds surrounding Capone's villa, past the swimming pool and bath house, out to the private pier that facilitated a boat house, a high-powered speed boat and a lavish yacht.

"Let's quit talking about the rackets," Capone suggested as the two strolled under the moonlight along the waters of Biscayne Bay. "You've seen the grounds, now, how about a tour of my home?"

Brundidge followed Capone inside. By the time they had walked through all 17 rooms of the house — from the bedrooms to the kitchen where a nice catch of fresh mackerel was chilling on ice — it was 1 a.m.

Capone escorted Brundidge out to the front gate. After saying their goodbyes, one of Capone's men drove Brundidge back to his hotel. On the way back, the two struck up a conversation that lasted almost until the sun came up.

Back in Chicago, a mountain of press amplified daily with the investigation into who killed Lingle. Under "nine hundred million tons of pressure" from the public to resign, Lingle's pal, William Russell, stepped down from his post as police commissioner within a week of the murder.

"Someone had to be the red meat," Russell admitted. "I have had an insurmountable obstacle, by that I mean Prohibition, and I don't give a damn who knows it."

Also out was Chicago Police Deputy Commissioner John Stege, who had flaunted his rank to keep underlings from hassling bookmakers and gamblers who bought racing information from "Race Track Service" put out by the General News Bureau Inc. J.M. Regan, general manager of the General News Bureau, had been a close friend of Lingle's for years.

The Lingle murder had also exploded into a massive scandal for the Tribune. Chicago Mayor William Hale Thompson, a perennial target of the newspaper's scathing editorials, used the killing to go on the offensive by referring to the Tribune as the "Lingle Evangelistic Institute."

Frank Wilson, a federal agent for the Internal Revenue Service investigating Capone for tax evasion, wrote in his autobiography that Tribune owner Col. McCormick was well-aware of Lingle's gangland connections. The Colonel, according to Wilson, had even taken it upon himself to personally set up a meeting between Lingle and Wilson that was supposed to have taken place the day after the murder.

McCormick vehemently denied Wilson's accusations, while others close to the Tribune proprietor said Wilson only contacted McCormick after the murder.

The scandalous accusations lobbed toward the Tribune and the newspaper's brass overshadowed news reports that a priest had been spotted running from the scene. A police officer, and civilian Patrick Campbell, both claimed the priest was a "fake" who may have been involved in the murder. The police went public with widely circulated advertisements calling for the priest to come forward.

Father Reynolds was nervous and uncertain what to do. He prayed for spiritual guidance. When the priest met with his superiors at Notre Dame seeking advice, they gave him their blessing.

Father Reynolds was free to contact the authorities in Chicago and tell them what he had seen.

... Lingle's lavish lifestyle ... spelled out succinctly during Brundidge's interview with Tribune publisher Col. Robert McCormick.

Police knew Jack "Jake" Zuta all too well ...

6

MOB STEPS

Police hounded the streets of Chicago around the clock to pin down a suspect. More than 1,000 criminals of record were hauled in for questioning while detectives narrowed the motive for the Lingle hit down to circumstances surrounding two competing dog tracks — the Hawthorne, owned by Capone, and the Fairview, controlled by Moran.

Street sources revealed a promise Lingle had made to help Moran put another track in operation on the West Side. Moran had paid Lingle $2,500 up front in return for using his clout to get The Stadium open without any interference from the law. But like so many times before, the promise of favor fell by the wayside with Lingle pocketing Moran's down payment.

The investigation was only a few hours old when the name of the hit's suspected orchestrator fell into detectives' laps. Police knew Jack "Jake" Zuta all too well.

Zuta operated several brothels on West Madison Street before going to work for Capone in the mid-1920s. He helped contribute $50,000 of Capone's money to Chicago Mayor William Hale Thompson's re-election campaign in 1927, but when the infamous gang war broke out between Capone and Moran, Zuta defected crosstown to Moran's North Side Gang.

Zuta was known as the crafty "brains" and vice ring director of the North Side Gang run by Moran and Giuseppe "Joe" Aiello, a bootlegger who for years perpetuated a relentless bloody feud with Capone. Aiello masterminded several failed attempts to kill Capone, and he fought former business partner and Capone ally Antonio Lombardo for control of the Chicago branch

Police ... suspected Aiello and his crew.

of the Unione Siciliana benevolent society.

Aiello and Moran both sanctioned the contract murder of Lombardo. Capone retaliated by ordering the St. Valentine's Day Massacre.

Moran's North Siders generally despised Zuta as a coward who would sacrifice his own mother to save himself under intense interrogation. They tolerated him because of his reputation for being a smart underworld businessman.

To Capone, Zuta was a traitorous pimp. A rat.

Police at first suspected Aiello and his crew. Acting on a tip, their suspicions shifted to Zuta, and they quickly moved to bring the Capone turncoat in for questioning.

Zuta was accompanied by a girl and two teenage members of the Moran gang when he was picked up by police on June 10, the day after the Lingle murder. The interrogation lasted nearly 24 hours.

It didn't matter that Zuta kept his mouth shut without incriminating anybody. Once word hit the streets that Zuta was talking to police, every wise guy in Chicago tagged the brothel keeper as a snitch to be taken out at the first opportunity. Nobody knew that

Zuta's life was in danger of the same fate that befell Jake Lingle than Zuta himself.

"I'll be killed the minute I leave this building," Zuta told police the moment he was arrested. "Don't stand around looking sleepy. Do you cops want me killed? Here's the time I'll get it, if you're going to leave me to it. All of my people are hiding away. You cops have got to look out for me...

"My God," he pleaded, "I'm a goner. I know it."

Police got nothing from Zuta, and they told him to go home. He asked Lt. George Barker to drive him and his companions to the safety of his house on the North Side in Barker's own car, which was parked in the alley behind police headquarters.

Zuta and the three others piled into Barker's car. Zuta crouched on the floor in the rear to hide from street view. Barker slipped out of the alley successfully. A few minutes later the police lieutenant was driving toward Moran territory on the North Side where Zuta figured to be safe.

As Barker made a turn at Quincy and State streets, Zuta was on the floor jabbering in fear of his life. Barker no sooner edged the vehicle slowly into the traffic of the Loop when a blue Chrysler sedan swiftly drove up on them.

"They're after us!" Zuta screamed.

The sedan crashed squarely into Barker's car, causing it nearly to overturn. Barker drew his gun and started firing immediately at the sedan. The Chrysler swung around at full speed with guns blasting out all windows. A hailstorm of bullets turned the street into a thick, fiery fog.

A slew of police in separate squad cars rushed to the scene to try to pursue the blue sedan. But the gangsters' car sped away, miraculously avoiding several vehicles in the roadway and ignoring all signal lights in a high-speed escape westward.

By the time Barker had rushed back to his own vehicle, Zuta and his friends were gone. Smashed glass from store windows transformed State Street White Way into a crystal maze. Barker spotted a revolver in the middle of State Street which one of the killers had apparently tossed from the sedan. He picked it up and placed it in his car to take to Goddard Laboratories for ballistic tests.

A crowd had gathered around a nearby streetcar. The motorman, Elbert Lusader, lay dead after being shot with a stray bullet. In his final conscious act, Lusader had turned off the power of the crowded car. Another group surrounded Olaf Svenste, an employee of the Standard Club, who also caught a bullet in the crossfire and sat seriously wounded at the side of Barker's car.

Zuta had vanished. It was apparent to the State Attorney's office chief investigator, Patrick Roche, that Zuta's verbal fears prior to the attack and the verification of his despair in the shootout on State Street revealed, at the least, some knowledge as to who had pulled the trigger in the Lingle murder.

The following Saturday, Zuta failed to appear in court and his bail was forfeited.

"Needless to say, my client must protect himself," Zuta's attorney, Benjamin Cohen, explained to the judge. "He is certain of death if he appears in Chicago at this time. In view of recent developments, he can hardly expect adequate protection."

The gun Barker picked up off the street was tested at Goddard Laboratories. Ballistics results pointed to the South Side. The gun was revealed to have had the serial numbers filed off and covered with the symbol "#" —

a Capone technique discovered previously on two guns used in a mob shooting that had been traced back to Capone crew members.

Rumors swirled that Zuta had fled Chicago and was hiding out in Kentucky. Zuta got out of Chicago all right, but he drove north to Wisconsin's Upper Nemahbin Lake, a few miles west of Milwaukee. He settled in at the Lakeview Hotel under the name "J.H. Goodman, of Aurora."

His cover identification was short lived.

On August 1, 1930, Zuta enjoyed himself in the dance pavilion adjoining the hotel. Twenty couples were dancing, and Zuta was the life of the party filling the mechanical piano with handfuls of nickels.

"Every time she stops, the nearest one will feed her a nickel," Zuta called out. "Let's go! This is the life!"

As Zuta made his announcement, three men walked up to the front entrance of the pavilion. They quietly picked up the doorman, Joe Selby, and carried him bodily to a nearby automobile. One of the men poked the doorman's ribs with a gun and sat next to him in the backseat. Selby counted eight well-dressed men who made their way to the outside corner of the pavilion.

Five went inside. One carried a machine gun.

Zuta was dancing. As he passed the door of the pavilion with his partner, five men grabbed Zuta by the shoulders. Zuta fell to the floor, his face white as paste. The men picked him up calmly without saying a word. They carried him to the piano, sat him down in a chair and flanked him. The man holding the machine gun stood about 10 feet away. Two others, both with guns drawn, herded the dancers to another corner away from the door.

Without as much as a glance toward the gunman toting the machine gun, Zuta sat stone-faced, rigid and silent. He started to fall from the chair when the men beside him stepped away.

The machine gun fired off a cavalcade of bullets that cut across the piano with a crash of glass and haphazard musical intensity. Zuta fell limp to the floor, dead on impact, his lifeless body riddled with 28 bullets.

"Don't come out of this place," the killer warned the rest of the dancers.

The hitmen abruptly exited the room and walked back to the getaway cars without the slightest attempt to hide their faces. Once the dancers realized the danger had subsided, men scurried to revive the unconscious women who had fainted.

A few weeks later, a barrel containing the remains of Pasqualino "Patsy" Tardi washed up in a shallow portion of Lake Michigan. Rumors immediately surfaced that it was Tardi who fumbled the gun and nearly botched the hit on Lingle, but those rumors died out quickly without any substantiation.

Amidst a slew of murders that gripped the city through newspaper headlines every day, Chicago police detectives continued to work under mounting pressure from the public to make an arrest in the Lingle hit. Every time police brought in a suspect for Father Reynolds to see, the priest would catch the South Shore and make the two-hour train trip from South Bend to get a look at a new face.

Some of the men brought in for Father Reynolds' eyes were small-time hoods being hassled out of mere police formality and otherwise had nothing to do with anything. Others were more notorious. Some were famously notorious.

"And, because I'd go in... I met all the best killers there, like Baby Face Nelson," Father

Reynolds recalled. "He looked like a little dwarf, see, and then the most innocent face you ever saw, but the biggest killer in Chicago."

Chicago investigators didn't have a solid suspect. What they had was the weapon that had killed Lingle, a .38 caliber handgun dropped at the scene. The gun's serial number had been filed off, but ballistics expert Col. Calvin Goddard had a process for raising the tattoo — the second-deep impression left by the dye that stamped the serial number on a gun.

Within an hour of receiving the gun, Goddard traced the origin of Lingle's murder weapon to the Colt factory in Hartford, Connecticut — the gun manufacturer that in June 1928 shipped the same .38 caliber and five similar revolvers to a sporting goods store on Diversey Parkway. The store's owner, Peter von Frantzius, was also known as the "Armorer" because of his reputation for being Chicago's most prolific arms dealer to the underworld.

While von Frantzius had committed no crime under the city's lax gun laws, a detective and accompanying Chicago Tribune reporter John Boettinger threatened to jam von Frantzius up in the public eye if he didn't cooperate. With no other options at hand, the gun dealer produced a sales receipt showing the gun was sold to Frankie Foster.

Police pushed von Frantzius for more information. The gun dealer also revealed that Foster had been accompanied by a man who insisted that von Frantzius file off the serial numbers on each of the guns. The man with Foster at the time of the gun purchase, Ted Newberry, had already been fingered by witnesses as one of the gunmen in the Lingle murder. But the mere accusation didn't hold enough water for investigators to make a case against Newberry.

Frankie Foster, on the other hand, was a solid suspect.

A short, stocky, dark-haired bootlegger of Romanian-Jewish heritage also known by the names Frank Frost, Frank Citro and Frank Bruna, Foster was a former member of Moran's North Side Gang who had defected to Capone's ranks with Ted Newberry. Two days after Lingle's murder, Foster fled to Los Angeles, where Capone and Moran were both rumored to be attempting to establish new operations on untapped West Coast turf.

The gun receipt provided Chicago authorities with ample legal ammunition to bring Foster back. He was indicted in absentia as an accessory before the fact to murder, picked up in Los Angeles, and extradited back to Chicago where Foster was held in Cook County Jail for four months.

Foster's lawyer's demands for trial went virtually ignored three times. By the time his attorney filed a motion for trial a fourth time, State Attorney John A. Swanson conceded that, despite the gun receipt in Foster's name, there was insufficient evidence to warrant any further prosecution. The case against Foster collapsed.

As the investigation moved forward, Tribune lawyer Charles F. Rathbun and Patrick T. Roche, chief investigator for the State's Attorney's office, began to sense that moves were being made on the South Side to mislead investigators to target Zuta as the orchestrator of the Lingle hit in an effort to put the focus of the investigation on Moran's North Side Gang. Since the St. Valentine's Day Massacre, Moran had been virtually powerless to order a hit as monumental as the Lingle killing.

Capone was at his palatial home in Miami lying low from the Lingle investigation brewing in Chicago and a federal Internal

(Known as "The Armorer") ... Peter von Frantzius had committed no crime under the city's lax gun laws.

Revenue Service probe heating up over his income sources, but both Rathbun and Roche knew he remained the undisputed boss of Chicago's underworld in the wake of the St. Valentine's Day Massacre. He might have been out of sight, but Chicago was still Capone's city. Capone continued to be the chief benefactor from any and all of the city's organized crime business.

Roche's suspicions that the Lingle hit stopped at Capone's South Side doorstep intensified when Zuta's ledger fell into his possession. The ledger was a last laugh from the grave that meticulously documented $400,000 in bank notes and canceled checks from men who either paid or owed Zuta money. Among the names listed included municipal court Judge Joseph Schulman;

Judge Emmanuel Eller; Nate De Lue, assistant business manager of the Chicago Board of Education; Illinois State Senator Henry Starr, who claimed the $400 check he received from Zuta was for "legal services"; and former Illinois State Senator George Van Lent.

One letter from Zuta's records caught Roche's eye, a note from one-time Capone bootlicker Louis La Carva who had fallen out of favor with his former boss and had contacted Zuta to help exact revenge. "Dear Jack," the note read, "I'd help you organize a strong business organization capable of coping with theirs in Cicero."

Roche could barely contain his elation over Zuta's ledger. When a reporter asked if arrests were imminent in the Lingle investigation, he responded: "A lot of men

... Foster ... picked up in Los Angeles and extradited back to Chicago ...

will be leaving town... We are following the trail of many of Zuta's dollars, and there is no telling where it will end."

In September, the trail for Lingle's killer led Roche to Louisville, Kentucky, where Indiana gangster Ted Geisking had been tracked down on the loose tip that he may have been the "left-handed man" witnesses saw shoot Lingle.

But two witnesses failed to identify Geisking as the shooter. Both claimed to have seen a blond-haired gunman fleeing the scene. Geisking had dark hair. When Geisking passed the shampoo test given by Roche and proved

he didn't dye his hair, the Indiana mobster was cleared of any link to Lingle's murder. He was returned to Indiana under police custody where he was wanted on numerous other charges.

In December, with the trail for Lingle's killer still lukewarm, Roche enlisted a former bank robber, beer runner and associate of the South Side Genna brothers' crew to return to his old gangland haunts as an undercover operative. It didn't take long for John Hagan to ingratiate himself with an old pal, Pat Hogan, who had been rumored to be vaguely connected with the Lingle murder.

Foster's lawyer's demands for trial went virtually ignored three times.

Hagan took Hogan out night after night and plied him with food, drink and cabaret action in the hope that Hogan would spill something good. After several nights of carousing, a drunken Hogan blurted out a nickname.

"Buster."

Hagan played nonchalant toward Hogan's name-drop. Over the next few weeks Hagan continued to treat Hogan to a succession of nightclub-filled evenings while trying to casually pull more information about "Buster." Finally, during one night of particularly heavy drinking, Hogan divulged Buster's actual name, or at least the name Hogan knew.

"Leo Bader."

Hogan mentioned that Bader stayed at two apartments about a block away from each other: One at the Riviera Apartments at 4906 Blackstone Avenue; the other at the Lake Crest Drive Apartments at 4827 Lake Park Avenue.

When Roche learned that their suspect kept two addresses, the savvy sleuth knew he had a problem. It would be far too risky for investigators to move aggressively and make inquiries about Bader with staff members at either building. Roche was certain that if word got back to Bader that cops were asking questions around his residence, their main suspect would vanish in the wind.

One night after Roche had returned to his office from dinner with his captain, he sat in his chair with his feet perched on his desk puffing on a black cigar. Suddenly, it hit him: His former secretary at the Internal Revenue Service had also lived on Lake Park Avenue.

"Sam..." Roche called to his captain, who was chatting with another investigator in the office. "Hand me that telephone book, will you? It seems to me I know a girl who worked for me in the federal building several years ago who lives near that number on Lake Park Avenue."

Roche took the book and shuffled through some pages. He stopped and ran his finger down a column to one name: Rose Huebsch.

For several years when Roche served as the ace of the IRS's Special Intelligence Unit, Rose Huebsch had worked as his secretary. It had been three years since he left the IRS to become chief investigator for State's Attorney Swanson, but Roche knew that Huebsch had stayed on with the IRS, and that she still worked at the Federal Building. She was 30 years old, barely 5 feet tall with a plump figure and dark hair, and possessed a quiet manner, but Roche remembered his former secretary as being keenly smart, exceptionally competent, and courageously confident.

He looked at the address listed next to her name in the phone book: 4827 Lake Park Avenue, the same address as Bader.

Roche picked up the phone and dialed Huebsch's number. She answered and expressed mild surprise at hearing from

Rose Huebsch... had no idea whom she had just helped her former boss capture.

Roche. A brief conversation ensued, and the two readily agreed to meet at his office in the Temple Building. Roche held off from giving Huebsch any details about the gangster they were seeking, nor did Huebsch ask. She was just glad to help her former boss.

Thirty minutes later, at about 8:30 p.m., Huebsch sat in Roche's office giving Roche and Rathbun a detailed description of the Lake Crest Drive apartment building — a five-story structure considered modern for its time that facilitated 75 furnished apartments, mostly one-bedroom kitchenette-style units.

A quick check on Bader's name at the building revealed that the suspect did not have

63

... Rathbun's and Roche's orders had come to an end ...

a private telephone in his apartment. Those who called were instructed to leave a message for Bader with the building's clerk. That bit of information gave Roche an idea: He asked Huebsch to return to her building, but instead of going straight to her apartment, she was instructed to check the building directory in the front entry corridor for Bader's name.

At 10 p.m., the phone rang in Roche's office. He picked up to Huebsch's excited voice on the other end. She had found Bader's name — and apartment number. Bader lived in Number 410, directly across a narrow, 6-foot-wide hallway from Huebsch's apartment in 411. Huebsch could open her door and look straight into Bader's front door.

"Watch the door closely and let me know if you see or hear anything," Roche advised.

Ten minutes later, Roche's phone rang again. Huebsch's voice, again, was charged.

"I had my door standing open, and I sat beside a floor lamp reading a magazine," she said. "Then I heard the door of the elevator slam, and footsteps sounded in the hall. I looked up just in time to see a man pass and stop before Apartment 410. He pulled out his keys and entered."

"What did he look like?" Roche asked.

"Well, he was blond," Huebsch replied. "He looked like a bad man. He was fairly tall and well built."

Huebsch had only gotten a quick glance of the suspect, but the description matched perfectly with the man Roche and Rathbun were after. When Roche passed Huebsch's details on to another law enforcement investigator who confirmed the description, Roche and Rathbun both knew they had their man in their sights.

Rathbun and Roche also knew they had to move quickly if they were going to catch Bader on the spot. If the gangster got wind of their tail, he could disappear in a flash. And if news hit the streets that the heat was on Bader at his address, his associates would spread the word and the entire investigation could be jeopardized.

On December 21, Rathbun, Roche, fellow investigators Fred Joyner, Walter Wendt and Samuel Lederer, and Tribune reporter John Boettinger, walked through a heavy snow fall to the Lake Crest Drive Apartments and set up posts in the front and rear of the building. Two men were also posted in the shadows beneath Bader's window in case he discovered the sting and tried to escape down a rope. A third man walked slowly up and down the sidewalk as cars, street cars and taxi cabs passed. His eye never left the front doorway of the apartment building.

Inside Huebsch's apartment, Roche gave her the signal to dial the number of the apartment building and ask the clerk to call Bader. The plan was for Huebsch to tell the operator to ring Bader's buzzer to say there was a message left for him at the front desk.

... a gangster to convict.

Hopefully, Bader would leave his apartment so the investigators could move in and capture him.

But it was past 11 p.m. — the plan hit a snag.

"We called the apartment building office," Huebsch told Roche after hanging up the phone. "They told me that the call service was discontinued at 11 o'clock at night, and that they would be unable to call Mr. Bader to the telephone. I asked the girl to ring his buzzer, but she said she couldn't do it."

With snow falling heavily outside and

Father Reynolds knew better...

Bader seemingly settled in his apartment for the night, there was no further need for guards posted at the front and rear of the building. The men outside had grown impatient, so they climbed a back stairway and quietly made their way up to Huebsch's apartment on the fourth floor. With the door cracked open a mere two-to-three inches to serve up a full view of Bader's apartment door, the investigators took turns throughout the night posted in Huebsch's kitchenette with an eye out for any movement coming through the front door of the apartment across the hall.

The sun came up following the all-night stakeout. Roche decided once again to have Huebsch call the front desk and leave a message for her neighbor. Huebsch dialed the phone from her own apartment. She told the operator to contact Bader with a message that a call from a woman was waiting for him at the building's office.

All eyes were on the front door across the hall when it opened. A tall, powerfully-built man with light hair emerged partially dressed from the apartment and made his way down the hallway. Before the occupant known as Leo Bader could get to the elevator, Roche, Rathbun and the rest of the stakeout crew converged on Chicago's most wanted murder suspect and arrested him without a fight.

The lady who lured Leo V. Brothers into a trap had no idea whom she had just helped her former boss capture.

"There isn't anything to tell about it," Huebsch told reporters who tracked her down at her office in the Federal Building later that day. "When Mr. Roche was in the federal service, I was his secretary. I was glad to help him... I used to transcribe reports in criminal cases, but this is the first one I've had anything to do with."

Leo Bader's real name was Leo Brothers, a Capone crew member who went by several aliases. Brothers had started out as a small-timer with the Egan's Rats crew, a ruthless organized crime gang that exerted considerable power in St. Louis for nearly 35 years. Brothers had worked his way up in the Egan's Rats organization as a labor-union buster and contract murderer specializing in arson, bombs and explosives. In 1929, while under indictment for murder in St. Louis, Brothers had fled to Chicago where he quickly found work with Capone.

Brothers was booked and charged with Lingle's murder, then whisked away to a secluded spot in the custody of the state's attorney's office. Rathbun and Roche both made it clear in no uncertain terms that it was mandatory for the continuing investigation to remain secret or else apprehension of other men suspected in the plot could be jeopardized.

Other than a handful witnesses who told police they saw a "blond man" running away from the train station after Lingle was shot, there was no solid evidence to identify Brothers as the gunman. With a receipt for the actual murder weapon in hand, there was

more evidence connecting the Lingle murder with the man police had just released, Frankie Foster.

Nevertheless, Leo V. Brothers, a.k.a. Leo V. Bader, or "Buster," was Roche's guy.

Father Reynolds knew better.

After numerous trips to Chicago to view a seemingly endless slew of photo lineups, Father Reynolds remained certain that Frankie Foster was the man who had shot Jake Lingle. Even the one other direct eyewitness to the shooting, a woman standing with her husband when the killing went down, agreed with Father Reynolds. She, too, had viewed a wide array of photos. She told the priest she was also certain Foster acted as the shooter.

"And it shocked her so much, she went out for a glass of water in order not to faint, and when she came back the police had removed the picture," Father Reynolds said.

Father Reynolds was suddenly caught between the rock of God's truth and a dubious indictment. It was obvious to the priest that Chicago's law-enforcement crew was manufacturing a sure-fire conviction to answer for a high-profile murder. Foster was free and Brothers was in custody to answer for Lingle. To appease the public and justify another unsolved homicide, they would sell Brothers as Lingle's killer to a highly charged public starved for a conviction.

The Tribune congratulated Rathbun and Roche — and patted itself on the back for orchestrating the Brothers' arrest. Yet, the city's other newspapers remained just as skeptical in doubting Brothers' guilt as Father Reynolds. Editorials insinuated that Brothers was either the innocent victim of a frame-up, or he had allowed himself to be framed for money.

Word got out that Capone had handed

up Brothers to the state as a sacrificial lamb. Capone, already the prime target of a heavy examination by the IRS, didn't want his name tied to any illegal business operations that could be exposed during the course of a federal trial. Two men with explicit knowledge of Capone's illegal financial sources — Lingle and Zuta — were both dead, and all the incessant raids and arrests of suspected gangsters conducted by police on Rathbun's and Roche's orders had come to an end.

Brothers' capture gave police, prosecutors and the local press what the public demanded — a gangster to convict, a blond gangster no less, like the one spotted at the scene. Most importantly to Capone, Brothers had no knowledge whatsoever of the notorious gangland boss's finances.

The fall guy did not come without a price. Capone was rumored to have promised Brothers a substantial payout for his time and trouble. Whispers on the street also implied that Capone was greasing the palms of police friends and his crooked pals in Chicago's judicial system to leave Foster alone. Capone would need Foster to counter Moran if a new turf war between the two Chicago mob bosses broke out on the West Coast.

Patrick Campbell, the bystander Father Reynolds had bumped into on the way out of the station, was alleviated of any obligation to serve as a witness by prosecutors. The woman, her husband, and Father Reynolds were set to be among the prosecution's eight key witnesses against Leo V. Brothers — that is, until the woman's nerves got the better of her and she begged her way off the witness stand.

Six witnesses were set to testify they saw Brothers fleeing from the Michigan Avenue tunnel, although not one could positively identify Brothers as the gunman. Lead prosecutor C. Wayland Brooks let Father Reynolds know in no uncertain terms whom they wanted him to point out as Lingle's murderer: It wasn't Frankie Foster.

"I want you to say this boy that we picked up is the one you saw running away up the alley," Brooks told the priest.

"No," Father Reynolds replied. "I won't do that because he doesn't correspond. If I was casting a play and I wanted a character representing the blond boy, I would pick him if I couldn't get any other better representative."

"No, it's alright," the prosecutor urged. "We want you to."

"He has a kind of faint resemblance," Father Reynolds noted reluctantly.

"Then we can't use you," the prosecutor countered.

"That's just fine," the priest said. "I have a lot of work to do back at Notre Dame and I'll catch a train back."

"Oh, no," Brooks retroceded with a laugh. "We can use you."

Section 1: The Hit

He might have been out of sight, but Chicago was still (Al) Capone's city. Capone continued to be the chief benefactor from any and all of the city's organized crime business.

7

IN THE EYES OF CAPONE

F ather Reynolds returned to South Bend to await the trial.

Prosecutors were content to let Father Reynolds go about his business at Notre Dame. They put their trust in the priest to show up on Friday, March 27th, 1931, the day he would take the witness stand and help them convict Leo Brothers in the shooting death of Jake Lingle.

Word got out that Father Reynolds had already identified Frankie Foster as the shooter. Investigators had Foster's name on the murder weapon's receipt, which only confirmed what had leaked out to the streets: Father Reynolds had already fingered Foster in a photo lineup as the dark-haired assailant who had snatched the gun away from the fumbling blond accomplice and fired a bullet into Lingle's head. On the word of a priest under oath in front of Brothers' jury, the charges could shift to Foster, and Capone could lose one of his most valuable cogs in his plan to move West and challenge Moran for control of new turf that was being established in Los Angeles.

Whacking a double-crosser like Lingle or a rat like Zuta was mob business as usual. But to kill a priest? That was against the rules for even the most ruthless of criminals. Consequences would rain down in a holy hailstorm from all directions of the law, the press, the public, and rival gangsters who regularly sought out the blessings of the Catholic religion, not to mention the powerful institution that served as Father Reynolds' employer — Notre Dame.

Capone's men had orders to scare Father Reynolds into staying home, far away from the

Capone was a frequent visitor ...

witness stand. Already the target of a massive IRS probe into his finances, Capone couldn't afford the blood of a Catholic priest on his hands, too. Intimidating Father Reynolds into staying in South Bend and shunning the witness stand in Chicago was another matter.

Capone's bootlegging business stretched from Chicago to Canada back to his hometown of New York City, so he was no stranger to Michigan. He owned at least one home in his name in the Upper Peninsula city of Escanaba, but for privacy purposes Capone kept several hideout residences in associates' names, two of which were located just north of South Bend in the towns of Paw Paw and Berrien Springs. .

*Capone was a frequent visitor to South Bend. One favorite haunt, Martha's Midway Tavern & Dance Hall, was a small watering hole tucked on 4th Street in a predominantly

72

... the target of a massive IRS probe into his finances ...

Belgian neighborhood in the neighboring town of Mishawaka.

Once, upon sampling Martha's special batch of homemade corn liquor the tavern owner conjured up in her back yard, Capone offered a business opportunity.

"Let me sell your liquor in Chicago and you could make a lot of money," Capone suggested.

Martha declined politely. "I only make it for the neighbors," she replied. "I want to keep it small. It's just for my neighbors."

Later, when Martha relayed Capone's offer to her husband, she admitted the blunt truth for her refusal. "There's no way I'm going to do business with that man," Martha insisted.

Sending iniquitous men out to lurk in the shadows to follow Father Reynolds in an attempt to intimidate him into not testifying at the Brothers' trial proved an easy logistical mode of operation for Capone. Father Reynolds was an extremely intelligent man with an acute sense of his surroundings that some would describe as "street sense." Once he committed to help police identify Lingle's killer, Father Reynolds firmly grasped the stark reality that he couldn't step foot out of his residential quarters at Morrissey Hall without watching his back.

The priest also suspected that if

A familiar face climbed out followed by six intimidating goons who lined up behind Father Reynolds.

something were to happen to him, it wouldn't happen anywhere near the scene of the crime in Chicago. "Chicago is all Catholic," Father Reynolds reasoned.

But not even Chicago provided a safe haven for the potential witness in the city's most high-profile murder trial. In one incident, the wife of an acquaintance met Father Reynolds on the street and invited him up to their apartment for a drink.

"That smelt high of murder," Father Reynolds declared. "I knew if I didn't take it, that would offend them, and if I did take it, I would

be under a certain obligation, see, to them."

Never one to back down from a drink under any circumstance, Father Reynolds took the whiskey. "Of the two evils I chose the lesser one by taking the pint of whiskey and still living. You have to make a decision like that on an occasion like that."

Thanksgiving Day, 1930, Father Reynolds had just finished saying mass for students at Morrissey Hall. Leaving everybody in the dining room, Father Reynolds walked outside alone, where he was approached by a man dressed in a long coat. The suspicious man took a picture of Jake Lingle out of one pocket, then pulled a photo of Leo Brothers out of his other pocket.

"Are you going to testify against this man?" he asked.

"Well, " Father Reynolds replied, "my lawyer told me that if anybody asked a question like that, I was to tell them that they must see my lawyer."

The priest's brazen retort caught the man by surprise. He turned and disappeared back into the shadows.

During trips to Chicago to view photo lineups, Father Reynolds left the police station and headed to temporary quarters that appeared to be set up for him at the German House Hotel. The German House served as a smoke screen. Every night after he had checked in to the German House, a police officer arrived in a car to pick up Father Reynolds at the German House and take him to the Polish Catholic parish on the North Side, zooming in and out of traffic through the Loop with a police signal.

Capone's street soldiers still seemed to know when the prosecution's star witness was in town. One afternoon, while waiting to catch the train at the Harrison Street station, Father Reynolds was startled to see a car pull up next to the station. A familiar face climbed out, followed by six intimidating goons who lined up behind Father Reynolds. One pulled a gun from his side pocket and shifted it inside his coat in full view of the priest.

"And this fellow kept looking at me," Father Reynolds recalled. "And I kept looking at him. And they knew that I knew that he was the killer, see."

Frankie Foster stood face-to-face with Father Reynolds. But the priest, being the tough kid who grew up handing out his share of beatings in Bellows Falls, stood his ground. He remained outwardly calm, reserved, yet keenly aware of the immediate surroundings, trying to calculate a defense with one eye on a nearby metal chair.

"Well," he said, "I looked at the back of the chair and I was wondering whether that would stop a bullet or not because I was going to duck if they started firing. But I knew I had two things going for me, two strikes on them. One, I was a priest. Secondly, I was Irish, and if he killed an Irish priest in Chicago, the whole city would turn against him."

Seeing a strength in the priest he hadn't fully prepared for, Foster instantly packed it in without as much as a nod. "Come on, " he said to his goons. Foster turned around and returned to the car with all six men following close behind.

"Like little children, see, " Father Reynolds recalled. "And I breathed easily, see?"

The intimidation tactics didn't stop at shady characters following the priest from the streets of Chicago to the campus of Notre Dame. Two anonymous letters addressed to Father Reynolds arrived at Morrissey Hall on two separate occasions. Both carried the same ominous message:

"Notre Dame will be more sorry than it realizes if they allow you to testify."

Father Reynolds gave a passing thought to turning the letters over to his superiors at Notre Dame. Then he tossed them in a waste basket.

... the undisputed king of the college football world.

8

A TICKET

K nute Rockne was a champion again.

Rockne's Ramblers brought an end to their 1930 season with a stunning thrashing of archrival Southern California, 27-0, a good old-fashioned Fighting Irish butt-whooping in front of a massive crowd of 90,000 at the Los Angeles Coliseum that sealed Rockne's third undefeated and untied national championship in 13 years as head coach of Notre Dame.

The star of that title-winning domination served as testimony to Rockne's untethered prowess as a leader and motivator of young men. Of all the legendary players to take the field for the Fighting Irish under Rockne's command — George Gipp, Dutch Bergman, Adam Walsh, the Four Horsemen — it was a third-string running back, Paul "Bucky" O'Connor, from Bellows Falls, Vermont, who carried the load for the Irish on Dec. 7, 1930, rushing for 142 yards on 11 carries and scoring a touchdown.

In the season's immediate aftermath, Rockne helped organize a charity game in New York against the New York Giants to raise money for the city's food lines overwhelmed by unemployed New Yorkers victimized by the Great Depression. Rockne made a promise to O'Connor: "Play in the charity game, and I'll help you get into medical school at Yale University at no expense to your family." It was a promise Rockne kept.

Rockne was the undisputed king of the college football world. His fabled career record stood at 105-12-5, a mind-boggling winning percentage of .881. Once the trophies were handed out and the offseason was underway at the outset of 1931, Rockne was a hot commodity. Chronic health issues exacerbated by severe exhaustion plagued the coach, but he stubbornly planned to embark on a strenuous nationwide tour giving speeches to salesmen working for the Studebaker Corporation, the South Bend-based automobile manufacturer that provided Rockne with a very lucrative side income as a promotion manager. Already in the planning stages was Studebaker's next model, the "Rockne."

Flying was the only way for Rockne to travel around the country and meet the time demands of his grueling schedule.

"What's the use of wasting time on trains and automobiles?" he quipped to a friend. "This is a fast day and age. I've got to get around to do things and reach places."

Rockne's first offseason priority was to catch his breath with some rest and relaxation in Florida with his wife, Bonnie, their daughter, Mary Jeanne, 10, their youngest boy Jackie, 4, and their oldest sons, Bill, 15, and Knute Jr., 12, both of whom were on spring break from their boarding school at Kansas City's Pembroke Hill.

Two years of suffering with phlebitis that landed Rockne in a wheelchair for an extended period of time during the previous football season had not subsided. Doctors constantly warned him that the relentless stress of coaching football at a national championship level on top of a grueling personal business calendar was taking a severe toll on his soon-to-be 43-year-old body.

Traveling to Florida, Rockne caught a plane out of Chicago with stops in Atlanta and Jacksonville, then it was on to Miami. When the plane was in the air, Rockne turned to fellow passenger L.W. "Chip" Robert, a trustee at Georgia Tech and friend of the coach, and remarked: "I think that each of us has a time to go, and when that time comes, no matter where we are, it strikes. So, I figure I might as well be in a plane as anywhere else."

The Rocknes vacationed at their winter home in Coral Gables. On Saturday, March 21, Rockne and Bonnie hooked up with friends, Frank and Mary Wallace, for a relaxing evening at Hialeah Race Track. Afterwards, he told a writer the vacation was agreeing with him, he was feeling much better, and he was looking forward to the upcoming football season. He also found time to kick around a football in the front yard with his young son, Jackie.

With the opening of spring football practice set to begin at Notre Dame, Rockne left Bonnie and his four children in Coral Gables, hopped a plane and returned to South Bend to preside over the team's first spring drills.

Two days into the sessions, Rockne fielded a phone call from his agent, Christy Walsh. There was a $50,000 offer on the table to come to Hollywood to work as an adviser on the planned Universal Pictures film project, "The Spirit of Notre Dame."

Walsh added that the Hollywood filmmakers wanted Rockne in California the following week to sign a contract. In addition to movie business, the two-day trip was crammed with personal appearances: Rockne was set to be inducted into the L.A. Breakfast Club, and he would be the featured speaker at a convention for Studebaker executives to promote the soon-to-be-named "Rockne" Studebaker car. Chicago pal John H. Happer, comptroller for Great Western Sporting Goods, also wanted Rockne to help open a new Great Western store in Los Angeles.

Flying to the West Coast was the only way Rockne could meet all his Los Angeles business obligations in two days. He could also return to Kansas City on April 12 to speak at Pembroke Hill's athletics banquet, the military school sons Bill and Knute Jr. attended.

It didn't take long for Rockne to realize that he needed a plane reservation, but a ticket was difficult to find at the last minute. Faced with the need for a plane ticket to Los Angeles with no other alternative except for a long time-consuming train trip, Rockne's only recourse at the moment was to let Christy Walsh handle ticket arrangements.

Rockne had other pressing concerns. Spring football practice was his top priority.

Father Reynolds was anxious to get the Brothers' trial over with and behind him. Badly in need of some rest and relaxation far away from the threat of mobsters following him from Chicago to South Bend, far away from the pressures his Notre Dame superiors had been applying to get him out of this trial and avoid the school's name being splashed all over the headlines of one of the most notorious gangland murders in recent memory, the priest had already secured a plane ticket to the West Coast where he planned to get away from it all by enjoying his favorite hobby: hiking in the forests of Oregon.

Those plans were in jeopardy. Father Reynolds was the prosecutors' main witness. He had to make himself readily available at a moment's notice until the trial was completed. And he had to teach his American History class at Notre Dame the following week when students returned from spring break.

On Thursday, March 26, the night before he was scheduled to take the stand, Father Reynolds caught the South Shore train in South Bend and headed to Chicago. It was the usual routine of the past nine months: Check in at the German House, then slip out secretly under the protection of a police officer who drove Father Reynolds to the North Side to bed down at the local parish.

The trial was nearing the end of its second week. Eight witnesses called by prosecutor Curly Brooks described Lingle's killer as a man nearly 6-feet tall, well-built, young "like a college senior," wearing a gray suit and straw skimmer over light brown or blond hair. The blond man, according to the witnesses, was seen walking quickly toward Lingle moments before the fatal shot was fired in the tunnel, then doubling back the way he had come and dashing out of the tunnel after the shooting.

Six witnesses had pointed to Leo Brothers sitting at the defendant's table and identified him as the man who shot Jake Lingle. Seven witnesses testified to not seeing Brothers at the scene.

Before Father Reynolds took the witness stand on Friday, March 27, a photographer shot a photograph of the priest sitting in a chair in a waiting room down the hall from the courtroom. Seeing the camera, he tried to hide his nerves but the lens captured a frightened look that could not conceal the truth: Father Reynolds' eyes were filled with the fear of God.

That fear subsided on the witness stand. With Leo Brothers sitting at the defendant's table next to his attorney, Louis Piquett — the same Louis Piquett who had met with Lingle the night before Lingle was shot to death, and the same defense attorney who would later gain national prominence defending John Dillinger — Brooks fired off a series of questions before asking Father Reynolds to look Brothers in the eye and identify him as

... a stunning thrashing of archrival Southern California ...

the gunman who shot Jake Lingle.

"He answered the description," Father Reynolds replied obtusely.

It's the most honest account Father Reynolds could give without defying his Bible-sworn oath, but hardly the rock-solid ID the prosecutor sought from the priest in front of the jury.

For months, those random threatening confrontations and anonymous letters had made it perfectly clear that the underworld didn't want Father Reynolds to testify. But his civil duty was completed. Father Reynolds got off the witness stand, walked out of the courtroom, and left the courthouse with the sole intention of catching the next train back to South Bend and putting the entire ordeal behind him.

The next day, Father Reynolds decided to unwind with a peaceful Saturday afternoon stroll on campus. Walking in front of the main building, the Golden Dome, he spotted a familiar face approaching from the opposite side of the courtyard with a smile on his face.

Father Reynolds recognized his pal Knute Rockne immediately. The two had been friends since 1916 when Rockne was Notre Dame's track coach, and Father Reynolds was a star of the track team who had set a national record for the 2-mile run.

The two greeted each other with open arms. After a brief chat about the trial, Rockne mentioned the Universal Pictures offer. The filmmakers wanted him to travel to Hollywood the following week to lend his expertise during production of "The Spirit of Notre Dame," a film starring Lew Ayres and Andy Devine. Rockne mentioned that there had been other film offers the past few years, but each one focused on Notre Dame football, and each was met with opposition from the Notre Dame hierarchy who wanted to distance themselves from football in favor of portraying the school as an academic institution.

This offer was different. Rockne told Father Reynolds how excited he was to get out to Hollywood and finalize his contract to work on this movie. There was a jam-packed two-day schedule planned the minute he arrived. But it was difficult to find a plane ticket to Los Angeles in such a short time, and a train would take too long to get to the West Coast.

Father Reynolds looked Rockne in the eye. He pulled out the flight reservation to the West Coast that he was unable to use.

"Take it, Rock," Father Reynolds said. "I'm in no hurry to get to Los Angeles."

The ticket was for Transcontinental & Western Flight 599, a passenger/postal delivery flight set to leave Kansas City for Los Angeles on Tuesday, March 31.

It was a perfect flight to accommodate Rockne's tight two-day West Coast schedule: He could travel to Chicago on Sunday, take the overnight train to Kansas City Monday night, and arrive just in time Tuesday morning to have a brief rendezvous with his sons, Bill and

Knute Jr. The boys were still with their mother in Florida for the family's spring vacation trip, and they were expected to return by train to Kansas City at 8 a.m. on March 31. The timing was tight, but it did allow Rockne a few precious minutes with his sons before the plane departed Kansas City at 8:30 a.m.

This flight put Rockne in Los Angeles by nightfall — where his two close friends, "Navy Bill" Ingram, head coach of California, and his old pal, Pop Warner, who had moved on to coach Stanford, had already flown from San Francisco and were awaiting a reunion.

Rockne stuck out his hand and thanked the priest for the ticket. Father Reynolds grasped his pal's hand without mentioning anything about the mob intimidation tactics that had followed him the past few months.

The trial was over for Father Reynolds.

Two anonymous letters he received on two separate occasions at his residence at Morrissey Hall, the last of which arrived in his mail just a few days before he took the witness stand, were in the trash and all but forgotten. "Notre Dame will be more sorry than it realizes if they allow you to testify" was a message that was gone with the wind.

Rockne was grateful for the priest's generosity. The two said goodbye and went their separate ways.

SECTION 2
THE CRASH

"... if I hadn't given Rock my tickets, he would have been alive." — *Father John Reynolds*

9

DELAYED FLIGHT

U sing the plane ticket purchased in Chicago by Father Reynolds, Christy Walsh handled the transfer of reservations for the flight leaving Kansas City on Tuesday into Rockne's name.

Before catching the train in South Bend and heading to Chicago on Palm Sunday evening, Rockne drove from his home on East Wayne Street and stopped in to visit his former neighbors, Tom and Kate Hickey, at their home on East St. Vincent Street a few blocks away from the Notre Dame campus.

After living next door to each other on St. Vincent Street for six years, the Hickeys and the Rocknes had become close friends. Tom Hickey accompanied Rockne on several road trips, and the two often shared sleeping compartments during those trips. Hickey had even served as Rockne's godfather during Rockne's baptism in Notre Dame's Log Chapel on November 20, 1925, when Rockne converted to Catholicism.

The Hickeys had a driveway to park cars, but Rockne, as was his custom, parked on the street and walked up the stairs to the front door. It was a nice visit. Rockne was his usual jovial self, down on the floor playing football with the Hickeys' 3-year-old son, Joe.

Toward the end of his stay, Rockne positioned himself by the home's front entryway and hiked the ball to the toddler. The ball sailed over the boy's head and smashed Kate Hickey's favorite Chinese vase.

Rockne shrugged his shoulders. Smiled an apologetic grin. Then told his friends good-

Martha Gjermo Rockne's 72nd birthday was filled with cake and champagne.

bye and Tom Hickey watched his pal saunter down the walkway to his car and drive off.

*Rockne caught the South Shore train in South Bend headed to Chicago. Upon arrival, he went straight to his mother's house. Martha Gjermo Rockne's 72nd birthday was filled with cake and champagne.

On Monday, Rockne stopped in at the Chicago Herald-Examiner for a conversation with the paper's sports editor, Warren Brown. That evening before catching the train to Kansas City, he met up with Christy Walsh and Chicago playwright Albert C. Fuller over dinner and cigars.

"Soft landings, Coach," Fuller said in farewell as Rockne hopped into a cab.

"Yes," Rockne replied. "But, you mean, happy landings."

The cab dropped Rockne off at the train station in time to catch the overnight train to Kansas City that departed Chicago just before midnight.

Rockne rode the train through the night. When he arrived in Kansas City at about 7 a.m. the next morning, his pal and former Notre Dame teammate on the 1912 and 1913 squads, Dr. Dominic Michael "D.M." Nigro, greeted him at Union Station. The two longtime friends had breakfast in the Union Station dining room while they waited for the train carrying Bill and Knute Jr. to arrive from Florida.

But the boys' train was late. Rockne's flight was scheduled to depart Kansas City Municipal Airport at 8:30 a.m., he didn't have time to wait. Figuring to see his boys when he returned April 12 to speak at the Pembroke Hill athletic banquet, Rockne and Dr. Nigro took off for the airport to catch the T&WA flight in time.

After arriving at Kansas City Municipal Airport, Rockne took a few minutes to wire a telegram to Bonnie, who was still on vacation at their home in Coral Gables.

Rockne's friend, John Happer, was also ready to board the flight to Los Angeles. Rockne planned to help Happer set up a new Great Western Sporting Goods store in Los Angeles. The other passengers on the 10-seat airliner included C.A. Robrecht, a produce businessman from Wheeling, West Virginia; Waldo B. Miller, of Hartford, Connecticut, an assistant superintendent of sales promotion in the group life and disability department of Aetna Insurance company; Spencer Goldthwaite, a young New Yorker traveling to Pasadena to visit his parents; and with the exception of Happer, the only other passenger from Chicago, H.J. Christen.

Christen, who worked as a dime store interior designer in Chicago, was traveling to California in an effort to reconcile with his estranged wife. Just before leaving Chicago, Christen had cashed a check for $55,000, a massive sum of money for a storeroom designer to be carrying in 1931. The Chicago Tribune, the Chicago Herald-Examiner and the Chicago Evening Post had just paid out a combined $55,000 in reward money to the unknown informant responsible for the arrest and conviction of Leo Brothers, the Capone hitman on trial for killing Chicago Tribune reporter Jake Lingle — the trial Father Reynolds had testified as a witness just four days before the flight.

But there was a problem. Passengers were notified that T&WA Flight 599 had been held up to wait for a late mail shipment due to arrive at any time. Jack Frye, T&WA's vice president of operations, pushed the flight's takeoff time back to 9:15 a.m.

Rockne was anxious to get to Los Angeles. Frye's refusal to order the pilot, Capt.

Robert (Joe-Pete) Fry, to put the plane in the air on schedule did not sit well with the fiery football coach. In full view of T&WA station operations department worker Wes Bunker, Rockne cornered Captain Fry and exerted some of his famous motivation on the experienced former military fighter pilot.

"I paid for the ticket and you're paid to fly, let's go!" Rockne insisted loudly enough for everyone within earshot to hear. Fry stared at the ground. He shuffled his feet. A few seconds later, the pilot shrugged his acknowledgement.

Finally, the mail shipment arrived. Four seats on the plane were removed to make room for additional mail pouches that carried nearly 95 pounds of weight.

The passengers boarded the plane. Rockne was the last passenger to settle into a wicker chair with a leather cushion and no seatbelt. At about 9:45 a.m., Transcontinental & Western Flight 599 — a Fokker F-10 Trimotor, three-engine monoplane made out of laminated wood — was in the air.

Bad weather with rain, thick clouds and poor visibility between Kansas City and the

One of the Fokker Trimotor's wings ripped away and fluttered to the ground like a giant piece of paper.

first scheduled stop in Wichita prompted Fry and co-pilot Jess Mathias to navigate the first leg of the flight under low-hanging clouds. With reports of clear skies ahead, both pilots switched back and forth on the radio checking weather conditions with air traffic controllers at Wichita airport.

Rockne and the passengers were oblivious to the activity in the cockpit. Rockne peered out the window, but it was too cloudy for visibility. He felt the plane shake under his seat with turbulence. Numerous cross-country flights had made Rockne an experienced air traveler. He didn't think twice about the mild turbulence under his seat.

A radar map tracking the flight in Wichita indicated suddenly that the plane was altering its direction. Wichita flight controllers speculated a possible return to Kansas City. At exactly 10:45 a.m., a terse radio transmission from Mathias sent a chill through their airwaves.

"No time to talk," the co-pilot said.

Radio communication went dead.

Ranchers R.Z. Blackburn, Edward Baker and Clarence H. McCracken were working their daily farm chores on the ground when they spotted a large wooden aircraft flying at only about 600 feet. Young Edward Baker looked up from feeding cattle and recognized the plane as the mail airliner that frequently flew over his father's farm.

What Edward Baker witnessed next was something out of a bad dream: "A terrific explosion in the foggy sky..." is how a newspaperman would describe Baker's eyewitness account later that day in the March 31, 1931, evening edition of the Sedalia (Mo.) Democrat. "Looking up, the youth saw an airplane burst into flames and rocket toward the earth..."

One of the Fokker Trimotor's wings ripped away and fluttered to the ground like a giant piece of paper. The plane spiraled out of the cloudy sky and crashed into a wheat field owned by Edward Baker's father, Steward H. Baker, near the tiny community of Bazaar, Kansas.

The impact was violent, loud and ground-shaking.

"The plane was flying low and seemed to explode in the air," Edward Baker's mother told a reporter. "My son watched it spin in flames and bury itself in the soft pasture."

After shelling corn with his parents and brothers in their kitchen, 13-year-old Easter Heathman headed out to the barn on an errand when he heard a raspy, coughing roar that sounded like cars racing on the highway about a mile away. A phone call from a neighbor informed the Heathman family that a plane had crashed nearby at 10:37 a.m. The Heathmans jumped in their Model T and were among the first to arrive at the scene.

"My Uncle Clarence seen it come out of the clouds," Easter Heathman recalled. "He said the wing was broke off. The plane was turning end-over-end. You can picture in your own mind what that ride was like.

"There was the smell of gasoline and hot oil," Heathman said.

The crash scene was catastrophic. Pieces of airliner furnishings, wood and debris scattered through the air for hundreds of feet. The impact was so tremendous, the tail of the plane was twisted and broken, resting at right angles to what was left of the fuselage — a fuselage made of solid steel tubing, bent, twisted and broken far beyond salvageable reclamation.

Edward Baker walked up on five bodies lying in a line about 30 feet from the tail near a long pile of broken wood, torn fabric and pieces of the aircraft, all reeking of gasoline and hot oil. The bodies of both pilots and John Happer were still in the plane's nose cone.

Another body came to rest on the ground near the wreckage. The left hand of the unrecognizable remains of Knute Rockne clutched a rosary.

Stunned responders had no idea who the victims were; no clue that the mangled body pulled out of the wreckage by three teams of horses — with his spinal column split wide open, his head mutilated beyond recognition, and his right arm driven into the pit of his stomach — belonged to the most famous football coach in the land, beloved by fans all over the world.

The Heathmans remained at the site until the coroner arrived about an hour later. Easter and his family helped carry bodies on stretchers to the ambulances that transported them to Kansas City. They also helped pick up scattered mail around the site. Once Baker notified an undertaker 30 miles away in Cottonwood Falls, ambulances rushed to the scene over muddy roads, which slowed their travel time to a crawl.

By the time ambulances arrived, word of the crash had already spread like wildfire throughout the area. Crowds of locals, drawn to the site by morbid curiosity, snatched up bits of the plane. Large pieces of the wing, fuselage, and other significant plane parts that might have otherwise revealed the actual cause of the crash were loaded as souvenirs into cars and pickup trucks.

Some locals got in and out of the crash scene quickly enough to make their way to hotel lobbies in nearby towns and sell the wreckage souvenirs before ambulances carrying the morticians and caskets arrived from Cottonwood Falls to collect the remains of Rockne and the rest of the victims.

Christen's body was found with $400 in his clothes. Just two days later on April 2, newspapers across the country reported that mystery surrounded the disappearance of $55,000 Christen was said to have withdrawn shortly before boarding the plane. His attorney, Murray Miller, reasoned that Christen could have deposited the money in another bank or invested it in securities before he left for the trip. The possibility of a souvenir collector coming across the money wrapped in a briefcase or similar pack and running off with a cash windfall amid the onset of the Great Depression was never mentioned in newspaper follow-ups.

Harold V. Lyle, a rookie photographer for the Wichita Eagle, had previously met Rockne in Newton, Kansas, when the coach and the Notre Dame football team were eating breakfast while waiting for a train. When Lyle arrived at the Eagle office early on the morning of March 31, he was greeted by a brief teletype saying Rockne had left Kansas City on a Transcontinental & Western flight bound for Wichita. It didn't take long for the bulletin bell on the teletype machine to ring with a wire report of a plane going down in Chase County, Kansas.

Lyle and the newspaper's sports editor, Bill Cunningham, immediately chartered a plane and headed to the area. Their pilot couldn't locate the wreckage from the air until he spotted a cowboy on the ground wearing a red bandana on a horse waving them toward the southeast. Once over the wreckage, Lyle snapped photos of the tail and the devastation of plane wreckage surrounded by a large gathering of people and several black cars. He also shot photos of circular tracks of tire trails in the snow left behind by local souvenir scavengers who had snatched pieces of the wrecked plane and taken off.

"I knew then, by the size of the airplane, it was the Transcontinental and Western," Lyle recalled 37 years later on the anniversary of the crash. "I knew Rockne was dead. I took the aerial photographs then. I hated to, but it was my job."

Since nobody knew the identities of the eight victims, responders on the ground could only ask one question: How did it happen?

The Associated Press was the first news outlet to break the story. Every late edition of every newspaper across the country, which printed the AP account of the crash on March 31, 1931, cited witnesses on the ground who heard an "explosion" in mid-air. Several newspapers reported eyewitness accounts that saw the plane "in flames" as it "cartwheeled" to the ground.

Same-day headlines screamed 'explosion' on the front pages of both afternoon editions in Pittsburgh. "Knute Rockne, 7 Others Die As Plane Explodes, Crashes," blared the Pittsburgh (Pa.) Sun Telegraph. "Knute Rockne, 7 Others Die As Plane Explodes," clamored The

... the tail of the plane was twisted and broken ...

Pittsburgh (Pa.) Press. A bold-highlighted subhead on the front-page crash story in the Red Bluff (California) Daily News revealed "Explosion on Plane Reported By Farmer Watching Flight" then cited Edward Baker's eyewitness account with the description, "Suddenly, he said, there was an explosion and the ship fell to the earth."

Three hours later when crash investigators from the Aeronautics Branch of the U.S. Commerce Department arrived on the scene, details of the plane coming down began to soften from the first "explosion" accounts. The following day, newspapers made no mention of a mid-air explosion. "Wing Drops From Clouds, Plane Falls," read the New York Daily News headline on April 1, 1931.

The version told by the property's owner, Steward Baker, differed slightly from his son's on-the-spot eyewitness recollection of hearing an "explosion" in mid-air and the plane "falling in flames" from the sky.

"We heard the plane flying over this morning, but couldn't see it for the clouds," Steward Baker said in nationwide reports that splashed headlines of the plane crash the following morning. "A minute later it sounded like the motors were missing and then we couldn't hear them at all. It seemed like five minutes after the ship passed over the house that we heard the crash. It landed in the pasture about a mile from the house and when it hit, it sounded like a muffled explosion. It didn't catch fire after it hit."

(Above) First-day headline for the Rockne plane crash on the front page of The Pittsburgh Press, March 31, 1931

(Page 94) First-day headlines of the crash on the front pages of the Pittsburgh Sun-Telegraph and Red Bluff (California) Daily News that appeared on March 31, 1931.

Some newspapers were quick to report investigators' claims that ice on the wings brought the plane down. Other newspapers indicated that the pilot's visibility was blinded by clouds, and that the plane's instruments had been rendered useless by ice that formed on the wing's air tubes. When the pilot realized the plane was in a death spiral, it was too late, and part of a wing pulled off when he tried to pull out of the dive, reports speculated.

News conjectures were countered by eyewitnesses on the ground and air traffic controllers in Wichita who claimed the pilots knew where they were. Weather conditions were not ideal, but Wichita airport's radar system showed no signs of severe weather systems.

Also noted was a NAT Mail plane piloted by Paul E. Johnson that flew safely without any problems just ahead of the Fokker F-10. A preliminary investigation revealed that although temperatures were slightly above freezing on the ground, no ice had been found on any part of the plane.

Today **Kline Named Jobholders, Lang Says**

Pittsburgh Sun-Telegraph WALL ST CLOSE

VOL. 8—NO. 38   40 PAGES   TUESDAY, MARCH 31, 1931   THREE CENTS

KNUTE ROCKNE, 7 OTHERS DIE AS PLANE EXPLODES, CRASHES

LANG ADMITS PRESSURE BY KLINE

QUAKE ROCKS MANAGUA; 40 DEAD

FOOTBALL'S GODFATHER KILLED!
—See Pictorial Studies of This Strong Character on Page 3—

FAMOUS NOTRE DAME COACH MEETS DEATH IN KANSAS WRECK

Red Bluff Daily News

RED BLUFF, TEHAMA COUNTY, CALIFORNIA, TUESDAY EVENING, MARCH 31, 1931   ESTABLISHED 1885

ROCKNE KILLED IN PLANE CRASH

...ker Dies In Highway Explosion

ROAD BILL IS ENDORSED BY SENATE

NOTED FOOTBALL COACH AND SEVEN MEN DIE INSTANTLY

Five Pupils Die in Blizzard

DUFFUS WINS GOLF CROWN THIRD TIME

Baboon Amuck Injures 5 Before Killed By Officers

CABARET SINGER IS ACQUITTED OF MURDER CHARGE

BERTHA CROCKER DIES IN BAY CITY

FAST HORSES FROM SANTA ROSA COMING HERE FOR ROUND-UP

Section 2: The Crash

Rockne's secretary, Ruth Faulkner, wept openly.

10

IDENTIFICATIONS

Word leaked out that Rockne's name was listed on the flight log's passenger list.

The press not only had a national disaster to report, but also that the most famous football coach in America was among the dead. Every newspaper and radio network across the country jumped on the news that Rockne was killed before the coroner confirmed the identities of any of the victims.

In a fateful twist of irony, Jess Harper, the former Notre Dame coach Rockne replaced in 1918, was living about 100 miles away from the crash site. Harper heard the news, jumped in his car and drove to Cottonwood Falls to officially identify his longtime friend's body.

Martha Gjermo Rockne learned of her son's death from a radio news bulletin, as did Martha Stiles, one of Rockne's four sisters. Mrs. Stiles phoned WGN Radio in Chicago for an update, but she was told her brother's body had not yet been identified; the station was still awaiting confirmation.

When the news was confirmed to Martha Rockne that her son was among the dead, her calm words were spiritually subdued: "It's God's will and we must not question it."

Martha snapped off a cable to Bonnie Rockne, who was still in Florida. But Bonnie never received the wire from her mother-in-law. She was at the beach spending her last day in Florida with daughter Mary Jeanne, and Tom O'Neil and his wife — the Rocknes' friends from Akron, Ohio.

At about 2:30 p.m., Bonnie and Mary Jeanne rode in a car with the O'Neils back to the house in Coral Gables, where a handful of friends had gathered along with telegrams that began to

CLASS OF SERVICE		SIGNS
This is a full-rate Telegram or Cablegram unless its deferred character is indicated by a suitable sign above or preceding the address.	WESTERN UNION	DL = Day Letter NM = Night Message NL = Night Letter LCO = Deferred Cable NLT = Cable Night Letter WLT = Week-End Letter

NEWCOMB CARLTON, PRESIDENT J. C. WILLEVER, FIRST VICE-PRESIDENT

The filing time as shown in the date line on full-rate telegrams and day letters, and the time of receipt at destination as shown on all messages, is STANDARD TIME.

Received at   1931 MAR 31 AM 9 56

MZ17 10=MP KANSASCITY MO 31 841A

MRS BONNIE ROCKNE=

2202 NORTH GREENSWAY CORALGABLES FLO=

LEAVING RIGHT NOW WILL BE AT BILTMORE LOVE AND KISSES=

KNUTE..

... Rockne's last words to his wife.

arrive offering condolences. O'Neil no sooner pulled the car into a garage when an attendant recognized Bonnie. The attendant pulled O'Neil aside and told him about the crash.

Shocked and devastated, O'Neil maintained his composure long enough to approach Bonnie. "I've got some serious news for you," he said gently.

A look of disbelief crossed Bonnie's face. No way her husband was dead. Just a few hours ago she received the telegram Knute had wired before he boarded the plane in Kansas City.

"LEAVING RIGHT NOW WILL BE AT BILTMORE LOVE AND KISSES... KNUTE." were Rockne's last words to his wife.

"I just don't believe it," Bonnie repeated softly, over and over. Only after sitting down with O'Neil and a priest, Father David Barry of Miami Beach, did Bonnie accept the tragic news as fact.

She turned to her son, Jackie. "Your daddy has gone away. He loved you so."

Bonnie put forth a brave face. With urgency to help her family pack for the long trip back to South Bend, Bonnie began to fill an old trunk with the initials "K.K.R." printed inside. Among the items Bonnie made sure to take home — the small football Knute and little Jackie kicked around the front yard before he left. The trunk was nearly filled, with barely enough space for the ball. Over Neil's suggestion to let the air out of the ball, Bonnie made room for her husband's last bastion of life without deflating it.

"Knute blew that up himself," she said.

Chicago Tribune Sports Editor Arch Ward had spoken with Rockne over the phone earlier that morning before the coach boarded the plane in Kansas City. Ward was at his home in Chicago when he received a call from Tribune

A look of disbelief crossed Bonnie's face ...

Managing Editor Loy Maloney.

"Where's your friend, Rockne?" Maloney asked. "There's a report that this might be the plane he was on. You better get down here. There's nothing official, but it looks like Knute Rockne's dead."

Ward was stunned. Rockne's passionate voice talking about his plans to take a jazz band on a tour of Europe to raise money for the cancer-stricken mother of one of his players was still fresh in Ward's head. Rockne had also mentioned that Hearst newspapers were offering to pay him $75,000 to retire from coaching and write a syndicated football column.

Ward had hung up the phone from Rockne thrilled over the thought that prosperity was finally on the horizon for his friend, a beloved icon who had given away more money to help people in need than he had ever made coaching at Notre Dame. Rockne's sudden death was no mere tragedy — it was a paralyzing injustice.

Ward picked up the phone and dialed the number at the Rockne's vacation home in Coral Gables. Bonnie answered.

"Mrs. Rockne, there's this crazy story going around," Ward said. "I don't mean to upset you, but the wire services think something awful has happened to Rock."

"It's true," Bonnie replied. "They just called."

The phone clicked off in Ward's ear.

"Gentlemen, we have lost the best friend that a man could ever have." — Father Charles L. O'Donnell

That night, Bonnie, Mary Jeanne, Jackie, the O'Neils and the Rocknes' maid caught the train. The ride was a long, somber trip home.

Word of Rockne's death spread like wildfire throughout Notre Dame and South Bend. "Have you heard?" was a question that started every conversation on campus prompting the common reply, "Can it really be true?" As initial reports confirmed the death, the Basilica of the Sacred Heart filled up quickly with a stream of students, faculty members and campus workers, many crying openly. Telephone lines were flooded with students calling family members to relay the tragic news.

Eugene "Scrapiron" Young, the first full-time trainer in Notre Dame history, left his home at around 1 p.m. and strolled along Eddy Street Road toward the campus. Two blocks into his walk, he heard footsteps approaching. Young turned to see who might be running to catch up. One of Rockne's players, John "Big John" McManmon, lumbered toward him at a fast speed before he stopped next to the trainer huffing to catch his breath.

"Have you heard, Scrap?" Big John's usual jovial Irish nature gave way to a voice that sounded like it was coming from a tomb.

"Have I heard what?" Young asked,

expecting McManmon to break into one of his customary practical jokes.

"Oh, dear God," McManmon said. "I hope it isn't true. They say Rock is dead."

Young's heart stopped beating. His legs sagged. A cold chill formed in his toes and shot upwards through his body like a lightning bolt that pierced his brain.

"Dead!" Young gasped, looking directly into McManmon's eyes. Genuine horror was etched in Big John's face.

McManmon filled Young in on the sketchy details of what had been reported of the crash, then the two headed over to the Administration Building, taking the steps two at a time. When they got to the door of the Athletic Office, both froze in their tracks. Young's stomach contracted into what felt like a fist-like knot. Bracing themselves as best as they could, Young and Big John entered the office.

Rockne's assistants had already gathered in the Athletic Office. Hunk Anderson, Jack Chevigny, Ike Voedisch and Tim Moynihan talked quietly amongst themselves. Rockne's secretary, Ruth Faulkner, wept openly.

News spread throughout campus as the seconds turned to minutes. Phones rang occasionally at first, then rapidly became an incessant clamor of calls from newspapermen and radio stations from around the country. People crowded into the Athletic Office, including the football team. Players' emotions ran the gamut. Some talked excitedly, while others tried to whisper quietly. Others clenched fists and alternated pacing the floor pounding their fists into their hands or against the wall. Some just stood and prayed.

The office door opened and the secretary to Notre Dame President Father Charles L. O'Donnell entered the room. "Will you all please follow me?" she asked.

Young followed the team and everyone else into the president's office where Father O'Donnell was waiting. He waited until the last team member arrived then closed the door. Father O'Donnell removed his glasses; Young noticed red-rimmed eyes.

"Gentlemen, we have lost the best friend that a man could ever have," is all Father O'Donnell could say before his voice broke on the last word and he was rendered speechless. The only sound in the room was the sobs of players.

Father Reynolds was supervising a recreation period with students. When the news hit, he dropped to his knees. His body went numb. The priest listened in silent shock as radio reports told of an eyewitness, "a little farmer boy," who heard an explosion in the clouds and watched "a pillar of fire rise up near where the wing attached itself to the machine... and then the wing flew off..."

It was all Father Reynolds could do to bow his head in prayer.

"I can do that standing on my head ..." — Leo Brothers

11

GUILTY

Two days after the crash, headlines of Rockne's death and tributes to his remarkable life and coaching career overshadowed the end to what had been the biggest story in Chicago for the better part of the year:

After three weeks of witnesses testifying at Cook County Criminal Court in the high-profile trial formally entitled "The State of Illinois vs. Leo V. Brothers," a jury found Leo Brothers guilty of murdering Jake Lingle.

The Brothers' trial, which lasted from March 16 to April 2, nearly ended in a hung jury because of evidence that had been just as evenly balanced in Brothers' favor as it was against him. The jury deliberated 27 hours before coming back with what many viewed as a compromised verdict — a guilty verdict that would be challenged unsuccessfully a year later in Brothers' appeal to the Illinois State Supreme Court titled "The People v Brothers."

"The principal controversy relates to the identification of (Brothers) as the man who shot Lingle and fled from the scene of the crime," Illinois State Supreme Court Justice Norman L. Jones wrote in his lead opinion filed in response to defense attorney Louis Piquett's appeal in February 1932. "Various witnesses positively identified defendant as being in the tunnel and as the man who dropped the gun and ran up the stairs and across the street. Other witnesses testified with equal positiveness that they were present and that defendant was not that man."

Of six prosecution witnesses, five positively identified Brothers as the man they had seen run from the tunnel of the train station and flee across Michigan Avenue. Warren Williams,

Otto Swoboda ... paid by the state attorney... on several occasions.

Daniel Davidson Mills, Marcus David, and Patrick Campbell — the man who bumped into Father Reynolds as he started to chase the assailant — each testified that they got a good look at Brothers' face. Williams claimed the man passed within a foot of him as he ran out.

Otto Swoboda told jurors that he was in the public library shortly before the shooting and noticed a man, whom he later learned was Frankie Foster, leaning against the wall of the library with another man standing nearby. A short while later as Swoboda was crossing the street to go to Grant Park, he walked into the tunnel when a man rushed past him and knocked a lighted cigarette out of his mouth. Swoboda testified that he recognized Brothers as the man who had knocked his cigarette out.

Red flags had popped up on these prosecution witnesses as soon as the trial began. Swoboda had been paid by the state attorney sums ranging from $2 to $25 on several occasions. And he had been compensated to travel to two out-of-state prisons where Brothers was held, including Leavenworth, which bordered on prosecutorial witness tampering.

Williams was on the payroll of the state attorney's office as an investigator to the tune of $200 a month. Campbell — known by two names, Patrick and John — was free on $2,500 Cook County bond for conspiracy to commit robbery. Campbell had also been working on a plea deal with the same Cook County prosecutor's office when he was called to testify against Brothers.

Chicago Police Officer Anthony Ruthy had followed one of the suspects out of the train station onto Michigan Avenue. Ruthy, initially, had identified Frankie Foster as the man he had chased. But when he took the witness stand and it came out that he was mentally unbalanced due to a previous brain injury, and that he had been assigned by the Police Department to light duty at the time of the Lingle murder, Ruthy was ruled to be unreliable and his testimony was suppressed.

Seven witnesses with no strings attached to either the defense or prosecution freely testified that Brothers was not the gunman.

Lawrence O'Malley, a railroad switchman, said he was in the underpass "within six feet" of the triggerman when Lingle was shot, and that Brothers was not the shooter. Real estate broker Harry J. O'Connor, fv who was in the tunnel when he heard the shot, told both sides of attorneys that he could not identify Brothers as the assailant. Albert Stein, an employee in the Cook County Office of the

"Do you see anyone in the courtroom now that you saw that day?" prosecutor Curly Brooks asked...

Brothers attorney, Louis Piquett, never pressed Father Reynolds for clarity.

Samuel Lederer ... whose hobby as a criminal investigator landed him on the team of the Lingle murder investigation ...

Recorder, was with O'Connor and another man in the tunnel at Randolph Street when he heard a gunshot and saw a man running with two men chasing him up the stairs. Stein told jurors the man he saw was "not as tall, or as heavy," as Brothers.

Abigail Wilson, Madeline Whitehurst, Paul Thomas and Pasquale Clarizio each testified to seeing the gunman running away, but that the man they saw was not the defendant. Whitehurst told jurors that she "got a good look" at a "young man coming up the stairs" at the same time she heard someone in the tunnel shouting, "Get that man!" She told jurors that she had never seen the man before in her life — and that she had never seen Brothers before the day of the trial. Clarizio, a stock clerk with the Dennison Manufacturing Company at 62 East Randolph Street, recalled seeing Officer Ruthy and several people chasing a man through an alley. Brothers, Clarizio maintained, was not the man Ruthy was chasing.

Despite the witnesses' denials under oath in front of the judge and jury, Leo Brothers was found guilty of pulling the trigger on Lingle.

Conviction of first-degree murder called for the death penalty. Yet, Brothers was sentenced to 14 years in prison, a sentence commutable to eight years for good behavior. As the rest of the country mourned Rockne's death, Brothers laughed off the light sentence for killing a Chicago Tribune reporter whose secret life working as a bagman for Al Capone was still being unveiled to an unwitting public.

"I can do that standing on my head," Brothers said with a smirk upon hearing his sentence.

Post-trial newspaper accounts revealed that prosecutors, police, Chicago politicians and even the Chicago Tribune considered Brothers' conviction as a turning point in the city's battle with gangsters.

In the months after the Lingle murder, the city's top brass found themselves on the receiving end of heavy public backlash screaming that criminals, namely Capone, were ruling the city through violence. The same law enforcement bosses and high-end politicos who lauded the Brothers conviction as a big win for the city were the same figureheads who manipulated circumstances surrounding the trial so Brothers could be convicted in the Lingle murder and give the public what it was clamoring for: a guilty verdict and closure to a high-profile case.

Among all the witnesses to take the stand, only Father Reynolds had seen the actual gunman pull the trigger. When he took the stand on March 27, the priest remained ambivalent in his identification of Brothers. The priest testified to seeing a "blond young chap with a gray suit and blond hair" running from the tunnel between "the safety island and the curb" while being chased by a policeman.

"Do you see anyone in the courtroom now that you saw that day?" prosecutor Curly Brooks asked.

"Mr. Brothers answers the description," Father Reynolds carefully replied.

Brothers attorney, Louis Piquett, never pressed Father Reynolds for clarity. The priest's nebulous choice of words left the question of "reasonable doubt" open for the jury to mull, which satisfied the defense lawyer who made a nice living defending gangsters in Capone's crew and, later, John Dillinger. Father Reynolds' fuzzy description that left Brothers' guilt or innocence wide open for interpretation was also satisfactory to the judge, the prosecutors, and everyone else in the courtroom, including the press.

Brothers was, at the least, a formidable sacrificial lamb. During the months prior to the trial during questioning of suspects, investigators learned that St. Louis mobster Fred Burke, a former charter member of Egan's Rats, had hired Lingle's killers. It was Burke who brought in Brothers to don a different disguise each day and trail the Tribune reporter to get an idea of his schedule so the hit could be planned with a time and place. On at least one occasion, Brothers followed Lingle disguised as a priest.

Brothers may not have pulled the trigger, but he had been involved in the murderous conspiracy. That was good enough for city officials determined to secure a conviction in a high-profile case and save face in a city where an outraged public demanded protection against organized crime.

Capone, meanwhile, had been the subject of a growing investigation into his finances by the IRS. Several of Capone's friends and associates on his payroll, including politicians and reporters such as Jake Lingle, maintained intimate knowledge of the gangster's illegal financial sources — most notably from bootlegging, gambling and prostitution. If Capone went down for not paying taxes, politicians and anyone else connected to his illegal enterprise would go with him.

Politicians aligned with Capone needed his help in putting Brothers forward (and paying for his high-priced defense attorney) to make everybody look good in the public's eye. Convicting Brothers was beneficial to both city officials and Capone, who was able to protect his close confidant and crew member, Frankie Foster, the man Father Reynolds positively identified as the actual gunman.

Father Reynolds could have easily turned the whole plan to convict Brothers upside down. The priest refused to lie on the stand, yet still managed to skirt the edge of truth. But how much longer could he remain quiet while Brothers served his nominal time in prison? There was a lot at stake for the most powerful people in Chicago, and it was riding on a conviction of Brothers that would put the entire public relations nightmare to bed once and for all.

If only Father Reynolds had buckled to the intimidation tactics and stayed at Notre Dame. Instead, a holy linchpin got off the witness stand, walked out of court and caught the first train back to South Bend with a bull's eye on his back.

Four weeks after Brothers entered the penitentiary to begin serving his sentence, two boys found the charred remains of an old brothel keeper who had been demoted to a relatively minuscule position in the Capone organization. Angry and resentful before he was murdered and his car set on fire, Mike de Pike Heitler had fired off an anonymous letter to State Attorney John Swanson disclosing everything he knew about Capone's bordello operations.

In a second letter to his daughter, Heitler expanded on the information he penned to the State's Attorney. The letter also included instructions to deliver to Pat Roche for use as evidence in the Brothers trial, but the posthumous testimony proved too obscure for the judge to admit so a jury could hear.

Heitler's correspondence did strengthen what investigators had suspected all along. The letter named eight gangsters who had conspired to kill Jake Lingle, all members of Capone's crew, and he described a meeting where Capone lambasted Lingle as a double-crosser.

"Jake..." Heitler quoted Capone as promising, "... is going to get his."

Several years later, Johnny Roselli, a Capone affiliate famously known as "Handsome Johnny" who had moved to Los Angeles soon after the Lingle murder where he became one of the most influential mob muscles in Hollywood, put the final stamp on speculation as to who had actually pulled the trigger on Jake Lingle.

Roselli named Frankie Foster and Ted Newberry as the true killers of Jake Lingle.

The great bell of Notre Dame's picturesque Gothic Basilica of the Sacred Heart tolled solemnly ...

12

FUNERAL FOR AN ICON

D r. Michael Nigro took it upon himself to gather Rockne's physical remains in Kansas City and assemble them in the casket. He drove Billy and Knute Jr. out to see the crash site where their father had died, then returned to the train station in Kansas City to accompany the boys and the casket on the long ride back to South Bend.

Billy and Knute Jr. were in a state of confusion. Because their train was late getting back from Florida, they had missed seeing their father for the last time by mere minutes. Now, the two young boys, 14 and 11, stood reluctantly alongside Dr. Nigro, Jess Harper and other strangers who knew their famous dad, posing for insistent newspaper photographers seemingly paralyzed in dazed, grief-stricken silence.

The train pulled out of Kansas City early Thursday morning on the prayers of a shocked country engulfed in a national outpouring of grief usually reserved for the death of a president. President Herbert Hoover called Rockne's death "a national loss." King Haakon VII of Norway posthumously knighted Norway's favorite son and sent a personal envoy to Rockne's massive funeral.

The train from Kansas City rolled into Chicago Thursday at 7:45 p.m. Floral arrangements and tributes flooded the Chicago residence of Rockne's mother, Martha Rockne, who had already traveled to South Bend to be with her son's family at their home on Wayne Street in the city's Sunnymede section. Following a brief stop in Chicago, the train was back on the rails carrying Rockne's casket to his final resting place in South Bend.

Billy and Knute Jr. ... had missed seeing their father for the last time by mere minutes.

Out of respect for the legendary Notre Dame coach, Charles H. Jones, general manager of the South Shore railway line, announced that all trains and motor coaches of the Chicago South Shore and South Bend railroad would be halted for one minute at the hour of the Rockne funeral services.

At the request of Bonnie Rockne, the funeral was set for 4:30 p.m. on Saturday — the day before Easter — despite the Catholic Church's dictum that no funeral could be said on Holy Thursday, Good Friday, Holy Saturday or Easter Sunday.

Thousands showed up Saturday morning at Rockne's simple brick home on Wayne Street to view the casket holding Rockne's body situated somberly near his fireplace.

The casket remained closed, another decision made by Rockne's widow due to the severity of her husband's injuries.

Among the roster of guests — a virtual "Who's Who" of notables from the sporting and coaching world plus a cavalcade of prominent politicians and statesmen — were New York Mayor James Walker, who was returning from Los Angeles and ordered his special car to stop in South Bend so he could pay his final respects. The mayor of New York City did not forget the man who assembled a team of Notre Dame stars from past years to play an unemployment benefit football game in New York.

"My words would be worthless if I were not speaking for 60,000 families whose wage-earners, out of work, had been materially aided

New York Mayor James Walker ... ordered his special car to stop in South Bend so he could pay his final respects.

by the charity game last winter," Walker said in an impromptu eulogy to Rockne. "Knute Rockne came clear from California, where he had closed a glorious season, and at the risk of his personal health gathered the team that battled for charity on a cold and forbidding day. New York recognizes the benefactions his life has made in the training of manhood, but it realizes with an unforgettable memory the service this man gave to us in a time of need."

South Bend City Hall and Notre Dame's campus were draped in black. Flags of the city fluttered in the breeze at half-mast. Business was shut down as University and municipal authorities made funeral preparations while trying to convince themselves that their city's national icon was gone. Cab drivers solemnly asked passengers if they had come to the city for the funeral while recalling tales of driving football fans to the train stations to greet Rockne's Notre Dame teams. Hotel porters lingered obliviously over routine duties, speaking, instead, of banquets and meetings the coach attended.

"People have heard so much about his speed and dash that they think he must have been unreasonable," one hotel porter reminisced to the Indianapolis Star. "He wasn't. I have seen the time he wouldn't let me bother the manager of the hotel until his turn came to be admitted, and he just sat on the davenport and waited, smiling. And you never heard of Rockne snubbing anybody."

At 2 p.m., Rockne's casket was loaded into

Grief spread from South Bend to Chicago, stretched from coast to coast, and was felt abroad from Australia to Rockne's native Norway — a magnanimous sendoff normally reserved for a president, king or statesman that prompted press accounts to openly question whether Rockne had gained the largest personal following of any man in the United States at the time.

the back of the funeral car and taken from his home on a solemn cortege through the streets of South Bend. Lining bedecked roadways, thousands stood bare-headed in reverence as the procession rolled by. As it passed the Notre Dame football stadium, the grandiose football mecca Rockne himself had built, there was a silent pause cast in solemn salute.

Grief spread from South Bend to Chicago, stretched from coast to coast, and was felt abroad from Australia to Rockne's native Norway — a magnanimous sendoff normally reserved for a president, king or statesman that prompted press accounts to openly question whether Rockne had gained the largest personal following of any man in the United States at the time.

A lone sound rang through the air. The great bell of Notre Dame's picturesque Gothic Basilica of the Sacred Heart tolled solemnly as students and faculty knelt before the altar. Father O'Donnell, president of Notre Dame University, celebrated mass and gave communion to every Catholic student in attendance.

The funeral service inside Sacred Heart was limited to 1,400 members of Rockne's intimate circle. In its span of more than 60

The same group of Ramblers who carried Rockne's teams to football glory on the field carried his casket ...

years, Sacred Heart had been the scene of numerous services for Notre Dame's beloved, but none of those previous services came close to approaching the impressiveness, sadness or sorrow over the loss of the iconic Notre Dame football coach.

Rockne's mother, mere days past her 72nd birthday, sat with his children, Billy, Knute Jr., Mary Jeanne and Jackie, along with Rockne's four sisters. Bonnie passed through the solemn crowd on the arms of Notre Dame Assistant Coach Jack Chevigny and Dr. Nigro.

As the choir sang "Popule Meus," the casket was wheeled to the foot of the altar for final blessings administered by a trio of priests — Bishop John F. Noll of the Fort Wayne diocese; the Rev. Thomas Steiner,

C.S.C., dean of the school of engineering; and the Rev. John F. O'Hara, C.S.C., prefect of religion. The Rev. William Connor, C.S.C., served as master of ceremonies.

Father O'Donnell's eulogy rang out through the church.

"He was a man of the people. A husband and father, a citizen of South Bend, Indiana. Yet, had he been any one of these personages that have been mentioned, the tributes of admiration and affection which he has received could not be more universal or more sincere."

The same group of "Ramblers" who carried Rockne's teams to football glory on the field carried his casket out of Sacred Heart and loaded it into the funeral car for the final

113

two-and-a-half-mile leg of Knute Rockne's extraordinary journey on earth. Tommy Conley, Tommy Yarr, Marchmont Schwartz, Frank Carideo, Marty Brill and Larry Mullins each wept openly as they tenderly embraced their immortal leader's ravaged remains and carried the casket from the hearse to his final resting place beneath the spreading branches of Old Council Oak's Highland Cemetery. The St. Joseph River flowed peacefully nearby.

It was a simple farewell, carried out by the boys who fought for him on the field, blessed by the holy fathers with whom he worked and worshipped. It was a final procession that gripped the heartstrings of Notre Dame, colleagues, rivals, a stunned nation, and a world

> *It was a final procession ... that shed profound tears in collective grief when Rockne's casket was lowered into the ground.*

that shed profound tears in collective grief when Rockne's casket was lowered into the ground.

Two thousand miles away, Robert "Joe-Pete" Fry, a 32-year-old former military pilot who flew several recon missions for the Marines in China just four years prior, was also laid to rest in Los Angeles. The T&WA pilot's bride of only eight months, Mary Breeden Fry, and his parents, Mr. and Mrs. John Fry of Milwaukee, were among the few present at Fry's military funeral.

Rockne, Fry and the six others who perished in the plane crash felt 'round the world' were all laid to rest in eternal peace. The cause of the crash, however, did not rest in peace with the Aeronautics Branch of the Department of Commerce.

A Good President.
A Fourth Perplexity.
Efficient Japan.
The Brontosaurus Teaches.
— By ARTHUR BRISBANE

FOR CLASSIFIED ADS PHONE
CHERRY 8800

THE WEATHER

TIMES

MAIL EDITION

DETROIT, MICHIGAN, SATURDAY, JANUARY 7, 1933   26 PAGES   THREE CENTS

BOMB KILLED ROCKNE, PUT IN PLANE BY GANG

★ ★ ★ ★ ★ ★ ★

Reveal Coolidge Premonition of Death

PLOT BARED BY SECRET SERVICE

Timed Blast Intended for Witness to Killing Whose Ticket Noted Coach Used

Coolidge's Office Now an Empty, Silent Room

ONLY PAPERS ANNOUNCING DEATH DISTURB QUIET ORDER OF EX-PRESIDENT'S DESK IN HIS STUDY
(Telephoto from International News Photographic Service)

'MY WORK DONE,' HE WROTE FRIEND; BURIAL TOMORROW IN HILLS OF VERMONT

President Hoover, Cabinet and Members of Congress to Attend Rites as Ex-President Is Laid to Rest in Family Plot; Body Will Lie in State in Northampton, Mass.

More Coolidge News and Pictures, Pages 2, 3, 4, 8, 9

WASHINGTON, Jan. 6.—Calvin Coolidge may have had a premonition of death.

"I know my work is done" was a highly significant phrase contained in a letter received from the ex-President only yesterday by his former private secretary, Edward T. Clark.

FORD CAMPAIGN GIFT $25,000

Detroit Bank Systems Praised in Senate

LOWER INCOMES FACE TAX RISE

Hitler Is Ready To Aid Fatherland

Free Press 'Yellow,' Bishop Blake Says

BETTY COMPSON TIED, ROBBED

How Dems Plan Increased Tax On Incomes

Al Capone's Cousin Guilty in Gun Case

"Should an Unwed Mother Keep Her Child?"

Darrow's Plea for Boy Killer, 17, Fails

ELSIE ROBINSON'S

"They don't kill you for nothing." — Ted Newberry

13

PAYBACK

Father Reynolds remained hopeful that The Chicago Tribune would pay him at least $25,000 in reward money for his part in the arrest and conviction of Lingle's killer. The only money he'd seen so far was $25 in expense money shelled out by police and prosecutors when they had called him to Chicago to view a suspect.

The expense money was all he would get. Nine months of dodging mobsters' threats, traveling to and from Chicago to view police photographs of suspects, risking life and limb to testify in a pressure-cooked trial, praying for strength every minute of every day, and wracking himself with guilt after hearing the news that his friend Rockne had been killed on the very airplane he should've been on... would wind up being worth $25.

"There was a $25,000 reward by the Tribune; they were trying to cover up, I think, for the one who would help to arrest, get the one who did the killing arrested and help to convict them, see..." Father Reynolds said. "But after time was over, there was a Notre Dame boy in charge of the program for the Tribune. I phoned him and said, 'How about the $25,000? Because my testimony kind of put the trial over, see?'

"And he said, 'Well, you got your share of all those trips you came in when we paid you $25 and it only cost you $2 to come in.'"

Father Reynolds hung up the phone. If anyone needed a spiritual course in upholding the truth, it was the folks responsible for convicting Leo Brothers in a murder actually committed by Frankie Foster. The priest had toed the line of courtroom justice and stayed true to the Bible he swore upon when it mattered the most.

"See, I wouldn't tell them that he was the man. I told them plainly that if I couldn't get any other better-looking character than him to fulfill the characteristics of the man I saw running away, I would take him, see?"

The Chicago Tribune paid out $25,000 to an undisclosed source in total confidentiality through the Illinois State Attorney General's Office. The Chicago Herald-Examiner added $25,000 to the reward pot, and the Chicago Evening Post kicked in another $5,000, for a total of $55,000.

Within two days of the Rockne crash, newspapers splashed reports that one of the victims, H.J. Christen, an interior designer in Chicago who earned a modest living setting up floor fixtures for downtown department and sporting goods stores, had cashed a check for $55,000 the day before boarding the plane. Crash responders found only $400 in Christen's clothes when his body was recovered.

The post-crash spotlight fell on a bigger inquisition: How did newspaper editors know immediately to report in first-day accounts that a modest interior designer named H.J. Christen, a virtual nobody in the world of fame and fortune occupied by Knute Rockne, had cashed a check for $55,000 one day before the plane went down? Was it coincidence, that $55,000 was the same combined amount paid out by their own employers?

And for whom was the money earmarked? Christen? Could Christen have been a bag carrier flying under the radar of vengeful mobsters to deliver the reward money to its rightful benefactor in a place far away from Chicago where the transaction could be conducted out of sight and mind?

It was unlikely that the reward money was for Rockne. But Rockne had been traveling with John Happer, comptroller for Great Western Sporting Goods, another victim of the crash. Did Christen have a business relationship setting up floor fixtures for Happer's sporting goods store in Chicago? Could the two have been flying to Los Angeles with Rockne to set up a new Great Western Sporting Goods Store? Or was there other, more covert business planned? Christen and Happer were the only two actual residents of Chicago flying on that plane.

How Christen obtained $55,000 was a question that died in the crash with him.

Father Reynolds moved forward with his life at Notre Dame teaching American History and serving as rector at St. Edward's Hall. He wanted nothing more than to serve his students and live quietly in a spiritual manner in the aftermath of the trial and the crash that had killed his beloved friend. Simply, he had had enough.

But two years later, Father Reynolds was back on the front page of the news.

On a cold January afternoon just after the turn of 1933, Father Reynolds was hanging out in a bar in South Bend drinking beers with a few friends. Their conversation was drowned out by loud shouts of a newsie boy out on the street hawking the day's edition of the South Bend News-Times. Father Reynolds took a swig of beer when his gulp was interrupted by the sound of his name.

"Read all about it! Special edition! The underworld tried to kill Father Reynolds!"

According to the News-Times, an "unimpeachable source" told the newspaper the federal Secret Service was investigating reports that a bomb had caused the Fokker Trimotor aircraft to crash and kill Rockne, five other passengers and the two pilots.

On Jan. 6, 1933, a headline in the

Washington Times blared: "Rockne Died Gangsters' Victim."

The Washington Times story echoed the South Bend News-Times account: A bomb planted on the plane was meant for Father Reynolds in retaliation for his testifying in the Brothers' trial.

"This is the first I have heard of such an astonishing angle in the tragedy," Major John Griffith, commissioner of the Big Ten Conference and head of the Coaches Association, was quoted as saying in the Washington Times article. "I hope, and I'm sure all other lovers of football hope that if it is true that gangsters were responsible, the government captures them and gives them the punishment they deserve."

The following day, Jan. 7, 1933, headlines put the South Bend News-Time's exclusive on full blast in newspapers across the country.

"BOMB KILLED ROCKNE, PUT IN PLANE BY GANG," screamed the Detroit Evening Times over an underlying subhead that rocked the sports world from Rockne's grave.

"Government operatives were in South Bend this week investigating several angles of the case. It was reported they were working with airline officials in the hope of getting some traces of the mobsters who were believed to have caused the plane crash."

The Evening Times' story concluded that Father Reynolds was at the forefront of the investigation.

"Father Reynolds was an important witness at the trial of Leo V. Brothers, who was convicted of the sensational Lingle slaying and was sentenced to 14 years in the state penitentiary. Credence was given to the theory that Rockne's plane was wrecked by a bomb when it was recalled that witnesses declared a violent explosion preceded the crash."

Newberry's belt buckle had also been a gift from Al Capone.

The Santa Ana (Calif.) Register story delved even further into who actually planted the bomb under the headline, "Claim Rockne Air Crash Due to Gangster's Bomb."

"Secret Service operatives were in South Bend a few days ago rounding out their evidence... and had it complete even to the name of the man suspected of placing the bomb in a mail pouch in the plane," the Register reported in its Jan. 6, 1933, edition.

"The name of the suspect was not revealed to our informant, the (South Bend) News Times said."

Father Reynolds took another swig from his beer. The shocking news of the day was what the priest had known all along.

Neither the New York Times nor the Chicago Tribune were certain enough to run the story. Both newspapers contacted the FBI to see if a government investigation was being conducted into the crash. Indiana Congressman Samuel Pettingill, representing the state's 3rd Congressional District, also reached out to the FBI to inquire about a federal probe.

One FBI agent denied the existence of any investigation to The New York Times. The Tribune was told that the publicity spokesman the paper needed to speak with "could not be reached." J. Edgar Hoover himself responded to the congressman's query indirectly through another FBI agent. The FBI director's note to the agent passed on to Pettingill did not completely deny the investigation.

"I said we were not conducting any investigation of this, insofar as I knew or had been advised," Hoover replied in a memo, "but that I understood the investigation was being made by the Commerce Department."

Two days after the crash's mob-linked headlines splashed across the country on January 8, 1933, the body of Edward "Ted" Newberry was discovered on a lonely stretch of road in Indiana, south of the Chicago line. Found around the waist of Newberry's body was a belt with a diamond studded belt buckle. Like the identical one gifted to Jake Lingle, Newberry's belt buckle had also been a gift from Al Capone.

"He must have done something," Newberry once said of a murder victim. "They don't kill you for nothing."

SECTION 2: THE CRASH

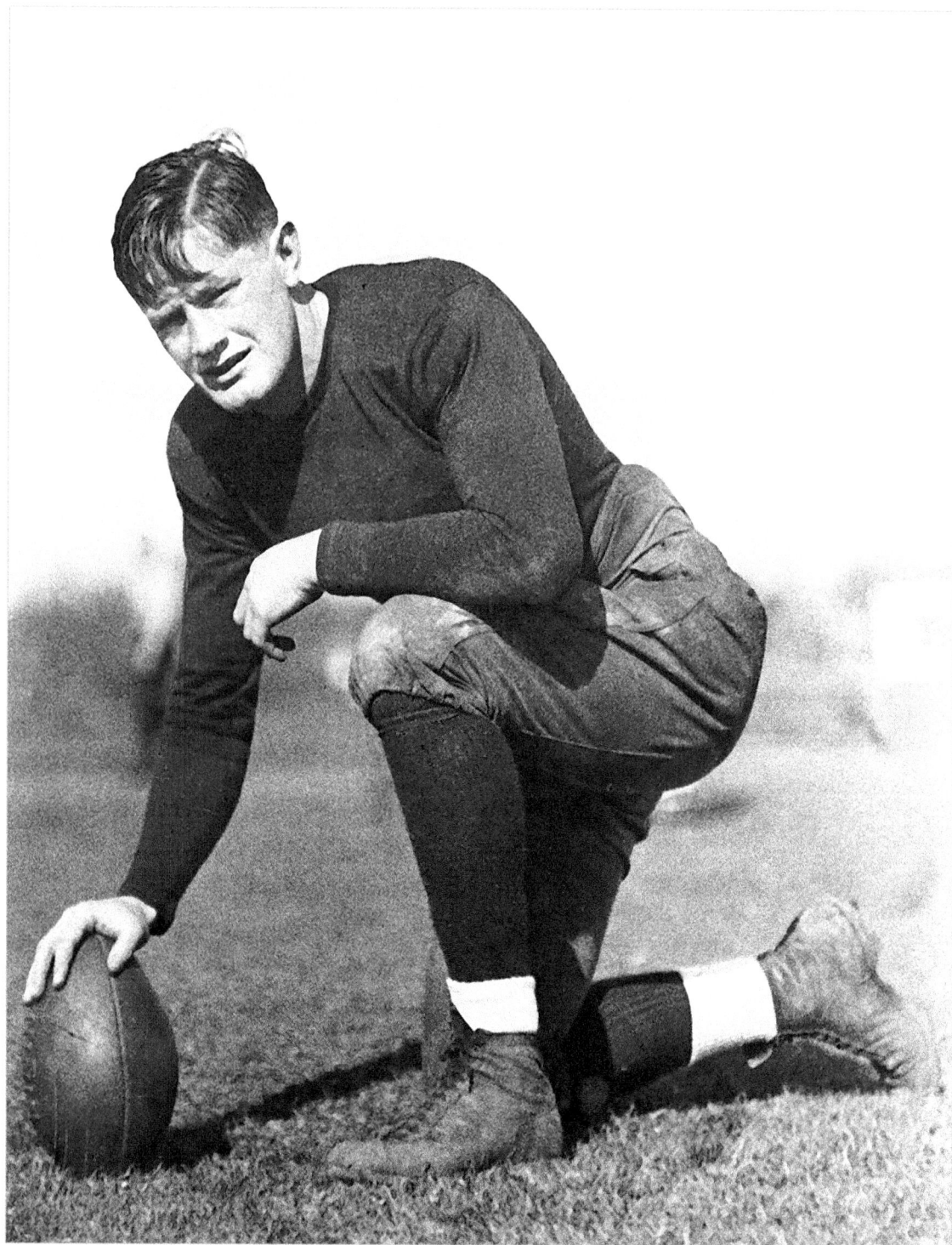

Kitty Gorman ... the football team's center and a favorite student among Notre Dame priests because he was a Minim.

14

MADE IN HOLLYWOOD

The news that a gangster's bomb may have been linked to the Rockne plane crash barely lasted two days before it died out.

By 1933, most of the country's populace had two years to recover from the collective grief of Rockne's death. More important concerns crippled Americans devastated by the height of the Great Depression. And in Germany, a notorious dictator was rounding up Jews and putting them in death camps while his Nazi military gained strength by the day and threatened to throw the entire world into an earth-shattering war.

One evening in 1934, Notre Dame sophomore James Bacon was hanging out with pal and Notre Dame football captain Kitty Gorman drinking beer with the rector of St. Edward's Hall where Bacon and Gorman resided as roommates. Bacon would later move to California and establish himself as one of Hollywood's most notable newspaper columnists. In his 1977 book, "Made in Hollywood," Bacon recalled that Gorman was the football team's center and a favorite student among Notre Dame priests because he was a Minim.

Gorman grew up attending school through the Notre Dame Minims, once the elementary and high-school branch of Notre Dame, before entering the University of Notre Dame. Being one of the few Minims still left at Notre Dave provided Gorman with privileged and exclusive friendships with the university's priests not afforded to other students. Gorman was frequently welcomed to hang out and drink beer with the rector of St. Edward's Hall, Father John Reynolds, even though the drinking of alcohol by students on campus was a

123

strict violation of campus rules.

"So that explains how I was in the rector's office drinking beer," Bacon wrote in his book. "I came with Kitty."

That night over beer and chitchat, Father Reynolds made small talk before he slid into an astonishing tale that stunned the two awestruck students — a story that began in the early afternoon of June 9, 1930, when he administered the last rites of the Catholic Church to a Chicago Tribune reporter by the name of Jake Lingle.

The boys listened intently as Father Reynolds put them in Lingle's shoes — leaving the Sherman House Hotel to catch the 1:30 p.m. train to a racetrack in Homewood where Lingle was planning to lay bets on the horses. They were all ears as the priest walked Lingle toward the Illinois Central platform at the foot of Randolph Street, where Lingle noticed he was being followed by two men.

There was a blond man with blue eyes in a straw hat who fumbled a .38 caliber pistol., the priest recalled vividly. And there was a short, stocky, dark-haired man who snatched the gun and fired a bullet into the back of Lingle's head.

Father Reynolds explained how he rushed to the mortally wounded Lingle just in time to give him last rites ... how Lingle barely whispered something in the priest's ear before he took his final breath.

Father Reynolds told the boys he remembered the exact words Lingle whispered.

Bacon and Gorman sat spellbound as Father Reynolds recounted testifying in the Brothers' trial.

Those words, he insisted, would forever remain between Father Reynolds, Lingle, and God.

Bacon and Gorman sat spellbound as Father Reynolds recounted testifying in the Brothers' trial. He recalled being caught between pressure by police to testify against Brothers, and enduring months of threats and intimidation tactics from mobsters lurking in the shadows outside his residence at Morrissey Hall, trying to keep him from testifying.

"Father Reynolds then told Kitty and me a horrendous tale of his harassment by gangsters, all of whom wanted to know what Lingle had divulged to him during that last confession," Bacon penned in "Made in Hollywood."

The priest informed the two students that he had given every inquisitive mobster the same answer: He was bound by the seal of confessional to keep Lingle's final confession to himself. The longer Father Reynolds stayed tight-lipped about the confession, the more phone calls and mysterious visits from shady characters he had received.

The priest shifted his recollection to his friend, Knute Rockne. Gorman and Bacon sat stunned.

"Father Reynolds told us, 'My name was on Rock's tickets and reservation. He didn't have time to change them. And then all those threats on my life. Did those people plant a bomb on that plane for me? I don't know.

"I know if I hadn't given Rock my tickets, he would have been alive."

Section 2: The Crash

SECTION 3 ROCKNE ON ROCKNE

Born Knut Larsen Rokne on March 4, 1888, in Voss, Norway, Knute Rockne and his three sisters emigrated to the United States at the age of 5 with their father, Lars Knutson Rokne (1858-1912), and mother, Martha Pedersdatter Gjermo (1859-1944), settling in Chicago. After arriving in America, the family Anglicized the surname spelling to Rockne. The two-syllable pronunciation of the forename was "Ka-nute." His friends called him, simply, "Rock."

The following is a posthumous autobiography compiled from essays, books, magazines articles and personal writings presented in Knute Rockne's voice.

THE BOY

Mother took her three daughters and me, her only son, on the long journey to join him in Chicago. How she ever managed that voyage, which I still recall with uneasiness, is beyond me.

15

STRAIGHT OUT OF NORWAY

"A Chicago childhood and youth had to be lived ... The new spacious city with its endless corner lots was a great place for a boy to grow up in 'B.C., ' before Capone... neighborhood games were undisturbed by gunfire."

Knute Rockne

How anyone from Voss, a hamlet in Norway between the cities of Bergen and Oslo, could be captain of a Midwestern college football team may require an explanation. Suffice to say, it has occurred so often it has become commonplace. Whether in business, politics, athletics, or in some other endeavors, it begins with coming to America. For me, a number of breaks came my way when I had sense enough to take them. And, while that's an unromantic way of explaining a career, it has the advantage of being the truth.

Queen Margaret of Norway had something to do with it. According to a student of Norse genealogy, it's written on an elaborately inscribed piece of parchment that resembles a map outline of all the football plays ever invented. It states that I'm descended, among others, from Filippus Erlendsen of Losna, Norway. He and his tribe were landowners of some consequence.

When Queen Margaret merged the three kingdoms of Norway, Sweden and Denmark, she

Pleasant recollections of skiing and skating in the Voss Mountains, and the fervent memory of home cooking were my sustaining tools early in life.

invaded Ireland looking for trouble, then returned to Norway with colleens for wives.

My Irish heritage will surface on occasion. It showed itself in my father when he crossed the ocean to enter a carriage in the World's Columbian Exhibition. By profession he was a stationary engineer, and by avocation he was a carriage builder.

Mother took her three daughters and me, her only son, on the long journey to join him in Chicago. How she ever managed that voyage, which I still recall with uneasiness, is beyond me.

We arrived in New York, where we were duly admitted through Castle Garden. She guided us through the intricacies of entry, without knowing English, and took us into the heart of a new, strange and bewildering country without mishap. How she achieved the first step in our Americanization without anyone's help is one of the millions of minor miracles that are the stuff and fabric of America.

Pleasant recollections of skiing and skating in the Voss Mountains, and the fervent memory of home cooking were my sustaining tools early in life.

When my dad was elated by an award for his carriage at the Chicago Exposition in 1893, he failed to check my curiosity. At length, and it must have been a long time, I wound up in the midst of a sort of miniature Indian reservation. Perhaps it was a trick of fate that the natives of the new country to register favorably with me were not only natives, but aborigines — American Indians.

In this wonderland, with its glittering sights and amazing crowds, a tow-headed Norwegian boy was lost.

The fairgrounds police came to "Item 181-B" in their nightly hunt for youngsters lost or strayed, specifying a Norwegian boy who knew no English but might respond to

did not retain the best features of the three. The Erlendsens refused to have anything to do with the merger. They retreated in a collective fit of anger to Voss, and there they established themselves in the hills. Generations elapsed, and it became increasingly difficult to make a good living.

The traditional adventuring Norsemen were bolstered by periodic infiltrations of Irish blood. This happened because the earlier Vikings had

We lived in the Logan Square neighborhood, which was inhabited predominantly by Irish and Swedes.

the name "Knute Kenneth Rockne" — if pronounced with pressure on the k's.

The contrast — between me, a white-haired Nordic fresh from the homeland and the jet-haired Indian papooses — must have struck some Indian chief as odd. A weary policeman passing by the make-believe reservation beheld a blonde head ringed in feathers bobbing through a noisy mob of Indian kids wielding a wooden tomahawk and yelling for scalps. They promptly collected me, stripped me of Indian finery, and reunited me with my puzzled parents.

I've held Indians in affection and high esteem ever since that childhood adventure, unaltered even after a collision on a football field years later with Jim Thorpe. A Chicago childhood and youth had to be lived before I was to see Indians again.

The new spacious city with its endless corner lots was a great place for a boy to grow up in 'B.C.,' before Capone ... neighborhood games were undisturbed by gunfire.

Chicago's broad ethnology called Scandinavians "Swedes."

16

THE SANDLOTS

The first big thrill of my life playing football came when, at 13 years of age and weighing 110 pounds, I was placed on the scrubs of the Northwest Division High.

We had light coaching on the scrubs. Teachers called sandlot football "eclectic," because we pinched whatever plays we had seen and could remember. Half the fun of the game was the solemnity with which our corner-lot quarterbacks would shout, and we would receive the long litany of signals.

We lived in the Logan Square neighborhood, which was inhabited predominantly by Irish and Swedes. Chicago's broad ethnology called all Scandinavians "Swedes." The Irish and the Swedes were both clubby. My lot was naturally with the latter. Boys of the two nationalities would meet on Wednesday and Saturday afternoons for impromptu and sometimes violent contests.

O'Goole, a husky middle-aged copper, kept a paternal eye on us.

When the Irish lads were pounding us "Swedes," O'Goole strolled up and down the sideline grinning. To onlookers who protested that he should stop the free-for-all, he said, "Nonsense! It's an elegant game, good for the youngsters. Look at Patsy Regan there knock that Swede lad from under a punt."

A few of us, dissatisfied with the constant lickings at the hands and feet of the Irish, took it upon ourselves to scout other neighborhoods for bigger Swedes. When bigger boys couldn't be found, we enrolled a couple of bruiser-like Italians on our side.

Legends like George "Rube" Waddell... how, attired as a scarecrow, he drove a wagon pulled by a team of mules up to the players' bench, jogged onto a crowded ballpark in Harrisburg, and struck out 12 men in a row.

O'Goole strolled up when we were giving the Irishers a free and liberal taste of mud. O'Goole wouldn't have it. He walked into the thick of it, grabbing Swede boys by their necks. "This won't do at all," he said. "This game is altogether too brutal and unfit for small boys!"

We could only even matters out by appealing to the precinct captain to send us a Swede cop as well as O'Goole to supervise our games. Then the mayhem would be balanced.

My first real baptism by fire was received in one of those neighborhood corner-lot games. I was an end on the Tricky Tigers — historic rivals of the Avondales — so-called because we had a beauty of a triple-pass back of the line play when we wanted to impress opponents and onlookers.

Equipment wasn't elaborate: We had no helmets. One shin guard per player. And we covered our ears with elastic tape to prevent injury.

Many of us graduated to play for a club with older boys who were mostly Irish. Trouble came in handfuls when we played the Hamburg Athletic Club for the district championship. We played in a huge lot opposite the White Sox ballpark. Crowds lined the gridiron and broke into the game as it progressed. Irish sympathizers grew militant. There were only a few policemen present to hold back the mob. Things grew unpleasant as the more pugnacious spectators slipped away every now and then for refreshments at nearby saloons.

My part in the game was not brilliant. I had spindly legs, which I've retained, and speedy feet, which left me long ago. Whenever the call came for me to carry the ball, I'd lay back my ears and sprint. In one play I was spurting in an end run with the Hamburg boys after me. My path to a touchdown was clear, not a Hamburg player was in front of me.

But the Hamburg fans came to the rescue. They ran onto the field and grabbed me, snatched the ball from my hands, and threw me down. A minor riot ensued, with players on both teams being pummeled impartially. There were so many players' noses punched that a police sergeant allowed only players with nose guards to wade into the crowd.

Most of us returned home that evening with the physical markings of a strenuous sport. This was a serious matter for me. I played the game surreptitiously because my parents held the general belief that football was a system of modified massacre. I had to smuggle my prized moleskin football pants in and out of the house to play the game, but scars from the battle with the Hamburg team betrayed me. My football career was squelched.

It was nearing winter, so this punishment didn't matter as much.

I went out for baseball with the rest of the sandlot boys when spring arrived. My parents were more than happy to approve of my participation in the game of baseball.

Legends like George "Rube" Waddell and Mordecai "Three-Finger" Brown were figures to inspire any youngster with the easy glory of athletic games.

We knew something of Rube's tradition — how, attired as a scarecrow, he drove a wagon pulled by a team of mules up to the players' bench, jogged onto a crowded ballpark in Harrisburg, and struck out 12 men in a row.

The Rube always played up to the youngsters. He'd guide droves of us into the ballpark free, and we'd even follow him for miles and miles in his eccentricities. He'd take "French leave" from his club, go to Libertyville or some other town, and pitch for a local semi-pro team. Rube was a great showman. In one game, we saw him turn dramatically on the pitcher's mound, wave in all the outfielders, and strike out every batter.

Playing the Maplewood boys in an extra-inning game, a hot argument developed. Being blessed or bothered by hidden strains of Irish ancestry, I found myself in the thick of it.

A bat smacked me on the bridge of my nose and flattened it.

I went home blinded, but uppermost in my mind was not sorrow, but logic. Ironically, my family had banned football because it — not baseball — had been deemed the dangerous game. When my parents asked me what happened, my triumphant reply was, "I got this nose from playing baseball!"

I made the track team as a half-miler when high school days arrived. I also went out

I yearned to follow in the footsteps of baseball legends like Three-Finger Brown, but my dream to be like him required extraordinary skill.

for football with full parental approval.

High school football in those days had all the enthusiasm, but none of the finesse of today. Coaches were few.

Two teachers volunteered to coach our high school squad. They did a good job of it, if only by holding me back, making me realize there was something more to football than the ball.

It took me until my senior year to make the first team. We beat the powerful Marshall High, tied with Crane, and bowed only to North Division High, whose second team

licked us. The first-string, led by Wally Steffen — now Carnegie Tech coach — heckled us from the sidelines.

I earned a spot on the Chicago Amateur Athletic Junior Team while in high school after making the grade in one of the numerous athletic clubs dotted around Chicago.

Youngsters were quickly initiated into the tricks of the athletic trade. In minor meets, the chance to win sometimes would depend on quick wits as much as stopwatches. One timer was known for his distaste for perennial Irish victories. When he was officiating and our teams faced stiff competition, somebody on our side would stand near this official and holler at a winning opponent named Schmidt:

"Watch that O'Brien run," or of a Thorgensen, "Look at that O'Reilly jump."

I was subbing for an absent teammate in one track meet, running the 880-yard sprint. I thought it was for a record time, but the non-Hibernian official overheard some malicious bird yell, "Come on, Kelly!"

The interim between high school and entering college, four years to be exact, was the principal period of my not-too-celebrated career as a track athlete. I carried the colors of Irving Park Athletic Club and Chicago's Central YMCA, for which I managed to win the half-mile in 2 minutes, 20 seconds; it was a good mark then.

I graduated to the Illinois Athletic Club.

The half-mile was my specialty. In various meets, I ran against old-time stars like Knut Lindberg, Harvey Blair, Craig McLanahan and Frank Belot. Martin Delaney and "Dad" Moulton were our coaches. And we newcomers were able to touch shoulders with Olympic stars like Ralph Rose, James Lightbody, Bill Hogenson and Frank Irons. Gold medalist Johnny Hayes came to Chicago, but not to

*I went out for baseball with the rest of the
sandlot boys when spring arrived.*

compete because he had turned professional.

Persistence running track paid off. It earned me a small reputation, and when a whimsical switch to pole vaulting placed me in the news by setting an indoor record of 12 feet 4 inches (which today wouldn't qualify a boy to be a mascot), I began to think I had arrived.

"With the fondness for coincidence, people ask me whether or not Stagg and I met in those days. If we did, it must have been under the stands when I dropped out of the marathons as invariably occurred.

17

DISCOVERING
STAGG AND ECKERSALL

The name of Amos Alonzo Stagg rose on my horizon, but not in connection with football, although I knew something of his fame. With the fondness for coincidence, people ask me whether or not Stagg and I met in those days. If we did, it must have been under the stands when I dropped out of the marathons as invariably occurred.

We saw his teams play on the University of Chicago football field whose names were almost mythical to us, teams like Northwestern, Haskell and Michigan.

Chicago's famed quarterbacks Wally Steffen and Lee Maxwell had a snap to their style that made the quarterback the focal point in the football drama that was right. But a good quarterback needed all of many qualities, only a few of which I had, the principal one being speed.

The first time I learned that a football was not an object to kick or throw, but a way to think, was when I saw a great football player in action. A sandlot youngster who regarded the game of football as a pleasantly rough pastime, I had no hero worship for any particular player and no interest in any one team.

But when the Eastern High School champions challenged the Western High School

I sat spellbound watching Chicago's Hyde Park High play Brooklyn Polytech December 6, 1902. Quarterback for the west team was Walter Eckersall. With his 'Prairie Football,' running wide sweeps around the ends, he hit the heavier Brooklyn linemen until they were dizzy.

champions, the meeting of the two teams in Chicago was a noteworthy event. Brooklyn Polytech represented the Eastern team and Hyde Park High the Western team.

My most vivid memory of the game was the strikingly heady play of Hyde Park's quarterback, Walter Eckersall. His sharp, staccato calling of signals and the way he handled the team with the rhythm of an orchestra leader gave football a new meaning to me.

When the game was over, the victorious Western team went clamoring from the field shouting Eckersall's name. I tried to get close to the hero of the day. Two- or three-thousand other youngsters were trying to do the same thing.

I went home without a handshake. Yet, for the first time in a young and fairly crowded life, I had a role model. I imagined dreams of being like him one day.

Eckersall, in subsequent years, became a sensational star at the University of Chicago. In sharp contrast, my path took me from high school to nothing more physical than being a mail dispatcher working nights.

I had hoped in high school to make my way to college.
... Athletic fame was secondary to me.

18

ODD JOBS

If anybody wonders why it took so long for me to get from high school to college, the answer is easy: I was obliged to earn a living. Football, except as a spectator, was neglected, and I relied on track competition to keep in physical shape.

I had hoped in high school to make my way to college. To that end, I learned how to earn money and save it.

I was working one summer cleaning our high school's windows at good pay. But other boys — possibly jealous over my appointment — would invade the school, break windows, switch door signs from doors with coarsely diabolical wit, and commit other vandalism. I, being the amateur window cleaner, was blamed. Naturally, I was fired.

I received an appointment as a mail dispatcher after taking the civil service exams. I was eager to go to the University of Illinois, setting a goal to save $1,000 and then march onto a college education.

Athletic fame was secondary to me. College players loomed as supermen to whose heights I could never aspire.

As the days and months passed by, it seemed more and more unlikely that any college would have the opportunity to matriculate or reject me. As years of night work ensued, my prep school was the sorting room of the post office.

The most a mail clerk could earn was $100 a month. He could make his job mundane or difficult by assuming simple or complicated routines. I chose the more difficult routine of dispatcher, to have something to do in an environment which led to much loafing.

If a clerk took the southern territory, he wouldn't have much to commit to memory because few railroads feed the south from Chicago. I chose the more difficult Illinois, or Eastern Territory dispatching job. Every main line and branch line train had to be memorized, and this knowledge had to be amended with all the timetable changes made by the railroads. It took me a full year to learn the dispatching routine.

Most of the old-timers called me a fool to tackle the toughest job. But it was excellent for training my memory. This decision was a good investment. If a football coach needs one thing more than another, it's a memory for the myriad details of plays and combinations of plays.

For the rest of my time in civil service, working at the post office taught me little. Going to the job with a zeal to make good and be promoted, I wondered at first why veterans smiled at my youthful ardor and industry. Enthusiasm could hardly survive the discovery that a dispatcher who worked hard for eight hours a night earned less than the fellow who did nothing more arduous for eight hours a day than sell stamps from a stationary seat on a stool.

I was on the path to becoming the smartest shirker of all, having reached a point of lethargy where it took me an hour to distribute as many pieces of mail that in the first enthusiastic days would have only taken me 10 minutes.

Two friends of mine, Johnny Devine and Johnny Plant, both runners of more than local note, were going to Notre Dame. When we discussed our plans during a Chicago meet and I told them I was bound for Illinois, they suggested I go along with them to the Indiana school.

I remember exclaiming, "Why, whoever heard of Notre Dame? They've never won a football game in their lives."

What persuaded me to go was the argument that I could probably get a job and certainly get by cheaper than at the University of Illinois. So, I went to South Bend. I'd hardly seen more than two trees at one time anywhere, so my first impression of the school was its sylvan beauty.

Later, came a serendipitous afternoon when Notre Dame was playing in Chicago, with the former sandlot boy/ex-mail dispatcher as captain of the squad. The referee for the contest was none other than Walter Eckersall.

In his smart referee uniform, he looked hardly a day older than when he led Hyde Park in its victory over Brooklyn Poly years earlier.

Grasping at his hand, I said, "I've been waiting years for this."

"For what?" he asked.

"To shake your hand."

I, then, recounted how his brilliant performance for Hyde Park High turned my mind seriously to football.

"Stop," said Eckersall, cutting me off as I spoke, "or Notre Dame will be penalized five yards for speech making."

Section 3: Rockne on Rockne

THE PLAYER

... my first impression of the school was its sylvan beauty.

Main Building 1890.

19

WELCOME TO NOTRE DAME

"What persuaded me to go was the argument that I could probably get a job, and certainly get by cheaper than at the University of Illinois. So, I went to South Bend."

Knute Rockne

When I arrived at Notre Dame I felt the strangeness of being a lone Norse Protestant, if word must be used, an invader of a Catholic stronghold.

I was assigned to Brownson Hall. The school had 400 undergraduates, physical training was compulsory, and a fellow wasn't thought of as much unless he joined his hall's football team.

What persuaded me to go was the argument that I could probably get a job, and certainly get by cheaper than at the University of Illinois. So I went to South Bend. I'd hardly seen more than two trees at one time anywhere, so my first impression of the school was its sylvan beauty.

A varsity man, Joe Collins, recommended me for a chance with the big boys, though Coach Shorty Longman wasn't enthusiastic. Freshmen were played in those days, and with a small enrollment we needed them.

Coach Longman sent me out with the scrubs in a test game with the regulars. He made

"Playing football didn't seem possible. But the fact remained I could run, and running was an important part of football."

me fullback. They should have changed my position to drawback. Never on any football field was there so dismal a performance. Trying to spear my first punt, I had frozen fingers, which caused me to fumble the ball. It rolled everywhere it wasn't wanted. Longman kept me in that agonizing game.

Finally, I tried to punt. I might have just as well been a statue of a player. Nothing was coordinated. I was half-paralyzed. A 200-pound tackle smashed into me. My 145 pounds went backwards for a 15-yard loss.

Shorty Longman knew much about football, but he talked even more. Our offense was typical for the game then, principally, a punt and a prayer varied with an occasional line plunge.

Longman's method of coaching included an old-fashioned oratory before each game. He would enter the dressing room dramatically, toss back his shock of black hair and burst into rhetoric.

"Boys," he declared, "today is the day. The honor of the old school is at stake. It's now or never, we must fight the battle of our lives. I don't want any man with a streak of yellow to move from this room. You've all got to be heroes... heroes, or I never want to see you again. Go out and conquer. It's the crisis of your lives!"

I was tremendously impressed when I heard his speech the first time. The team went out and all but pushed the opposing team, Olivet, over the fence.

The next Saturday, Coach Longman entered the dressing room. "Boys," he detonated, "today is the day of days. The honor of the old school is at stake. The eyes of the world are on you. Go out and bleed for the old school, and if anybody has a yellow streak, let him . . ."

I sat there awe-stricken. Then I saw two veterans, Charles Dorais and Al Bergman, casually yawn. "What do you think of the act today?" asked Bergman. "Not so good," said Dorais. "I thought he was better last week."

One oration a season is quite enough for any football squad. Action brings reaction, and if the coach talks too much, his words lose weight.

Longman was a sturdy man and useful with his fists. He decided one day that the best way to impress his charges was to demonstrate that he was physically our master. With this in mind, he prescribed boxing lessons, which he himself would give, beginning with the lightweights and working his way through to the heavies of the George Philbrook displacement.

Respectfully, the squad gathered to see the first demonstration. Several of the less heavy boys, including myself, were to be operated on with boxing gloves. Shorty selected a mild-mannered chap named Bob Matthews, a light end, for the first object lesson. That was a bad break. Matthews stepped out expertly, ducked and weaved and hooked and jabbed. After three minutes, Shorty had enough. There were no boxing lessons for the rest of us.

The University gave me a chance to work off my room and board as janitor of the chemical laboratory, cleaning out the slop buckets and doing minor chores. An incident occurred that almost got me expelled. Someone stole a gallon of experimental wine from the pharmacy laboratory. I was blamed and ran the risk of expulsion. My reputation was not glamorous.

I had the most unusual experience of meeting an athlete, whose name then was Foley, although he had played for many schools under aliases. He was typical of young men who roamed the country overflowing with college spirit, regardless of the college. His tongue teemed with professional jargon.

Foley knew all the techniques and practiced none of them. He was so slick yet believable that it invariably took a shrewd coach half a season to get wise to the fact that this fellow had only one principle in football, which he pithily expressed: "Avoid 'em."

Foley opened my eyes to the state of affairs in college football, which has since been reformed— of the journeyman players who'd leave new names behind them wherever they went and live from foot to mouth, so to speak, taking loyalty and sometimes talent with them to whichever alma mater would give them the best break.

There were natural hurdles for me to jump in a social sense, for a lone Norwegian always mistakenly dubbed a Swede, had difficulties among so many Irish. These anxieties were largely dissipated, when once, with flushed face, I was called on to talk at a football rally and having heard somebody call somebody else just a dumb Irishman. I had the good fortune to remark, "There's only one thing dumber than a dumb Irishman." Before the bricks could fly, I explained, "A smart Swede."

Playing football didn't seem possible. But the fact remained I could run, and running was an important part of football. I reasoned if I tried for a chance at end, my old spot on the sandlot and high school teams, I'd have better luck. The first step was to get on the varsity track team, which I did. A track letter gave me the confidence to try out again for the varsity squad. This time I was successful.

Persistence running track paid off ... and when a whimsical switch to pole vaulting placed me in the news by setting an indoor record of 12 feet 4 inches ... I began to think I had arrived.

Section 3: Rockne on Rockne

20

'GUS' DORAIS

When Jack Marks coached our team, he made us over from a green, aggressive squad into a slashing, driving outfit.

We played with poor equipment. One of our guards was so severely injured in one game that we had to use up our lone roll of tape. Later, his substitute in the line cracked up, so we had to take tape off the first boy to bind up the second.

Alexander trampling the Persians, Napoleon defeating the Austrians at Jena, and One-Eye Connolly crashing the gate at Toledo, all are faint carbon copy thrills when compared to the beat and jump of a young man's pulse when running onto the gridiron for his first big-league performance.

Our coach for my junior year was Jack Marks, the former Dartmouth back. Pittsburgh was my first big game. Before meeting the Panthers, we scored 182 points in four games compared to six by our opponents. True, the opposition was not strong, although Ohio Northern and Butler — two on the list of four — were never pushovers.

The Panthers were a powerful outfit under Coach Joe Duff. They had beaten some of the best in the East. But we were rather cocky because we had been used to piling up points. The experience of not making a score in the first quarter was so novel it flustered us.

What seemed like a big crowd watched the game, and the local press had spoken much,

157

*Charles "Gus" Dorais… only weighed 140 pounds,
but he had both smarts and speed.*

perhaps too much, about the brains and speed of our quarterback Charles "Gus" Dorais. He only weighed 140-pounds, but he had both smarts and speed.

In a plan to break the scoreless tie after the first half, we tried to show the cagey Panthers that we could outguess them. We did. Catching them napping with an onside kick, I scooped-up the ball and raced to make a touchdown. But officials called us offside and ruled a penalty of five yards.

Disappointed with the referee's call, Gus, always the quick thinker, decided to give the crowd another sample of the tricks in the Notre Dame bag by eliminating called signals. His plan was to play our right and left halfbacks, Al Berger and Alfred "Big Dutch" Bergman, without further notice, depending upon which side, right or left, the Panthers aimed their punt.

This decision was new and smart stuff. Huber "Hube" Wagner, Pittsburgh's 190-pound ace, kicked a long ball to Bergman's side. After the runback, we went into scrimmage. Gus called no signals. But our center, a big husky chap who, up until then, had been eminently satisfactory, failed to snap the ball back.

Precious seconds passed and our chance for a surprise play was lost. Officials cautioned us to hurry. Gus prodded the center, and the linesmen yelled at him. "All right," he barked, "What's the signal?"

Gus calmly called one of our routine plays, and the game went on. In the huddle, Gus berated the defaulting center, reminding him how it had been agreed to have a surprise play around end without signals. "Next time you plan a trick," the center shouted back at him, "don't whisper it. I'm half deaf."

Failure to discover that fact before the game cost us a chance to score against the Panthers. But Wagner's play also had something to do with it. Wagner was a big, strong, speedy man, and he seemed to have made it his life's work that afternoon to stop Gus.

Anybody who saw Gus play will agree that he had the best open-field legs in football. The news reporters, who were digging into dictionaries for labels at that time, called him the "Will-o'-the-Wisp." Usually he was just that, but not against Wagner. Wagner, an All-American, had All-American brains. Instead of diving at Gus's legs, he ran at him and threw his arms around his neck, stopping him dead.

Information on football will always vary, depending on whether you get it from a coach, player, student, alumnus, or newspaperman, or whether you are one of those lucky chaps who got it direct from the barber himself. I remember the critically important information, which was carried to us in this Pittsburgh game.

Coach Marks, becoming rather irascible with Gus and the score locked at 0-0, turned to his bench and sent in a third-string quarterback with instructions to "open up." The poor chap's knees were knocking, because the only thing he had ever opened up was an umbrella.

Taking the instructions literally, on our own 20-yard line with 80 yards to go, he called for a very complicated play, a double pass followed by a long backward lateral pass. Well, we tried the play and the double pass was all right, but the long backward lateral pass found no receiver. Chris Lindsay, Pittsburgh's left end, pounced on it on our one-yard line.

As we lined up on defense, it felt as though it was all over. It didn't seem possible to stop them with a touchdown only a step away. Suddenly, Coach Marks sent in a frolicking sub to replace our regular left guard. The rules stated very clearly that an incoming player may not speak to his teammates until one play has elapsed, so as he lined up with us, he said nothing. But he gave us a look out of his serene, beaming countenance as though to say, "I carry valuable information from the coach."

Immediately, our morale came back. We figured if we could hold them for one more down, the afternoon might be saved. This old boy was carrying the mystic nexus from the coach himself. The next play all of us charged so low and so hard that afterward we picked ourselves off the ground one by one. Still there on the one-yard line was the ball.

Enthusiastically, we hurried back to the huddle, and with our ears up like a lot of donkeys, all of us said: "What did coach say? What did coach say?"

We took time out and the new sub took us back five yards to make sure the opponents and the referee wouldn't hear him, and said, "Boys," then he paused… "the coach said to hold 'em."

That evening we were a disappointed bunch; our game with Pittsburgh ended with a scoreless tie. I learned two things in that initiation into big-league football. When you catch your opponent's napping and pull a fast one — as with the onside kick that should have won the game — officials may also be napping and call offside what was actually onside.

My second lesson that I took from the game is that a large crowd was no thrill to me. I was over-awed by what looked like tens of thousands in the stands as we ran onto the field for the kickoff. The moment the ball

... news reporters... called him the "Will-o'-the-Wisp." Usually he was just that..."

went into play, I had promptly forgotten that anybody was looking on.

It was puzzling to me that the crowd, as interpreted by the news writers, felt that we had failed to pull off any miracles of forward passing, the new and then little-understood aerial game.

When we played Wabash College two games later, we had the pass in full play. The Rules Committee had placed numerous and various restrictions on the forward pass going back to 1906 when it was ruled legal.

Wabash Quarterback Kent "Skeet" Lambert was also using the forward pass. He had us beaten on a long and perfectly executed pass to his receiver Brooks Howard. But the officials measured it, and because the ball was thrown more than 20 yards, it was ruled illegal and Wabash was penalized. The ball had to cross the line of scrimmage five yards out from the center or it would have also been a penalty. If you can make sense of that rule, you're much better than I am.

Through a circuitous happenstance, Lambert was partially responsible for a restriction being placed on the forward pass. When we rushed him, and chased him behind the line of scrimmage, he would fool us by purposely throwing the ball on the ground when we were about to tackle him. The ball was returned to the spot where the play had started, with a loss of down, but not

Wabash quarterback Kent "Skeet" Lambert... had us beaten on a long and perfectly executed pass... it was ruled illegal and Wabash was penalized...

of yardage. Gus borrowed this tactic from Lambert. Vernon Prichard of Army in turn copied Gus. Prichard, however, got the credit as the gridiron fox for this quarterback ruse, which a subsequent rule penalized.

Many football tricks of offense and defense have had similar genealogy. The player who performs them before the most newspaper witnesses was credited as the "originator."

Coach Marks was always a quiet mentor, but he liked to run up scores. In his final instructions before playing Wabash, he turned to Ray Eichenlaub and said, "We're playing Wabash this afternoon, Eichenlaub. Jones,

Feeney and the rest will make the holes. You tear through them."

"But I'm only a poor high school boy," said Eichenlaub. Marks turned and walked away without saying a word.

Coach Marks proved he knew his stuff with Ray "Eich" Eichenlaub, our 200-pound torpedo. He ran through the Wabash line that afternoon for more than 400 yards. When the game was over, the Wabash squad, badly licked, piled onto the streetcar taking them to the train depot. An elderly lady carrying parcels was working her way through the limping Wabash players, when a wag cried:

*Coach Marks proved he knew his stuff with Ray "Eich"
Eichenlaub, our 200-pound torpedo ...*

"One side! Here comes Eichenlaub's mother!"

When we led Adrian 81 — 0, and the Adrian coach had used up all his substitutes, he asked Marks if he would agree to let him send men back in the game that had already played. Marks agreed. He returned to the sidelines.

Sometime later, Marks saw a strange player on our bench. "You're on the wrong bench," he said. "I know it," said the lad. "I've been in that scrap four times already, and they're not going to send me back if I can help it. I've had enough." Marks laughed quietly, and let him remain.

Again, during a game with Butler, our big halfback named Meyers, who was strong but shy, was missing. The umpire yelled to Coach Marks, "You've only got 10 men on the field."

Marks looked over the field in anger. "Where in heck is Meyers?" he demanded.

"Here I am, coach," Meyers replied from under his blanket. "I got bumped right on my knee." Marks smiled quietly and said nothing.

The team stepped out under Marks's leadership. Gradually, we came to be noticed a little beyond the Midwest. I won a regular berth at end, and I had the pleasant surprise of seeing myself discussed in the paper as an All-American. Almost imperceptibly, it seemed, I was established in football.

Section 3: Rockne on Rockne

The West Point boys were the background for Notre Dame's first big Eastern appearance.

21

PERFECTING THE FORWARD PASS

Gus and I spent our summer vacation at Cedar Point. We earned our money as restaurant checkers and whatnot. On the Lake Erie beach, we made ourselves familiar with the innovation that changed the entire character of the game.

Through daily, tedious practice we perfected the forward pass. Gus would throw from all angles. People who didn't know we were making painstaking preparations for our final season of college football may have thought we were crazy. This impression would have appeared especially true when a bearded, older gentleman wanted to get in on the fun. He took off his shoes, seized the ball, and kicked it merrily with his bare feet, until a friendly caretaker came along to return him to where he belonged.

In those days, the football was thrown and caught much like a medicine ball. A football weighs 14 ounces and a medicine ball 14 pounds. I practiced catching the football with a grabbing, hugging motion, and mastered the technique of catching it with hands relaxed.

I had hardly got off the train in South Bend that autumn to start my senior year when I was greeted by Jess Harper. He introduced himself as Notre Dame's new coach.

"I'm grabbing you football men off the trains as fast as I can. We've got to work our

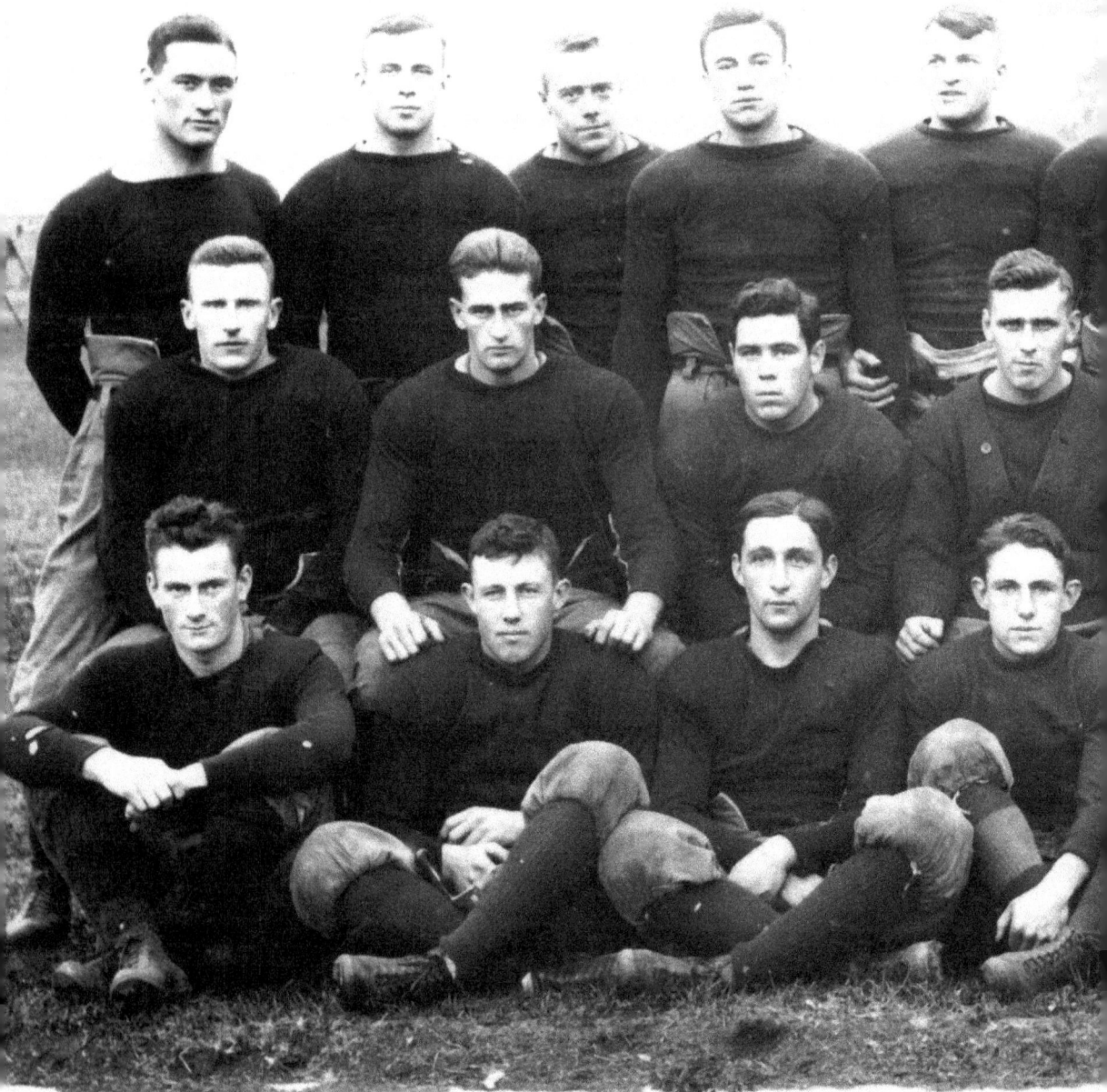

heads and legs off."

"What's the excitement?" I said, trying to be calm.

"They're letting us play in the East. Army has agreed to play Notre Dame."

The West Point boys were the background for Notre Dame's first big Eastern appearance. And while the game was not all-important to them, to us it was the supreme test of our playing careers. The Army had a formidable line, with two All-American stars, John McEwan at center and Louis Merrilat at end, while Vernon Prichard at quarterback also had an All-American rating.

The morning we left for West Point, the entire student body got up long before breakfast to see us to the day coach that carried the squad to Buffalo, a dreary, all-day trip. From

> *There was no pampering in those days. We wanted none of it.*

Buffalo, we enjoyed the luxury of sleeping car accommodations—regulars in lowers, substitutes in uppers.

There was no pampering in those days. We wanted none of it. We went out to play Army like crusaders, believing that we represented not only our own school but the whole aspiring Midwest.

West Point, as always since our first meeting, treated us most hospitably. We were housed in Cullum Hall and given the freedom of the Officers Club. There was a fair crowd to see the game on the Plains, and the New York newspapers were interested enough to send second-string football reporters.

The cadet body and most of the other spectators seemed to regard the engagement as a quiet, friendly workout for Army, and for

Freeman "Fitz" Fitzgerald... took special interest in Army's center, John McEwan. Fitz closed in on him and socked him square on the jaw...

... it is no wonder that they could not solve the problem of a team using the forward pass in a single hour...

the first part of the first quarter it looked that way. An Army line, outweighing ours by about 15 pounds to the man, pushed us all over the place before we overcame the reality that we were actually playing the Army.

I recall Merrilat shouting: "Let's lick these Hoosiers!" So I asked him, during a lull, if he knew how the word "Hoosier" originated.

"We started it at South Bend," I informed him, John Markoe, and what others of the Army team would listen. "After every game, the coach goes over the field, picks up what he finds and asks his team, 'Whose ear is this?' Hence, Hoosier?"

My joking didn't go over so well. Something else did though. After we had stood terrific pounding by the Army line, and a trio of backs charged in on us like locomotives, we held them on downs.

Then Gus said in the huddle, "Let's open up."

It was amusing to see the Army boys huddle after our first snappy 11-yard pass had been completed for a first down. Army's guards and tackles tried to stop a line buck or plunge, but Gus simply stepped back and flicked the ball to one of our receivers. We did this twice in a march up the field, gaining three first downs in almost as many minutes.

Gus was successful with passes for short gains. Then Gus called my number, meaning that he was going to throw a long forward pass to me as I ran down the field and out toward the sidelines. I put on full speed and left my defender standing flat-footed. I raced across the Army goal line as Gus whipped the ball. The grandstands roared at the completion of

CATHOLICS DOWN ARMY SQUAD, 35-13

Rush Cadets Off Feet in Final Quarter of Bitterly Fought Contest.

N. D. LEADS AT HALF TIME

West Point. N. Y., Nov. 1.—[Special.]—The Army was outclassed in eevry department of the game today by Notre Dame and went down to defeat by a score of 35 to 13.

The westerners played the fastest game of football seen on the local gridiron in years. Their open field running, brilliant forward passing, and sure handling of the ball was pretty to watch, but was a source of much discomfort to the cadets, who seemingly never had a chance. The Catholics proved they could play straight football also, for through the big holes opened in the Army's forward wall they drove their backs for long gains. When the whistle ended the gabe they were smashing the Army defense to pieces.

Eichenlaub, Dorais, and Pliska were the stars of the Hoosier team. The visitors essayed fourteen forward passes and succeeded twelve times. Dorais' one attempt at field goal from the forty-five yard line was short, but the western quarter was a sure kicker of goals from touchdowns, scoring them from difficult angles. He did not miss a single one.

For the Army Hoge at half back and Merrill at end did the best work. Notre Dame took time out only once and used only one substitute during the entire game. Lineup:

Army.	Notre Dame.
R. E..Merrilliat, Brittor	Rockne ....L. E.
R. T........... Weyarc	Jones ....L. T.
R. G........... Jone	Keefe ....L. G.
C....McEwan. Waddeil	Feeney ....C.
L. G...Meecham Good-man, Woodruf	Fitzgera'd ....R. G. Lathrope ....R. T.
L. T....Wynne, Packard	Gushurst ....R. E.
L. E............. Jouett	Dorais ....Q. B.
Q. B......... Pr'chard	Pliska ....L. H. B.
R. H. B...Hobbs. Hess Woodruf	Finnegan, Lar-
L. H. B....Hoge, Ford	kin ....R. H. B.
F. B.....Hodgson. Lanphier, M'lburn	Eichenlaub ....F. B.

Touchdowns—Hodgson, Pritchard, Rockne. Eichenlaub [2], Pliska [2]. Goals from touchdowns—Hoge, Dorais [5]. Referee—Morrice [Penn]. Umpire—Roper [Princeton]. Head lineman—Luehring [Northwestern]. Time of periods—12 and 15 min-

George Philbrook, our gigantic tackle, weighed 220 pounds and he gave me good reason to come up with a new blocking technique.

a 40-yard pass to score 6 points. Everyone was astonished. No one had ever seen a touchdown scored this way before.

We also used "boxing" tackle for the first time in this Army game. George Philbrook, our gigantic tackle, weighed 220 pounds, and he gave me good reason to come up with a new

blocking technique. I practiced for hours the head bob and shoulder drop that the lightweight champion Albert Griffiths, "Young Griffo," used so successfully in the ring. It's a feint followed by instantly applied power. By employing this strategy, it was practicable for one man to block one man, no matter the discrepancy in weight, instead of using two men to block the big boys.

The contest grew personal as Army lost ground and we gained it. Super-heated between scrimmages, wild words flew. Freeman "Fitz" Fitzgerald, our guard, took special interest in Army's center, John McEwan. Fitz closed in on him and socked him square on the jaw, and then he yelled, "Hey, referee!" The referee turned around to see McEwan crash home a right to Fitz's nose. McEwan was promptly ordered from the game. I had to explain that both boys had been too boisterous, and so the referee let both of them stay in. From then on their behavior improved.

Hard fought to the end, this first Army game with its score 35-13 in our favor does not quite represent the difference in the playing quality between the two teams. The Army was much better than the score showed. It was, however, the first signal triumph of the new open game over the old battering-ram game played in the East. And the Army was quick to learn.

Both the press and football public hailed this new game, and Notre Dame received credit as the originator of a style of play that we had simply systematized. We had demonstrated, by completing 14 out of 17 passes gaining some 200 yards, the forward pass could be an integral part of offense and not merely a threat.

There was no crushing of muscle and sinew by the 1913 team. We didn't rely on hurdling, tackling, and plunging, just a lot of touchdowns by rapid transit.

Looking back over that match and its surprising revelation to Army players versed and skilled in the old-style game, it is no wonder that they could not solve the problem of a team using the forward pass in a single hour. Indeed, after 20 years of making and directing forward-pass attacks, I know of only one genuinely effective way of stopping it (beside the obvious precaution of covering the five eligible receivers — the ends and backs), and that is to rush the passer, a tactic at once crude and unreliable.

If this account seems to confirm a once prevalent impression that Western football was legalized rioting, that's far from the truth. Moguls of the game in the East seemed to have thought that the football boundaries were limited by the Alleghenies on the west, the Berkshires on the north, and the Philadelphia City Hall on the south. Likewise, they thought the principal — indeed, the only — inhabitants of this kingdom of football were the Big Three — Yale, Harvard and Princeton, with Penn and possibly Cornell and Dartmouth as neophytes in the sacred circle. Only when Western teams had the audacity to invade the East and beat Eastern teams did football consciousness expand nationally.

There were scores of fine players in the West and great games every week that received little but local publicity. Only when a Western team fought a big Eastern team did it stand a chance for headlines.

Later, when the football public converted to the idea that while East is East and West is West, the twain had met somewhat to the advantage of the West — a new sensation in football, such as Willie Heston, Eckersall, the Praying Colonels of Centre College, or the "Galloping Ghost," Red Grange, could be front-paged and made famous overnight. I could name a dozen players who, had they the opportunity to do their stuff against schools with better-known names but certainly with no better brand of football than the schools they played, would have been as celebrated as long-remembered stars.

Paul Simmons was generally remembered as the terror of that team because of the astonishing and dangerous dives he made over the heads of the would-be tacklers.

22

THE LAST GAME

In all my experience as a player, one of the toughest games I ever survived, apart from a professional game in which Jim Thorpe participated and nearly tore me in two, was the Notre Dame-Texas game on Thanksgiving Day, 1913. It was my last game playing college football.

The temperature in Austin was 86 degrees. When we left South Bend, the temperature was freezing. It nearly ruined us, but the Texan boys seemed to like it.

Paul Simmons was generally remembered as the terror of that team because of the astonishing and dangerous dives he made over the heads of the would-be tacklers. He would run rapidly with the ball after receiving it from center and dive headfirst, regardless of what, where or when he might hit. It ended in a complete somersault unless somebody got him, which was not often. When caught, he was lucky not to break his back.

Simmons caused me no end of trouble. Our team was dog-tired. Al Feeney, Gus and the others stood about the field like weathered statues. I, too, was on the verge of collapse. Finally, I grew so tired that when Simmons started on one end-run, I faded out, stopping dead through weariness. He cut back and ran right into me. I hung onto him, and as I got up I looked around and saw that not a single man on our secondary had moved to help me. They all burst into an ironic cheer: "Atta boy, Rock!" (What I thought need not be printed here.)

Paul Simmons's famous somersault hurdle was solved in the second half. As he came thundering at Joe Pliska, Joe crouched, lifting his shoulders at the moment of impact. Eichenlaub then hit him in mid-air. Simmons had to be carried from the game, which we all regretted. He was a great back without the diving that left him open to injury.

A giant tackle had been roughing me up when he was sent in as a sub toward the end of the first half. He left me with a limp, so that in the rest between halves I dreaded returning, getting myself prepared mentally for another thirty minutes of hell.

I've played against many strong linesmen, but never against one as strong as this one. In that terrific heat (to us Northerners), he smashed into me like a ton of animated ice. I was glad when the half ended. I might mention in passing that in the dressing room a strange newspaperman regaled us with the tale of a Texan, a spectator not a player, who saved a game once by actually shooting down a drop-kick before it could cross the bar.

I was happy when my friend, who apparently belonged to the wrong social set and so was not played as a regular, was not in the lineup for the second half.

Fate was with us. A "cool norther," as they call them in Austin, blew in between halves, and we went out for the second half with the temperature comfortably lower.

Opening up with passes, we scored two touchdowns. Everything was rosy. Another touchdown for us made us think the game was in the bag with only 10 minutes to go.

But the Texas coach returned the giant tackle to the line, and he again was paired with me. He knocked my poor, sweating, ill-treated carcass sideways, backwards, and nearly every which way. Suddenly, I came up with an idea. Mal Elward, my substitute at end, was just 10 minutes short of the 60 minutes big-game play necessary to win a football monogram, the emblem of team membership.

I called out to Coach Harper, "Send Elward in, he needs 10 minutes for his monogram."

"Darned nice of you," said coach.

I replied after Elward ran past me, "If that tackle does to him what he's done to me, he won't think I'm so nice."

Section 3: Rockne on Rockne

... football remained at Notre Dame, and later the same President Cavanaugh appointed me head coach.

23
NOTRE DAME HITS THE MAP

Acquisition of fame stimulates individuals and organizations. Nationwide discussion of Notre Dame by football fans after the first Army game had a tremendous effect on our own varsity spirit. Everyone in the school, with the exception of the old professors, wanted to be a football player.

We won all of our games that season, defeating Army, Penn State and Texas. Winning the Army game gave Notre Dame some recognition in the East. It marked all of our players. I know of only two instances where it didn't. Against Penn State, Joe Pliska, a fine player otherwise, had an off moment. A Penn State end went scrambling by Joe while he stood rooted to the ground, staring into the grandstand. The end scored. We tore into Joe in the dressing room, and he took it. He had to.

Joe confided to me saying, "I was wondering about a girl in the grandstand. I heard her holler: 'Atta boy, Joe!' I looked for her and missed that end going by me."

It was an expensive distraction for us, but excusable. Certainly, it was more so than in another case when the surge of college spirit missed its mark. And it was a colossal mark. His name was Frank Milbauer, and hundreds of players who bumped into him will bitterly recall him as Notre Dame's 280-pound tackle.

In a game our B team had with DePaul in Chicago, Frank Milbauer was sent in at a critical moment when the ball was on our three-foot mark with about 30 seconds to go. A large crowd of DePaul fans were hysterical with excitement. Just as signals were called by the De-

His name was Frank Milbauer, and hundreds of players who bumped into him will bitterly recall him as Notre Dame's 280-pound tackle...

Paul quarterback for the final play, Milbauer looked over at the guard next to him and said, "I hope they've got a big dinner tonight. I'm gettin' kind of hungry." The words had barely left his mouth when the play smashed through him.

Winning of our spurs had a heady effect. But at Notre Dame we had a pretty good tradition for what they called "knocking down the ears" of conceited football players or students. Coach and professors supplied the balance between achievement and self-esteem when the ordinary vicissitudes of the game failed to do so. In my case, I felt the cockiest when the Midwest papers spoke glowingly of my chances to be named on the All-Western team. I heard that an impressive crowd of football writers had gathered to see Notre Dame play Marquette in Chicago. This seemed like a good opening to show them they were not far from wrong in mentioning my name.

Although I had been in a score of matches, my own mother had not seen me in a game. I invited her to watch me play in the Marquette game. I was sure she would not be disappointed in her son. This was perhaps a touch of vanity, but no boy wants his mother to see him try anything athletic, unless or until he thinks he's pretty good at it.

Quarterback Ray Huegle of Marquette caught a long punt, and I chose the play to show my stuff. Laying my ears back, I tore down the field to tackle him, putting on all the speed I had to impress the newspaper boys and my mom. Approaching the ballcarrier, I should have slowed down and spread my feet for the tackle. I didn't. I kept running fast. Huegle just sidestepped me and I went flying by, feeling foolish. Conceit of any kind is a handicap to an athlete.

Marquette was a comparatively easy game for us, and I had plenty of openings to make individual plays, long runs, and so on. All of which I did. After the game was over, my mother asked me a question. "That player," she said, "isn't he wonderful?" "Which one," I asked. "The one doing the pinwheels." He was the cheerleader.

When Notre Dame played Northwestern in 1905, the line-play closely approached assault and battery. Football is not or should not be merely a game for the strong. It should also be a game for the smart, the swift, the brave, and the clever.

The roughest game I ever saw, and one I played in, resulted in victory when the fighting spark was blown to flame by a taunt. It was our game with a certain Eastern college in 1913. The Easterners, outweighing us considerably, figured the best way to beat us was to keep as many of the Notre Dame men as possible on the ground at the same time.

We were being soundly licked until an Easterner said to one of our halfbacks, "Why don't you fellows bring your own mattresses?" Between halves, our halfback spoke wisely. "Don't you guys think that if we keep these chaps busy picking themselves up they won't have time to knock us down?"

That sounded logical. I venture to say the second half of that game was the liveliest, if not the loveliest, ever seen on a gridiron. We won.

At the training table, we football players were forbidden to eat pastry. Nonetheless, pies were served to stimulate strength of will by avoiding them. Non-players, knowing the pies were present and would not be consumed, invaded the training table room to steal the pies. Objecting to this intrusion, we would beat them off with a barrage of buns.

Running interference for Eichenlaub was one of my contributions to a successful game with Marquette.

Especially luscious pies — strawberry pies — were served one day and thrust aside. Envious eyes lighted on them, and hungry hands reached out. Then a violent bun throwing attack ensued, and at its highest moment, the door opened and suddenly someone stepped in the room. He got a bun squarely in the right eye from me. He was President Cavanaugh of the University. Instantly, he demanded that the football squad be disbanded and the football schedule for that season canceled. We quickly formed an impromptu committee to apologize and explain matters to the president.

"I cannot reconcile," he said, tapping a damaged eye gently. "Men, like you who are good, with ruffians who throw footballs and buns."

We made more explanations that were satisfactory to him, because football remained at Notre Dame, and later the same President Cavanaugh appointed me head coach.

SECTION 3: ROCKNE ON ROCKNE

... one hard day stands out above all others — the day I was playing professional football and tried to stop Jim Thorpe.

24

THORPE

In a review of my playing career, one hard day stands out above all others — the day I was playing professional football and tried to stop Jim Thorpe.

My job was to tackle him, which I did two times successfully, but with much suffering. After the second time, Thorpe smiled genially at me.

"Be a good boy," he said. "Let Jim run."

Thorpe took the ball again. I went at him. Never before have I received such a shock. It was as if a locomotive had hit me, followed by a 10-ton truck, rambling over my remains. I lay on the field of battle while he pounded out a 40-yard run for a touchdown.

He came back, helped me to my feet, then patted me gingerly on the back. Smiling broadly, he said, "That's a good boy, Knute. You let Jim run."

I did not see Jim Thorpe in his college days. The first time I saw him play was at Canton, Ohio, in 1915, several years after he had left Carlisle. He was playing professionally for the Canton Bulldogs in a game with the Massillon Tigers.

I saw Jim several times during the next few years and am convinced he was the greatest of them all. He could do everything all the other backs have been able to do, and he could do most of these things just a little better.

On the first play of this game against Massillon, Thorpe stood on his own 10-yard line and punted the ball. It was fumbled by the receiver on his nine-yard line. There was no wind. High as a skylark, the ball had traveled 81 yards.

A little while later, I saw him flash off-tackle with a speed and change of pace that Red Grange might have envied.

Thorpe threw passes. He caught passes. And when he interfered, he knocked them down and they stayed down. When he tackled them, they stayed tackled.

It was impossible to complete forward passes in his territory. Early in the second-half he dropped back and drop-kicked a ball from the 58-yard line that seemed to have 15 yards to spare as it passed over the goalposts.

Shortly after this score, one of the Massillon players began violating the rules and started playing rough. Several times Jim cautioned and remonstrated. The Massillon player gave the retort discourteous, and, further to show he was no gentleman, on the next play committed one of the most muckerish fouls out of football.

Jim said nothing, but bided his time. When the game was safe in the hands of Canton, Jim obtained the ear of the quarterback. The quarterback barked out the numbers and the ball came back to Jim. It was

evident he was going to throw a forward pass.

The man who had been abusing Jim was a Massillon center. He dropped back to the side known as the weak side. The ball left Jim's hands and traveled in a soft arc right toward the Massillon center. He caught it. An instant after he caught it, he was tackled by a Canton player. The tackle was so loud that it was heard throughout the stands.

The Canton player was Jim Thorpe, who got up smiling.

The Massillon center did not get up. He was carried from the field with several torn muscles and a severe shock. It was a clean tackle, but, my, what a leg drive!

Thorpe got even, and no one can say that he was not within his rights.

There was nothing Jim couldn't do. Frances "Red" Fleming of Washington and Jefferson, who tackled many great players in his time, said he would rather tackle anybody than Thorpe.

"When I tackled him, I felt it all the way from my big toe to the fourth ventricle! The next time he ran with the ball, I slowed up and stayed out of his way."

THE COACH

Boys must have an outlet for animal spirits. Their education must contain a training in clean contests, otherwise they'll be lost in a world that thrives on competition and in which those who cannot compete cannot hope to thrive.

25

STUDENT ATHLETES

I was asked the bromidic question the other day as to what we men in athletics do for the students who are not varsity athletes.

I am so tired of re-telling this that I hope it will be the last time, but it won't. I might reiterate that the plan we follow at our school is the same one that is used at most institutions.

The student not so physically inclined, be he from Portland or Anoka, can take home with him the knowledge of various athletic exercises such as how to swim, play tennis, golf or handball.

A student partially interested in athletics may obtain, besides the advantages listed above, a place on one or more of the intramural teams. It will not take much of his time, as he has to practice but very little. We have intramural contests in basketball, baseball, track, or one of the other sports and, for those who are physically strong enough, even football. Each student will be fully equipped, and members of the varsity will provide instruction.

Then there is the boy who would like to be an athlete — wishes he were an athlete — but has no ability and still wants to play on our school's football team.

We will outfit him completely if he will come out to practice three times a week. He can stay on the team and receive the benefit of football coaching just as long as he cares to stay out. There are no cuts on the varsity squad at Notre Dame anymore and the result is that we finish the football season with a hundred and fifty or sixty men. Teachers in their classes, for the sake

189

If the newcomer decides to try out for football, he realizes from the beginning that he must make his mark in the face of much competition.

of efficiency, have to end the dubs, but on the varsity athletic squads, the dubs are allowed to stay out until the very last day.

If this program, along with the intercollegiate events, is not a sane adjunct to a sound educational program, then perhaps we are on the wrong track and had better be giving varsity monograms for a long run on a saxophone or for dancing a full program at the Prom.

A student entering Notre Dame finds himself at once a part of an entity complete in itself and united by a single spirit. There is, of course, no compulsion to play football, although quite naturally it is insisted, for the sake of health and character, that every student should take part in some sort of athletics. It does not seem to be generally known that in many other sports other than football — such as track, basketball, baseball — the school has an enviable record.

There has been detected a tendency, especially in elite schools, to substitute social life with caste implications for athletic prestige and campus activity — a movement led by lounge lizards. One year a group of mezzanine-floor high-hurdlers presented their candidate for president of the senior class. His opposing candidate was a campus leader — not an athlete — an orator, debater, and a hard worker in many extracurricular activities. But he waited tables. The other boy with the help of his friends won the election.

To me in my thinking, Notre Dame had gone soft. At the football mass meeting the

190

following fall, I announced that Notre Dame, in harmony with the spirit prevailing on the campus as evidenced by the senior election, would pursue a new football policy. Notre Dame would play their highly respected rival Northwestern as usual in 1935. However, I added, the boys would be alumni by that time, and those living far away and picking up the morning paper the day after the game to read about it, would turn, not to the vulgar sporting sheet — oh, my, no — but to the society column. It will be an impressive game, with spectacular, unbelievable proportions.

We are all conversant, of course, with the benefits that the man indulging in athletics derives from that source. Enumerated briefly, they are: improved physical health, confidence, initiative, self-control, sportsmanship, concentration, keener analytical powers, and courage.

How about the average student who does not have the time or the ability to indulge in athletics to the extent of trying to make a varsity team? I feel quite sure that the qualities of the varsity team that make for a successful aggregation — such as courage, initiative, confidence, irrepressible fight, and ability to think keenly and quickly under fire — I believe all of these qualities are imparted more or less to the student body as a whole.

I also believe that one of the finest attitudes which any student or alumnus can have toward his school, namely that of loyalty, is developed almost entirely around the athletic teams.

Statistics compiled by athletic directors all over the country prove conclusively that in those schools where there are successful varsity teams in the major sports, the students lacking the physical and mental make-up for the big teams go out enthusiastically for other healthful sports such as tennis, golf, gymnasium work, swimming and walking.

These reports will also show that schools which have no interest in their varsity teams also have no interest in any exercise of any sort for the student body at large. Instead, the interest of this student body seems to concentrate entirely around social activities with attendant effeminacy which always accompanies all excesses towards the social life. The mental attitude of manliness is lost, and the student body tends toward the feminine point of view on things in general. This is not the product of anyone's imagination but is the result of the observations of men who have spent their lifetime analyzing the psychology and activities of students in colleges.

Our universities are copied after the Greek universities, and the ideal, of course, is to have the academic, social and athletic activities in the proper proportion. We are all agreed that we come to school primarily to study, and that academic work comes first. We are also all agreed that a certain amount of social activities is absolutely necessary in developing a well-rounded citizen.

Athletics, however, are also an "essential desiderata" and form an integral part of any educational system which aims to turn out a full, well-rounded alumnus.

Let me say at once that Notre Dame's scholastic discipline creates the right atmosphere for a coach. There is no coeducation. By far the majority of the 3,000 students live in halls and dormitories on the campus. All but seniors are obliged to eat their meals in the school refectories. Strict hours are kept, and class attendance requirements are stern.

The latter I know, to my sorrow, for several fine football players have been suspended in my time. It's bad procedure for

You can't make drudgery of it and get anything out of the boys. It's a game, a hard game, but a game just the same.

a coach to appeal to the faculty on the behalf of an inadequate student. I did this one time and the boy was reinstated. He went into an important game and fumbled us to defeat, illustrating a general rule that a careless student is a careless player.

The average class grade of the Notre Dame football team for the first semester of this year, as given to me by the Director of Studies, was 82.3, and only one man on the squad of monogram men was classed as a "flunker." This is somewhat higher than the average of the student body as a whole and is just one example of showing that figures prove that athletics and studies do mix, and that athletics do not in any way hamper a man's academic work, but to the contrary, prove a stimulus in many cases.

From the beginning of my coaching career, with whatever faults I brought to my profession, I at least possessed the intelligence to recognize that the faculty must run the institution. The school is their school, and the coach must bear in mind that his is an extracurricular activity like debating societies, campus politics, publications, and so forth.

If a player fails in class, he's no good to the coach or to the school, and the coach who goes around trying to fix it for athletes to be scholastically eligible when mentally they're not is plain wrong and a waste of valuable time. The school wants a good team and so, of course, do the ever-vocal alumni. And the boys want to make a good team.

Sometimes a coach may be handicapped by the passion in human nature for prerogative and authority that, on occasion, leads the faculty to interfere. But meddling is never the policy of top-notchers. They're too busy perfecting themselves in their own work.

At a luncheon, I was answering questions that were written and handed across the table to me. One question read: "Why does a Notre Dame football player sing 'Home, Sweet Home' every time he sees a Pullman car?"

It was a sharp dig at "the Irish" as a constantly traveling team. The conference teams, playing their own round robin, haven't room on their schedule for us. If we don't want to play teachers' institutes and dental colleges, we have to go traveling. We have good teams, and we want to play good teams.

But I'll also tell you this: We lose very little time from the classroom. I don't believe our football players lose three days a season from class in spite of the traveling we do. Our Coast trips are usually made during the Christmas holidays. And when we play at home on Saturdays, our football players are in class until noon on Fridays.

In the fall, our training program includes enough scrimmaging to keep the boys tuned in and sharpened up, but not enough to bog them down and have them bruised and battered for Saturday games. You can't make drudgery of it and get anything out of the boys. It's a game, a hard game, but a game just the same. The natural love of the sport and the competitive spirit are enough to keep the boys on edge. We have signal practice and dummy drills and blackboard talks.

In the minds of many who do not know the facts, there seems to be an idea that athletics and studies do not mix well, and also that athletics of themselves are of no particular value to the student body. Having been in athletic work for almost ten years, and having during this time become acquainted with conditions not only at the University of Notre Dame but also at many other schools throughout the United States, I am absolutely convinced that anyone holding any such idea is either grossly ignorant or narrowly prejudiced.

A coach must study pedagogy and be able to give out facts in such a simple and clear way that the men can assimilate them.

26

PEDAGOGY

For some inexplicable reason, physical educators seem to have the idea that they have a monopoly on all the big words in athletics, so that when a football coach mentions "pedagogy," the average physical educator responds by chuckling. The football coach will allow the physical educator a monopoly on such words as "kinesiology," "somatic," and "anthropometry," as those don't impress too many folks anyway.

An experienced coach knows that motor coordination is developed through drills and exercises of the right kind, and that distance discernment of the eye and muscle of the arm can be developed and improved upon by practice. As for producing large, bulging muscles, that is absolutely devoid of any particular meaning.

But when you come to pedagogy — that is a football coach's real dish.

The average professor goes into a classroom, gives his lecture, and leaves. His attitude is distinctly one of "take it or leave it." He may flunk half the class and everyone is awestricken. The coach, however, has to be a super-teacher. He must see to it that the class learns what he has to teach. If he flunks half his class, he flunks with them.

It is not what a coach knows, it is what he can teach his boys, what he can make them do. Therefore, the coach must take every possible means to give the candidates a clear and concise picture of what he has in mind. Then he must convince the candidates of the importance of perfecting every detail.

There are similarities teaching in a classroom setting and teaching on a football field in

Keep your eyes up and your stern down, so your drive is concentrated and at the same time you can see where your opponent is maneuvering.

that both strive to cause the student to use his mind. As an example of teaching football, imagine that I am talking to a group of guards and that I am going to explain to them the double-coordination movement.

Say the guard is a right guard playing against a balanced line with the opponent's backfield shifted to our left, making the guard the weak side guard. The right guard stands with his left foot to the rear, both toes pointed straight ahead and balancing on the balls of his feet. He should bend his knees so that his seat is low, so that he is comfortable and his position firm. He lets his arms dan-

gle loosely in front of him so that he gives no intimation in any way as to what he intends to do or how.

It is third down and four or five yards to go, and therefore he is suspecting the play will be coming back to the weak side. His position as guard is such that he must maintain it or guard his own territory. In other words, he is expecting a play right over him and so he is alert for it, for previously he may have used, under the same conditions, the submarine or the flying squirrel over the top.

Also, since the offensive guard and tackle, from their stance, appear to be susceptible to it, he decides he is going to use the "double-coordination" movement.

The instant the ball moves, his two hands are brought from underneath sideways near the ear of the tackle with sufficient power and vigor to deflect completely the tackle in his charge. His left knee is moved from the rear right along the ground between the guard and tackle as far as he can. In fact, the knee is fairly shot forward with a sort of loose hip movement, using the hip action and the upper thigh muscles of the left thigh to effect this. The reason that the movement is called double-coordination is because the two parts must be done simultaneously.

In game action the two parts must be done at the same time together in a split second. The instant these two first movements are completed as one, he uses his left shoulder and right leg to brace himself as he slips off the charge of the guard. And with the use of his left elbow he heaves the guard to one side as he continues his path into the backfield unhampered, free, with both hands ready to make the tackle.

His knees are under him to spring, if necessary. He should stay loose and relaxed and doesn't tense until the moment of contact. He should believe that he will be successful. His two opponents don't know which of the three or four stunts he intends to use.

I line the players up personally and give a demonstration in both "slow motion picture" style and full speed, as under game conditions. The guard candidates then line up and I have two offensive men line up against each one, as I said previously, to charge very little or passively. I then watch the guards closely and criticize one fault at a time. I do not call the attention of any one candidate to more than one fault, and he stays with this fault until he has corrected it.

Then I call his attention to his next fault, and he corrects that, and so on.

The boy can concentrate on only one thing at a time, and the teacher must remember that. I do not give them any long, detailed description of what is wrong with them, and my line of conversation is something like this:

"Anderson, bend your knees down!" ... "Smith, you are bringing your knee along the ground too high!" ... "Jones, your hands have no power, and you are not using the straight forearm shiver!" ... "Miller, your hands are hitting the opponent from above, not from underneath!" ... "Lockhart, you are not driving your knee forward fast enough or far enough!" ... "Noonan, you are not reacting fast enough, and you are not using your elbows with enough power!"

This same form of instruction should be carried on in detail when instructing the candidates for the various positions in any form of fundamental play. Don't forget that the only way to achieve perfection is to keep them practicing until it becomes second nature. Whether it is teaching charging, blocking, or any of the other hundreds of things that have to be taught, each skill has to be performed perfectly for the team to be able to play the game of football well.

A coach must study pedagogy and be able to give out facts in such a simple and clear way that the men can assimilate them. Put your information across slowly and repeat over and over again. Take a difficult point and study how to make it so simple that it will become palatable mentally even to the dullard.

You must be able to weigh values to a nicety. Know what to stress and pay particular attention to it. Know what to gloss over lightly. This is what distinguishes a good coach from a poor one. Some coaches are always stressing the unimportant things and passing by the big things. Keep everything simple, and particularly stress the fundamentals. Do not give much credit to the star who carries the ball, but give the credit to the men who knock out of the way the potential tacklers. Develop a tradition of blocking and tackling at your school.

And so the coach's work is really refined pedagogy, as the results of his teaching are put to a test every Saturday. He should immediately take the proper means of correcting everything which he sees wrong in the scrimmage or the game. The best time to do this teaching is in three or four weeks of spring football when there is plenty of time without tension or emotion hurrying the process unduly. Teach slowly and build brick by brick, so that when the job is completed you would have built surely.

And I'm convinced the technical in football should be adapted to the popular. That is, the essentials, which are all any intelligent follower of the game cares about. It's possible to build up a mysteriously significant vocabulary of technical terms regarding anything.

At coaching school in Dallas a year ago, a coach from a Texas school sought me out in my room to ask advice. "I've got a problem where I teach football," he said. "The alumni don't think I speak authoritatiously. Neither do the students."

"You should explain your plays as simply as possible," I said. "For instance, beginning with shift."

"Please elucidate," said the coach.

"Well, your backs move into place at the signal. They are arranged in juxtaposition..." I could get no farther, my friend arose beaming.

"Tha's a word," he said, "tha's a word. All I need, Mister Coach." He grasped my hand warmly. "You've made me."

Just as in the classroom, so in managing college athletes, firmness and consideration, and the knack of letting the lad know that you know his capacities and failings better than he does wins implicit confidence for the coach. Boys are generous in their loyalty when they are convinced of your fairness.

I do not believe in abusing a team or using any means that a gentleman would object to. I believe a coach who uses profanity at all loses the respect of his men.

A very good player named Charles Bachman gave me my first test of authority when I was an assistant to Jess Harper. Bachman was being put through blocking practice, but someone had evidently given Bachman what he considered better advice than mine. I worked with him for half-an-hour that afternoon, only to see him discard the blocking method I had taught him — a quick spread step and low crouch.

There was only one thing to do, so I did it.

"Come out of there, Bachman," I called.

He came out. "Turn in your suit. We won't need you anymore," I said.

There was the expected consternation at an assistant coach firing a varsity squad man. But Harper sustained me. Later, Bachman explained that somebody had told him Rockne might be a good end, but his knowledge of blocking was limited. Bachman apologized and was allowed back on the team. He went on to play with credit in many big games.

This example gave me the reputation of being a martinet, a label valuable to any coach if he doesn't work too hard to keep it. As you work along with your team during the fall, you must cultivate a cheerfulness of mind in all of them. A good trainer with a fund of witty stories is invaluable. Confidence is another

The best time to do this teaching is in three our four weeks of spring football when there is plenty of time without tension or emotion hurrying the process unduly.

thing that you are always trying to instill into the men, although this must not be carried to extremes.

In the first half of the season it is very difficult to build up confidence, but a team which has it is very difficult to defeat. The team must not be allowed to worry much about the games, but should take them more in the spirit of play. Every man on the squad must have the point of view that he has a fair and equal chance to make the team regardless of fraternity or any other politics. Do everything to allay their fears along any line and to increase their hopes.

Some coaches try to scare their teams every game, and scare them Saturday after Saturday. I think this is a serious mistake because after a while the team refuses to scare and a decided opposite reaction will set in. As long as you go along with your practice, you must keep stimulating the team to the idea that the thing which wins football games is the "will to win." Show them that the difference between defeat and victory in many cases is merely that one team has more will power, more determination, and the margin of difference is, in many cases, just a matter of inches.

The history or traditions of the school are a great thing to recite to your team and to keep before them. Exaggerate these as much as you can and set somewhat exaggerated standards to emulate. A school without traditions will find it very hard to build up a successful football team, as tradition is a powerful factor. Putting up in a dressing room one or two appropriate signs, such as "Notre Dame Fights" or "Nothing Else

Counts But Guts," are helpful factors in bringing a team around to a mental attitude where they will do their best because they know that it is expected of them.

Be absolutely square with your men and never call one down unless he has it coming to him. Never call a man down for a mechanical error, but you must keep insisting on fight, alertness of mind, and that the men must be enthusiastic, trying to do their best at all times.

The time to key up a team is the week previous to the big game. By keying up a team, I do not mean any emotional frenzy, but just merely a grim realization of the immensity of the task ahead. Bring them along quietly and gradually by telling them just what they are up against. I never underrate an opponent but I am a little inclined to overrate them. A team which goes into the game underrating their opponents is an easy team to beat. In fact, I can imagine nothing worse than an over-confident team.

Talk to the men individually during the week.

A team should never be coddled in regard to their physical ailments, but rather should be made to adopt a Spartan attitude. Every man should report an injury so as to make sure that a more serious injury may not follow and also to make sure that no man who should not play is allowed to get into the game or scrimmage. No man should ever be played if he has an ailment of a chronic type, as playing a rough game such as football is might very easily give him a permanent injury.

Every team should have several comedians among them so that the squad is always in good humor. If my football squad is not laughing, singing, or horse-playing in a shower bath, I am alarmed. On the day of the game they should be raring to go and all on edge for the opening whistle.

The football coach's greatest asset is the reliance placed upon him by the boys in his charge. Whatever secret of success there is to it can be reduced to a simple formula: Strict discipline in training and on the field of play must be combined with kindly interest in all other relations with the boys.

SECTION 3: ROCKNE ON ROCKNE

... every football coach knows that there is nothing more important for victory than the mental attitude of his players before a game.

27
PSYCHOLOGY

Psychology has its place in football, but not to the degree of importance many football fans believe. When I hear a football coach of some mental capacity referred to as a deep and serious thinker, as a mastermind who evolves game-winning strategy, and that with a single brain wave he can conquer tremendous opposition, excuse me if I have to smile.

The word "psychology" nowadays may mean almost anything. We still have some adherents of the old introspective school of William James, but most of our modern psychologists belong either to the behavioristic, endocrine or eskalt schools. It will probably be many years before the leaders in this science will be able to agree on something definite after meeting on a common ground.

The freak psychologists will tell you that a shot of adrenalin will cure cowardice in the case of a football player who is afraid, etc. The practical football coach knows that this is a lot of bunk. He knows that if a man is yellow, he is yellow. Whereas, the boy with character and will power will overcome his fears and will go into the game showing those qualities we know as raw courage. Courage is largely a matter of breeding, environment and development of the proper mental habits.

However, every football coach knows that there is nothing more important for victory than the mental attitude of his players before a game. He appreciates the fact that the wrong mental attitude has lost more football games than fumbles, intercepted forward passes or bad decisions. He appreciates the fact that a player mentally fit and emotionally keyed up will

Psychology is very important to the coach in his relations with his players, his opponents, and the alumni who seem to be so influential with both.

play a far better game than he would were he mentally unprepared and emotionally dead.

He appreciates the fact that a boy cannot change emotionally or mentally after the game has once begun. If he enters the game in the wrong mental attitude, it is too late; the chances are that if the opposing team is good, it will win.

My mind goes back to a story of two great thinkers and their monumental game. It happened in a small town in the Wabash Valley when there was an outbreak of football fever. It reached its crisis in a love affair between the town belle and two young men who had spent four years in high school and the 10 years thereafter talking about their prowess as substitute backs on the high school team.

One was named Joe, and he was principally distinguished for the most artistic chrysanthemum haircut in the county. The other was named Ed, and he planned to be a dentist if his dad didn't insist on his going to a veterinary college.

Joe wanted to show the girl that his list of high school achievements was more authentic and glowing than Ed's. And, likewise, Ed desired to demonstrate that his record had been better than Joe's.

Ed was the more resourceful, at first. He organized a football club and they met two or three local towns and vanquished them in contests evidently staged to determine who knew the least about the game. This enterprise on Ed's part, however, made him solid with the girl.

Joe was about to be shelved when he had

a mental attack, and a subtle one. Shut out of organizing another football team to rival Ed's in that town — for Ed's outfit, after winning three games straight, had received enthusiastic endorsement from the chamber of commerce — Joe went to a nearby town to form his own team. This town was famous as the seat of the county asylum. Joe sold the authorities the idea that football would be an excellent thing for the inmates. He was promptly appointed coach, manager and quarterback.

Almost as promptly he issued a challenge to Ed's club, which was accepted.

The day came when the grandstands were filled to overflowing. Joe's team of odd ducks lined up against Ed's combination of local talent. The girl sitting in the field box added color to the occasion. Ed wore a bright red sweater to baffle the players on Joe's team.

Through three quarters, the teams played each other to a standstill. Excitement was high, and while orthodox football was more or less pushed aside, all the customers had a good time.

Between Joe and Ed, however, there was more than a mere game at stake. The winner of the contest would also, by the laws of romance, be winner of the girl.

They redoubled their efforts in the final quarter, driving their teams on with inspirational cries and nifty slugging in the scrimmages. In a burst of energy, Ed got the upper hand on a fumble by an asylum player who imagined he was a Spanish ring bull and dropped the ball to charge at Ed's red sweater.

Ed's team scored a touchdown. Only five

minutes remained to play and Joe's forces were furious. Precious seconds slipped by. Defeat stared Joe in the face nearly as mockingly as Ed's bright red sweater.

Joe had another idea. On the sidelines he saw a member of the odd rooters, hissing and pumping his arms, giving a perfect imitation of a Big Four locomotive. Indeed, had you asked this gentleman what he was, he would have replied that he was a Big Four locomotive. As a matter of fact, he had been an engine driver until a fireman did something unfriendly with a shovel.

Calling timeout, Joe went to the sidelines and addressed the human locomotive.

"Special ordered down the line," he said, "from Logansport to Wabash. Steam's up and we're ready to go."

The big fellow seemed hypnotized as he followed Joe on the field and took his position as fullback. Joe cried signals, got the ball and handed it over to the newcomer.

"Green lights," Joe thundered. "Blow the whistle, let her go!"

For a moment only the human locomotive stood still while Ed's players moved back. Spectators marveled in anticipation of what was to occur. The fellow hissed, spouted sounds like escaping steam. He pumped his arms like pistons, and with a mighty roar started down the field yelling, "WOO, WOOOOO!"

He ran over player after player that got in his way. One after another they dropped in his wake. Only Ed remained with his bright red sweater as if a shining target in the sun.

Ed was stunned. The human locomotive ate up the yards, and behind him was Joe grinning from ear to ear. His chrysanthemum head was butting over any opposition players who were indiscreet enough to arise. Joe skipped along in joyful anticipation of his triumph. All appeared lost for Ed. The human locomotive was 20 yards away, 15, and then 12.

Suddenly, Ed had a masterful inspiration, the sort that can come only to the naturally great psychologist. As the human locomotive, eyes fixed ahead at the goal line, came snorting up huge and irresistible, Ed didn't tackle. He quickly tore off his red sweater and made a noise like a foghorn. "Waaaa."

Then Ed waved the sweater in the breeze. The human locomotive let out a loud screeching noise as if he were applying his brakes. "Eeeek!"

He let out a hissing noise as he came to a stop in front of Ed. Then he reversed his path, pumping his arms like pistons. He shunted back . . . back . . . back, trampling Joe in his reversed path. He wound up on the wrong side of the goal line, causing a safety and two more points for Ed.

While, as they say on Wall Street, I have the facts of this unique game on good authority, I cannot guarantee them. Still, the story illustrates the highly dramatic brand of psychology, which the master football coach is supposed to have at his fingertips.

Psychology is very important to the coach in his relations with his players, his opponents, and the alumni who seem to be so influential with both. He must have some understanding of the minds of the various types of boys if he is to elicit the best there is in any lad who tries to make the football grade.

Every season, for instance, I find material that shines on the practice field but falls down in the test of a real game. Last year I had a typical case. A Western youngster had all the earmarks of a great broken-field runner for the halfback spot. He was a sensation in practice games where visiting alumni saw him.

The same alumni wondered why this boy was never used in big games. It was because he failed in small games. When he got the ball, he tightened up, lost control of his nerves, and as the grandstand bellowed, he also lost his speed. He received innumerable chances. It wasn't his fault, yet, although he never played in a major game to win his letter, that lad did a very real service for the school because his fleetness as a ballcarrier in practice games gave the first team a first-class opposition.

The type of high school athlete that every coach dreads to meet is the high school star who has been petted and pampered by press, townspeople and high school students. These boys come to college with an exaggerated ego regarding their importance and their worth. Whereas, as a matter of fact, in that condition they are worthless not only to themselves but to anybody else.

Wearing the high school monogram on a big sweater, they stroll onto a strange college

As captain, it was an honor and privilege to lead the team on the field at the beginning of every game.

campus and are pained that no one knows who they are or that no one seems to care. This is probably the best thing that can happen to this type of boy as it merely brings him down to earth much earlier than he would have come down otherwise.

Some campuses, however, make much over this type and the boy becomes worse than ever. He will not take part in the team-play. He will not stand for the coach trying to teach him anything. And he will not learn how to block or interfere.

Who is he? He is the bi-triple threat who kicks, passes and runs. Every smart coach, as soon as he finds one of these boys under his charge, will use every means conceivable to deflate the ego, but it isn't always an easy job to do it.

So many boys are ruined in high school by this petting and pampering and being-made-much-of, which is regrettable. But if they recover from their swell-headedness and get down to earth with a serious and sensible knowledge of their own values and of values in general, they will have had an experience they will never forget. They will have had an experience that will stand them in good stead, and I don't believe there is any better teacher for any young man than experience.

The opposite psychological case to the practice athlete is the firing-line competitor. We meet several of these each season. In his way, George Gipp was one. By firing-line competitor, I mean a lad who may be indifferent during tests and tryouts, but who comes through in the acid test of competition against quality.

The facts of perception, attention, action, instinct, emotion, habit, association, thought, memory and will-power have their place in a treatise on psychology. However, I do not claim to know anything about psychology, and anyone interested in the relation of these things to athletics from a purely academic point of view will have to get it from some textbook and make his own deductions. My observations are purely the result of practical experience and whatever observations I have to make on the boy and his emotions, hopes, resolves, fears, memory, will-power and spirit come entirely from a layman's point of view.

Also, the psychological limitations and possibilities of the game I will note purely from the point of view of a practical coach making no attempt to be academic. I have met coaches who have gone to extremes on psychology.

I remember particularly a track coach in one of our Midwestern schools with whom I became intimately acquainted. This fellow trained his runners by sprinting them against dogs; his theory was that a runner would run faster because he was in competition with a faster animal. He tied his long-distance men by means of a rope to a Ford car, and they broke world's records. He painted the lower half of the vaulting standards dark and the upper half light so that the bar didn't appear so high, and therefore presumed the vaulter would vault a great deal higher not knowing how high he was going. Figuring along the same line, he stated that hurdling was a matter of rhythm, and so he trained his hurdlers to the tune of a Victrola record. He used for a record a waltz, "The Nights of Gladness," which seemed to tune in very nicely with his hurdlers. It gave a sort of a little life at just the right time to help the hurdler over the hurdles. As the season progressed and he wanted the hurdlers to hurdle faster, he merely tuned up the Victrola to a higher speed.

He took his psychology very seriously. But the sad part of the thing was that when the big track meet of the year came along, this team didn't score any points. I mention this story just to show that psychology can be carried to ridiculous extremes.

However, I do believe that every boy has to be considered as an individual. The sensitive high-strung boy cannot endure many sarcastic remarks, nor can you ever call him down in front of the team. If you do this, you hurt his feelings to the extent where he may never again play the same kind of football for you. The dull, phlegmatic fellow may respond to sarcasm and tongue-lashing in great shape, and I always have one man on the squad to whom I give nothing but abuse. He thrives on it and cannot play well without it.

You can also get points on how to handle the individual from his nationality and his race. I believe that a coach on the field should be a very strict disciplinarian, and a man with a lot of pep and enthusiasm, and who puts a lot of hard work into his activities. Football is a game of emotions and it is sometimes necessary to make a lot of noise in order to keep up emotional activity, and men will work twice as hard under the stress of emotion as they would otherwise.

An assortment of teams using different styles of attack and defense give a coach plenty of opportunity to test the qualifications of different players, especially those whose temperaments he finds it not so easy to analyze.

Take the boy who is so high-strung and so nervous that from Wednesday-on to game day, he cannot sleep because he is worrying about the coming game. What shall be done with him? A good coach tells him on Wednesday that he's not going to play. The high-strung lad is disappointed and naturally sullen or resentful, but he relaxes and sleeps well at night. Twenty minutes before game time the coach tells him, "I've changed my mind. You're going in."

Immediately the lad becomes anxious and keyed up, but this is the proper time for that. The coach might also keep this fellow out of the game until, we would say, the start of the second quarter.

Then there is the big, powerful, phlegmatic chap. He will just not be aggressive. He is just too friendly with everybody to play football well, and in business later on will probably be known as a good-natured sap. What can be done to arouse this lad from his self-satisfied, lethargic state of mind? A good coach will go to him just before the big game and say, "John, your teammates and the student body and the alumni think you're afraid. I'm the only friend you've got. I'm sticking with you and putting you in that game today. Now what are you going to do? Show me up? And have these other people give us the horse laugh?"

John Mohardt had heard that I was on the lookout for an A-1 blocker for George Gipp. Mohardt became that blocker, and in addition he developed into an accurate forward passer.

209

If the lad has any character at all, the result will be an irresistible, pile-driving, head-long charging, irrepressible fighting machine. He will surprise everyone, and himself most of all, by what he can actually do when fired up. Many big linemen have found themselves by this process.

When a coach has a practical knowledge of the psychology of his own players, his mental equipment is still far from complete unless he learns something of the temperament or psychological mannerisms of players — particularly of star players — who are on teams he is to oppose.

As captain, it was an honor and privilege to lead the team on the field at the beginning of every game. But my experience running onto the field my first year on the varsity squad was a humiliating experience. It taught me a valuable lesson. Running onto the Notre Dame gridiron as a starter for the first time, a one-man greeting committee yelled out, "Who's the homely Swede at end?"

Roars of laughter followed this taunt. I was disconcerted. It was like being hit with a missile. Although fairly thick-skinned under criticism, this personal jab in public carried a sting. It had its influence in helping to formulate one of my first principles in coaching: You can kill a young talent by a smart crack at the wrong time.

In my early days as coach, we tried a trick designed to intimidate our opponents that was later discarded. More than a hundred boys would race onto the field in football uniforms before a game to give a picture of Notre Dame's reserve strength. This stunt used to surprise smaller squads, so much so that one smart coach correctly said to his boys, "Keep your eyes on the ground till you line up."

While it was true that many of the players in our impressive army never got into the game, it seemed to serve the purpose of acclimating beginners to the roar of the crowd, although it had a less desirable effect of spreading the legend that Notre Dame was first and last a football school. This myth has never been true and never will be. Many schools are richer in material than Notre Dame, which observes all conference rules as to eligibility, training, practice, and the rest.

I have often been asked why I start a whole second team and then later, generally at the end of the first quarter, insert 11 new men — the varsity. In a schedule like Notre Dame's, I am continually faced with the problem of saving regulars.

The second team acts very much in the capacity of shock absorbers. We know by experience that two football teams generally hit the hardest in the first quarter. With a light backfield, like the Four Horsemen particularly, why aren't they saved from this bruising and unnecessary thumping?

The second reason is psychological. The varsity, sitting on the sidelines and watching the second-string play, becomes keyed up unconsciously. The third reason is to enable the varsity quarterback to look over the defense carefully and decide his plan of attack.

This result, however, is incidental. The main reason is to save them as much as possible from Saturday to Saturday, for boys will be boys, and often they must be guarded against their own zeal for play.

One particular sophomore, I recall, was much too eager for the fray. He could hardly be blamed. His sweetheart was watching the game. He came to me, time after time, and asked to be allowed to go in for at least one play.

"I'm saving you," I said.

This reason didn't hold him. Back he came, pleading to get into the game, overlooking the fact that if he had been vitally important, he would not have had to apply. Also, that he was a sophomore with two years of play ahead of him.

"I'm saving you," I said again.

In desperation, as he saw the third-string boys rush in for the final few minutes, he resumed his annoyance. By this time, it became evident that this young man needed a quick, clear lesson in deflation.

The game ended. Morose, he trudged by my side as we left the field.

"The game's over," he complained. "The season's over. What are you saving me for?"

"The junior prom," I said.

A wisecrack — if you call it that — of this type is a necessary adjunct to a coach's verbal contacts with his players. Youngsters in their late teens and early twenties take more meaning from a pointed quip than from prolonged sermons, and if a coach seeks a sure way to have control of his boys, he'll be quicker, if not sharper-tongued, than they are.

One of the best lines uttered at the right moment by the coach assuaged the grief of his team, smoothed the ruffled feathers of its opponents, and prevented a possible rift in relations.

Wisconsin was playing Minnesota and the score was 12 — 6. In the last minute of play, Wisconsin tried a long pass, which a Minnesota back knocked down. But the field judge ruled that a Minnesota man had interfered illegally with the receiver. Wisconsin was given the decision and the score was tied. There were growls and murmurs. The captains of the two teams, as per custom, claimed the ball. There was an impasse, in which Coach Spears of Minnesota good-humoredly solved

by remarking, "Give the ball to the field judge. He won the game."

Every good coach I know spices his relations with his own personnel, with his opponents, and with officials by the injection of humor. In the thousand and one details of contact with everybody connected with the sport, unless the coach has a saving grace of humor, he is certainly to be counted among the lost.

Every team has its whims and weaknesses. I remember when we had a superstition at Lincoln, Nebraska, that if we walked backward into the stadium we would win. As a matter of fact, we won twice because of this superstition, or so we thought. Until, in a third game with ceremony, we entered the stadium face-last and we were beaten. The superstition was duly squelched.

Humor is sometimes costly. As when the Carlisle Indians went down to play St. Louis, to be welcomed by the St. Louis fans with the spectacle of a funeral hearse containing a cigar-store Indian, followed by a cortège of wailing mourners. A boomerang joke, for it infuriated the Carlisle team, who beat a superior team by 3 — 0.

I've known of rivalries between star players that would inevitably have developed into bad blood, jeopardizing the prospects of the team and breaking the morale of the entire squad and student body by producing factions and cliques — unless the coach employed good humor plus firmness in handling the situation.

There have also been times my fairly well-trained patience became exhausted. Two of the finest players who ever wore the blue and gold of Notre Dame provoked one such situation. They were John Mohardt and Norman Barry.

Mohardt was the most industrious of

... It is not what a coach knows, it is what he can teach his boys, what he can make them do ...

players. He was always the first man out to practice and the last man in. He tried hard to make the team in 1919 but wasn't quite good enough. In the spring of 1920, it was reported to me that Mohardt would spend hours on the practice field alone trying to specialize in blocking.

But Norman Barry, not so hardworking, was brilliant in his own way. Uncertain as to the ability of either boy to sustain his quality through the season, I decided to alternate them as halfbacks. This decision made them rivals.

In a game with Nebraska, Barry played

well but Mohardt lagged. Then in a game with Army, Mohardt shone while Barry looked poor. Things reached an impasse when the two boys were glaring at each other during practice the Monday following the Army game. So, I called them out and ordered them to return their suits.

Realizing that this action — banishment from the squad — was too severe a punishment for two boys whose frustration arose from their eagerness to shine for their school, I relented. On Friday before the Indiana game they were told they could rejoin the squad. Reports had come to me that the two had been close to

A football coach must also understand public opinion regarding the school and its athletic reputation as it exists in the community where the school is located.

starting a fistfight on campus, so it was up to me as coach to prevent further trouble.

Yet there was a problem: how to control them in the game for the benefit of the whole team.

I started Mohardt and Gipp at the halves. It was a game we expected to win easily, but Indiana gave us a surprise. At the end of the third period the score was 10 — 0 against us, and George Gipp, our best offensive and defensive star, was injured. The team didn't seem to be going anywhere. The only time any player was off his feet was when he was knocked down.

What should I do? I took Gipp out of the game.

"Barry," I called, "here's your chance. Go in there and insult them if you have to."

"Yeah," said Barry, tearing off his blanket, "and especially Mohardt."

Barry had no sooner taken position than the quarterback called Mohardt's number for an off-tackle play where Barry was supposed to block the end. Barry blocked him with a vengeance, carrying him almost to the bleachers on his back to let Mohardt through for an 18-yard gain.

On the next play it was Barry's turn to carry the ball. He said to Mohardt in the huddle, "Listen you, take your end out the same way I did mine when I carry the ball or I'll sock you so hard on the jaw you'll have fallen arches."

SECTION 3: ROCKNE ON ROCKNE

Jack Cannon, the All-American guard, presented for a brief time one of those studies in temperament that a coach must gauge carefully before deciding whether or not he'll tease the player with a humorous remark or prod him with some other psychological weapon.

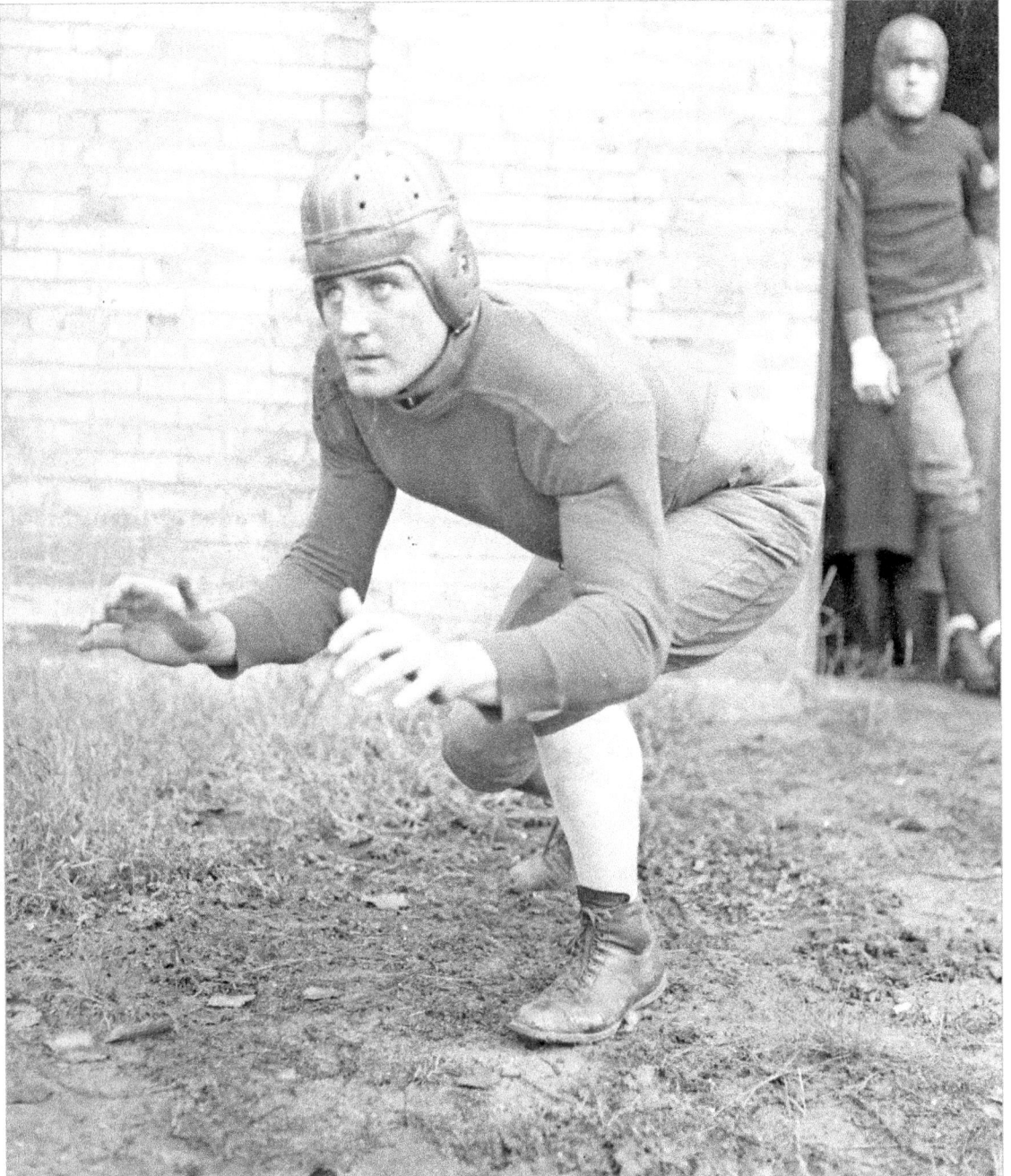

The play came. Barry carried the ball and Mohardt carried the end out to where the head linesman carries the sticks. Barry gained 25 yards. Four more plays between those two and Notre Dame had a touchdown. The game was pulled out of the fire in the last minute by 13 — 10.

I planned to make Norm Barry and John Mohardt shake hands in the dressing room after the game. That turned out to be unnecessary. All the bile in their systems had been worked off clearing paths for each other to carry the ball. They've been the best of friends ever since.

Jack Cannon, the All-American guard, presented for a brief time one of those studies in temperament that a coach must gauge carefully before deciding whether or not he'll tease the player with a humorous remark or prod him with some other psychological weapon.

Everybody who saw the game between Army and Notre Dame will remember the bareheaded guard who happened to be in every spot where he was most needed to stop the Army ends and backs. By actual count, Cannon took out more than 25 rushers that afternoon, skipping like a lamb in pasture on a gridiron that was literally as hard as iron.

Yet, Cannon was not always a whirlwind at play. Even after he had made the team he seemed halted at times by lethargy. At practice before one of our biggest games the entire first string performed beautifully — with the exception of Cannon. This was on the day before the game. I was going to take him out of practice, but that might have been misinterpreted merely as a move to save him for the game.

Some sharper tactic was necessary. In the middle of the third practice period, I called a halt.

"All right, boys," I said. "You might as well go to the showers now before Cannon spoils any more plays."

My comment to Jack Cannon had the effect of hitting him with a brick — a psychological brick. He said nothing. I thought he might call at my home, as the boys sometimes do on the eve of a big game, to seek advice or argue with me. He didn't. This proved I had sized him up correctly. Just before we went onto the field for the game, I walked up to him where he stood, calmly wondering whether or not he'd play.

"You go in with the first string, Cannon," I said.

His eyes lighted. When the first string was summoned for action, Cannon went in — and what a job he did.

SECTION 3: ROCKNE ON ROCKNE

... Pop insisted that the old kicking game was dead.

28

DIFFERENT STROKES

I have sat down with other coaches on many occasions to talk about tactics in football. These discussions have often ranged along the lines of the evolution of generalship as it applied to a quarterback in systems of football.

In a meeting with Glenn "Pop" Warner and several other coaches, Pop insisted that the old kicking game was dead. He said, "I like to have my team receive the ball on the kickoff and carry it all afternoon. It gives them lots of practice in perfecting the execution of their plays. The better the execution becomes, the better the team. Generalship in my opinion merely means the ability of my quarterback to play the opponents' defense, the ability to take advantage of the weak points and avoid the strong spots."

Vanderbilt coach Dan McGugin spoke up and inquired as to what he would do if his team had marched the length of the field several times but had always been stopped in the zone of intense resistance, that is, the zone inside the 10-yard line. Each time, the Vanderbilt coach added, the opponents had punted the ball back deep down the field again.

"We would come back and do it all over again," said Warner. "You can't stop a good team all the time and it is no more tiring to play offense than it is to play defense."

A young coach from Bradley Institute, A.J. "Robbie" Robertson, then inquired whether it was not extremely valuable for a quarterback to know every detail regarding the personnel of the players on both sides.

"It is," said Warner. "Some people seem to think that football scouts are after the plays.

Billy Roper at Princeton... is liable to open up with a daring forward pass attack when it is least expected.

Nothing could be more erroneous. All I want my scouts to bring back regarding the opponents' plays is the formations. I can dope out the plays. I do want to give to our quarterback all the values I can regarding the strength and weaknesses of each individual, and we discuss among ourselves the relative merits of our own men."

Personally, I agree with most of these observations of the "Old Fox," as Pop Warner is sometimes called by his rivals. But the most difficult thing for any quarterback to be able to do is to visualize clearly what he is observing.

Pop said that the biggest part of tactics lies in the ability of the quarterback to play the opponents' defense. The most difficult thing that I have found in coaching quarterbacks has been to develop the ability to find out what the opposing defense really is. Smart teams change their defense from Saturday to Saturday and often during the game. Constant practice in scrimmage against a scrub eleven changing its defense now and then is necessary before a quarterback begins to be at all aware of the details that are in front of him. Just about the time he gets good, he graduates.

Clarence "Doc" Spears ... will put on a grueling through-the-line Army style of game for the greater part of the afternoon ...

The average fan seems to think that if he knows when a quarterback should not forward pass and if he knows when a quarterback should punt, that he knows a lot of football. The average boy on the sand lot knows this and a lot more.

What a boy must know to play quarterback on a college team would fill a book. Field tactics of football, however, are far from being standardized, and they never will be. Coaches differ in their opinions on this broad subject just the same as they do on any other phase of football. There are many little salient features regarding peculiarities in tactics that I have noticed from playing many of the teams across the country.

Howard Jones of Southern California will have his quarterback invariably forward pass on second down. On the critical third down, you can figure that the Army team will use its best back on its best play. Billy Roper at Princeton is a great hand for a kicking game and playing for the breaks, but is liable to open up with a daring forward pass attack when it is least expected.

Clarence "Doc" Spears at Minnesota will put on a grueling through-the-line Army style of game for the greater part of the afternoon, apparently trying to wear his opponents down. At some stage, look out for a fake line plunge followed by a forward pass or a double reverse.

Bill Ingram always uses the reverse on the goal line. Glenn Thistlethwaite of Wisconsin is strong for weak side plays in a pinch while a forward pass to his best receiver is the thing that the defense will have to look out for, whether it is first down 10, or third down 10.

H.O. "Pat" Page, when at Indiana, made much of the onside kick on the kickoff, the shoe-string play and long forward passes from the spread formation. Page believes that the first blow struck is the most important and is always trying to score just as soon as he can, sometimes taking extreme chances to do so.

The genesis of the Notre Dame system can be traced to when Jess Harper and I were on our way back from the Yale debacle ...

29

THE NOTRE DAME SYSTEM

People ask me about the origin of the system of football as we now use it at Notre Dame. Quite a few of the Notre Dame alumni use it in various part of the country. The system has been affected by many influences, particularly as regards blocking, tackling, and the execution of the other fundamentals. But the flavor, the peculiar twist which differentiates it from other systems, originated with Alonzo Stagg, Yale alumnus and veteran coach at the University of Chicago.

In the fall of 1914, having graduated in chemistry, I was made assistant coach to Jess Harper, and our first big-league game was with Yale. Faculty, student body, townspeople, and team were confident that it was just a question of the score. We hadn't been beaten in three years, and everybody, including myself, was suffering from a bad case of what we call "fathead." That is, all except Jess Harper. Jess pleaded and stormed like a lone voice in the wilderness, but all in vain.

"Absurd," everyone said. "This Notre Dame team can't be beaten!"

I saw on the sidelines at New Haven that Saturday afternoon and saw a good Yale team captained by Bud Talbot, with a crack halfback named Harry LeGore leading the attack. They made Notre Dame look like a high school squad. They lateral-passed Notre Dame out of the park and knocked our ears down to the tune of 28-0 — the most valuable lesson Notre Dame ever had in football. It taught us never to be cocksure. Modern football at Notre Dame can be dated from that game, as we made vital use of every lesson we learned.

The genesis of the Notre Dame system can be traced to when Jess Harper and I were on

223

our way back from the Yale debacle. He called me into his office and announced that we had to break into something new, something different in the way of offense, or the year would be a failure. He began drawing on a piece of paper, describing a backfield shift similar to what Chicago had used in the old days when he was quarterback, but Harper's variation was that he made the shift cover twice as much territory.

I added the idea of shifting ends in and out with a stationary line. Mr. Harper wanted the line to shift also, but after a day or two of experimenting, the line from tackle to tackle was left stationary and this simple shift, with some forward passing ideas that were a little different, was the beginning of what is now known as the Notre Dame offense.

The Notre Dame shift has changed since 1914. Many Notre Dame men now coaching the shift have added embellishments of their own. Most of the sound fundamentals, which Harper found at Notre Dame when he was coaching there, were probably inherited from Tom Barry. But systems of football, like nationalities, are all somewhat of a mix, though one of the most interesting things about the game today is the fact that there are many difference conceptions of offense, many of them successful. It is this that adds the variety and spice to this autumn sport.

In the case of the shift attack — I mean by this a team, the defensive team has had a chance to look over for information — the defensive team cannot pick up any tipping signs, nor will

it have to see whether it is a V formation, Z, or square, and if it is cleverly done, the defensive team cannot tell whether the quarterback is going to handle the ball or not.

The set formation coach, however, will argue that the shift is a blind offense because one cannot foresee how the defense is going to shift against it. This may be true to small extent, but with a clever line in front of you carrying information to a clever quarterback, the shift attack can be made into a definite proposition. The offensive end can tip the quarterback where the defensive tackle is shifting; the offensive tackle can explain how the defensive guards are shifting, while the offensive guards can tell whether or not the nose tackle is staying in or pulling out. If the nose tackle pulls out they can tell under what tactical situation he stays in and under what tactical situations he pulls out. The backs can tell the quarterback whether or not the ends are coming in smashing, or playing square.

Assimilating this information, the quarterback can get a picture in his mind pretty definitely as to just where to find the defensive line. By keeping his eye on the secondary and tertiary defense, he gets the entire picture of the outlay of the defensive team. By keeping the tactical situation in mind — the picture of how to expect to find the defensive players playing — he can choose with a certain definite assurance whether to execute a plunge, delayed plunge, reverse, flank play, or forward pass. Since the shift is fast enough, the opponents cannot tell whether the offensive has a square, V, or Z

Section 3: Rockne on Rockne

You may talk about defense until you are blue in the face...
the thrill, the big picture in football, is in offense.

30

SYSTEMS AND TACTICS

M ost high school and college football teams resemble one another rather closely in detail. Where the variety comes is in the methods of attack, the formations, and the plays.

When you talk about the Warner system, the Haughton system, the Stagg system, the Jones system, and the Spears-McGugin-Roper systems, what you mean principally is their offense, their formations, and their key methods of advancing the ball.

There has always been a lot of conversation in football circles regarding systems.

The Warner system involves two wingbacks and consists very largely of a crushing power attack by a big plunging fullback along with single and double reverses. The Warner system calls for a big powerful fullback, a large back-2 for blocking, while one of the wingbacks also must have some size. The other wingback that carries the ball on reverses and double reverses may be small.

The deception in the Warner attack comes from the half-spin. It is a mighty fine attack, particularly when the timing is accurate. It requires big men and lots of practice. It is also effective as a forward-pass formation since four of the eligible receivers — the two backs and the two ends — are in a good position to get out into the open.

The second system in wide use is the kicking and passing game from punt formation. This system has been carried on very effectively by such teams as Michigan, Vanderbilt, Missouri, Princeton, and others.

227

*... There is a fifth system of play, which depends
very largely on spread formations ...*

Their style of game is to keep trying long forward passes and, if they don't succeed, to kick long and accurately down the field. Their idea is to complete long forward passes if they can. If these are unsuccessful, the idea is to put the other team's offense in a hole by means of a well-placed punt. They punt for position and they hope either to recover a fumble of the opponents or to tempt the opponents into some audacious tactics in order to pull out of the hole into which they have been placed. This sort of a game isn't much to look at, but it has been very successful, and teams using this system, although they may be outrushed a great deal, will very often get the breaks and have the score in their favor.

The third is the Howard Jones system,

also very similar to Dr. Spears's system, which consists of a 10-man shift ending up with only one wingback. A wingback is one who lines up just back and outside of the offensive end. Both Howard Jones and Dr. Spears, off this shift, may finish up with about eight variations of the same formation. This makes their attack very effective unless the Rules Committee decides to make the shifting team stop for four or five seconds in order to give the defensive team time to read the details. In stopping a shade over a second, however, to lose momentum, the system has still been very effective.

Both Jones and Spears have developed fine fundamentals of line play, which makes the power plays through the line just as much to be feared as the sweeping end runs, or the well-masked forward passes.

The fourth system of play, which also has been quite successful, is the man-in-motion, used from either close formation or a spread. In the latter case, the flank man is in motion before the ball is snapped. This has been developed very successfully both by Alonzo Stagg at Chicago and by Walter "Wally" Steffen at Carnegie Tech. This system requires expert timing so that the man in motion can turn forward the instant after the ball is snapped. He may block either a tackle or an end, or he may go down the field as a pass receiver.

There is a fifth system of play, which depends very largely on spread formations. A spread formation, however, is not as effective as it used to be, as smart defenses have been built up to meet value with value. However, with a very clever chap back 10 yards who can kick, pass and run, the formation may still be dangerous. It is mainly used, though, in killing time — to execute a punt if your kicker is small, or to impress the downtown coaches who are more or less awed by the apparent complexity when a team is spread from sideline to sideline. A team using a spread, however, is helpless when it comes to the 10-yard line — the zone of intense resistance — and a spread formation therefore is not used except in midfield.

Sometimes it does and sometimes it doesn't ...

31

THE NOTRE DAME SHIFT

The Notre Dame system is in contrast to the Warner system, which depends on power and deception.

Notre Dame shifts just the backfield and the two ends. The team can shift into one of eight variations off the same formation. Blocking is entirely a matter of having the proper angle. The main idea of the shift is to place men in positions where they get the proper blocking angle on the defensive men. The proposition becomes, then, more a matter of finesse than of bruising.

You may say, "Well, what if the defensive team shifts and gets in just the proper place?"

Sometimes it does and sometimes it doesn't. But when the defensive team does shift correctly, then of course the value of the offensive shift is lost to a great extent. However, when you have eight variations off the same formation, the defense cannot and does not shift correctly all the time. And that is where a smart team, all the players carrying information to the quarterback, is able to take advantage of any player on the defense being out of position.

If this isn't smart football, then I'll eat your new fall hat without catsup. And I don't mean maybe.

Personally, I wish there were more systems of football. I wish more men would branch out into individual lines and construct offenses that are entirely different from those in vogue today. It would add a lot of color and renewed interest. If every team in America were to use the

Warner system, football would become a very monotonous game.

We would probably have the same results if every team in America used the Notre Dame system, or the kicking game. However, with six variations of offensive play now more or less in college football, there is plenty of diversity to keep both spectator and player interested. Then we have such men as Zuppke, Page, Alexander and Morrison, to name just a few, who are always springing new variations and new angles that are not only effective but highly colorful.

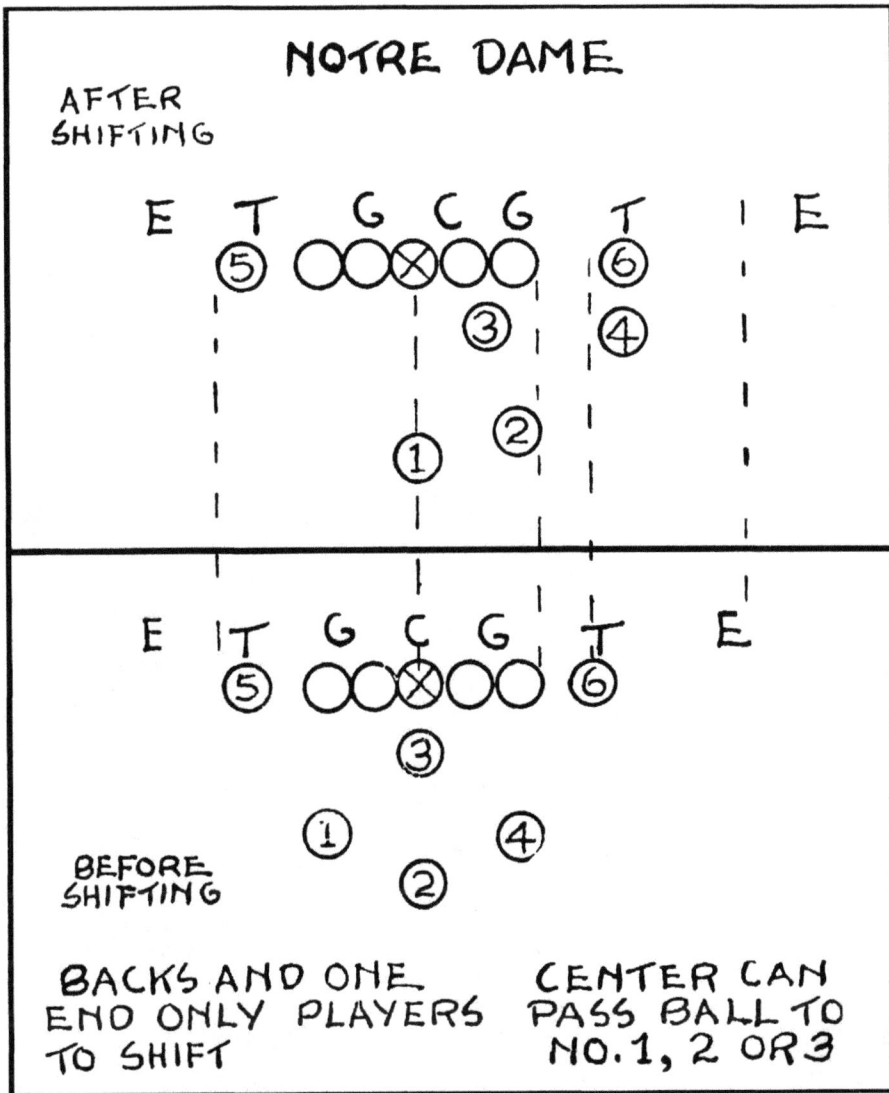

NOTRE DAME

AFTER SHIFTING

E   T   G   C   G   T   E
⑤ ○○⊗○○ ⑥
          ③ ④
          ②
       ①

BEFORE SHIFTING

E   T   G   C   G   T   E
⑤ ○○⊗○○ ⑥
       ③
    ①   ④
       ②

BACKS AND ONE END ONLY PLAYERS TO SHIFT

CENTER CAN PASS BALL TO NO. 1, 2 OR 3

THE SHIFT. Every one knows that Notre Dame uses the shift. The team lines up as in the upper panel of the diagram, the signal being given by No. 3, quarterback. Note that the line and backfield are perfectly balanced. No tip is given as to which direction the shift will go. On e a second signal the backs will shift either to the right or left. I have sketched the position of the team when it shifts to the right in the lower panel of the diagram. After the necessary lapse of time required by the rules the plan then starts from this formation. The Notre Dame ends also shift. That is, the move in toward their tackles or out toward the side-lines, depending on the play

---

Author's note: In the above text excerpt, taken from a book, the author mixes up the panels in the description of this diagram. As the diagram states, the before-shift line-up is in the bottom panel and the after-shift play, where the players are signaled to go right, is shown in the above panel.

233

A good passer must be able ... to find the eligible receiver just the right amount of distance so that the receiver can barely reach the ball.

32

THE OFFENSE

"I always pay a little more attention to offense than defense, as it is more difficult to get results. Offense involves more finesse in timing, judgement, and more complex team play."

Knute Rockne

There is always a doubt in the minds of coaches as to which is the more important, offense or defense. Both are important, but I do believe it wise for a team to pay more attention to offense.

In case you have an early game with a rugged opponent, your defense may stop them dead. However, along in the second half with the score nothing to nothing, there may be a fumble and one of the opponents may run a long distance for a touchdown and kick goal. The score would then stand seven to nothing against you, and the thing you would have to call upon under these conditions would be the offense. If you have only defense, you would be helpless.

The essentials of offense are blocking and interfering. Just because you work some trick stuff against an easy team it does not follow that it will work against a good team. Of course, you ought to have a few trick plays to be used at the right time, but the backbone of your

Keep eyes open, tail down, and hands out in front, and be on toes.

plays should be interference, or collective blocking.

This is the essence of offense in football, and no man no matter how good a ball carrier he is should be allowed to play on the team unless he also knows how to interfere and block. I would far rather have a good interferer than a good ball carrier, insofar as the team is concerned. Interfering and blocking is done in many different ways, depending upon where it is executed, the kind of play used, and the type of opponent.

There are, however, six different ways

which I shall enumerate. The purpose of blocking and interfering is to keep the opponent away from the man carrying the ball without the use of arms or hands.

The development of the quarterback depends very largely on hard work and practice, but forward passers are born. The boy without any sense of rhythm, coordination, or measuring value in the eye, leg or arm can never make a forward passer, or a kicker for that matter. There must be some natural ability to begin with. However, the boy with natural ability must practice diligently and work hard in order to develop to a fine point these two specialties.

UNDERSTANDING OFFENSE

To have complete versatility of attack in football means that a team must be grounded in all branches of offense. It must be able to take advantage of any weakness shown by the defense anywhere, and it must be able to gain ground against any type defense, under any conditions. Ten or 12 plays well learned will give a team a much better offense than 40 or 50 plays half-learned. I don't believe any team can use more than 30 plays and have perfection in execution.

There are a lot of formations used in football, but I don't believe I would use a formation unless I could use all four methods of offense from it. These four methods of offense are: Thrust, Flank, Kick and Forward Pass.

Your plays in a regular attack must have the following qualities: (A) All play, including fakes, must be strong plays in themselves — deception alone is not enough. (B) On forward pass plays, the ball must never be thrown at a dangerous angle. (C) The play must fit in with a sequence of plays from the formation.

The success of a good play as far as the offense is concerned will depend on: (A) Superiority of line charge and interference; (B) Fast starting and getting to the point of attack fast; (C) Proper timing; (D) Every assignment fulfilled by all the 11 men.

Some coaches prefer the Balanced Line and other coaches prefer the Unbalanced Line — as follows:

The balanced line gives the offensive team a powerful attack behind the four linemen on one side of the center. The center is not a good point to hit, of course, because the snapper-back is too engrossed in passing the ball accurately to be able to charge effectively. The unbalanced line, however, is not quite so strong outside of tackle, nor is it so strong back on the weak side. The balanced line has not as much strength driving from the strong side. This is compensated for, however, because it has more strength outside of tackle and back on the weak side. I would say, generally speaking, to use the unbalanced line if you have driving backs, and the balanced line if you have fast shifty backs.

Coaches are also differing in their opinions as to the respective merits of opening a hole by means of the shoulder-to-shoulder charge or by the quick opening method. Each method has its advantages. Against a line playing high and waiting, the wedge method is best. When playing against a defensive line which is down low and against the ground, the quick-opening method is the best.

A good college team should therefore have both methods of opening holes. It is probably asking too much to have a high school team use both, and I would determine whether I would use one or the other by the kind of material I had. If I had a big powerful line, I would use the quick opening.

The key man to take care of, of course, under either method, is the defensive player backing up the line. If the man back of the line is not taken care of, no line plays can gain. In the case of the wedge, he is taken care of because the wedge is supposed to go on through intact, so this man and the defense will have difficulty breaking through it.

In the case of the quick opening plays, one back will have to go through the hole in the front of the man carrying the ball in order to take care of the defensive player. He

can also be taken care of in a large measure by deception in the backfield.

Square Formation is better around flanks. It also gives you the possibilities where the quarterback may come in at times and handle the ball.

Z-formation gives you a better punch-back into the middle of the line and back to the weak side.

V-formation is good to kick from and run the ends, but not so strong into the line.

Some coaches use all direct passes and other coaches use no plays in which the quarterback does not handle the ball. Both methods have their advantages. Forward pass plays and plays off tackle are better when the direct pass is used. When the quarterback handles the ball, however, we have certain

In a game of football, the chief thought of both teams is to get the ballcarrier across the goal line, as this means six points for the scoring team.

hidden plays, split bucks, delayed bucks, etc., which cannot be used otherwise. The most versatile offense, therefore, is one which combines the strong points of both the direct and indirect passes. I would not use too many formations on offense, but instead would use just a few good formations and exhaust all the possibilities.

I shall now try to diagram plays to hit these seven holes. And in order to make the plays successful, these plays will all start very much alike and are therefore what we might call a sequence. This sequence also means that they depend one upon the other and that their successful use lies in their being used in an intelligent and logical sequence. In other words, the use of one play may not gain much ground but has the effect of making another play, which looks much like it, very strong.

In modern game of football, every one of the 11 men on offense must take part in the play. Every man must fulfill his own important assignment to the best of his ability. It must be borne in mind that a good interferer never looks back.

Always cover on all forward pass plays, particularly if they are thrown out at an angle to the side in any way. Have forward pass plays from every formation you are using. Punt formation is still the best all-around formation. The passer is the most important man in a forward pass combination, and the hardest man to find.

A good passer is rare. There are many men who can throw a ball far, but very few throw forward passes in the strict sense of the term. A good passer must have fine mental poise and complete control of himself physically, and he must not be disturbed by anything that might happen. A forward pass attack, in case you have a rattle-brain passer, might boomerang against you at any time. In the hands of a good forward passer, a forward pass attack is a very powerful weapon at any time. A good passer must be able instinctively to find the eligible receiver just the right amount of distance, so that the receiver can barely reach the ball.

THE QUARTERBACK

Victory goes not only to the strong and brave, but to the smart team made up of men who think, who are alert mentally, men who never pass up an opportunity.

The game is played with the arms, legs and shoulders, but principally above the neck. If he has a good voice with a bite and snap that lifts his backfield, and if he has a good mind and the ability to stay cool under fire —

"sangfroid," the French call it — then there can be no question that this is the logical man to lead the team.

The quarterback should not get panicky or excited in a pinch. These types of boys may play football at some other position, but not at quarterback.

The quarterback should, of course, make a study of football from every angle so that he will not make what are known as tactical errors. He should be a keen observer because his principal job will be to play the defense. A quarterback must have keen intellect, resourcefulness, initiative, ability to analyze and size up the situation regardless of the excitement of the moment, resiliency of mind so that he can adapt himself to all conditions, a razor sharp memory, and daring imagination. Then you have the making of a quarterback.

The quarterback must keep in mind the tactical situation and play the defense. He must study his plays, his teammates, and his opponents to have the right sense of tactics. A good quarterback will lead his team to victory over physically superior teams which, however, lack a tactical mind.

A knowledge of the personnel of his own team and the strength of his own plays will come after a few scrimmages. A sensitivity toward strength and weakness in the defense will come from the experience of playing a season. It is not fair to expect a young man to develop any faster in this exacting position. The coach must be careful not to call down the quarterback in front of the team. Whatever mistakes are made should be corrected in private because the quarterback must develop respect for himself, confidence in himself, and must earn the respect of his teammates.

A quarterback of mine very seldom calls upon himself to carry the ball. In order to

"A lad who is the natural leader, full of personality and confidence to a point that he might be said to be chesty, is the one that can make a good quarterback."

Knute Rockne

have a clear mind functioning to its fullest efficiency, it is necessary that the quarterback save himself from all unnecessary shocks, bumps and collisions.

When receiving punts, if he sees that the offensive ends are right down on him, he must signal for a fair catch. On returning a punt, if he gets near the side lines, he must get out of bounds in order to avoid punishment. Some spectators erroneously call this cowardice. A team, as a rule, has but one quarterback, and he owes it to his school, to his coach and to his teammates to avoid injury as much as possible. His job is to run the team on offense absolutely, and he cannot do this if he has to undergo the hard, physical plays which the men in the other positions have to undergo.

A couple of days later this quarterback, because he is a leader, may want to know why in the coming scrimmage he cannot forward pass more or take more chances. Every live, red-blooded boy likes to play the game for all it is worth. You can then show him this point. Tell him that if he has everything to gain and nothing to lose then he can afford to gamble.

In other words, if he is way behind in the second half, or if he is one touchdown behind and the time is short, he might as well start using the forward pass and trick plays. If they work, well and good, they may save the game. And if they don't work, there is nothing lost.

It is the same as if the quarterback himself had one dollar and he met a chap with a thousand dollars. Certainly the quarterback would be wise if he had suggested a gambling game, for he has everything to gain and nothing to lose. But if he has everything to lose and nothing to gain, then he is foolish to gamble. He must play it safe. He must not forward pass as every time the ball is thrown into the air it gives the defensive men a chance to intercept it.

Or going back to the other far-fetched comparison, if the quarterback has a thousand dollars in his pocket and he meets another chap who has only a dollar, he would be exceedingly foolish to gamble. I think it will come to the quarterback now why we have gone to such pains to show him when not to forward pass. After his second scrimmage, you might sit down with your quarterback and show him what, against a normal defense, are his strongest plays. And you might also suggest to him that he should save the fullback for his necessary short gains when a yard or two must be gotten.

A smart quarterback on any football team, high school or college, in his choice of plays is always governed by his position on the field, time left to play, score, down and yards to gain, personnel of both teams, defensive formation opponents are using, what has been working, and what has not been working. He must keep in mind his position like a pocket billiard player and try to think what the defense is expecting and get the play off in less

241

than 30 seconds. He will make mistakes when just starting to gain experience.

Regardless of the fine work he may have done earlier in the year, sometime he may use what the experts call "poor judgment." As far as the coaches are concerned, if he calls a play and had a good reason for calling it, he is right and the coach will stand by him.

It has been my experience, however, that no college quarterback has ever been able to compete with the Sunday morning quarterback. This latter species is always correct. He insists on the right of playing Saturday's game on Sunday, whereas the poor little quarterback has to play it on Saturday. However, I wouldn't be without the Sunday morning tacticians for the world, as they are always interesting, they add color, and they are the barometer of interest.

The quarterback's job of handling an offense consisting of about 30 plays is a big one. The coach helps the quarterback understand how to handle the plays judiciously, and he helps the quarterback develop his sense of values so he can use that rare quality known as judgment.

There are some intangible parts of the quarterback position that a candidate must practice. He must be a leader and he must be the only man to call plays. There can be only one quarterback on the team. He must believe in himself, and the team must believe in him.

A quarterback has many responsibilities. If the team is to be successful, he must know what to do in any given circumstance. He must always be thinking three plays ahead of the defense to keep them on the jump.

When will he not forward pass? He will not forward pass in his own part of the field, except possibly a real long pass when he is behind. He will not forward pass when his team is on the opponent's goal line. He will not forward pass when his team is ahead. He will not forward pass against a strong wind. He will not forward pass unless he has a good center. He will not forward pass when the defensive team is evidently laying for such a play.

And when in doubt, he will punt.

If a quarterback will learn these fundamentals, and if in the game he will remember what plays have been working and what plays have not been working, and if, as a result of these observations he will keep using only the plays which have been working and are working, he will make a mighty fine quarterback.

To be successful, he must know the right strategy and tactics to use. He must know when to play it safe, when to take a chance, when to play fast, and when to play it slow. He must know which to do, and he must do it with confidence.

Play Calling

The quarterback must watch his opponents carefully and size up their weak spots. The coach can help the quarterback here immeasurably if he will sit down sometime after the quarterback has learned his plays fairly well and classify these plays according to the following table or something similar to it:

1) The strongest plays: Plays to be used on first down and that are likely to gain four or more yards and safeguard possession of the ball. These are generally plays aimed on the outside of tackle, though against a team using a roving nose tackle or a six-man line, it might be a cutback over center.

2) Short, sure gainers which are also good for from one to three yards and which

... He must be a leader and he must be the only man to call plays. There can only be one quarterback on the team...

safeguard possession of the ball: These are plays to be used when you have only a small number of yards to go for first down. They are also necessary to keep the defensive line in tight so that the strong plays will continue to work.

3) Check plays: These are plays which are not good until the defense changes its position to stop your strong plays. For instance, a wide end run around the defensive end is not a good play by itself. However, when the defensive end comes smashing in tight to stop your strong plays then a run around him becomes a good play for two reasons: First, it will gain ground, and second, it will tend to

drive the end out where the strong plays will again become more effective. A split buck is another type of check play.

4) Gamble plays: These are generally long forward passes and short forward passes where you gamble for great yardage but jeopardize possession of the ball.

5) Position plays: This may include the punt or a wide end run which will be used to get position for another play, or to get position to punt or place kick.

6) Sideline plays: The team should have one or two plays designed to gain ground if possible, but mainly designed to get out of

And when in doubt he will punt ...

bounds when near the sidelines. A cutback play might belong here. Sometimes a cutback may be used when close to the sidelines.

7) Goal line plays: Every team should have three or four plays which should be used only on the goal line in what is known as the zone of "intense resistance." These are generally plays which start the same as other plays but end up differently.

8) Psychological plays: These are generally long gainers to be used at the psychological moment, such as a long forward pass as the first play of the game, or a trick forward pass as the first play in the second half. Or supposing the opponents have just fumbled and their minds are mostly on their bad luck, a long forward pass here might be the psychological thing to do, or a long forward pass against a defensive team which has gone up in the air and has not had sense enough to take time-out.

9) Trick plays: Every coach should have a couple of trick plays. It is well to let the opponents know that you have a couple of trick plays as it will keep them in a state of mental unrest which renders them less effective against your regular attack. Trick plays are also very useful when a team is in a hole at the end of a game and everything else has failed.

10) Time-killing plays: These are to be used when you are ahead near the end of a game and you want to kill time. Here is where spread plays come in mighty handy.

11) Sacrifice plays: These are plays which are used to make other plays good. An example

of this is the common, ordinary reverse play which, while it may not gain much ground, may help to make the other plays good. Then there is the smash over guard. This smash may not be so very effective, but its continued use may draw the tackle and end in where a sudden use of a wide end run might now become very effective. This continued smashing might have the effect also of drawing the linebacker up, making him vulnerable at the right time to a fake guard smash followed by a forward pass over the fullback's head.

12) Long gainers: These are your forward passes which go a long distance and which can be used sometimes in lieu of a punt, or can be used in midfield to score near the end of a half or in other similar situations. They'll bring many a touchdown.

13) Change-of-pace plays: These are plays involving change of rhythm, change of timing, or plays without a signal, as in a series play. This type of play is particularly effective near the goal line and may catch the defense napping or they may find the defense offside.

Choice of plays can sometimes be based on the obvious. It can be beneficial to quickly call the same play twice if a defensive lineman is dizzy and he needs time to recover. Throwing a pass into the zone of a limping linebacker or running a play directly at a substitute lineman could be a good strategy. On the other hand, it is a mistake throwing too many forward passes in the first half, as this will give the defensive coach between halves a chance to make corrections in the defense.

Most plays in the repertoire will, of course, be found under three or four of these classifications, but I do believe that this kind of a classification will immeasurably increase the quarterback's sense of values.

The main thing, however, is to develop a desire on the part of the quarterback to think, to learn how to think, and to develop confidence in his ability to think. If the coach can do this, experience will do the rest. All the coach needs to do is to correct the mistakes quietly and privately as they are made, and the quarterback cannot fail to profit from them.

In the huddle the quarterback calls the play. No one is to leave the huddle until every man is sure of his assignment. Everyone must be careful not to be nervous or overanxious. Remember to charge with the ball, not ahead of it or behind it. When the man carrying the ball is knocked over, it isn't the fault of the play. It's because somebody failed to do his job.

SIGNALS

Systems of signals used by different teams have varied quite a little. Before the days of the forward pass most teams used a system of numbering the offensive backs and of numbering the offensive linemen. The line always charged shoulder to shoulder with slight variations.

If a certain halfback's number was called followed by the number of the linemen, the latter number merely meant that this lineman was apex of the wedge. The numbers were, of course, covered up in such a way that the defense could not tell when the two digits denoting who was to carry the ball, and where, were given.

Another method would be to number the offensive backs and the defensive holes. However, in my opinion, modern football has outgrown both of these two methods. In the two methods I have just mentioned, and which, I think, are obsolete, you will have to adopt key numbers and complications in the key of numbers if you intend to include in your repertoire different kinds of forward passes, trick plays, double passes, triple passes, delayed plays, in and out plays, or any plays of an unusual nature.

The system of numbering each play is now more generally used as being the most simple. We can say, for instance that number twenty-one is an end run by the halfback to the left, number twenty-two an end run by the halfback to the right. You can give each man a definite assignment in this play so that when this number is called by the quarterback there is no confusion in the minds of any player as to just what he is to do.

The question of a snap signal is quite important to a team using the set offense. The old-fashioned method of having every man on the offense watch the ball is not effective, as the offensive team charges after the ball has been passed and they do not get as good a look at their opponents as they might. The advantage of the snap signal is that it gives the offensive linemen a chance to watch their opponents, and also it gives them a chance to anticipate the passing of the ball so they can charge with the ball and not after it has been passed.

The best method of putting in a charging signal is to put in a key number. The number following the key number in the first series will denote at what number in the second series the ball is to be passed.

In case our quarterback was at all suspicious that some on the defensive team were hep to the signals, our offensive quarterback could call his team in a circle and could change his system of bringing out his play number by a very simple means.

For instance, we call the halfback off-tackle to the right, and we call "32, 42, 56, 45." The first digit, "3," meant that the shift was to the left, and the second digit of the first

number and the second digit of the second number gave the play number, "21." The quarterback will now come back and tell the members of the team that from now on the first number is blank.

The thing which the quarterback must avoid is allowing himself to get into a rut by calling continually the same numbers in trying to bring out certain numbers in the digit system. He must watch himself constantly so as to guard against this tendency.

He must also guard against the tendency towards putting any unusual accent on the important numbers and then slurring over the unimportant numbers. He must not look in the direction in which the play is called, except once in a while, but usually he will look in some other direction. The numbers must be called out clearly and distinctly so there is no chance for ambiguity in the minds of any of the offensive players. He must particularly avoid trying to call fifty-something, or sixty-something, as it is rather hard to distinguish between the two sounds.

IN THE HUDDLE

The huddle system of calling signals has been rising in popularity. As far as I know, Robert Zuppke of Illinois was the first man to use it in public. Since then, many others have adopted it.

There is no doubt that it has assumed strategic importance in football. But before any coach decides to use it, I believe it would be worth his while to consider both pros and cons. The inability of a team to hear the signals from the quarterback in a large stadium with a large zealous crowd was probably the primary reason for the beginning of the huddle system. With the

The system of numbering each play... You can give each man a definite assignment... when this number is called by the quarterback there is no confusion in the minds of any player as to just what he is to do.

team huddling around the quarterback, there is no doubt that every player hears the signal designating the play in general and his specific assignment. This would, therefore, tend to do away with any conflicting offensive signals and absolutely eliminate any fear that an unscrupulous scout might have given the signals to the other team. These points are important and no one can deny them.

Zuppke and the other coaches using the huddle have also utilized its strategic value. It is quite possible for a team coming out of the huddle to line up in one of several formations, and the ball can then be snapped before the

defense has had time to analyze the formation to meet value with value.

It is particularly useful in surprise formations in the second half — and by surprise formations I mean those formations which the other team's scouts have never seen. It gives the offensive team a chance to mix up backfield men and linemen indiscriminately without the defensive team being able to detect the fact. It is possible, for instance, to put the best offensive linemen together or to put some clever back in almost any position, and the play is off before the defense is able to determine it.

One team coming out of a huddle swung

*My big exception to the huddle system is based on
the fact that it lacks continuity of punch.*

into the various formations. It would seem that a defensive team would certainly be hard-pressed to analyze and meet such contrasting formations sprung suddenly and quickly from a huddle. However, the coach using these formations evidently did not figure on the limitations of the boys. He forgot that he was dealing with boys from 18 to 20 years of age with no background of experience and with 101 other data about football to master.

In other words, the offensive failed to function on account of the human equation. A boy in college can learn just so much and no more. The team using these five formations did not gain, not because the defense was particularly keen, but because the boys on the offensive stopped themselves. They had too much to learn and, therefore, they were in doubt about most details. They had no background of experience as to how to meet the various defenses presented against these formations, their timing was inaccurate, and every play lacked the plan of execution necessary for success.

I do believe that somewhat along this line lies the future development of the huddle system, but I also believe that any team, regardless of its brilliancy, cannot master thoroughly more than three formations. A defense can successfully meet three formations, whereas meeting five or six would be well nearly impossible. So the possibilities of the huddle system are tremendous in theory. It remains to be seen what possibilities are practical.

The objections to the huddle system are many. Some critics claim that it slows down the game. This is not true, as a stopwatch would reveal that a team using it properly would run off just as many plays from the huddle as from the other system. Most spectators, however, object to it on the grounds that it looks like a lot of old women gathered around at a sewing circle.

Some coaches say, "to hang with the public." This is not a bright remark, as every coach must realize that it is the public who is paying his salary. If it were not for public interest, football coaches would not be getting their present salaries.

Some teams use the huddle system to stall, but this is not possible with a good referee. The referee has the right to stand in the middle of the huddle to make sure that there is no stalling. One big danger of the huddle system is that a team may suddenly develop 11 quarterbacks. There is a strong temptation for every one of the boys coming back into the huddle to offer advice to the signal caller, which of course would be fatal for the success of an offense. However, a good strong captain backing up a signal caller can very easily eliminate this.

My big exception to the huddle system is based on the fact that it lacks continuity of punch. I like to pick a quarterback with a wonderful voice, magnetic personality and unquestioned qualities of leadership. This sort of man looking over a defensive team, looking them right then in the eye, overwhelms the defense with his voice, personality and drive. He stimulates the offensive team to an intensity of enthusiasm that gives the offensive team, when they smell a touchdown, an irresistible drive that will sweep across the goal line. These assets in a team are invaluable. They are lost in the huddle system. The strategic advantages of the huddle system may all be derived from a shift attack.

Personally, I would advise every young coach to look over the huddle system carefully before deciding to use it. I will say that should I be caught somewhere without an ideal quarterback, I shall then use the huddle system.

No matter what system of signals you use, keep them simple so that the association is clear, and so that the play numbers stand out very clearly in the minds of everyone. Do not be so simple that the defensive team can analyze them.

Some coaches prefer the huddle system as there is no doubt at all but that every member on the offense has the signal, and there is no danger that the defense has it at all. However, I like the moral effect of a live, snappy quarterback who barks out his numbers at the defensive team, and I have always found that a team with this kind of quarterback will have fifty-percent more punch than it would the other way.

There is too much danger in the huddle system of having more than one quarterback. The quarterback, if he has a fine personality and clear, powerful voice, should be allowed to use this great asset. Personally, I believe the disadvantages of the huddle system outweigh the advantages.

Teaching the quarterback position is perhaps the most difficult. I have found that the less you try to teach the quarterback directly, the

The quarterback should, of course, make a study of football from every angle so that he will not make what are known as tactical errors.

better. The position of quarterback is not like trying to learn something by memory or rote from a book. He learns mainly by experience. The coach should always keep before him certain fundamental principles to help him in his analyses and in making his decisions.

In fact, the longer I coach, the less artificial means I use in teaching football.

QUARTERBACKING BASICS

1) Bark out your signals distinctly and loud.

2) Observe all the time and let nothing escape your attention.

3) Be daring in your imagination.

4) Have confidence, believe in yourself.

5) Be boss of the team.

6) Call plays from the way the defense is positioned, as well as from the tactical situation.

7) In offensive territory, use your best play on first down, that is, your biggest ground gainer.

8) Use one play to make another play strong. Various strengths of plays will depend

on using them in the best sequence.

9) Study your backs and know their strength and weakness on all plays.

10) Always be sure every player on your team is ready before you call a play.

11) Remember who your strong offensive linemen are.

12) Look and see who breaks up a play and who makes the tackle; it may suggest plays to fool them.

13) When you discover a weak spot in the opposing line, don't forget it. Use it just enough to keep going, but nurse it for a time when it will count the most.

14) Disregard a tactical situation whenever the defense presents a glaring weakness. An unorthodox defense is an opportunity, don't pass it up.

15) Give the defense what they are apparently not looking for.

16) Cover the long man with forward passes.

17) Always stay low on hidden ball plays.

18) Watch for the psychological moment to pull your trick play.

19) Try a trick play or a "long gainer" after recovering a fumble, as the defense team will then be in the air.

20) When a new substitute comes in, shoot the first play at him.

21) Throw a pass at a limping back. Shoot a play at a dizzy lineman.

22) When the defensive line tightens up, use end runs. When the defensive line is spread, use line plunges.

23) Never call-down backs, always encourage them.

24) Save your best forward pass plays for the second half.

25) When ahead play safe — when behind take a chance.

26) Against a very strong defensive team, kick often and play for a break.

27) On a wet, muddy field let opponents carry the ball and do the fumbling; kick, kick, kick.

28) If worried, hide it.

29) Use punt formation deep in your own territory. Save your close attack until you get past the middle of the field.

30) Stall against the wind and run plays quickly with the wind.

31) Stall when you are ahead. Run plays quickly when you are behind.

32) If you have a weak kicker, try a long forward pass in your own territory.

33) Against a team with a powerful offense, hold the ball as long as you can.

34) Always have lots of ginger, pep, and enthusiasm, and don't bawl anybody out. Instead, encourage everybody.

35. Learn to relax, stay cool, and retain your mental poise regardless of the excitement.

With these axioms serving as a foundation, the quarterback begins and has his experiences. Since every cell in his being has memory, he will remember when he has done things correctly, and he should remember when he has made mistakes. It is well that he should make his mistakes as early as possible.

BACKS AND LINE

A man is born either to play the line or the backfield. Physical makeup, the trend of football thinking, the ability to absorb grueling punishment, the quickness of reflexes, the ability to throw and catch a ball, whether one's talent is in his legs or in his in arms, all have a part in determining a boy's playing position.

Nature didn't gift every lad to be a back fielder. Football would certainly be a sorry

The center should have a sense of touch in the hands for passing correctly.

game if that were the case. As it is, it is often a difficult task to convince some marvelous prospect for the line that he was never intended by nature to throw forward passes or wriggle his way through a broken field.

The question as to whether football stars are born or made has been argued by hundreds of well-versed sports authorities, and almost as many arguments have been presented on both sides of the debate as there are so-called experts to argue. It all seems to come down to the question of whether any artist — for football is an art — is born or made.

I have seen backfield men of small stature, of the type generally described as easily injured, who, through their brains and their ability to get the most out of their arms and legs, make mighty good ground-gaining material. I have also seen boys who lacked everything but ruggedness and determination develop in that supreme asset essential to a blocking back.

On the other hand, I have seen big bruisers, whom you couldn't injure with an ax, sit on the bench throughout the entire season simply because they lacked football knowledge.

THE SKELETON

I believe that the most desirable thing to do in choosing a first team is to build on the skeleton framework. This skeleton framework or backbone is made up of the quarterback, center, and two tackles.

A man playing center must be rugged. The prime responsibility for this position is the ability to pass the ball accurately. The center should have a sense of touch in the hands for passing correctly. He must never lose the feel of the ball. Pass it. Catch it. Kick

it. Even carry it around if necessary. He must never lose the feel of the ball.

In some instances, it's simply by chance that I find the right position for a lad. We had a boy come to our school who was a fullback in high school. During spring practice this man accidentally got over the ball and was passing it back to the kickers. I happened to observe him. I could see at a glance that he had the touch, so I immediately suggested to him that I was going to play him at center. He went in there, but did very poorly as evidently his heart was not in it. He was just an average fullback, but I could see the makings of a greater center.

I went to the local sporting editor and convinced him to help me with my idea and he put it over for me. The next day the local sport-sheet came out with a long story to the effect that X had been promoted — had been moved from fullback to the most important position on the team, the position of center. This writer then went on to describe how the center was the man who started every play, and if the ball was passed well, the play was already one-third successful.

The next afternoon, this lad X was the first man out for practice and he was over the ball working at perfecting himself in this difficult art. Suffice it is to say he played center and he did a good job of it. He could have ended up no better than a mediocre fullback. He was invaluable to his team.

The boys trying out for center position should try passing the ball on all kinds of plays. For instance, supposing there are four centers, whoever is coaching the team will first tell these centers how to stand and how to pass. He will then demonstrate these techniques, completing the picture for the boys. The boys line up to practice the stance and pass the ball. The coach then criticizes the boys constructively.

There is one thing that the center must develop: consistency. There must be no changing of pace. The ball cannot be passed too high, or too low; not too fast, or too slow. It should come back at exactly the same height, same speed — faultlessly every time.

The coach leaves the group of centers and moves on to the guards or tackles, placing his oldest and most mature center in charge of the practicing centers. These boys then practice for proficiency, remembering the things which have been told them by the chap who is coaching them.

I would now look for the two huskiest, most rugged, most aggressive lads to play the very important position of tackle. The biggest boys generally play this position, provided they have powerful forearms, are aggressive fighters, and have just a little shiftiness in their feet. Speed is not so essential for this position. The two tackles, of course, are the team shock absorbers.

The defensive play of a tackle is often undervalued. On defense, he crashes back into the backfield, piling up all the interferers, "stripping" the ballcarrier, so that the latter comes out alone where he is easily tackled by the end or the man backing up the line.

The defensive backs are often credited for clever defensive play when the other team uses a forward pass. In reality, it is the tackle "rushing through," chopping the arms of the passer, that makes for about 75 percent of the defense against the pass. He is always guarding his own territory and yet making his presence felt all over the field. No team can get along without tackles of unusual merit.

The tackles should practice defensive stunts against themselves, and they can also practice learning how to charge against themselves. However, it might be wise to first teach blocking against the dummy. The simplest block is the "hip and armpit" block. It is done by getting contact with the part of the body between the hip and armpit, while straddled on all fours. This block is particularly effective against a player who is stationary or only slightly moving.

HALFBACKS AND FULLBACK

With the skeleton of a team now chosen, we have the easy task of picking the man who is generally put in the position of left halfback. The task of picking a man for this position is comparatively easy, because he can kick and throw well, besides having that fine sense of balance and elusiveness needed for the open field ballcarrier. He will stand out like a beacon light.

We now have three linemen and two backfield men. I will next go about picking a right halfback, whom we will also call the blocking back. He is the man who works on the tackle or the end and, by blocking effectively, makes it possible for our triple-threat man to do his stuff.

As a rule, the right halfback should be a more rugged type of back because of his arduous duties. He should, however, be fast enough to get into the open to receive a pass, and he should be quick enough to make the reverse play effective. But, just the same, his main qualification should be the ability to block.

Of course, it is unfair that fans seldom give due credit to the blocking right halfback. We all love to cheer for the loose-hipped, high-knee-actioned, triple-threat man who weaves and wiggles out of the grasp of the would-be tacklers and thrills us by long runs down the field. Any time a great triple-threat

Joe Savoldi, who was so popular on the Notre Dame team that the Chicago newspapers refer to him as "the people's choice," was also put to a test.

man startles the world by his performances, you can put it down in your book that there is a blocking right halfback unnoticed, and perhaps unappreciated, but he's playing his position like a dedicated solider.

We remember Harold "Red" Grange, Morley Drury, George "Stroop" Strupper, Christian "Red" Cagle, Edward "Eddie" Mahan, Christie Flanagan, Aubrey Devine, Jim Thorpe, Elmer Oliphant, and other triple-threat men who have made history. Hundreds of columns have been written about the scintillating performances of these stars. But who remembers Earl Britton, John McEwan, Glenn Devine, Harry Thomas, Lester Hearden, Joe Guyon, Ed Harlan, Frederick

Paul Castner ... one day I tried him at passing and punting and discovered that he was a real find.

Bradlee, or Norm Barry? Joe Guyon, probably of all on this list, is remembered because he could also do other things.

The others of this last list are the men who "made" the first list, but they also rarely receive proper recognition. They usually work in obscurity. The coach and their teammates appreciate what they contribute to the success of the team more than the public will ever know.

Joe Savoldi, who was so popular on the Notre Dame team that the Chicago newspapers refer to him as "the people's choice," was also put to a test. A sturdy, muscular chap, I confess to having had doubts as to his gameness. I confided this to Tim Moynihan, our center, and told him to test Savoldi in a scrimmage against the scrubs.

Moynihan relished the assignment. At the first opportunity, he walloped Savoldi — undercover, of course. On the next play, Savoldi tried to rip through Moynihan again and took another hit for his pains. A third play and Moynihan once more cracked him. This time Savoldi knew it was no accident.

Turning to his quarterback, Savoldi said, "Just keep calling for me to carry the ball through Moynihan — he can't stop me."

And the way that terrible Tuscan tore through Moynihan for gains of five to ten yards was an eye-opener for everyone.

A fullback should be a pretty good-sized lad, one with speed. The main thing to keep in mind — in plunging from the fullback position — is to hold the ball, keep the eyes open, and lift the knees high to drive hard. The fullback is the plunger. He is generally the type of man who does not reel off particularly large gains but who is generally good for the short, necessary gains. Some teams employ slow, ponderous fellows because they hit the line hard. However, I believe the smaller type of fullback with speed, who will depend more on picking the hole, the one with dash and nerve in getting through the line, is the better.

I remember well the experience of Paul Castner. Paul looked like line material when he reported, yet in line play he seemed to lack something. Then one day I tried him at passing and punting and discovered that he was a real find.

Castner was a natural backfield man. He developed into one of the best all-around backs we ever had. His kicking, passing, and running with the ball were all of a high order, yet if we hadn't found his specialties, he would have been just another scrub. As a rule, though, a triple-threat man is the easiest boy of a group to find because his excellence in his specialty is so obvious.

In getting ready to start with the ball, the back must begin in the most optimum position. His feet are spread, but not too far apart. Both feet are placed on the same line. The player steadies himself by placing one hand on the ground. Just previous to the start of the play he rises on his toes. On end runs and wide tackle plays the ball should be tucked under the armpit. In that spot there is the least possibility of having the ball "knocked loose," resulting in a possible fatal fumble.

There is much discussion as to whether the backfield men should use the sprinter's crouch, with one or both hands on the ground, or whether they should merely be on the balls of the feet, legs well spread, knees bent, and with the hands resting on the knees. I believe that with a heavy, ponderous backfield using the set formation, I would use the sprinter's crouch with one hand on the ground. For a fast, shifty backfield employing the shift, how-

ever, the sprinter's crouch is not necessary.

Jack Elder was weak on forward-pass defense; he couldn't block. But out in California, the last game that year, he found himself. It will be remembered that his most spectacular play was a forward pass he stole from the Army to turn into a one-man touchdown. Elder was a firing-line competitor.

Jack Chevigny, a great Notre Dame halfback, used to give an imitation of Leon Errol when he was with the scrubs. His idea of a broken-field run was to trip on a blade of grass and fall. But he came through splendidly when the big games stirred his heart.

Size is not necessary in hitting the line, the ability to do this depending upon ability to pick holes, leg drive, and nerve. The finished halfback is a man who can intuitively sense how to elude defensive players by change of pace, sudden change of direction, use of straight-arm, and by dodging.

Clever halfbacks I have known never worried about the first defensive man coming at them, but their minds were actively at work on how best to elude the second and third and even the fourth man coming up. Above all, a halfback must learn how to hold on to the ball, and he must NEVER fumble. In order to make sure that there is no fumble, the halfback when tackled must not put the hand out to break his fall to the ground. Rather he should put the other hand also on the ball and, falling relaxed, must keep keenly in mind the importance of holding on to his precious burden.

The offensive fullback is the plunger. He is generally the type of man who does not reel off particularly large gains but who is generally good for the short, necessary gains. Some teams employ slow, ponderous fellows because they hit the line hard. However, I believe the

Size is not necessary in hitting the line, the ability to do this depending upon ability to pick holes, leg drive, and nerve.

smaller type of fullback with speed, who will depend more on picking the hole, dash, and nerve in getting through the line, is the better

It is best to teach a back the technique of the three different dodges which are: the side-step, cross-over, and the pivot. In using the side-step, the halfback holds the ball in the arm away from the tackler, shows him a leg, and then by means of the hip muscles pulls the leg away by jumping to the side.

There are three things to be borne in mind here regarding putting down the leg which is used as a bait for the tackler. This leg must be put down so that the weight is on the toe, no part of the heel touching. The weight of the body must be forward and the knees well

bent. The straight arm is used along with this to make it more effective.

The "cross-over" dodge is more easily learned. The back fakes one way and then by crossing one leg over as sharply and as far as he can, he changes direction and also sort of fades away from the tackler. The straight arm can also be used here, but the important thing is running relaxed and having a pair of very supple hips.

The "pivot" dodge which is generally used by line plungers, though it is also used by small men, consists in holding the ball in the arm on the side the tackler is coming. Just before he is tackled, he places down his outside foot, hitting the tackler on the head gear with the outside hand and at the same time spinning away from the tackler. Big men find lifting the knees adds to their effectiveness. The objection to the pivot dodge lies in the danger of injury and in the fact that the man carrying the ball turns his back to the defense for an instant or so. This may prevent a long run, but the pivot dodge may add many extra yards to the ball carrier's gain.

Fullbacks, of course, have all been made by good lines. Johnny Maulbetsch of Michigan, while a very fine fullback, was made by his line. In 1914, working behind a veteran, polished line, Maulbetsch plunged almost the entire length of the field against Harvard. He was picked by most experts for All-America teams that fall. The next year, in the fall of 1915, when he played behind a green sophomore line, Maulbetsch didn't look as good, through no fault of his own. I merely mention this to show the relative values.

ENDS

Now we come to the ends. An end should be fairly fast for blocking. He should be rather short and rugged, and perhaps not a particularly good forward-pass catcher, but he would have to be able to block a tackle. The other end, however, should be the tall boy with good speed and with the basketball ability to go up into the air and spear forward passes.

As a rule, the rugged blocking end would be played on the right side of the line on offense. The tall forward-pass catching end should be played at the left end on offense and on the right end on defense. This is due to the fact that most teams run four out of five plays to the right. The ends must also have the speed and elusiveness to be able to cover kicks well, and in this regard elusiveness and ability to use hands are just as important as speed.

The groups of ends are brought together to learn how to box tackle, or block tackle, or practicing defense against a backfield. The backfield can practice running inside or outside the end using prearranged signals. The defensive end tries to get to the ballcarrier. This activity gives practice to the offensive backs learning how to block the end out or in, and it gives practice to the defensive end in learning how to meet interference. They get lots of combat work in small groups without any danger of injuries. The comparative ability of the boys in the various stunts can easily be determined by whoever is in charge of the team.

In the popular mind, ends are classified according to their ability to catch passes. In the minds of the football coach, the most important thing the end does offensively is to box the tackle. If the end is not clever at "land-locking" the tackle, no offense can function.

Defensively, the end must be able to turn every play in, and also watch for passes into the "flat zone." The "flat zone" is the territory along the line of scrimmage extended toward the sidelines. An end must be elusive, powerful, nimble of hand and foot, and must never allow himself to be "sucked in" or "knocked off" his feet.

GUARDS

The group of guards is brought together. The coach will place two guards on offense against one guard on defense. The two guards on offense practice charging, using short, digging steps. With a bull neck, with his legs well apart, he practices carrying on through against this one defensive guard.

The guards should be strong and physical, yet fast enough to pull out and run interference

Johnny Weibel ... was one of the greenest chaps I ever saw come out on our field. But he was a strong boy, so we used him in the scrubs, although he impressed me as being preternaturally lazy.

on the flank and on forward-pass plays. The boy who plays guard is more or less a martyr, because he receives quite a lot of physical abuse, more so perhaps than the player in any other position. A green man on the ordinary team can fill in here better than he can anywhere else.

You may think that your team won't be able to use plays where the guards pull out. I believe you will improve your offense at least 33 percent if the guard will learn to come out fast enough to be effective as an interferer on forward passes, or through the secondary on an off-tackle play. I have found that the short, squatty, heavy chaps fit in better at guard with the tall, heavy men fitting in better at tackle.

How many see the offensive guard pull out quickly and precisely, down low like a bloodhound on the trail, and move out around the tackle? The linebacker is just about to tackle the ballcarrier when he is swept off his feet by this same guard. The ballcarrier goes on his way unhampered with the crowd cheering him for his clever bit of work. No one cheers the guard but his coach and teammates. They appreciate the play.

Defensively, the guard is always underneath the pile like a submarine, yet never staying down. What I mean by that is he doesn't play ostrich. Instead, after the charge, he comes up with his head and arms free, ready to grasp the ballcarrier in case he tries to go over his territory.

I studied Weibel for a long time and decided that he had contempt for practice. He evidently figured — as most competitors do — that he should save his energy for the real games. And this almost defeated his ambition, for it is doubtful if Weibel would have had a chance to play for Notre Dame among all the talent. He had been relegated to third-string guard. Even then I was not inclined to use him. But in a game with Army, Harvey Brown, a regular guard, had his elbow twisted in a play and had to be taken out of the game. The second-string guard withstood three hard plays and limped off the field with a sprained ankle. Having nothing else to do, I sent in Weibel.

George Smythe was the Army quarterback — and a smart one. He must have seen my stoic look of disappointment when two guards came to the injured bench one after the other. Army was battering its way toward our goal line at the time. They were about 12 yards from a touchdown when Weibel went in.

I watched the play closely and saw Weibel crouch low, teeth gritted, when Smythe shot a play at him. Army gained a little. Smythe tried another spot in the line and gained more. Then he went back to Weibel with the ball on Notre Dame's four-yard line. Army fans sounded like a massive mob yelling for the score. Weibel steadied himself for the shock. He was able to stop the determined Army's charge from scoring again.

Then it was fourth down, two to go. Smythe smiled. I knew his next play would go right at Weibel. It did — and what a piledriving smash! I expected to see Weibel flat and finished. The whistle blew and there was Weibel — the Army back prostrate before him and the ball still two yards from Notre Dame's goal.

The guard practicing defense will experiment in diving underneath as he would in playing defense in a game. He must learn how to jam his body through as far as he can, being careful not to go on his stomach, but having his arms clear at all times so he can make a tackle if a ballcarrier aims at him. The same system holds true teaching them their other techniques and, in fact, holds good for every position.

The "shoulder charge" can also be taught on a dummy and consists of hitting it with the shoulder without the use of the arms. Smack the dummy squarely where the shoulder of the opponent would be and keep the head back, with the bull neck, and legs well apart, feet straight ahead, and the seat should be kept low. The arms should be practically behind the blocker so he will not have any tendency to use them — using the arms by an offensive

Kicking a football before it hits the ground is very much like playing golf — the younger you start, the better you become at it.

player is against the rules. If the player will learn these fundamentals, he will be a good shoulder charger.

The "open field" block used against a defensive player who is running is called the running dive with a roll. The tackle makes a dive at the defensive player just above the knees, turning his back into him just as they hit. If the boys all master these types of blocks, the team should be a dandy.

KICKERS

Kicking a football before it hits the ground is very much like playing golf — the younger you start, the better you become at it.

A famous coach once said punters were born, not made. This may or may not be true, but the fact remains that most great punters began at an early age.

In learning how to punt, the first thing is to hold the ball properly. The ball should be held in the fingertips of both hands, with the right hand covering the rear point of the ball and the left hand a little bit behind and to the left of the front of the ball.

The leg should always be turned to the right for a right-footed kicker. The front point of the ball should be turned inward and the axis should be about parallel with the ground. The arms are then both straightened and the ball is held as far away from the body as possible and about three and a half to four feet off the ground, but no higher.

The ball is shaped and dropped carefully — never tossed. Just as the ball begins to leave the fingertips, the kicking leg should be brought up swinging freely from the hips, and the instep of the kicking foot should be clubbed against that spot on the ball between the two white lines.

To ensure this movement, the toe must be depressed so as to allow the instep to protrude. The kicking leg should describe an arc, cutting somewhat to the left. This seems to give the ball a sufficient cut to cause a spiral. The leg should follow through. This is the reason I use the one club in contrast to the one slap or "spank" which would be wrong.

The four points to bear in mind when learning to kick the ball properly are:

1. Drop the ball carefully and just right not too close nor too far away.

2. Keep your eye on the ball.

3. Depress the toe.

4. Follow through so the kicking foot ends up over the head.

A youngster should practice this movement for weeks before he tries to kick quickly, to kick with steps, for height, distance, or placement.

In fact, it is just the same as a golf player learning golf and lining up near a green with about 50 golf balls and simply practicing hitting the ball properly with the clubhead. After a boy has learned to club the ball properly with a free, easy swing, he is ready to practice receiving the ball from the center or snapper back and then punting.

There has been much talk about various kinds of kicking shoes, but always remember that a boy kicks with his foot, not with his shoe. In reality, there is no such thing as a kicking shoe. Some of the best kicking I ever saw was executed by barefoot boys in Hawaii. The best shoe is a light, glove-foot kangaroo shoe, which just shapes the foot, giving a better chance to club the ball with the instep. The best exercise to develop the kicking muscles is hitch kicking and squatting.

Be very careful to kick into the air a half dozen times before doing any actual kicking, so as not to pull any muscles. As a kicker becomes more proficient, he might pay a little more attention to such fine points as snapping the knee at the moment of impact. The leg should be brought up slightly, bent at the knee, and then just before the moment of impact, the knee is snapped, straightening the leg. This gives the feet added velocity. The question of the driving force depends entirely on the velocity of the foot that meets the ball at the moment of impact. You may question this judgment. Some may say that a heavy shoe is better to kick with than no shoe. In that case, why don't fungo hitters use a big steel bat instead of a light willow?

There are two methods of getting extra force under the kick by means of the body. One is to use the stomach muscles and double up forward as much as you can at the moment of impact. This is used by small men effectively. The other is to lean back as the instep is driven into the ball. This is preferred by large, tall men.

The passer is very important in kicking, and you must have a center who will pass the ball about halfway between the waist and shoulder, straight from the front. The two stripes on the ball are very important as they give the kicker something to watch as he goes through the motions of kicking. He must keep his eye on the spot he intends to club, ideally equidistant between the two lines.

In drop kicking, the ball is held somewhat differently. Hold the ball in the fingertips, one hand on each side, letting go with both hands at the same time. Lean forward as far as possible, so that the ball is dropped but a short distance. This posture allows for accuracy. The ball should be dropped with its axis perpendicular to the ground, and it will bounce right straight up again, as the longitudinal axis is the most resilient part of the ball.

The points I mentioned previously for punting are held to, except that in drop kicking, the ball may be kicked with the toe or with the instep. However, you must lean forward and drop the ball carefully: You must keep your eye on the ball and you must imagine that you are throwing the kicking foot right through the goalposts.

The center, in the case of a man trying a drop kick, should aim the ball at his knees, so he will be well bent over forward. Another good thing is, by means of the foot, to draw a line on the ground, aimed right at a spot between the goalposts. This gives you something to follow. You must not look at the goalposts but must keep your eye on the ball. A boy who makes the kick the instant the ball hits the ground kicks with the toe.

Frank Hudson and Charley Brickley were great drop kickers who used this form. Drop kickers who delay a little bit and allow the ball to bounce higher than that use the instep in kicking. This generally gives a little more distance. Jim Thorpe was a great drop kicker who used this latter form.

The leg must be swung in a vertical arc in drop kicking with absolutely no lateral cutting. Some punters who exaggerated the lateral arc and cut the ball laterally are unable to drop kick because of this. A lateral arc kills drop kicking. The leg must be swung in a vertical arc for accuracy. Keep your eye on the ball.

A capable drop kicker means much to a football team. Moving back the goalposts has resulted in fewer drop kicks now than in the old days, but many games are won each week by what writers describe as "educated feet." It is always a good idea to have a drop kicker handy.

The victories in football generally go to the
team which is the most aggressive.

33

THE DEFENSE

"Defensive players should always have in mind the number of the downs, yards to go, time to play, position on the field, and the score. From these facts and by watching closely for every sign shown by the offensive team, the defensive team can analyze probable tactics of opponents. They should never be caught napping."

Knute Rockne

Defense should not have the idea that the other team is carrying the fight to them. The victories in football generally go to the team which is the most aggressive. A successful team should, therefore, be very aggressive when they have the ball. They should, however, have the mental attitude when they have not got the ball that they will be so aggressive that in a very short time they will take the ball away from the other team. This psychology will tend to do away with a waiting defense and all the ills that go with phlegmatic playing.

Tackling is probably not emphasized today as strongly as it was before the advent of the forward pass. There are so many things to be done that a coach cannot give it the time that he could in the old days.

The nose tackle and linebacker each watch the various holes in the line into which the man carrying the ball can come... if the defensive line has done its work well, the man carrying the ball will come through free and alone...

It is still, however, very important. You cannot defeat a good tackling team very badly. The deadly tackler is a big asset. No man should be on the team who cannot tackle well.

The defensive safety man does not have to tackle often, yet when the time comes for him to make a tackle it is vital that he make it. A safety man must get his man or a touchdown results.

Some men with big high school reputations do not like to tackle. They will, however, when they realize that they cannot make the team by merely being ball carriers. A good tackler is enthusiastic about it and gets a lot of pleasure out of a neat job well done.

Tackling requires head work, good judgment of distance and timing, and plenty of nerve. After a week of instruction on the dummy, give him work in actually tackling a man carrying the ball.

TACTICAL SITUATIONS

A team on defense must keep in mind the downs, the yards to gain, position on the field, score, and time left to play. These conditions are called the "tactical situation." Variations of the "tactical situation" will of course cause the defense to change, as a defense will logically, of course, anticipate different kinds of plays under varying conditions.

For instance, if the other team has first down (and) 10 against a normal team, there is not much sense in expecting a line buck. With third down (and) 10, it is not good judgment to expect a line plunge. With third down (and) one yard, it would not be good judgment to expect a forward pass. Instead, it would be just the reverse of these.

Likewise, if a team is several touchdowns ahead in the second half there is not much need for the defense to worry about forward passes. If, however, the opposing team is several touchdowns behind in the second half, then you may safely expect a great number of forward passes. Teams as a rule will not forward pass deep in its own territory, and with less than a minute to play in the middle of the field there is little likelihood of line bucking.

A defensive team must be able to adapt itself to any offensive formation. Its individuals on defense must be able to adapt themselves to the "tactical situation," no matter what it may be, without squeaking. They must perform as a well-oiled machine.

Let us take up the defense under conditions where the game is even and around the middle of the field, and the offensive team has about third down (and) four. There are 10 or 15 minutes still to play. Under these conditions, we will take up first the several styles of defense which are now used.

First of all, we will take up the style of defense as it is generally used by teams in the East. In this style of defense, the guards, tackles and ends play a little wider than usual, and they all charge into space without the use of hands and drive everything in towards the middle. The linemen do not use their hands until after the initial drive and they charged the opponents with their shoulders and bodies.

The nose tackle and linebacker each watch the various holes in the line into which the man carrying the ball can come. Their theory is that if the defensive line has done its work well, the man carrying the ball will come through free and alone, and will be easily picked off. The safeties are laying back farther for longer passes, whereas the two men, nose tackle and linebacker, are of course responsible for short forward passes.

This defense used in the East presents several weaknesses, though of course this is not admitted by the advocates of this style. The first weakness is the fact that each of the six linemen has committed themselves by charging in a certain direction and therefore they cannot change their course. They become vulnerable to delayed sideswiping in-plays involving double handling of the ball, split bucks, etc.

The defensive end is, of course, covering the inside of his territory very well. But if the offense uses an open backfield formation, he becomes vulnerable to lateral passes and wide end runs as he cannot get more than one backfield man by smashing.

The secondary defense can be fooled by hidden ball plays which becomes impossible for a six-man line to be able to bear the brunt of the attack. However, this defense is very good against an offense without deception.

The guards and tackles line up slightly inside and charge outwardly, and the defensive center is allowed to roam at liberty. He may be in the line tight, he may be back several yards, or he may be in the line pulling out rapidly. The end comes in two steps perpendicularly past the line of scrimmage and then turns in at right angles.

This defense is very good against certain types of offense as it is practically impossible to gain inside of the guard and tackle or around end. However, it is possible to pinch tackle in, and the end, because of the width of his position, is easily held out. This end, in other words, cannot guard the inside half of his territory by this method.

The other weakness lies in the fact that the nose tackle becomes the key man of defense, and if we can outwit him, we can gain much ground and even demoralize his play.

The better defense, in my opinion, is what is popularly known as the cup defense. In this defense, the guards and the tackles charge straight back in their territory, and they do not charge in or out until their secondary reaction when they should instantly charge toward the man with the ball. The guards or tackles must not wait nor shall they pull out behind their own line of scrimmage. Each one of them must expect the play to be coming through his hole and play accordingly, converging towards the ball only after they have charged through the offensive line of scrimmage.

The defensive end goes in just as fast as he can, somewhat like the type of end in the defense commonly used in the East only he does not commit himself. Rather, he takes three steps starting with his inner foot advanced. With his hands held up in front of him he can meet the advancing interference in such a position that they cannot knock him out. And, if they try to circle him, he can, by crossing his inner foot in front and by a nimble use of feet and hands, fade out with the play. He cannot be knocked in. This type of end play does not present any weaknesses,

although it is of course very difficult to master.

Defensive End

There are many different ways of playing defensive end. Coaches who use what is known as the square end send the end in at right angles two or three steps, after which he turns in.

Another style is to play what is known as the smashing end. In this case, the end crosses the line of scrimmage as fast as he can and leaves his feet right into the backfield trying to spill two or more men if possible before the ball is under way.

My idea of end play is to combine the two, using the strong points of each style so as to be able to carry out the old adage heard innumerable times. "Turn your play in, let nothing get around you."

I also try to eliminate the weak points of both methods. Most any end, by playing wide enough, can turn a play in, but there is generally left now so much place between himself and the tackle that large gains are easily made inside the end. By placing a loose backfield, a smashing end is easily circled. He can get but one backfield man and is made a fool of by trick and open plays.

The best end is the man who can play fairly tight to his tackle, thus closing up that gap, and yet prevent runs around him. This style of end play I call a shifting end. The shifting end comes in fast and then stops with hands and arms outstretched on toes and feet back.

In this interval he has located the play and acts accordingly. He plays the man carrying the ball. He focuses on the man carrying the ball while the interference he sees and plays out of the corner of his eye. If an interferer dives at him, he steps in quick and then sidesteps wide. He is always on his toes, and after sidestepping he makes his dive to tackle the man carrying the ball.

If the interference comes standing up, and there are two of them, he tries to play one man or the other while keeping to the outside until the man carrying the ball is "showed." He may also play each interferer with an arm on each, and after the man carrying the ball is "showed" in or out, fight to him.

The end must use his hands and feet nimbly as possible, cuffing, riding the interference, and on wide end runs keeping the man carrying the ball at such an angle that he can get him whether he tries to cut or circle. There are times, of course, when the man carrying the ball follows his interference closely, and here a sharp, quick-leg-driving smashing dive will dump the whole bunch. This the end must learn by experience. He must never smash if he cannot get two or more interferers.

Experience teaches the end much. He gets so he can almost smell a play when it is coming his way. The end must study the kind of back carrying the ball his way, his tricks, tendencies, strong and weak points, and play him accordingly.

Small shifty-legged men may be tackled high. Against big powerful hard running backs, dive hard high at the shoe-tops. Keep your eyes open, and when you hit him swing your arms around him for keeps. Never let the interference get to your feet. By keeping hands well out in front, and keeping nimbly on toes, no end should ever be boxed or put off his feet.

However, you must watch the man carrying the ball. He is the man you are after while you handle the interference automatically by reflex action. This latter comes only after hard work and constant repetition. Watch the ball closely, and on the slightest movement go in as fast as you can to the relative spot. Learn by experience where you stop the interference. Keep eyes open, tail down, and hands out in front, and be on toes.

As the end is coming in, he can always diagnose a line buck before he comes to the place where he ordinarily stops. In this case he therefore keeps right on in and in many cases can, by a long quick dive, make the tackle. However, he must be sure of his diagnosis, or they may circle him with a fake buck.

A good end with his eyes open should, quick as a whip, smear anything that savors of a fake buck. Against delayed bucks, the end should be the thorn in the side of the offense. Delayed bucks work because of slow charging, slow thinking, or waiting ends. A fast charging, aggressive end who keeps right on going in even when he sees the play apparently going the other way should nail a delayed buck for a loss every time.

Against lateral passes, the end should cover the outside man. The end must never allow any man to get outside of him, except on spread plays, in which case the end may drop back and become a half back. If the end does this whenever he sees that the spread is wide, there is no chance for an end run.

MAN-TO-MAN VS. ZONE

A spectator once asked me what was the difference between the man-to-man defense against forward passes, and the zone defense.

It might be explained as follows: Supposing five boys were living in five adjoining houses and each boy was guarding his house against an airplane attack with an anti-aircraft gun. Also suppose that behind each house the backyards were fenced in.

If each boy had his anti-aircraft gun mounted on a mobile vehicle but stayed in his own backyard and shot only at the airplane, which came directly over his yard that might be likened to zone defense against the forward pass.

If, on the other hand, the fences between these five yards were torn down, making it one big yard, and each boy with his mobile anti-aircraft gun picked out a definite, particular airplane and followed it wherever it went, taking a shot at it whenever it came close to him personally, this could be likened to the man-to-man defense against forward passes.

On the football field, a coach may divide the defensive territory into five zones and hold each one of five men responsible for his particular zone. The coach using the man-to-man defense will cover every one of the five eligible receivers of the offensive team with a definitely assigned defensive man.

The reader will curiously ask which system is the best. Personally, I believe that either a straight man-to-man defense or a straight zone defense is weak.

We can block out with linemen certain of the defensive players, and if this defensive team is using a man-to-man defense these men who are blocking cannot cover their man. Against a zone defense, it is possible to send two or three men into the same zone and the man covering that zone finds himself completely whipsawed if the passer is a clever man.

In other words, it would be the same if two or three airplanes came over the same backyard at the same time. Of course, the question of forward pass defense will always be a bugaboo to coaches. However, the teams which have been most successful in defending against the pass have been the teams which have been using an elastic combination of the two.

The system which is interchangeable to such an extent that the quarterback cannot know the other team's forward pass defense is bound to be successful. A quarterback must play the defense. If he knows the other team is using the straight zone defense, he throws a certain type of pass play. Against the man-to-man defense, he throws another type of forward pass.

Against a combination defense, which is changed from game to game, the offensive quarterback is nonplussed because he does not know what he is up against, or how to meet it.

The typical fan who watches a game loves to follow the ball and the ballcarrier, and no doubt he gets an immense thrill now and then by doing so. It is my personal opinion, however, that he would enjoy the game more if he learned what really makes a play work.

DEFENDING THE FORWARD PASS

A) Man for man.
B) Zone.
C) Combination.

No matter which of the above you chose, the success will depend on the individual brains and abilities of your man in the backfield.

Zone defense is probably better against short passes, and man-for-man against long passes. A defensive player must watch the man until the ball is in the air — he should then leave his man and play the ball. Try and maneuver so as to give the receiver only one path to follow, and also try and keep the receiver between yourself and the passer. Do not let the receiver get by you.

Watch downs and yards to gain, as well as score and time left to play so as to be able to anticipate forward pass plays. A zone defense is probably the best against most formations, but a team should be prepared to use a man-to-man defense against any team appearing with a wide spread formation.

Against forward passes from regular formation, it is the duty of the ends to rush in as fast as possible, putting so much pressure on the passer that he throws hurriedly and haphazardly. He must be careful, however, not to allow the passer to dodge him and convert the play into an end run. Half the defense against passes is to hurry the passer.

Against forward passes from punt formation, on certain downs with certain yards to gain, the end will suspect a forward pass and, in this case, will play a waiting game, covering his own end along the scrimmage line extended against forward passes. Only near his sideline a defensive end can take a chance and dive into the offensive end as he goes by, as it is a favorite trick for the offense here to take a play wide and then pass to the end running down the sidelines.

Against spread plays, the end covers his own end for passes just as though he were a defensive halfback. Quite a bit of practice must be done in the fall if the end is to acquire the basketball intuition necessary to do this.

COVERAGE FOR KICKS

Coming down under kicks — I include this as part of the defensive play — involves some fine judgment of timing, distance and footwork if the end covering the kick is to do any brilliant open field tackling.

The end going down under the punt should keep the following points in mind: First, he must get down the field just as fast as he can, though he may use with intelligence a change of pace. He must use his hands-on would-be interferers, sidestep them, or jump over them if they dive, always turning the

receiver of the punt to the inside of the field. The end must slow up when within five yards of the receiver and spread his legs so as not to over-run the receiver.

If you have been slow in getting down the field and the receiver comes toward you with interference, play more conservatively but by all means turn the man in. Never loaf on a punt, but rather get off as fast as you can and turn the head at the neck to take one look after you have heard the thud of the kicker's boot against the pigskin.

After that, remember but two things — elusiveness and speed. As the rules this year do not legislate against a flying tackle there is nothing to prevent the end in open-field tackling from coming at his man with absolute abandon.

The best training for ends is boxing, sprinting with the sprinters, handball, and hitting a bucking machine so as to develop strength in the arms and power in what we might call the forearm shiver. All these things involve coordination of the eyes, hand and foot, and perfection of automatic coordination is absolutely essential to playing defensive end.

BASICS OF DEFENSE

1. Keep man with ball turned in towards center.

2. Use aggressive defense having in mind taking ball away from other team.

3. In meeting new formation ask yourself question: "What can they not do so well from this formation?"

4. Then meet their strong point by taking men away from point which is not threatened strongly.

5. Vary defense for each game according

to offense of the other team.

6. Use square defense inside own 30-yard line.

7. Every man charge in his own territory on first charge and then converge on man with ball.

8. Cup defense best as general rule.

9. Combination of man for man with some zone defense best against passes.

10. However, tackles rushing passer fast is half the defense against passes.

11. Against passes, play the man until the ball is in the air and then play the ball.

12. Against short passes zone may be used, but against long passes it is best to use man for man entirely.

13. Defensive man against passes should maneuver so as to keep both receiver and passer in sight, starting soon enough so as to lead man down the field. Never follow or

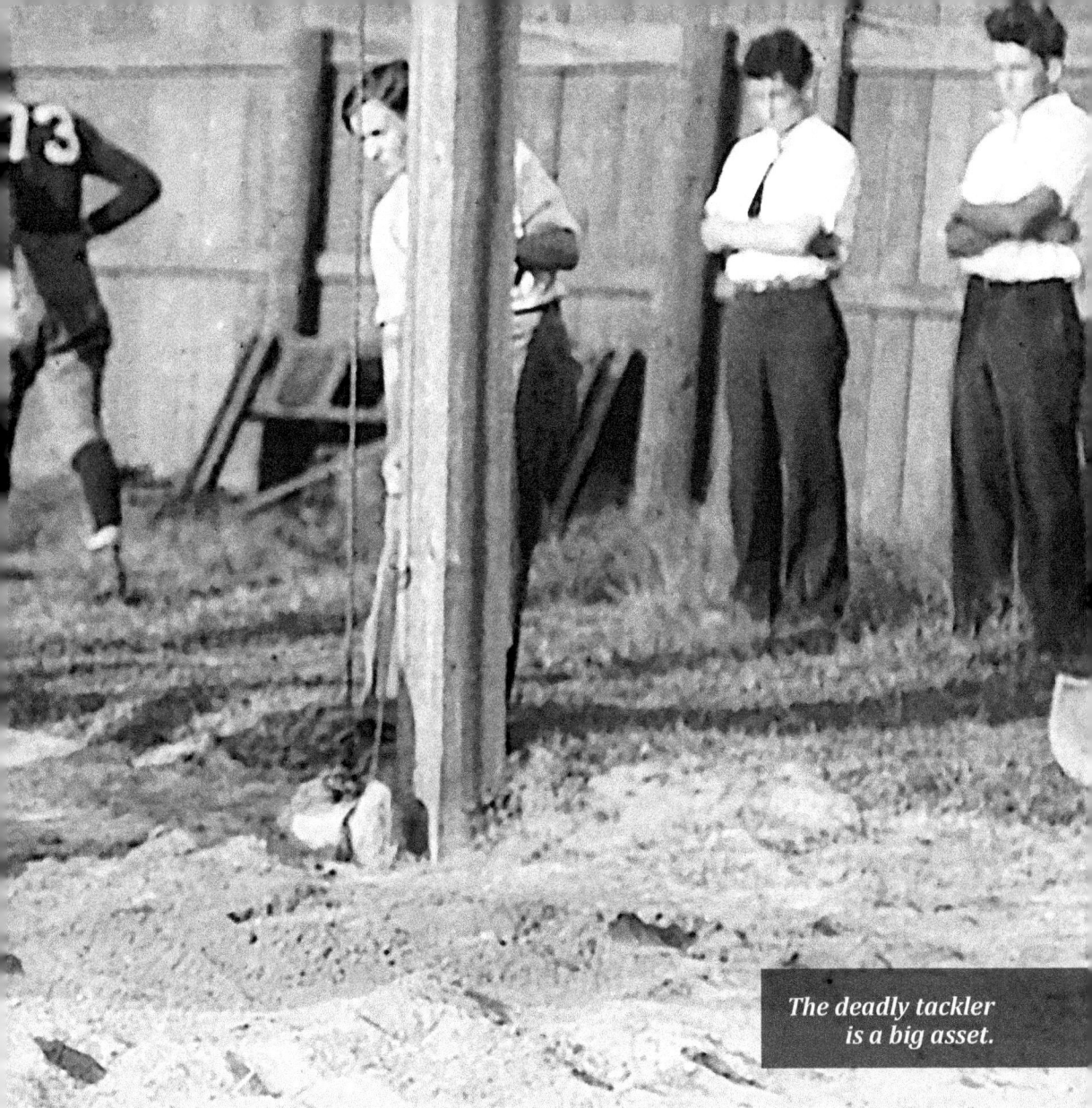

The deadly tackler is a big asset.

allow man to get by you.

14. Double up on extra good man.

15. Always talk it up so as to maintain contact and when changing defense captain makes it known by a word and this word should be one which means nothing to offensive team.

16. Always keep tactical situation in mind and don't let offense know what your thoughts are.

17. Defensive line must cross line of scrimmage and get into enemy territory.

18. Defensive full must move to the point of attack fast and fearlessly.

19. Six-man line can be used against many teams.

20. Conservative back must be CONSERVATIVE.

21. Every man go to the man with the ball on the second reaction.

22. Follow the ball all the time.

23. Always be ready, and do not be misled by talk of any kind on part of offensive team.

24. Wherever offensive team has tackle eligible, or any odd man, whole team should call it out loud.

25. Never let any man advance with ball or retreat with the ball under any circumstance unless it is an official.

26. Never stop until ball is declared dead, whistle or no whistle.

27. Relax physically but never relax mentally.

28. Be sure that your defense against passes is elastic enough to meet all conditions. A mixture of man-for-man and zone is good.

29. Secondary defense should see all the backfield so as not to be fooled easily.

30. Territory defense is responsible more for passes than for rushing. He should come up more cautiously than secondary and is also responsible for more tricks and wide-end runs.

31. Quaternary should help on good long man whether on strong side or weak side.

32. Center is responsible for back receiving pass to the weak side.

33. Tackle the ball whenever possible.

34. Always be alert for a quick play, series, etc.

35. Never allow an opponent to carry the ball forward or backward no matter what the circumstances. Tackle him.

36. If necessary, use signals to indicate changes in defensive system though every man should understand thoroughly why.

37. Do not allow yourself to be sucked into traps.

38. Sometimes leave openings so as to tease opponent into using a play that under the conditions you want him to use.

39. Use eyes, hands, and brains.

EXECUTION

Practically all the new ideas introduced into football in the last 10 years have had to do with innovations in advancing the ball. But don't forget one thing: What makes a play go is not merely that it is a sound play and that it has deception and power. It goes because of its execution.

Execution is everything. This adage is what the average boy forgets. I find that the average youngster just starting out in football believes he can always fool the other fellow. When one team plays another equally smart team and refuses to be fooled, trick plays become useless. In fact, they become a boomerang.

You'll find some plays work well for one team while the identical plays fail for another. Why?

In the case of the first team, the boys in the line out-charge the defensive line, the interferers in the backfield took care of the end and also helped on the tackle in a superior manner. The ballcarrier reaches the point of attack quickly, the men who are supposed to fake for the ball act as if they were actually going to get it, the team has a lot of dash, and of course every one of the 11 men takes his man.

Mark that down in your notebook: "Takes his man."

In the case of the second team using the same play unsuccessfully, this is due to the fact that they fall down somewhere on one of these points of execution. The line is not charging, the men in the backfield all want to be ballcarriers, no one wants to interfere, the ballcarrier is too slow, the man faking for the ball fakes so poorly that it is obvious he is not going to get the ball and therefore he fools no one. Someone either loafs or falls down because of inefficiency and therefore does not get his man.

Every individual on the team must shoulder his responsibility, whether playing on offense or defense. A certain play means that every one of the eleven has a certain duty, a certain assignment. Every man should take upon himself doing his own job 100 percent. If he should have a little success and perhaps be written up in the papers, he should never get swelled-headed.

Long jogs are bad for a football team ...

34

THE SEASON

SPRING TRAINING

This five-or-six weeks of spring football receives practically no publicity. There are no trips away from home, and no absences from classes. There is no student interest, beyond that of the boys taking part in the practice.

The coach gets a line on his material, and with five-or-six weeks' time on his hands he is able to give every boy on a very large squad a chance to show what he can do. This is impossible in the fall, as there is not time enough to give anyone but the first string a chance. So, spring practice makes for democracy and a fair chance for every boy.

In fact, I would be in favor of some spring games between schools, allowing only those boys to play who had not earned their letters, or who had not been members of the first string previously. This would provide a chance for the ordinary boy to represent his school in contests, whereas in the fall only the best, of course, will have the honor of representing their institution. Perhaps this won't be possible, however, until the word "overemphasis" will have been laid away among the mothballs where it belongs. From present indications, that won't happen for several years, but I believe it should come about eventually.

Just how much can be accomplished in spring football practice is entirely up to the energy, personality, and inventiveness of the coach. At Notre Dame, we practically do all of our

279

coaching and scrimmaging in the spring. In the fall, it is merely a matter of conditioning and polishing up — keeping the team fit mentally and physically.

FALL PRESEASON

Comes the time of the year when leaves turn brown and a cool breeze refreshes the air. The familiar thud of footballs being kicked can be heard around the country. About that same time, young men arrive at college, as I did years ago, anxious for a college education.

Researching all the many mental complexities of every conceivable type that occupy the minds of these young hopefuls would be interesting. They come to college with an earnest desire to study and learn all they are able. They don't know, perhaps, just exactly what they want to be, ultimately — businessmen, professional men, or what particular line of activity they are going to pursue — but they are eager for knowledge. They are filled with anticipation of what they are going to face in life, and the lives they are going to live.

I look forward with a great deal of expectancy each year to the opening of school. The new athletes arrive to begin their "last lap" per-se in preparation for the most important bigger "game" itself — life.

I firmly believe that football has a vital role to play in preparing boys for a successful future. The average high school graduate is rattle-brained. His education is superficial, and he has not the capacity to think of a single thing for more than one minute without getting a headache. Football teaches concentration. It also teaches responsibility as a representative of his college and his teammates. He learns responsibility in controlling his passions: fear,

hatred, jealousy, and rashness.

Requirements to play football are all about the same, whether played in grade school, high school, or college. It is no game for the weakling, the coward, or the egotist. The lad who hopes to be a good football player must have brains, courage, self-restraint, fine muscular coordination, intense fire of nervous energy, and an unselfish spirit of sacrifice for his team.

Men report in the fall in three different kinds of condition. There is the man who has worked hard all summer at trashing or firing and has overdone this to the extent that he reports underweight; secondly, there is the boy who has worked at rugged outdoor work all summer, not to excess, and he reports robust and in fairly good shape to start the campaign; thirdly, there is the "softy" who reports soft, flabby, and away out of condition.

Regardless of how the man reports, the work the first two weeks should be easy. If the man is underweight, easy work will be just the thing to give him a good appetite so that he will eat heartily and soon be up to normal weight. If he reports in fair condition, light work is all that will be necessary the first two weeks to keep him fit. Light work is all the "softy" can stand, because if you work him strenuously, he may either hurt himself or may get disgusted and quit.

After two easy weeks, however, the next four weeks should be concentrated and consist of the real hard work of the year. All the season's scrimmage should be packed into these four weeks, and the scrimmage should be done before the third week, and very little after the sixth.

A team should be in the best of shape after six weeks and after just enough work should be given the men to keep them fit and on the edge. Long jogs are bad for a football team as it makes them loggy. Short wind sprints are better. Five minutes of limbering up exercises daily help to condition the men, keep their muscles soft and limber, develop coordination, and quicken their reflexes.

There is nothing to worry normally about a man going stale, except to watch the weight charts. If a man doesn't pick up in weight in the twenty-two hours between practices, in other words, if he doesn't recuperate and if he appears languid, suffers from loss of appetite, has bad color in the eye, and is tired of football, it is then time to lay him off for several days. It would be well to work this man lightly for the rest of the season.

The work the day before the game should be quite light, and the work on Monday should not be very heavy. Some boys should not be worked as hard as others, as you cannot work them all the same. The nervous high-strung boys cannot stand as much work as the phlegmatic type. Every player should be careful to use antiseptics on any cuts or abrasions and should watch to see that his bowels are open three times daily.

Preseason training should consist of boxing, wrestling, track athletics, basketball and handball. Too much swimming is not good, as it softens one for football. Tennis and golf are good games, but there is not enough exercise to golf itself for pre-season work for football. Combined with tennis, it is OK.

The bucking machine and tackle dummy are all right as artificial devices, but I don't believe in the bucking strap. Neither do I believe in the apparatus for side-stepping, nor do I believe in any other artificial apparatus. We have to use the bucking machine to develop leg drive and the "forearm shiver" for linemen. We get along as much as possible without the tackling dummy, but we find we have to have it to teach tackling to the green men and also to toughen the squad. Later in the season, when we have acquired form and condition, the tackling dummy is no longer used, and the would-be tackler uses the live ball instead.

The football coach is faced with many challenges at the beginning of the season. The one that interests and amuses me occurs on the opening day of practice for the freshmen. Most schools have a separate freshman team, made up of boys just out of high school. These boys, for the most part, are unknown quantities as far as the coaches are concerned.

At our school, after the freshman coach has called all of the new prospects into a group, he separates them according to the positions which they profess to play. When the coach calls for backs, nearly three-fourths of the candidates step forward. Then the coach asks for the ends, and another one-fourth of the group steps out. This leaves only a few who humbly admit that they can play tackle, guard, or center.

From this illustration I would deduct that it is the ambition of every boy to play in the backfield. This backfield dream of the average American boy is a mistake. The young man should play what he is best fitted for by his physique, temperament and natural ability.

Each candidate must decide for himself, after a thorough analysis, what position he is best fitted to play. Whether it is quarterback or guard for which he is fitted, he should then practice diligently to make himself absolutely letter-perfect at that particular position, having no doubt in his mind that there is no better role on the team for him.

Of course, a football candidate must have at least some physique, but physique in the modern game is not as important as it was in the old days. Football is one of the games that requires fine physical condition. This physical condition is necessary for two reasons: First of all, it is necessary in order to have endurance. In the latter part of any football game, the player in poor condition will tire and lose his value to the team, whereas the player in fine condition will be performing as well as ever.

The player in fine condition can take hard blows without unusual shock or danger of injury; these same blows would probably injure the boy not in fine physical condition. This all-important physical fitness is attained primarily through hard work on the field during the long hours of practice.

In order to develop the endurance and stamina necessary to play the game, the player must practice hard. Football, like basketball, wrestling, boxing, running in track events, and swimming, requires endurance.

Practice should be rather easy the first two weeks, regardless of what the candidates have been doing during the summer. If the student has been working rather hard at some job during the summer and is right down to weight, he should work just hard enough to develop a good appetite — he should work just hard enough to get a little tired. He will then eat well and sleep well and put on that little extra weight which will stand him in good stead during the rest of the season.

If he starts practice fat, soft and out of condition because he hasn't been doing anything all summer, he will also have to start work easy. If he starts working too hard he may become discouraged easily and quit, or he might unnecessarily strain himself because of his soft condition in such a way as to unfit himself for football for the rest of the season. If he reports in fair condition, he will find that two weeks of light work is about all he will

need to keep him in condition.

For the first week, we have a competition in which every candidate is taught how to tackle the dummy, which should be considered a stationary ballcarrier. The first thing to learn is correct form, and to develop leg drive. The proper form is to run at the dummy, crouched well forward, with the head up and the eyes open, the knees well bent and the arms extended in front of you. Just before you hit the dummy, straddle your legs a little, crouch lower, and use all the leg drive you have, meeting the dummy squarely with the shoulders with the weight of the body solidly behind you.

Tackle on the dummy until you are letter-perfect. However, you are still not a real tackler. To develop judgment of timing and distance, and to learn to watch the ballcarrier's hips, making him show before you commit yourself, requires some practice in tackling a real ballcarrier. You can pad up one or two boys with some extra pads and use these chaps for the real ballcarriers, and practice tackling them.

The boys should not play a game or scrimmage until after they have had two or three weeks of practice. With two or three weeks of practice, they will have gotten themselves into a condition where they can go out and play without danger of injury. In other words, they will have been practicing until they have arrived at a point where their physical condition is such that they can withstand any ordinary blow without injury, and they will have practiced enough so that they will have developed the ability to know how to avoid unnecessary shocks. Knowing how to fall — absolutely relaxed — is a trick that a boy learns from experience, and I strongly urge every boy who wants to learn to play football that he concentrate on doing this.

A student with only average giftedness in physique and mental aptitude can aspire to and attain his niche in football if he receives careful, meticulous instruction, and he follows it equally, thoroughly, and painstakingly.

Some coaches use a lot of rigmarole and artificial apparatus to teach the various stunts in football, but I don't believe in them. Their greatest value lies in publicity and advertising. Coaches who do not use these devices get better results when it comes to actually playing football.

A football team that is practicing should rehearse those things which, as individuals, they must perform in the positions they are playing in the game. Players should become very proficient in every detail of their positions. A chain is no stronger than its weakest link. If there are no weak links, the chain is considered strong. This concept holds true for a football team as well.

OPENING GAME

We are now getting up to our first game of the season which, we will say, is an easy practice game. The only worry is that the other team will not furnish sufficient practice. Tell your quarterback to kick in danger zone on first down, and kick in kicking zone on third down, because he will have to do this when he gets up against a team as good as ours. Instruct him, in the game, to look for the other team's strong points, because in an easy game like this, it is not wise to play the weak points. Tell your quarterback that the idea in the first game is not to run up a big score and give the whole team an exaggerated idea of their ability, but to get some practice. The chances are that even in an easy game of this sort, the quarterback will make mistakes.

On the day of the game, breakfast should consist of a good steak, a baked potato, toast, coffee, or milk. The breakfast hours should be from seven-thirty until nine (ne heavy meal after ten o'clock). For lunch, a little consommé and toast (it is all right to give a very large man a little roast beef). If the game is called for two o'clock, eat lunch at eleven. If the game is for three o'clock, eat at twelve. An athlete should never eat anything which does not agree with him. Each individual should study his own idiosyncrasies. After an important game, let the men relax and break training to the extent of a dish of ice cream or a piece of pie. This will help them relax and recuperate for the next game.

SECOND GAME

As our next game is with a team that is very strong on defense but not very much on offense, it might be well to sit down with the quarterback once or twice this next week and go over again his strong plays against a normal defense, and then show him how, when the defense shifts to meet these strong plays, they make themselves vulnerable to check plays, delayed bucks, reverse, and other weak side plays.

If we have won the first game mentioned and the quarterback received a certain amount of practice in this work, all is well. You may now go ahead and tell the quarterback that if he tries his strong plays and it fails, that he might call exactly the same play, back over exactly the same spot. Show him where this is good strategy. Show him where in the last game the other team had a dizzy lineman, and he did not send the play right back at him before he had a chance to recover. Show him how he erred in not throwing a forward pass into the zone of a limping defensive halfback. Show him how it would have been good strategy, when the defensive team sent in a new sub-lineman, to have shot the first play directly at him. Show him how he made a mistake in throwing too many forward passes in the first half, as this gave the defensive coach between halves a chance to make corrections in the defense. Show him that the best way to play against a successful back such as the other team had was to put an extra man on him.

Of course, a great many things come along that he might indirectly suggest to the quarterback.

THIRD GAME

Suppose now in the third game you play a team which is very weak against the forward pass. The week previous you will spend a lot of time practicing up the pass attack.

The fact that on the previous two Saturdays we have shown a powerful running attack will be found of great help as the other team's secondary and tertiary defenses must be brought up if a forward pass is to be fully successful.

FOURTH GAME

If in the fourth game we find that we are up against a team with a wonderful defense,

We have to use the bucking machine to develop leg drive and the "forearm shiver" for linemen.

we then start polishing up our kicking game, and we instruct our team before the game to go out and play for the breaks.

Men with injuries must be nursed along. In the game against the team which is weak against passes, we will find that it is possible to get along without several of the men who are not in good physical shape.

Our scrimmaging for the year is now practically over, and we are doing just enough work to keep in top form. We are working towards a climax against the team we are playing in the sixth game. This will be the hardest game of the year.

FIFTH GAME

The fifth team we will play, we will say, is a very powerful offensive team, but quite weak on defense.

Against this team, our quarterback will have instructions to hang on to the ball as long as he can, and not to give it to the other team unless he absolutely has to. No matter what

285

the temptation may be to kick, he must not do so, but must keep rushing.

MIDSEASON

In the middle of the season, I have found it effective on the Monday after a hard game to give the team two or three outlandish plays, trick plays, which they probably will never use. However, they act as a mental tonic to the whole team.

A team will get a lot of fun and new lease of life mentally with these new toys. No plays, however, should be worked which have not been thoroughly drilled and rehearsed in actual scrimmage. It takes a lot of time to develop a play to a point where it becomes effective in a game.

When I see by the newspapers that a coach in midseason is changing his entire offense, I just take that with a grain of salt. There have been isolated cases, of course, where coaches have done things like this, but I have never heard of any case where this was effective. A coach must map out his offense before the season begins, and while he can, of course, put in a lot of variations and so forth, yet the offense must remain basically the same, or he cannot get results. The men on the team are just boys, and they have their limitations.

I do believe it is well to have three or four trick plays in the repertoire, besides the ones just mentioned, as they give the team a lot of confidence. They have something in reserve to call upon in case things get bad in the second half. It is much like a man carrying a revolver feeling much safer about meeting a hold-up man. However, he may be held up so quickly sometime that he will not have a chance to use his gun. And the same thing holds good for the team with the trick plays.

SIXTH GAME

We now come to the big game of the year, the sixth hard game in a row. We will have saved for this game two or three forward pass plays which we have not shown as yet, at least two trick plays, one of which we will try right at the start of the game for the sake of psychology. We will also save our team so that every man is in the pink of condition physically for this big game. If the team we are playing is well-rounded in all branches, we will have to play a safe game and play whatever weapons of attack we find, upon analysis and contact, will work best under the different conditions that arise during the game. Unexpected strength may arise where we didn't expect it, and the big thing is to be able to recognize this immediately.

Also unexpected weaknesses may appear where we least expected it, and the big thing is to be able to recognize these. However, if we have a quarterback and players who are heady enough to find these things and to recognize them, what remains is simple. Play the plays which will not hit the strong points, but which will take advantage of the weak points.

If the team against whom you are playing your first big game is weak at the ends, I would build my attack for the following Saturday along these lines. It must be borne in mind, however, that a powerful, crashing fullback is the threat which will make your ends-runs good.

I would leave nothing undone to win this first big game. This game will either make or break the season. If the team can win this first big game, it will be chuck full of confidence and enthusiasm, and they will play way over their heads whenever called upon later on. If they lose this first big game, it may dampen their ardor for the entire season.

It is true some teams have lost this first big game and then have come back in great form afterwards. This shows fine character in the boys. However, more teams are ruined by losing their first big game than are made.

SEVENTH GAME

Supposing, however, that you have won your first big game, and now find that you play the second big game against a team that is very weak on the line. The thing to do now is to rehearse, very faithfully, one-or two-line plays which were not used the Saturday previous. Concentrate on preparing this style of attack for the next weekend. However, we must keep in mind that a threat of a forward pass and a threat of an end run must be kept constantly in front of the team you are to play, to make your line attack strong.

Take all unnecessary padding off the men before the game, and tell the quarterback to use and play in the repertoire. Nothing is barred except that he must not take unnecessary chances. This is the one game where the team must put everything into it that they have and must leave no stone unturned for success.

Every school has at least one big rival, and if this rival is beaten, the season is a success. This is called THE game. As far as we are concerned, this sixth game is THE game. We may win every other game, but if we lose this, our alumni and student body will not count the season

After this contest we still have one hard game left on the schedule, but we must have gotten up enough momentum during the season to be able to win this game without undue preparation. It will be hard to win because, if we have had success so far, the last game against an easier team will not mean so much to our boys. It will be just a game. However, you must again overrate your opponents and must work just as hard as for any of the other games to have everything ready both on offense and defense.

I have been asked if I believe in resting a Saturday now and then in the middle of the season. I do believe in this very strongly, and in my schedule, I would leave an open Saturday if I could.

However, we have many problems to meet, and so we try to play seven hard games in a row. It would be better if we left one Saturday open after the third hard game so as to give the team a chance to recuperate mentally and physically for the remaining three games.

On the day of the big game keep all relatives, alumni, and well-wishers away from the team. They can do incalculable harm. The only exception to this might be one or two pet alumni who have the "gloom complex" and are therefore helpful as they will have a tendency to impress the men with the seriousness of the opposition.

As you make your talk to the men immediately before the game, do not make the mistake of throwing a barrage of frenzied oratory. Keep all alumni, particularly the weeping criminal lawyer, from making any remarks. Instead, just seriously and earnestly impress upon the men that this is a fighting game that they are about to play, but tell them that you have confidence in them as a fighting team, and as a team that never quits.

"The old guard may die, but it never surrenders."

Rehearse rapidly two or three important features about their offense and defense, and then with a final word on what winning the game means to them, send them out. The coach himself must not be nervous, irascible, and easy to shoot sky-high, but instead should have an air of coolness and confidence. This will also make the team cool and confident, but grimly determined. There must be absolutely no laughing or joking, but instead a solemn air of seriousness.

If you are afraid that a team is over-confident, you might try to impress upon them that their opponents are going to go through them here, there, and everywhere. Impress upon them that losing this game might ruin the whole season, and appeal to their pride. However, over-confidence, once it sets in, is a hard thing to counteract.

Between the halves, allow the men to rest and relax for eight minutes. After they have rested, then talk to them the last five minutes. Make constructive suggestions here and there, and work as hard as you can to keep up the morale. The whole thing is to get your team to realize exactly the situation. Tell them they must have more grit, and more pluck, and greater determination, or they will be beaten.

The coach during the game must be cool and collected, whereas during the constructive period of the season, when most of the coaching is done, the coach must be burning up, so to speak. He must be all enthusiasm, and fired with activity and pep. However, he must be just the opposite of this when the game is in progress. A team must have absolute confidence in his judgement, and they cannot do this if the coach throws any apoplectic fits or raves up and down the side lines about his players and the officials.

The campaign for the entire season should be mapped out ahead of time, though of course, the coach may adapt himself to whatever should arise during the fall. However, a campaign for the entire fall must be mapped out ahead of time and adhered to, to a certain extent.

It is quite easy to prepare for one or two games and win these one or two games. However, in the middle west where coaches have five, six, and seven hard games, the task becomes extremely difficult. This is one of the reasons why football coaches become so irritable that socially they are zero, at least during the ten weeks in the fall.

Section 3: Rockne on Rockne

Meeting all the demands that people put on the football coach makes it impossible for him to keep everyone happy ...

35

STAKEHOLDERS

FATHERS

Sometimes fathers are surprised when their son is not picked to play on the first team. I remember a gentleman who brought his boy to my office one day and gave me a great song and dance about what a great athlete this boy was going to be. I didn't pay any attention to him because all fathers talk the same way. But I do remember that the boy went out for the team, being a great big lad of about six feet, three inches. He made his numerals.

The boy did not come out for spring practice as his time was all taken up with laboratory work. The following September at the opening of school, the same fond parent again appeared in my office with his offspring and in a voice teeming with enthusiasm said, "Coach, look at him. I've had him working out all summer. He's brown as a berry and hard as a rock. There is the greatest end the old school has ever seen."

I became enthusiastic with the father and took the boy over to the equipment room so as to make sure that he got absolutely the best we had in the way of headgear, shoes, and so on.

The next day practice began. Starting out with a light workout, we don't do much the first few days, then gradually increase the vigor. On the eighth day we have scrimmage.

Anytime a boy puts on a suit and goes out and tries, he is all right. But this chap was the exception to the rule. I put him in the scrimmage on that eighth day and the only thing

Next to faculty and student support, I'm strong for alumni enthusiasm.

that kept him in the field of play was the high board fence. So, I moved him on down to the eleventh team and forgot him, as we were in a hurry to get three teams in readiness for our opening game.

We had played about two-thirds of our schedule when one afternoon the same fond father burst into my office and began abusing me all over the place. "What a shame. What a disgrace that a man in your position could be so petty, so little, as to allow personal prejudice on your part to keep the best athlete in school, my son, off the team."

For a few seconds, being caught totally unprepared, I just stared at him. But I finally stammered that if he would come out on the field at 4:30 that afternoon, I would allow his son to scrimmage against the varsity and then we would talk it over.

"All right," said the father as he went out, slamming the door.

At 4:30 the father appeared on the practice field, so I ordered scrimmage. I moved his son from the eleventh team, where he was being preserved in the mothballs, up to scrimmage with the varsity. The freshmen were feeling very peppy that afternoon. We gave this fellow's son the ball and put the varsity on defense. He then proceeded to play what we call a retreating end — no halfback could catch him. He had a look of livid fear on his face that would have made him his fortune in the movies.

"The most loyal support a coach can have — support he should cherish and hold — should come from the student body. ... Faculty may criticize, alumni may criticize, newspapers, and neighbors, but never have I heard the student body criticize in either victory or defeat."

Knute Rockne

I turned around to look at the dad intending to say, "I told you so!" But as I looked at him, I changed my mind. The poor old gentleman was slumped over and aged 10 years in a minute.

It slowly came to me that here was a father who had become all wrapped up in an only son until he had created in his mind an ideal. In high school, this ideal had never been tested, as the boy was a foot taller and 75 pounds heavier than his teammates. Could I have done it over again, I would have taken all the blame and tried to preserve the illusion for the dad, but it was too late.

ALUMNI

Next to faculty and student support, I'm strong for alumni enthusiasm. One of the biggest jobs any coach has on his hands is to take alumni enthusiasm and direct it into the right channels — to curb, for example, the zealous alumnus who takes it upon himself to visit the presidents of important schools and demand to know why they do not include his alma mater in their football schedule.

The head of an Eastern university once wrote me asking what he should do with such a fellow. I wired him pithily: "Throw him out."

THE OLD GRAD GROWLS

Toward the semi-paternal alumnus who follows the team wherever it goes, pursuing its star players with a fervid friendliness, the coach must be more charitable.

Notre Dame has several of these perpetual college boys on its roster of fans. One I know makes it his life work to follow the team. In a game once, remarkable for the verbal hostility leveled at our players, it didn't look as if we had a friend in the place when suddenly a raucous voice began a series of yells that let us know our alumni were not unrepresented. This one-man cheering section shouted so prodigiously that he won over a large number of neutrals and before the end of the game we were in possession of a lustily vocal proportion of the spectators.

This chap was a blessing. I have known alumni to be the opposite. When we played Indiana a few seasons back, it was hard going. The game should have been easily won if comparative scores in past games meant anything, and as a rule they don't. But the Indiana boys, to their credit, were handily winning. Sensing the loss of this annual game, the Notre Dame team stiffened and we managed to squeeze through with a victory.

It seemed to me to be an occasion for rejoicing at the banquet following the game, which turned out to be one of the hardest-won victories on our schedule. I observed a few fans at the dinner were anything but elated. Making inquiries I learned that these fellows had made considerable bets to the effect that

293

*A football coach must also understand public opinion
regarding the school and its athletic reputation ...*

their old school would win by at least three or four touchdowns. This was confirmed by the growling of the disappointed gamblers.

The good ole boys heard from me when I gave a speech. I was bristling, and, I fear, lit into those inconsiderate chaps with a vehemence that shocked them. They were reminded that boys who went on the gridiron and gave the best there was in them were entitled to better than money support. It didn't add to the harmony of the occasion, but it provided one fine chance for one coach to do what at some time or other every coach would like to do — put the gamblers in their places.

I believe a lot of our alumni, much more than our student body, are taking the game of football a little too seriously. I do not believe that this is fair to the coach or to the game itself. I believe that the alumnus who has just seen his team go down in defeat should take every factor into consideration before he puts too much blame on the coach or any of the individual players.

There are a lot of things which may lose football games. First, there is the fact that the team may have too hard a schedule, poorly arranged, and with a bad anticlimax. Secondly, a team may be crippled at just the wrong time through losing one or two valuable men. Thirdly, there may be bad breaks in the game, such as dropping forward passes or fumbling, over which the coach has no control. Again, the team may be tired and stale from too much traveling and may not be able to play its best in one or two games.

Last, and very important, is the fact that

what has appeared to be very fine material may prove to be very inferior material. If men who may have been coaching 20 and 30 years cannot tell whether or not a man is a good football player until he has been tested and tried, how can a lot of lawyers, doctors and barbers have such an expert point of view that they can look over a squad the first week out for practice and say with absolute certainty that "there" is a wonderful material?

There are many, many other factors which we need not go into here, and which our alumni would appreciate if they were brought to their attention. However, the alumni should realize that loyalty isn't worth a nickel unless it works both ways. If the team shows it has been well-coached, fights to the last ditch, and lives up to every tradition of the old school as regards to sportsmanship, morale and physical condition, the alumni should not feel bitter if the team is beaten now and then.

The most successful schools in athletics are those which have retained coaches over long periods. The most unsuccessful schools in athletics are those which allow their alumni to have them chasing rainbows. I mean by this that they keep looking for the "miracle man" to coach their team. Practical experience would show them that there is no such man. If they get a fairly good man, they had better keep him.

The alumni expect the coach and the team to be intensely loyal. The alumni can show their loyalty by their actions in defeat and standing by the team and coach, particularly when in other years this same team and coach have had a fair measure of success.

THE COMMUNITY

A football coach must also understand public opinion regarding the school and its athletic reputation as it exists in the community where the school is located. Likewise, he must — if he wants to be successful or even hold his job — analyze the alumni attitude and decide when he should give them what they want and when he should oppose them for wanting too much. A great deal of the coach's work and more than a great deal of the coach's woes await him far from the gridiron's madding crowds.

With the old grads and the neighbors, the coach must build goodwill for the benefit of his team. It's fatal to high-hat the people in the community where the school is located. It's good to accept the support of Rotary, Kiwanis and the rest, they provide a background of enthusiasm which is bound to inspire the players.

I make it a rule never to take criticism too seriously. Walking into a barber shop a day or two after a game, especially a game in which we've been defeated, it takes the edge off everything to bow to the assembled barbers and customers and ask jovially: "Good morning, how are all the coaches today?"

Meeting all the demands that people put on the football coach makes it impossible for him to keep everyone happy. I believe the public should be informed that the tickets are not handled by the coach.

The pasteboards are handled by the business office, always. For some reason, or other, every fellow who is late in purchasing his ducats for a game gets in touch with someone who knows the football coach. And then he either phones, wires, writes or personally accosts the coach with a long dry story about something or other. Gradually he leads up to the coup d'état, which is, "How about some tickets?"

These little affairs in themselves are not bad except when their numbers multiply.

However, I do object to being called up by long distance after midnight by chaps with Scotch instincts.

One coach I know has four form letters now which he sends out in reply to all ticket moochers. No. 1 is for those he doesn't know at all. No. 2 is for those he knows faintly. No. 3 is for those he knows very well. And No. 4 is for those he has to know.

I am suggesting that this teacher of football add a fifth form letter to include those he doesn't want to know.

However, of all the annoying pests, I have to award the brown derby to the chromo who obtains a couple of ducats on the morning of a sellout and then inquires in an egg-nog voice, "Are these on the fifty-yard line?"

The job of selling football tickets for a college football game is fraught with perils. The manager of ticket sales hasn't a chance. Someone has to sit around the goal line or even behind the goal posts, and what they have to say about the blankety-blank hound who sold them their tickets has fortunately never been printed.

No matter if the fans are alumni, neighbors or just plain customers at the gates, they seem to like bigger and better scores. For my part, they'll get the best games that can be given by the material in hand. But it is folly to pile up scores at the expense of weak opponents just to gratify the vanity of some unscrupulous fans. It's unfair to the opposite team and to one's own players. A game won by a point is nonetheless won, and better to watch than a one-sided contest.

I have found that the best relations prevail when opposing teams are treated with respect and fairness. When they lose, they appreciate not being martyred to make a football holiday. And when they win, there's nothing they admire more than an utter absence of alibis on the part of the defeated college and coach.

In football, as in everything else, it's impossible to please everybody. Bask in the sunshine of a winning schedule. But a difficult schedule is the only schedule worthwhile, for "buffer," or "rest" games, induce a letdown. You may even win your way through a half dozen tough assignments. And when you are congratulating yourself on results, remember, some busy soul is preparing a brickbat to aim at your lifted head.

DRAWBACKS

There is a time each year when much is said and written about the line, the halfbacks, the fullbacks and the quarterbacks. There is one position on the team, however, concerning which the comments are much neglected. The stars who fill this position have not received their just due by way of credit, eulogy, and special banquet.

I refer to the men who successfully play the position of "drawback" for many a high school and college team. Every team has its "drawbacks" and they come from many classes. Perhaps it would be better to define who are the "drawbacks" before picking the All-American "Drawback."

Drawback Coach: This is the hombre who has never lost a football game. His boys may have been defeated now and then, but this coach has never lost a contest. He has developed the alibi to a point of perfection where it will cover any shortcomings and any defeats, and he can explain any situation with the facile ease of a hen-pecked husband.

Big Hearted Alumnus Who Only Wants To Help: This is the fellow who always wants to know why so-and-so on the third string isn't

With the old grads and the neighbors, the coach must build goodwill for the benefit of the team.

playing regular. He talks to several members of the third string and convinces these third stringers that they ought to be regulars, creating a spirit of content and happiness on the whole squad that certainly is a great help to the poor coach who knows nothing about picking them.

The Tin-Horn Sport: This is the fellow who helps the team by betting on it. When the team wins, he is a great fellow and talks glowingly about the team, referring to the coach, and puts several of these young players, 19 and 20 years of age, severely on the pedestal.

If he should happen to lose 50 dollars, he deserts the team like a rat deserts a sinking ship. He generally becomes the new chairman of the committee of research with self-delegated power to hire a new coach.

Provincial Newspaper Writer: This man's loyalty to his own team in his hometown is so intense that he will admit that no other team can be quite as good as his, nor can his team or school ever do any wrong. He stands for breadth of vision and a square deal — for his team.

The Over-Fond Father: This is the proud parent who insists the coach doesn't know his business in case he doesn't put his son on the team.

Rumble Seat Cowboy: This is the member of the football squad who does not train and whose influence on the rest of the squad is to help them socially and sartorially. He could make the team if he ever had a chance. He celebrates with laughter and gayety just as hard when the team loses as when it wins — but "talks" a great game.

Professor Pop-Off: This very estimable gentleman generally chooses the month of January for his annual tirade against athletics of all kinds, and particularly against the salaries of coaches. At the time of the late unpleasantness with Germany, this gentleman was exempt from the draft because of flat feet and weak lungs.

The Sunday Morning Field General: This man is either a barber, a bank president or a dentist who gives out expert advice on Sunday morning as to what should have been done Saturday.

Assistant Coach Who Will Not Return Next Year: This man's work was unappreciated, particularly when he told members of the third string that if he were coaching, they would be playing regular. He also hinted to influential alumni that there would have been no games lost if he had been coach.

It can readily be seen, therefore, that the competition for the All-American drawback position will be remarkably keen, and with the aforesaid information there should be no difficulty for any readers to pick the All-American drawback in his particular vicinity. In case there is much difference of opinion, a committee should be formed that can score the competitors' points and, by the process of close elimination, determine the man who has been the greatest drawback.

I want to say that in all my experience, I have yet to see a lad with enough gumption to put on a suit and work out, trying to do his best, ever lacking in courage or could ever be rightly accused of having the broad light-colored streak up his back. I have sometimes seen boys who were shy and bashful, or perhaps phlegmatic and lacking in natural aggressiveness, who were sometimes called harsh names by the fearless spectators, but the spectators were all wrong and unfair.

WHY COACHES GET GRAY

Accidents can crowd thrills into a game even more than design.

Against Minnesota in 1926, Joe Boland, left tackle for Notre Dame, in trying to block a punt, had his leg broken by one of his own teammates.

It was our ball. On the first play after that, Freddy Collins, our fullback, hit the line resulting in his jaw broken in three places. Out he came to take his place in the ambulance alongside of Boland.

After replacing both men, I didn't know whether to cry or laugh at these savage breaks. The team lined up, and on our next play Ray "Bucky" Dahman, right halfback, ran 70 yards for a touchdown. I came down to earth. Over the telephone came a message from Boland and Collins.

"We're all through. All we can do is get the score when the game is over."

I repeated the message to the team. In the second half on the first play, Flanagan ran 70 yards for a touchdown.

The following year, there were more thrills from Doc Spears' steamroller team. Niemiec scored early in the game. It looked as if Flanagan might cut loose at any moment, but the Gopher tackling was sure and tenacious. It completely nullified our running attack.

Section 3: Rockne on Rockne

There's no trace of bunk when I tell you that turning out star players is not as thrilling as seeing these men go from the gridiron to make good in business and the professions.

36

WHEN THE IRISH FOUGHT

"With an even break the success at football will be a success when he faces the sterner contest of economic competition for jobs and sales, or what not. He learns more than how to kick and carry a ball on the gridiron. Courage, teamwork and quick-wittedness are developed there."

Knute Rockne

There are the situations in which the so-called expert — as a coach — does not revel.

A good Notre Dame team was literally swept off its feet by a good Northwestern team in 1925. It shouldn't have been. I was disgusted. They had played listlessly and without much spirit. At half, the score was 10 — 0 in favor of Northwestern. The team returned to the dressing room between halves, and shortly afterward I entered.

With a disgusted look on my face, and in my most sarcastic tone, I inquired:

"So, this is the so-called 'Fighting Irish.' You look to me like a lot of peaceful sissies. Well, I have been here too long to stand for this kind of nonsense, and I quit.

"I resign. Right now!

"Tom, take charge of the team. As far as I am concerned, I never want to see any of you again. And in my mind your names will always be mud!"

A good Notre Dame team was literally swept off its feet by a good Northwestern team ... It shouldn't have been. I was disgusted.

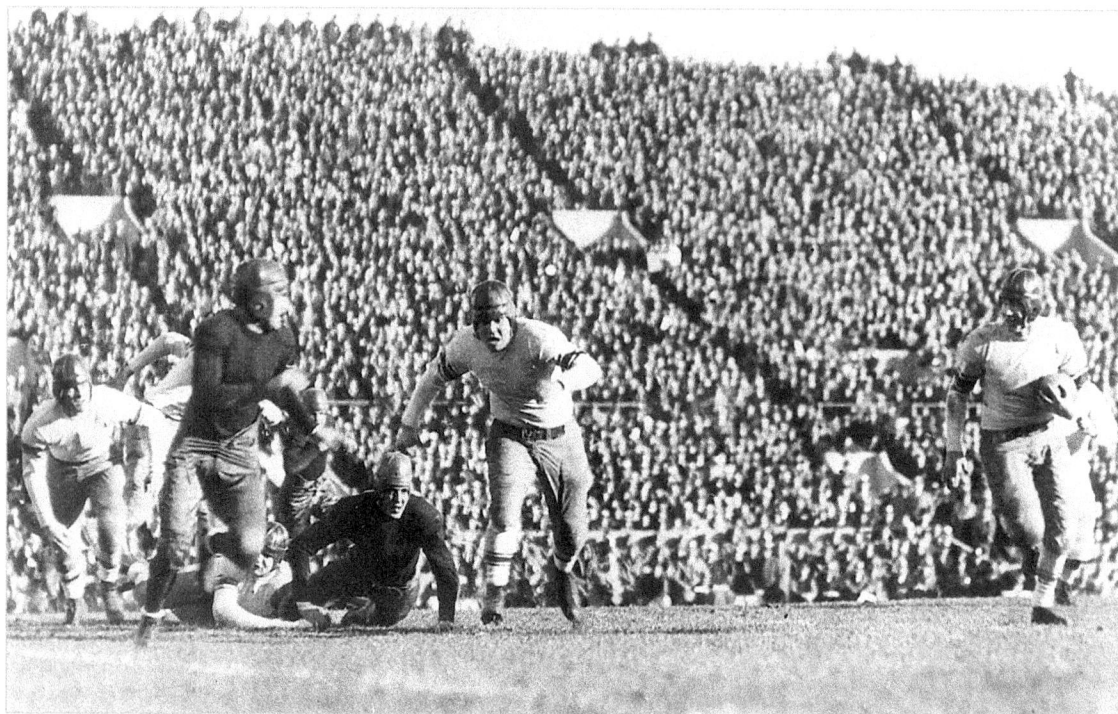

I left abruptly and stood near the entrance of the field. About six minutes later I felt a light movement of air beside me. I turned to see the team breezing through the gates with tears running down their cheeks and muttering to themselves.

Although they had made but one first down in the first half, in this next half they pushed Northwestern all over the field to the astonishment of the Northwestern rooters, not to mention the Northwestern players.

Down the field they went from the kickoff — 80 yards for a score.

Down they went, again — 80 yards again, and another score.

Only three types of plays were used in these marches for touchdowns. Christie Flanagan and Rex Enright alternately carried the ball.

In the final period, with the score 13 — 10, I replaced these lads; they were utterly exhausted. They had staged the superb thrill of a triumphant comeback.

No modern coach tries this sort of thing, because to every mental action there is bound to be an equal and opposite reaction. Playing with boys' emotions is a dangerous thing, and the coach who does so must pay for it.

Of course, there are times when the whole season may depend on winning a certain game, and in that case many of the old-time coaches have resorted to such tricks.

Our first big game of the season one year was with Georgia Tech. Winning the game was important as the loss would probably mean that our green team would go to pieces for the rest of the season.

So, I determined to win the game if possible.

Just before the game I read several telegrams to the team, and then one to the effect that my little boy, Billy, had suddenly become very seriously ill. Quite ill, in fact, and the telegram from my wife stated that the only thing that seemed to be worrying him was whether or not Daddy's team would win.

She added, as I read the imaginary telegram, that she felt that if the team won, it would be the best thing that could happen for poor little Billy.

Needless to say, the team went out keyed to a razor edge and their tackling was the talk of Atlanta for many a day. In fact, David "Red" Barron fumbled seven times that day from the effects of just sheer wild crushing tackles.

But I can never use anything similar to this again. In fact, now, years afterwards, whenever I meet one of the old team, his lips will break into a sardonic grin as he inquires:

"Well, how is your boy Bill?"

This is the first and last time I expect to do anything like this, as I receive many a jibe from the old boys who played in these games whenever I meet them. As I look back on it, however, they were sweet games to win, and perhaps in the exceptional circumstances the psychology was warranted.

A QUARTER'S WORTH

Pop Warner's team was a fine combination in 1925, the last appearance of the Four Horsemen.

Ernie Nevers could do everything. He tore our line to shreds, ran the ends, forward-passed and kicked. True, we held him on one occasion four downs on the one-yard line, but by that time Nevers was exhausted and I had sent in two fresh guards and a fresh tackle — almost as good as the regulars — to stop this fury in football boots.

Nevers labored mightily that day, and 80,000 people who saw the game do not realize that he was really entitled to a better break than 27 — 10. But for several unwise plays, that great Stanford fullback would have turned in different figures.

Twice, Stanford came 50 yards down the field with Nevers lugging the ball for first down after first down. Twice, out of a clear sky, the quarterback called for a dangerous pass-play throw to one side so that it couldn't be covered, which, on each occasion, was intercepted by Layden and converted into a touchdown for Notre Dame.

Just as a coach winces when he sees a faulty play, so he thrills at a great quarterback — even when this lad's fighting him. Howard Harpster of Carnegie Tech gave me fits in 1928.

After the kickoff, Harpster saw Freddy Collins, with a broken arm in a cast, limping badly, and in the first play he threw a forward pass to Rosenzweig, who ran past Collins for the first touchdown. This happened before I could remove Collins.

Two minutes later he saw our defensive guard out of position and he sent Rosenzweig on an end-around play, and cut back through that gap for another touchdown. I sent in a new guard and plugged up that gap, but the harm had all been done.

Harpster had done the thinking first. A great passer, a great punter, a great returner of punts, he had also the supreme confidence of a fine quarterback, his only fault being that he sometimes took chances when it wasn't necessary.

A MIGHTY ATOM

Naturally, teams take advantage of disabled players, but rarely do they violate the football code by purposely punishing a man apparently hurt. On the contrary, there is always a display of gallantry on the field.

In 1915, our center, Hugh O'Donnell, had a broken rib. He was to play against John McEwan of Army, supposed to be one of the roughest centers in football. Harry Tuttle, the Army trainer, heard of this injury and came in with a special pad for O'Donnell.

Just as play began, McEwan asked O'Donnell: "Which side is the broken rib on?"

O'Donnell pointed to it. There were 60 minutes of hard football, but not once did any Army player, least of all McEwan, touch O'Donnell's broken rib.

The code in football is: Take advantage of a cripple by running around him on forward passing, but never hurt him.

Big schools give the big thrills, but they can also come in small school games. Often in an obscure place, a great player will shine, unknown to headlines.

Such a man was Rody Lamb, quarterback of Lombard, who played against Notre Dame in 1924. He weighed 150 pounds and could do everything, an exceedingly dangerous man in open field. His spunk and daring were captivating. Where we had expected a trial pushover, we had a real football game that challenged all our resources.

Accidentally, on a head-on tackle,

this versatile human whirlwind had his knee wrenched and had to leave the game. Immediately, the game changed to a romp and Notre Dame added 40 points.

TOMMY FARRELL

Some years ago, I had a third-string end, a young lad by the name of Tommy Farrell. Tommy made all the trips East with us that year, when we played the Army, Princeton and Carnegie Tech, but he did not get in for a single play.

We wound up the season that year with St. Louis University at St. Louis. All day long, it was raining pitchforks and it rained all during the game. As is customary on such days, while we were in the dressing room before the game, I went to the trunk and took out a package of resin and spilled it on the floor in the middle of the room.

Turning to the team I said:

"Today, our tactics will be to kick, kick, and kick. Let the other team carry the ball and do the fumbling, and to make sure that we won't fumble, I want everybody to put plenty of resin on his jersey and pants so that when you get hold of the ball you won't lose it."

The boys started lining up and rubbing the resin on their jerseys and pants, "resining up" as we call it, and I stood to one side sort of musing about the game.

The last fellow in line was Tommy Farrell. When his turn came, instead of picking the resin up in his hands and putting it on his jersey and pants, he sat down in it and started wriggling around.

Our captain, Harvey Brown, stared at him and said, "What's the idea, Tom?"

"Gee whiz," said Tom, "didn't you hear what the coach said? What do you want me to

304

Ernie Nevers could do everything ...

Just as a coach winces when he sees a faulty play, so he thrills at a great quarterback even when this lad's fighting him... Howard Harpster of Carnegie Tech gave me fits in 1928.

do this afternoon, slip off the bench?"

This was very amusing at the time. Incidentally, we beat St. Louis 13 — 0 that afternoon, and I put Tommy in for the last minute of play.

Tommy was a senior that year. He graduated without having won his monogram. During his four years, three on the first team, he had gone out there and practiced, scrimmaged, and in every way gave the best of himself.

You may ask the question: What did he

get out of it? Well, first of all, if he hadn't gone out for football, what would he have gone out for?

Now, I have three boys of my own in whom I am highly interested, the same as your dads are interested in you. I am not worried about these boys when they are in school, in church, or with their Boy Scout Troop, or when they are at home, but I am worried about them when they are playing around. Their recreation can be either constructive or destructive.

The chances are, Tommy might have gone out for some of the other sports, or he might have gone downtown and got into the wrong environment.

Tommy could have decided to go around with a group of fellows who gambled and wasted their time, and if he wasn't expelled from the University the least that could have happened to him would be a lot of expensive and worthless habits.

But instead, he went out for football. He learned to take his hard knocks without whimpering. He learned to play the game fairly. He learned to give all he had and regardless of how hopeless the outlook, he kept trying.

Tommy learned the habits of clean living. He learned what things to eat and not to eat, and he learned how to keep fit physically.

He also learned not to be afraid. He learned by his various experiences, scrimmaging against the varsity, that courage pays. There were afternoons when Tommy had to scrimmage against the varsity, and he did not want to. But he found that it did not pay to run away, and that after all the scrimmaging against the varsity, it was just a lot of fun.

Tommy is a prosperous banker now. He plays golf in the summer time, and in the winter time he plays squash rackets. Whereas, many of our businessmen burn out at 40, the chances are that Tommy, because of the habits he learned while going out for the football team, will be good for 20 years longer than the chap who hasn't learned how to take care of himself.

Tommy has also learned how to think under pressure. If there is one place a young man in high school or college must have resourcefulness and razor-edge thinking qualities, it is in football, so as not to pass up any opportunities that might present themselves.

I have had games where my team has been decisively beaten, and yet such a team I had several years ago gave me the greatest thrill of my coaching history, even though it had lost several games.

Why? Because those boys came back against a great Army team, and playing better than they knew how, lived up to every fine tradition of their school. They kept trying in spite of some bad breaks, and finally, through sheer determination, beat this Army team.

And as they ran for me after the game, these lads seemed to say: "Well, Coach, we were down but we weren't out." And how they played together! Every player was helping the other to bring a united front against their opponents.

Tommy was one of those lads who did not play, but he worked just as hard as he could. In practice, he helped furnish the opposition and the competition that made the first team what it was.

There is an old saying that, "You can't take any more out of an organization than you put into it." Tommy had put his heart and soul into his college football team for four years, and he took out of it all these points that I have been mentioning. But, greater than that, he earned the love and the lifelong friendship of his coach and of those gallant lads who were out there struggling, playing, and giving — his teammates.

"Greater reward hath no man."

There's an old saying that, "An apple that is ripe begins to rot -the growing apple, chances are, will not rot."

In other words, we all keep learning and improving, or we decay. This truth applies to everything we do in this life and makes the game of football a game from which we can learn many valuable lessons to "carry on" after we are through school and are out playing the big business game, or playing the game in some profession.

No matter how tough the going, no matter how bad the situation may appear, remember this:

A winner never quits... and a quitter never wins.

THE ADVOCATE

Divided authority brought chaos into the administration of rules for the game until Walter Camp stepped into the breach and, by tact and judgment, reconciled the two rule-making bodies ...

37

THE RULES

I was sitting with a group of old-timers in the East enduring quite a bit of good-natured twitting from one of them who had played football for almost 30 years ago.

He jabbed me rather deftly with his remarks regarding modern football, describing it as a degenerate mishmash of rugby, basketball, pom-pom-pullaway, and correct social etiquette, compared to how rough the game was played in those days. He bragged about the good old he-man days of that period.

These things may seem semi-humorous when discussed by old timers 30 years afterwards, but I am afraid that this old-timer is doomed to disappointment if he ever expects those days will return.

There's no question that in the push-and-pull, mass-on-tackle plays, there was much rough stuff that added nothing to the game and that could well be eliminated — and with the hue and cry gathering momentum against football, something needed to be done.

The game of football has come a long way since the freshmen at such schools as Harvard, Princeton and Rutgers were informally kicking around an inflated pig's bladder, playing an impromptu game having few or no rules. Interest in this game developed, and as it grew, it became necessary to have definite rules, particularly when a group of students in one school informally challenged a similar group from another.

Up until 1876, Yale, Princeton, Harvard and Rutgers had played a few contests, using in some cases a modification of the association game and in other cases a modification of English

*... while the rules functioned smoothly... the game was
still exceedingly rough under those rules ...*

rugby. These same schools met with Columbia in a convention at Springfield, Massachusetts, in 1876, where American football was born by introducing two distinct departures from the English game of rugby.

The first of these was that the center should pass the ball to a quarterback, who, in turn, could pass it to any one of his players behind him — which differed considerably from the rather indiscriminate scrum as known in rugby. In that English game, the score was computed by field goals.

At the Springfield meeting, the Americans changed the rules so as to make four touchdowns equal to a field goal. This was the start of the game as we know it today.

The great Walter Camp, who did more for American football than any other individual, was a freshman on the Yale team that fall. For 40 years thereafter, he was largely responsible for the evolution of the game to its present form.

This informal Rules Committee began functioning in 1876 and continued to do so until 1899, when there was a severe rupture. Two football tribunals appeared on the scene, one composed of Navy, Princeton and Yale, the other of Cornell, Harvard and Pennsylvania. Previous to this time, the Rules Committee, while not representative of the whole country, made rules for the rest of the schools, and these rules were accepted around the country through recognition of the merit and labor of the committee.

Followers of the game — not many in those days — watched plays like the murderous flying wedge of Deland of Harvard and all the other attendant rough phases of the game. Divided authority brought chaos into the administration of rules for the game until Walter Camp stepped into the breach and, by tact and judgment, reconciled the two rule-making bodies, which merged into one committee, which functioned smoothly until 1905.

But while the rules functioned smoothly — that is, without divided authority in legislating for football — the game was still exceedingly rough under those rules. Examine the records available and you'll find that heavier teams invariably defeated lighter teams, and certainly that the lighter team suffered much larger casualties. The hard drive without recourse to deceptive tactics in and back of the line — except tricks of an elementary kind like the hidden ball — gave the bullnecked boys a devastating edge over smaller if brainier opponents.

By the winter of 1906, the game of football was in a bad plight. Long lists of fatalities and injuries, due to the heavy mass and wedge plays then in vogue, had aroused public opinion. There was a huge cry against the game. Some colleges had dropped football, and certain legislatures threatened to put a ban on the game.

About this time, a meeting of most of the large colleges was called and recommendations were passed about the game and sent to the Rules Committee. This meeting, by the way, was the start of the present National Collegiate Athletic Association.

As a result of these recommendations, the Rules Committee of that year initiated a series of radical changes designed to open up the game and get away from the horrific mass plays. The rule calling for five yards in three downs was changed to 10 yards. The onside kick and forward pass were introduced, the latter proving to be the vital innovation. True, it was hampered by a lot of restrictions, but nevertheless it offered great opportunity for an inventive game.

The fall of 1908 saw some innovations in the execution of the pass play. Three teams, St. Louis University, Carlisle and the University of Chicago used the pass successfully against all their opponents. They used the long spiral pass and the receivers caught the ball more as the ball is caught in baseball. The defense seemed absolutely unable to cope with this new weapon. The defense appeared not to know what to do to defend against this pass and a running attack at the same time.

The passes in those days were all advertised in advance, but even so, they were successful. The end ran down the field with no attempt at a change of pace or direction, but just apparently trying to out-run the safety. Some teams still use this tactic today, but these passes are easily broken up. In fact, the very next year, the defense caught up with the pass and the development of the pass was delayed for several years.

The impediment was due, however, as much to the rules as it was to the defense. In the fall of 1909, most teams made use of the fact

... All the muscles of the hands and the arms should be relaxed and they should give when the ball is caught.

that the rules still allowed pushing and pulling so that the game again became a brute strength proposition. The restriction on the pass limited its use to only in a pinch and as a threat.

An increase in the number of injured men prompted the Rules Committee the following spring to make another attempt to eliminate mass play and its attendant casualties.

They made what has since been shown to be the most radical change in football: They made it illegal for a teammate to help the carrier of the ball in any way except as an interferer. Pushing or pulling the man with the ball was eliminated and now, for the first time, the knell of the mass play was sounded.

The offense, however, found itself unable to advance against a determined defense. In the next two years, we saw most of the big games ending in a deadlock or being decided by goals from the field. Gaining 10 yards in three downs against a team of equal strength seemed an impossible task. It became apparent that the offense would have to be strengthened if the game were to hold the interest of the public.

Having in mind this strengthening of the offense, the Rules Committee, the following spring, made the last of the radical changes.

The 20-yard restriction on the forward pass was removed; in other words, the pass could now be thrown an unlimited distance. Another change made it possible for one to catch a pass in a 10-yard zone created behind the goal line. The real development of the pass can truly be said to have begun in the fall of 1912.

This part about the forward pass could go somewhere else as was done with the shift... The evolution of various kinds of passes has gradually progressed since 1912. First, we had the group pass, the fan pass, and later the spot pass. The screen pass, with its many modifications, began to be developed that year.

Later we have come to witness tackle-eligible plays, delayed passes, the use of men as decoys, the use of a screen for the protection of the receiver, the pass after an apparent line buck, the optional pass, the bifocal pass — all these had their origin in the years following 1912.

If a forward pass is to be successful, the eligible man must be able to get away from the defensive player.

No matter what kind of a pass is used, the method employed is one of six which, briefly enumerated, are as follows: using a change of pace; using a sharp change of direction; faking as if to block or actually blocking for an instant, and then breaking fast for an open space; hiding behind a screen; following a decoy at the proper time; revolving completely around and having the pass so timed that the ball is shot into a pocket at the proper instant.

In regard to the throwing end of the pass, no pass is going to be successful long unless the play is carefully covered up so that the intent is concealed until the moment of execution. The defense must be given no hint as to the nature of the play.

The several methods by which the offensive team can cover up are as follows: One man may fake a line buck and then shoot the ball back to another back, who forward passes; the passer may fake a run and then pass; the passer may fake a kick and then pass; the passer may fake a pass, then run a short distance as if panicky, and then pass; the passer may crouch down low so as to be hid behind interference and then pass; one man may take an end run and then pass the ball back to another man, who passes.

No matter which of these methods is used, perfection of execution is the thing that makes the play go.

The receiver of the pass should run, relaxed from the waist up, and should catch the ball in his hands like a baseball. The fingers of the hand should be spread wide, but not tensed. All the muscles of the hands and the arms should be relaxed and they should give when the ball is caught. The receiver must run fast and, when turning to look for the ball, should turn his head from the neck only. It is not necessary to turn at the waist. The defensive back can sometimes be fooled by the receiver cleverly using his eyes to deceive.

The passer must learn to throw a "light" ball, which is done by always throwing the ball over the shoulder, with the forward point up. The ball should not be spun, and the passer must learn to follow through. In getting the ball and faking an end run, the passer must learn to adjust the ball in his hands without looking at it. He must carry it in such a way that the ball can be thrown quickly.

Most passers have a tendency to hold on to the ball too long. The passer must be a man who does not get panicky under pressure, but instead is cool, collected and decisive.

The forward pass as an offensive weapon is of itself not worth much. Mixed in with a versatile offensive, which includes strong thrusts plays, powerful sweeps, and a deep kicker, it may become an overwhelming factor.

TAMING THE ROUGHING

The game was in modified shambles throughout its early history. It was Walter Camp, Alonzo Stagg and other leaders in the game who tried to devise rules against roughness — and did.

But what the game needed was not rules that could be violated with impunity in the rush and confusion of play, but a new device in the game itself to make its playing less hazardous.

Stagg at Chicago and Henry L. Williams at Minnesota pioneered the evolutions and gyrations of the football shift — the dramatic equalizer between "big" teams and "little" teams.

The shift quickly became popular. It was new and spectacular and gave the football fans a chance to see something of the game besides mass huddles, flying wedges, and then stretcher-bearers taking the injured off the field. Likewise, it stimulated coaches to real thought, for they had to devise defenses to meet the shift and variations of the shift to penetrate old-time defenses.

The shift and the forward pass have done much to popularize football. About a third of the teams in the country, high school and college use the shift in some form or other. Football fans from coast to coast love to watch it. Evidently, they realize that without the shift the game would often become dull and monotonous.

Boys who have played football on teams using the shift attack never can or will go back to the "set and wait" method of advancing the ball. This used to be called set and go, but set and wait is better. That's exactly what many teams do.

Many of the coaches that wanted rules against the shift tried to play it once themselves, but not with conspicuous success. The matter of timing, rhythm and counting is complicated, but not difficult when fully grasped. The shift provides the advantage of deployment — of catching an opponent out of position and off-balance.

The Four Horsemen could never have played football under the old rules without the shift. These four lads averaged in weight 158 pounds, and the qualities that made them remarkable were not bruising strength or crushing power, nor was it irresistible momentum — but brains, speed, cleverness, finesse and superb strategy.

The leading schools from the point of view of impressive records last year were the University of Southern California and St. Mary's on the Pacific Coast, Purdue and Notre Dame in the Midwest, Tulane and Florida in the South, with New York University in the East. All were shifting teams.

The shift is now an integral part of football. If it is ever restricted to more than a second or abolished, much of the spectacle of football will go with it. And the battering, bruising game may yet return to put beef at a premium and brains at a discount.

Or perhaps a shifting team will be driven to the necessity when the officials are timing the shift to time the timers. It complicates rules already somewhat difficult for the public, which supports the game, to understand fully.

One thing stands out in my football experience though: The officials who enforce the rules are almost invariably fair.

*In only a few cases... were the spectators treated to the colorful,
thrilling sight of a man catching the ball and ten others forming
themselves into an interference in front of him to dash down the field.*

I've seen cases where officials have erred, mistakes of judgment, and rarer cases where they have erred in their knowledge of the rules. But in all my years, I know of only one time an official was prejudiced and unfair.

In this game, we thought the official was somewhat biased. It happened when both teams were near the sideline and there came a fumble. First our opponents had possession, then Notre Dame took possession, after which the ball went out of bounds. Our captain came quickly forward and shouted to the referee, "Notre Dame's ball!" The referee strode forward belligerently and said, "No, no! Our ball!"

The Rules of the game, however, can make it or ruin it. It would be possible to bring up rule after rule and show how it might be improved. As things stand, however, we have a workable code, even if it is elaborate. The bane of coaches, officials, and the Rules Committee freaks with legal or legalistic minds — not one and the same thing, but many and different — who propound hypothetical questions seeking to add new rules as if there were not enough.

317

All the rules, as written, cover every conceivable circumstance or "break" in the game. This does not prevent the pundits from asking ludicrous questions.

For instance, what if Harvard has timeout and the water boy is on the field with the water bucket? Two minutes time allowed is up, and the referee blows his whistle that play must resume. The teams line up. Harvard is in punt formation and Yale in defense. The water boy is slow leaving the field. Before he makes it to the sidelines, the Harvard center snaps the ball back to the kicker and the kick goes to one side, the ball lands in the water bucket, and the water boy carries it off the field. What is the rule?

Suppose Stanford is playing California. Stanford is on California's 40-yard line and it's fourth down. They elect to take place-kick formation. The Stanford center snaps the ball and Stanford's quarterback places the ball on the ground for his kicker. The kicker, however, can't reach the ball before a California guard has broken through and run full tilt into the ball, causing the ball to go in the opposite direction and lo and behold, it goes between the goalposts. What is the referee's call?

Here is another example. Michigan is playing Illinois. The Michigan team takes punt formation and their punter punts 50 yards down the field to the Illinois receiver. He catches the ball, but instead of running with it, kicks it back 50 yards, where it is caught by the Michigan kicker, who hasn't moved an inch. The Michigan kicker now, instead of kicking back, throws a long forward pass down the field to one of his ends and the end crosses the goal line, scoring a touchdown. What will the referee rule?

These hypothetical questions can all be answered satisfactorily by any official who knows the rules thoroughly. But the average spectator should not worry about hypothetical questions of this kind, because they are not likely to ever happen.

Theodore Roosevelt, apostle and exemplar of the strenuous life, decided one day that football was far too strenuous. There was a public cry against a game that resulted in scores of casualties every year. President Roosevelt summoned to a White House conference, representatives of the then truly-called Big Three — Yale, Harvard and Princeton — and urged upon them the necessity of saving football from public disfavor by revising the rules to give brain a chance over brawn.

When somebody at the conference chided the president that as he personally lived a strenuous life he should let football players do likewise without his interference, Roosevelt made a characteristic reply: "These players are boys who must be protected against the natural recklessness of youth. I believe the game can be made more interesting and less brutal without in any way impairing its manliness."

I agree with the president, but a search of football annals does not show that his sound judgment was instantly recognized by others. The savage, battering-ram style of play went on, probably because that was all the coaches knew or cared to teach their players. Turtle-back, guard-back, and tackle-back plays with their solid smash and impact that always meant bruised bodies and often broken bones went on for a while as if the president had not intervened. Memory goes back to games witnessed at that time, and they resembled very much what we now call a battle royal where assorted gentlemen in a ring try to disassemble one another as completely and as expeditiously as possible.

Rules have been written and rewritten

over the years to improve the game. The reason I objected so strongly to the lateral pass rule is because some people were merely using it as an opportunity to change our whole American game to English rugby. I believe we have the right to demonstrate against this very strongly. Coaches should test the lateral pass with an open mind, but if it does not fit in with our American game, they should have no hesitancy in saying so to the Rules Committee.

A fan wrote a letter to me once and asked, "What have they done with the football rules again? I understand the Rules Committee has gone and made more changes. What's the idea? For what reason were these changes made? I have heard of no demand from the public, from the coaches, or from the players for any change."

Would the day of the thrill — the kind the American football public has experienced and enjoyed so much — be in jeopardy? My answer is, I don't believe so.

I've done a lot of experimenting and have had many discussions with other coaches over the years. I have come to the conclusion that football will go through rule changes, but it will always be a game with thousands of fans.

There was one change, however, the Rules Committee made that many other coaches and I did not approve of — the backward pass rule. This rule states that on all incomplete laterals, when the ball hits the ground it is dead and belongs to the side that had possession of it — that is, of course, except on fourth down.

This rule merely subsidizes the lateral pass. I was against it for many reasons.

We have always had the lateral pass play, and any team could use it if so desired. The reason it was not used is because it was not effective. It was easily stopped.

These rules subsidizing the backward pass have made officiating much more difficult. More complications could be added that will not add anything to the game. It's almost impossible under some conditions to tell a lateral pass from a fumble.

One of the golden rules of football has been, "Hang onto the ball." This incomplete backward pass rule may in time devitalize a great game.

It takes more than one season to develop the skill and perfection of execution necessary to make the lateral work in a play. Some teams that used the lateral pass effectively against easy opponents often regret it. The lateral pass acts like the opiate of easy money; it spoils the boys, so in the big games some of them do not have the experience to adequately block and interfere in order to gain yardage. Teams that have had an easy time using the lateral passes against weak teams — without using solid blocking or interfering — find it psychologically impossible to go back to the good old-fashioned solid block to pave the way for a ballcarrier.

The smarter teams have used the lateral pass merely as a threat or as a scoring play in the "zone of increased resistance," the territory close to the goal line. The American game has been predicated on blocking and interfering.

The lateral pass is a part of English rugby. English rugby rules do not allow the forward pass at all, and their line plunging is negligible. The game is based almost entirely upon lateral passing and kicking. English rugby does not permit blocking and interfering except in a certain zone.

In other words, the two games are antithetical; they are as different as night and day. The rule was put in our code through the ef-

I have come to the conclusion that football will go through rules, but it will always be a game with thousands of fans.

forts of two certain schools. I do not know what these two schools had in mind; perhaps they wanted to change the American game to English rugby so that they can indulge in international contests with Oxford and Cambridge. Now if these two schools should decide to play English rugby and play international matches, I am sure the American public would be pleased. At least no one could have any objections.

But football coaches, players, and fans throughout America do not see by what right two schools can change the rules of a game that is played by 20,000 schools, colleges, clubs, and goodness knows how many sandlot teams throughout the country.

California and Stanford dropped the American game many years ago and took up rugby. They came back to the American game. No one at either institution, so far as I can learn, has any yearning for the return of the rugby game. This is America, and we have a

320

right to play American games as our spirit and fancy dictate. If there are among us those who wish to play rugby and cricket, let them play it. For goodness' sake, let's have American games for Americans.

Moving the goalpost back 10 yards was the only rule that affected the spectators. The field had a different appearance; touchdowns were no longer made where the goalposts stood, but 10 yards in front of it. Quarterbacks had to adjust their mental picture of the field or some of them, without realizing it, would be throwing incomplete passes beyond the end zone.

Moving the goalposts back 10 yards was done to make teams trying for the extra point use some other means besides the place kick. It was also done to lessen the danger of injury when two teams are scrimmaging close to the goal line. I understand that changing the position was suggested by a certain member of the Rules Committee whose team for several years spent most of its time punting from behind its own goal line. The goalpost was often in his punter's way.

The rule moving the goal post back also helped my team.

I had a quarterback who suffered from goalpost fright. He would run his team beautifully up to within 10 yards of the goalposts and then when he looked up and saw how close he was, he would become rattled and his well-laid plans would go awry. But because of the change, he was over the goal line before his goalpost fright ruined his concentration.

One year, two radical changes in the kickoff were made. The tee, which all good kickers used, was declared illegal, and the ball had to be kicked from the 40-yard line instead of from the 50yard line. It was thought that eliminating the tee, and thus cutting down both height and distance of the ball's flight, would compensate for the 10-yard difference. But it didn't. High school and college kickers, accustoming themselves to a tee-less kickoff, sent the ball over the goal line for a touchback. That meant that it was often brought out to the 20-yard line and put in play. And one of the greatest thrills in football, the return of the kickoff, was almost entirely eliminated from the game.

In only a few cases — Red Grange's 95-yard run at the start of the Illinois — Michigan game was one of them — were the spectators treated to the colorful, thrilling sight of a man catching the ball and 10 others forming themselves into an interference in front of him to dash down the field.

A major result of this rule change is teams developed a strong kickoff return. My teams devote a lot of time to running back kickoffs, for I believe this will be a big part of games in the future. It makes it a lot more fun for everybody, between the sidelines and outside them.

Another important rule changed the penalty when the defensive team is offside. The penalty was five yards before, but the down remained the same. Under the old rules, which penalized the offenders five yards and made it first down, was an unfair hardship.

I remember a Notre Dame — Nebraska game of several years ago in which this was illustrated. Nebraska had the ball, and it was second down with 25 yards to go. As the next play started, a Notre Dame man got offside, and at once it became first down for Nebraska. The ball was moved up five yards and our opponents had only 10 yards to go! This was a case where the old penalty was far out of proportion to the offense. The new rule makes this impossible; in an exactly similar case, the ball would have moved up five yards, but it would have remained second down, 20 yards to go.

To clarify a technical point, the line of scrimmage was redefined as a vertical plane between the two teams, rather than an imaginary line on the ground. This means that the heads of the linemen, as well as their hands and all other parts of their bodies, must be in back of the line of scrimmage. It will help avoid misunderstandings and squabbles.

The penalty on clipping was standardized with the same purpose — to avoid misunderstanding. When a man "clips" an opponent — that is, throws his body across the legs of the other fellow from behind and brings him down — his team is penalized 25 yards from the spot where the clipping took place. Last year the captain of the side against which the clipping was committed had a choice of two penalties — 15 yards from the point of clipping, or 15 yards from the place where the play started.

The new penalty is not necessarily more severe, but it is now standard and will avoid trouble like that which came up in a Minnesota — Michigan game, when Michigan suffered a stiff penalty for clipping and thought the Minnesota captain overstepped his rights.

The rule on blocked kicks was the fairest yet devised. Its first provision is that a punted ball blocked behind the line of scrimmage belongs to whichever side recovers it, but counts a down against the kickers if that side recovers.

Formerly, a blocked kick recovered by the kickers meant first down. In a Notre Dame — Wisconsin game, Joe Boland, Notre Dame's left tackle, broke through the line and blocked a Wisconsin punt on fourth down. Wisconsin recovered the ball, and it became first down for the Badgers. Obviously, it was unfair.

Under the new rules, the ball would have gone to Notre Dame in that case, for Wisconsin would have lost a down and that would have caused the ball to "go over."

On a partly blocked kick which crosses the line of scrimmage, the ball is played exactly as if it had never been touched. This rule was intended as a clarification to prevent misunderstandings, such as which arose in the Michigan — Iowa game of 1923. Harry Kipke of Michigan punted, and the ball tipped the fingers of John Hancock of Iowa but went far across the line of scrimmage. This made it anybody's ball under the old rule, but nobody except one official and Jack Blott, Michigan center, had noticed that Hancock had touched the ball. Blott, like a flash, went down the field after the punt and fell on it, making it Michigan's ball. It was a deciding play in the game.

Under the new rules, however, the ball would not be eligible for Michigan to take until some other Iowa player, other than the blocker, had touched it. The prompt action of Howard Jones, then Iowa's coach, was all that saved serious trouble on that occasion. The spectators, thinking it a "raw" decision, had become furious and threatening, but Jones announced that the play was properly executed, and the crowd quieted.

The Rules Committee, in trying to eliminate unearned touchdowns, ruled that if a punt is fumbled, the kicking side may recover the ball, but no run may ensue on the same play. This change in the rule was well intended, but I don't believe punts are caught more often than they have in the past. The changes I just mentioned all have merit and improved the game.

Another rule allowed trainers and a doctor to go on the field as soon as a man is hurt, reporting to referee or umpire before speaking to the man. The old rule required doctors and trainers to get permission from an official before stepping onto the field, and in some cases,

Young men who are unknown today will be stars in another month, and will be offering color to the lives of millions of Americans ...

like when an Army player had to go through two plays with a badly smashed foot before the doctor could catch the umpire's eye, worked out badly.

The "time-out" rule was altered slightly to provide that when a man is injured, time is called and a substitute goes in. It counts as one of the team's four "time-outs" in the half unless the team has already called for time four times. This rule is intended to speed up the game slightly.

Using the shift has come under the scrutiny of the Rules Committee on several occasions. The objections that cropped up against the shift in the winter of 1929 were all under cover and were made by coaches who had lost. There is a rumor that opposition is now not against the momentum of the shift, which doesn't exist, but rather against the success of the shift.

I was very much opposed to the two-second stop suggested by some coaches. This change would have eliminated from football everything that is colorful and involves clever finesse. The two-second stop would ruin the value of the shift, as every defensive player could size up the formation in two seconds.

However, in the one-second stop, the defensive team still has just enough players off balance and just enough players lacking in observation to give deceptive shifts the same strategic advantage they have always had.

Notre Dame has continued using the identical same attack while the Rules Committee debated the legality of the shift. I believe the shift is legal. Like any other attack played by enthusiastic boys, there were times when the rule was broken. However, I have never seen the time when shifting teams were any more inclined to infringe on the rules than "set and go" teams. I know of no coach who teaches his men to break the rules. The day of that type of coach is gone and past, but young boys — in their over-eagerness — will sometimes do things that will call for a penalty. That's what you pay an official $100 to watch for. To say that the shift should be abolished because there is a temptation to be in motion is ridiculous. Over-zealous boys using the "set and go" attack may break just as many rules as a shifting team.

Once in a while, a set team using the anticipating snap signal has its line charging before the ball is passed. Would it be sensible to suggest that no offensive team be allowed to call any numbers? That both teams must watch the ball and the ball is passed with no member of either team being aware of it ahead of time? Some "set and go" teams who pull their guards leave ahead of time. Would it be sensible to suggest a rule saying that no guards shall run in interference? Some teams using a wing back often-times have this player crawl up to within one or two feet of the ball, when the rule distinctly says he shall be back 36 inches. Would it be sensible to suggest that no offensive team shall use any formation with backs outside the ends?

The Rules Committee at its 1930 meeting made a rule restricting the shift. The old ruling read that a shifting team must pause for "approximately" one second. The new ruling also gives the referee the suggestion of counting six, instead of four, to denote a second.

I want to go on record as being heartily in favor of this new change. This new ruling should not only eliminate momentum from the shift but should also eliminate the shift from any further "momentous" discussions.

Now, who is competent to time one-second accurately? No one that I know. I have been head timer at many a Big Ten track meet

*Once in a while, a set team using the anticipating snap
has its line charging before the ball is passed.*

and in almost every 100-yard dash the timers will vary two-fifths of a second. As all of the watches are synchronized, the error is in the finger of the timer. I timed our shift last year 100 times, and it averaged one and one-tenth seconds.

This new rule will not affect Notre Dame in any manner. However, I remember acting as head timer at a high school track meet in a town where they had a local "phenom" in the 100. Three of us were timing. The two local enthusiasts caught their boy in nine and four-

fifths seconds, while I was almost run out of town because my watch showed ten and two-fifths seconds.

Speaking of shifts — the coach of Siwash was in recent conversation with the coach of Washington. One of them would have won all his games but for poor material, injuries, and bad handling.

"Well, I see where the Rules Committee plans to abolish the shift."

"Well, it's about time they abolish this bootleg football."

Pop Warner, the Stanford coach, and I were expressing ourselves as being very much in favor of the changes ...

system and they crowd closer than the rules allow. At Igona, the man in motion is going forward illegally half the time!"

"Those are minor items."

"Well, maybe, but didn't I hear you talk on sportsmanship at the Club?"

"Yes, and it was good, wasn't it?"

"Yes, I liked it. But the law of self-preservation sometimes causes a weak memory, and don't forget that jealousy is a sign of inferiority."

"Maybe, but I'm glad the shift is going. It will make the game more simple, and if they put the coaches in the stands, we'll all hold our jobs because the alumni won't know whom to blame."

In my opinion, the Rules Committee handled the shift legislation both fairly and intelligently. The one-second stop required all shifting teams to come to an absolute stop for approximately one second. Shifting teams depending solely on momentum and not stopping had an unfair advantage. This rule ended that type of maneuver, but a shift based on deception still retained its strategic value.

The Rules Committee should be complimented for resisting the pressure of those coaches who evidently wanted to standardize football. Similar criticism is sometimes heard of baseball, that it is too mechanical, too much the same. Eliminate the shift in football, and the game will lose its popular appeal. The color and pageantry which comes with the shifting of backs and lineman into a variety of formations would have been gone. Practically all we would have left in the way of offense would be

"Why, do you think there is an unfair advantage in the shift?"

"No, not with the one-second stop, but it's too darn popular."

"Don't you think the Rules Committee ought to legislate against unfair advantages only?"

"Such as, for instance?"

"Well, your team uses the charging number and the whole line is off two feet ahead of the ball. The Ileana uses the double-wing back

PENALTIES COMMONLY INFLICTED

Loss of Two Yards

Time called more than three times during a half at the request of the captain of a team.

Loss of Five Yards

1. Violation of the off-side rule, which includes:

(a) Lineman or backs illegally in motion when the ball is snapped.

(b) Any player of the kicking side ahead of the ball when it is kicked at the kick-off.

(c) Attempts to draw opponents into charging before the ball is snapped.

2. Unreasonable delay by a team, usually evidenced by calling signals several times before the ball is snapped.

3. Running into the kicker after he has kicked the ball.

4. Failure of substitute to report to referee when entering the game.

5. Unfair play not specifically covered in the rules.

Loss of Ten Yards

Intentional throwing of forward pass to the ground.

Loss of Fifteen Yards

1. Substitute communicating with players before the ball is put in play.

2. Interference with a man who has signaled for a fair catch.

3. Throwing player to the ground after he has made a fair catch.

4. Offensive player pushing or pulling the man carrying the ball.

5. Offensive player holding a defensive player.

6. Players of the side making a forward pass interfering with defensive players after the ball is passed.

7. Deliberately roughing the kicker after he has kicked the ball.

8. Piling up on players who are down.

9. Tackling a man after he has run out of bounds.

10. Clipping.

11. Offensive player tripping an opponent.

12. Side-line coaching.

Loss of Half Distance to the Goal Line

1. Return of the player to the game who has previously been in that half.

2. Disqualification of a player for rough play.

3. Any foul occuring inside the opponent's one-yard line.

Loss of a Down

1. Illegal or incomplete forward pass.

2. Forward pass striking the ground.

3. Forward pass touched by two eligible players of the passing side.

4. Forward pass going out of bounds on the fly.

Loss of Ball

1. Ball kicked out of bounds unless touched in the field of play.

2. Illegal use of hands or arms to prevent an opponent from securing loose ball.

3. Forward pass touched by ineligible player of the passer's side.

4. Interference by defensive side under a forward pass.

5. Failure to advance the ball ten yards in four downs.

6. Kicking or kicking at a loose ball.

Forfeiture of Game

Refusal to abide by referee's decision or to play within two minutes after being ordered to do so by the referee.

Important Note Regarding Time Out

Time is automatically taken out during a try-for-point after touch-down; after a safety or a touch-back; after a fair catch has been made; after an incomplete or illegal forward pass; during enforcement of all penalties; when the ball goes out of bounds; or when for any reason play is suspended by the referee. Time shall not begin again, after any of the aforesaid, until the ball is actually passed back from center.

Haughton football, Warner football, and punt formation systems of football.

Retention of the shift meant football continued to be played above the ears. A small, light, fast, clever man with brains will still have the edge on the powerful, Neolithic caveman who has the physical figure of Eugene Sandow.

Notre Dame uses the same shift it has always used because we believe this shift is absolutely legal and fair. We have no fear of the 15-yard penalty. Why? Because we know if the shift is properly executed, it is absolutely according to the rules.

A group of high school and college coaches were sitting in the hotel room of a sporting goods salesman in Dallas in 1929 discussing the football rules. Pop Warner, the Stanford coach, and I were expressing ourselves as being very much in favor of the changes, and Pop Warner particularly observed that it made the rules more simple. A sporting goods salesman then remarked that this would be a great help because in the past only the coaches themselves had been simple.

Dr. Blackwell of S. M. U. said that the rules were all right as far as he was concerned, but he thought the point after touchdown should be eliminated. He said it had no direct bearing on the game. This point was discussed pro and con at great length, but it seemed to be the consensus of the group that without the point after touchdown we would have too many tie games, which would not be particularly interesting.

At this point, Big College coach broke in to the effect that he was very much against the fumble rule, owing to the fact that it took away one of the chances of the weaker team winning.

"I thought your prospects were rather poor this year," drawled the sporting goods salesman. "I can generally tell when your prospects are hot, because when they are, every week or so I get an extra order for a headgear and pair of shoes, and I haven't had as much as gym shirts order from you in six months."

"Just the same," remarked Big College Coach, "I believe the weaker team is entitled to a chance to win, and this new fumble rule eliminates that."

"That's just the reason why the new fumble rule is a good one," countered Pop Warner. "I don't see any reason why a weaker team should beat a stronger team. As a matter of fact, I have a couple of things I would like to see eliminated from the rules so as to preclude any chance of a weaker team beating a strong team. I would like to see them award a point every time a first down is made. In that case, if one team made fourteen first downs and the other team only made two but scored a touchdown, the score would still be fourteen to eight or nine in favor of the team that made the fourteen first downs, the touchdown counting six points as in the past, with the possibility of adding the extra point."

"Do you think this would be very interesting?" asked Coach Morrison of S. M. U.

"Yes, I do," replied Pop. "Didn't you ever hear the crowd cheer every time its team made a first down? I think it would add a lot of interest to the game and eliminate fluke victories."

"Well, I am against that," said Big College coach, "because first of all I've got a long-distance forward passer and when he forward-passes, boy! It goes fifty yards and I think a first down of that kind should count a lot more than a first down that only goes ten yards."

"That's where you are wrong," replied Pop. "The forward pass is just a necessary evil in football, and right now I think it is over-balancing the offense. Personally, I would like to see the forward pass eliminated from football, but I know that can't be done. The Rules Committee, in making rules, has in mind an even balance between running, kicking and passing. But today the forward passing game has entirely over-balanced offense. I think that something should be done to curtail the wild, promiscuous, glorified football that some teams now indulge in. They throw three long forward passes, and if none of these connect, they punt. They figure on a percentage basis that if one of these long passes connects, they will fluke a touchdown and win the game."

"And that's just what I'm up against," continued Pop. "I think a game of football should be strictly on a merit basis. Every time a team throws a fifty-yard forward pass and connects, it is a matter of luck."

"You are trying to eliminate the thrills of football," said Big College coach.

"No, I am not," replied Pop. "We will still have all the thrills without the flukes."

At this point, Coach Jennings of Baylor spoke up. "How about running the game by forty plays per quarter instead of by a time limit of fifteen minutes?"

"The idea has some merit," said Pop, "but it would mean some more eliminating in the rules."

Coach Bible of Nebraska then broke in: "We've got a pretty good game as it is, boys, I think we've got a mighty fine set of rules, and I feel that we are all going to find the game better than ever. I've enjoyed all of these remarks very much — they have all been very interesting, but you can readily see that if every coach has his particular pet peeve eliminated, there wouldn't be anything left to the game of football."

The sporting goods salesman arose to his feet, stifled a yawn, and eased the remark that he thought he was going to bed. But as the coaches prepared to depart, he was heard to say, "Well, you coaches can eliminate all you want from football, but there's one thing you want to be careful of — don't ever eliminate the touchdown or you'll be out of a job."

All in all, the game of football will continue on the path of one of America's great sports. There is still plenty of room for original thinking, original ideas and inventions which will cause the game to sparkle and scintillate more than ever. Young men who are unknown today will be stars in another month, and will be offering color to the lives of millions of Americans.

We have only a short time in which to teach the game ...

38
SCOUTING

The announcement by Yale that there would be no scouting by it or any of its opponents this year is a fine, idealistic move. The move will, no doubt, be made by other schools throughout the country, with the finest intentions and highest motives.

Personally, I believe the thing is impractical. In their attempts to get away from the "bogey man" over-emphasis, the coaches and directors are racking their brains as to the various means of quieting this specter. I don't admit that there is an over-emphasis, except in the minds of some people.

I believe the more practical solution of scouting is to continue as we have — to scout openly, frankly, above board, and on a fair and even basis. When two Big Ten teams play, the directors of each school wire each other that their scout is coming. And when the scout arrives, he visits the home athletic offices and secures a good seat in the press box.

Generally, the scout has dinner with the home coach after the game, and the scout then goes home with his impressions of strength and weaknesses and a lot of misinformation.

We can get along very well without scouting, however. I believe scouting is very much over-valued anyhow. Its importance has been exaggerated. It will be interesting to watch the results of the experiment by Yale and the other schools which adopt the idea.

One of our opponents one year wanted me to enter a no-scouting agreement with them. I refused. Yale and Princeton have such an agreement, and I know that they are governed by the highest ideals

One of our opponents one year wanted me to enter a no-scouting agreement with them. I refused. Yale and Princeton have such an agreement, and I know that they are governed by the highest ideals and the best of intentions. Perhaps between two such fine schools, with such splendid traditions of rivalry behind them in every respect, this utopian idea will prove successful.

However, I don't believe scouting is wrong. Football is supposed to prepare young men for life. Life is competition. In life, men in every profession and business spend much time watching the other fellow so that they can pick up whatever new ideas are prevalent. They must do so if they wish to compete in their particular profession or business. The man who isn't on his toes, diligently competing in his line, soon ends up in the discard.

I am also against the no-scouting agreement because it will bring into football suspicion and innuendo. For instance, suppose we accidentally stop a pet play of a team we are playing, and we have a no-scouting arrangement. Immediately, accusations and charges would be hurled back and forth that the no-scouting agreement had not been upheld. I don't mean that the charges would be made by the coaches, but by alumni and other adherents.

News today is too easily transmitted. Some clever football scribe, in writing about a team, might very easily give a graphic description of the plays this team runs. Can the coach and players on the other team be prevented from reading this newspaper account? Can players be prevented from listening to accounts of the other team by alumni who may have seen the opponent play? Or can the members of the team be prevented from listening to traveling salesmen, who, so far

as football is concerned, have large and vivid imaginations?

We have only a short time in which to teach the game. The amount of time allotted is too short in which to teach everything in football, yet it would be necessary to teach glittering generalities if there was no scouting.

With scouting, a coach can tell his team that this is just about the style of football it is going to meet. Hence, the boys will not have to try to learn all there is in football, but just enough to be prepared for an opponent. As far as I am concerned, we are going to insist on scouting — honestly, honorably, frankly, above-board — the in which our opponents are contestants.

The value of scouting has been very much overstated. All a coach wants is just a general idea about the kind of football the other team is playing. Utopia is still off in the far and distant future. Sportsmanship is a vital part of the game — sportsmanship is ethics. Scouting has nothing to do with either sportsmanship or ethics. Scouting satisfies a natural curiosity as to what our competitors are doing, and there is nothing wrong with it in any shape or manner. We find it in every phase of life.

I read in one of the student publications that the reason scouting was abolished between Yale and Princeton was because scouting overemphasized football. I wish to disagree strongly with the writer and others who share his views. In my opinion, people who don't understand football exaggerate the value of scouting.

I played for Notre Dame in the years 1911 — 1913, and during those three years we never once scouted an opponent. Incidentally, we were undefeated those three years. The point I wish to make is that the lack of scouting in no way interfered with our efficiency. I believe most football coaches will agree that they could get along very well without scouting.

When I send a scout out, all I want is the other team's formations and also a few ideas of personnel. A coach can figure out all the possible plays once he has the formation. Most teams change their defense from week to week, and hence I don't want any scout to bring back any information on the defense. Our quarterbacks will have to look over the other team and see for themselves what kind of defense they have to meet.

You may ask if it is better to play without knowing the other team's formations. Yes, but the knowledge of what formations they are using becomes so obvious that if we didn't send a scout out to see the other team play a game on Saturday and get the formations openly and honorably, the information would be bootlegged to the members of the team by some clandestine method. Alumni and traveling salesmen with valuable football information are always very hard to handle.

The institution known as "scouting" is supposed to be a source of all necessary information about the opponent. Enthusiastic alumni of a school are often self-appointed football scouts. As a rule, their enthusiasm is in inverse ratio to their knowledge of the game and their powers of observation in spotting innovations or clever deceptions in the play of the schools they are scouting.

Back in 1915, when I was the assistant to Jess Harper, part of my job was to do his scouting. We were to play Nebraska, and so Jess wired Ewald "Jumbo" Stiehm, Nebraska coach, that I was going out to scout their Kansas Aggie game. I did. I came back with what I thought was two mysterious bits of information that would give us an edge.

Nebraska's great threat was a fine halfback named Guy Chamberlin. In the Kansas Aggie game, he scored touchdown after touchdown on wide end runs. I came back with the startling information that Chamberlin did not cut back at any time.

What happened when Notre Dame played Nebraska? Right near the end of the first half Nebraska had the ball on our 40-yard line. Chamberlin took it on the next play. Our players all swung wide, over-committing themselves to what we thought we knew of the runner's habitual tactics. To our surprise, Chamberlin cut back, and with no Notre Dame player in front of him, he ran 40 yards for a touchdown.

I was responsible for that touchdown, not the Notre Dame team.

The second bit of startling information I conveyed to our boys was this: Chamberlin was lefthanded. I told our boys, when he licked his fingers he always forward passed. When he did not lick his fingers, he always ran.

What happened? Right near the end of the game the score was tied 13 — 13. The ball was in midfield in Nebraska's possession. Back it came to Chamberlin, who started off as if on an end run. Suddenly he stopped, whirled, and threw a long pass to his right end who caught the ball and ran for a touchdown. Where was our safety assigned to cover him? He had seen that Chamberlin did not lick his fingers. Therefore, feeling sure it was to be a run, up he came, with disastrous results to Notre Dame.

Chamberlin had crossed us up. The final score was 20 — 19 in favor of Nebraska.

In the fall of 1926, a scout reported to me that Carnegie Tech was ordinary against West Virginia, which sized up as strong opposition at that time. My plans made it necessary for me to be in Chicago at a Big Ten Conference and the Army — Navy game on the day we met Carnegie Tech.

Down in Pittsburgh, our boys were prepared for the usual tough battle. They got an unusually tough one. Carnegie Tech had been playing possum for the scout I sent there, holding Howard Harpster, their bright particular star, under wraps. He cut loose like a thunderbolt against us.

Sitting between Tad Jones and Pop Warner at the Army — Navy game, I received a wire from Pittsburgh. It bore the doleful news that Carnegie Tech had beaten a great Notre Dame team 19 — 0.

"Too bad," said Pop Warner.

"Tough luck," commiserated Tad Jones.

"Come behind the stands," I invited both, "and give me the kicking I deserve."

One year, many Notre Dame enthusiasts wondered why our forward-pass game was not very much in evidence. I knew, although ill in bed, that they were scouting all our major games — and we won all of the earlier ones without the pass. That was kept under cover until we met Southern California. Their scouts reported that Notre Dame's pass game was of no consequence. But we completed five long passes that won that game.

So, too — again earlier in my acquaintance with what scouting can do to fool both friend and foe — in 1921, we played exceptionally orthodox football for a purpose.

Our leading opponent was the Army, which believed what its scouts reported — that our game was strictly orthodox. This, in turn, meant that we would follow the rules that guide smart teams and never dream of passing in our own territory. When the Army defense, observing our orthodox game, stayed up to the line of scrimmage, they remained there once too long. Paul Castner, halfback, faked a line plunge, then our quarterback passed the ball to fullback John Mohardt. He shot it 40 yards to our end Roger Kiley, who then raced 30 yards through unoccupied territory for a touchdown.

While scouting has brought me, as it brings every coach, disappointments, I've had valuable tips that helped to win games.

In 1924, we learned through the scout route that Carnegie Tech had adopted a man-to-man defense, and that the center, fullback, left halfback and quarterback were fast runners. Their right halfback was a grand blocker but a slow runner. Play during the first half verified all this. So, Jim Crowley was sent into the defensive right halfback's territory, where he ran him ragged all afternoon, catching all the passes Harry Stuhldreher sent his way.

Football science has a place for legitimate scouting, just as it has a place for psychology. But where the emphasis is overlaid, these by-issues of the game defeat their own ends.

Really, the thing that is wrong with scouting is the very word "scouting." I suggest that we use the word "research" instead, or as it might better be defined, a football clinic. Everybody in every game is interested in what others do with it, especially when those others are future opponents at the game. When scouting is done over and aboveboard, and one school announces it will have an official representative to see a public exhibition by another school, we all know where we stand. Then there can be no innuendo that there was secret scouting, spying, or other betrayal.

We are all curious as to what our competitors are doing. The city editor of the New York Times is most interested in the first edition of the Herald Tribune. The grocer on one corner wants to know if his rival on the other corner is going to sell certain products. Physicians in a community are most eager to know what new medications some professional brother is introducing. Department store managers are persistently inquisitive as to what their competitors are putting on sale next week. So, research men are continually finding out what additions to scientific knowledge are being made by other research men —and increasing or improving the discoveries of others. Why shouldn't this same process prevail in football?

Naturally, a coach's ingenuity in improvising new plays is part of his assets. He can't patent his inventions, but he should be protected by mutual trust. Really, there are no new plays anymore than in humor there are any new jokes. All are variations of old principles, but it is in the new touch — as in the novel ways of performing old plays, in new deceptive tactics applied to old routines — that the surprise element, which is the best stuff in football, is to be found.

I have three sons ... I want all three to play football if they are able.

39
CHARACTER

I have three sons. I want all three to play football if they are able. I want them to learn the lessons of right living, because no boy can play on a high school or college football team who smokes or drinks or does anything else that might interfere with his fullest individual potential. He learns to take his hard knocks without squawking, without kicking, without knocking, and without becoming cynical. He learns to take them as a matter of course.

I would like to feel that one of the by-products of playing a hard contact game like football is character.

Character is a rather complex thing, but it is a mixture of temperament, habits and fiber. I would also figure that I have helped to safeguard the best interests of the country from a military point-of-view because every man would be physically fit and trained to obey orders.

...he cupped his hand and he called in a loud clear voice that could be heard all over the football stadium... 'I say there, dear Bickerdash, is that a terrible run in your stocking?'

40

T. MURPHY'S QUICK THINKING SAVES THE GAME

On a beautiful fall day, two of this country's most prestigious schools played an outstanding game of football. On the first kickoff, receiving for Northwestern was M. Bickerdash Pix III. The entire Northwestern team was fabulously clad in purple-mauvette tunics, and about the waist was a white girdle with a Louis XIV-buckle.

Kicking off for Notre Dame was T. Simmons Murphy, who is better known to his teammates as "Two Lump," as he always asks for two lumps of sugar in his orange pekoe. The Notre Dame team also presented a striking appearance with their green shirtwaists and their headgear resembling a woodsman's toque. Giving a very neat appearance without being at all gaudy was the fact that their hip-pads were trimmed with georgette. Hanging from the necks were pendants, lavaliere type, on which was engraved the motto of the university: "Fight fairly but furiously."

Precisely at 2:30 p.m. the referee, dressed in regulation costume of plus fours and crêpe de Chine blouse, blew his whistle. Two Lump met the ball squarely and kicked it down the field right into the arms of Bickerdash, who, catching it, brought it back 5, 10, 15 yards before he was tagged by a deft tag on the shoulder by Nouveauriche Gilhooey, the Irish left end.

Northwestern lined up and tried three running plays to no avail. Notre Dame's tagging defense was impregnable. So, on fourth down, Bickerdash kicked the ball back down the field to Two Lump, who was tagged right in his tracks. He couldn't move.

Then, Notre Dame took the offensive with the ball. They determined, to their dismay, that Northwestern was just as clever at defensive tagging as they were. Neither team could gain at all, so all throughout the first-half a punting duel resulted between Two Lump and Bickerdash, neither gaining any advantage.

Between halves, both teams sat at lovely decorated tables along the sidelines and sipped tea.

Up until five minutes before the end of the fourth quarter it looked as though it were destined to be a tie game, which they considered so unsatisfactory. Suddenly, out of rhythmical gavotte, a sort of a hidden-ball evolution, Bickerdash broke loose and went streaking up the sidelines with a clear field to the goal posts. The Northwestern stands were excited. The Irish stands were deathly still because it looked like sure defeat for Notre Dame. But they failed to reckon on the resourcefulness and resiliency of mind of Two Lump.

Now, when Two Lump — who was back playing safety, the last man on defense — saw Bickerdash running with style toward the goal line and no one there to stop him, he didn't give up and become panicky. Not Two Lump. With a savoir faire for which he was justly famous, he cupped his hand and he called in a loud clear voice that could be heard all over the football stadium: "I say there, I say there dear Bickerdash, is that a terrible run in your stocking?"

Imagine the intense embarrassment and mortification of poor Bickerdash. What could he do to hide his discomfiture but drop the ball and run for the clubhouse? Two Lump saved the game.

This story had the effect I hoped for, of restoring the normal balance in our masculine democracy, so that today while socialites and social events have their place, they are not paramount. The old school continues to turn out men of culture, character and courage.

Let's develop a fine sense of fair play ... respect the rules of the game and the rights of the opponents ... be as fair as we can in every way ...

41

COOPERATION

After reading the details of how each of the various units of our Army had to work together to be victorious, the strategy that they used was beyond me. Cooperation among the infantry, artillery, airplanes, and so on was sheer perfection.

I met with one of the leaders of American industry, and I asked him which factor he appraised most highly in men coming up in his organization: the spirit of cooperation or technical knowledge?

This man replied: "It used to be knowledge, but today I would say the spirit of cooperation. Much of the trouble in my organization has been due to men endowed with more than their share of knowledge but who would not cooperate."

He laid most of the blame for the lack of this cooperative spirit in our young men of today on the schools. He explained that today no man stands alone, and that no matter what line of work a man goes into, he must depend on contact and organization to affect his ends successfully.

However, I think this man is unfair in placing the blame for this lack of cooperation on our schools. The teachers in most schools do good work, but it cannot be expected that they can do everything.

The spirit of cooperation is a matter of psychology instilled into the young men in group experiences. It is here, I believe, that team games such as football, basketball and baseball have their greatest value. Golf and the other individual sports are fine sports and have their place in the recreation and training of our youngsters, but many times more so do our games where an organization is necessary and where the boy must, to a certain extent, submerge the ego of his individuality. He must forego his personal ambition for the good of the team.

As part of the team, a lad learns how to play his games with the proper value, and by that, I mean trying to win just as hard as he can and, if he does, not bragging. And should he lose, he learns no alibi.

Nothing destroys character more than constant alibis over failure. He learns to take his sports as a means to an end, not an end in itself. He learns the true element of sportsmanship, which is having a little respect for the other fellow or opponent's point of view. There can be no sense of fairness without this. He learns how to take care of himself and how to curb his primal emotions such as hatred, fear, passion, anger, and so on.

And last, but most important of all, he imbibes the spirit of cooperation.

Football is not an individual proposition. Eleven ordinary players, functioning together with an unselfish spirit of sacrifice for the team but without losing any of their real individuality, can beat 11 stars if the latter are merely 11 individuals, each man playing for himself with no regard for the team as a whole. The spirit of "all for one and one for all" as expressed by d'Artagnan and the Three Musketeers must prevail for the team to be successful.

While I was in France several years ago, I went to the YMCA in Paris one day to see a basketball game between two French teams. The league standing was inscribed on a blackboard in the hall, and I noticed that an American team, made up of some American students in the Latin Quarter, was leading the league with a 15 — 0 record. The five other teams were made up of French boys.

As I said, the game I saw was between two French teams. After the game ended, I went over to the physical director and told him that I had enjoyed the game very much, and asked, "You have different rules over here, haven't you?"

"No," he said, "we use the same Spalding Guide rules you have in the states."

"That's strange," I said, "for I saw little or no passing. Every boy who got hold of the ball, it seemed to me, either dribbled and shot or shot from where he stood, regardless of how far it was."

"Yes, that's true," replied my director friend. "But perhaps you don't understand. These French boys are highly individualistic, and they have been playing this team game only a short time. As it is now, of course, the American team runs over them roughshod with very little opposition because of your team play. But these French boys will learn. In a short time, they will be imitating the team-play idea of the American boys. They will be playing them even-up soon, but they will have to learn by experience. I can't tell them — it would be just a waste of breath now.

"In fact, if I were to say to Jacques, holding the ball in the middle of the floor too far out for any proper chance for a basket: 'Jacques, why don't you pass the ball to Henri standing down there under the basket?' the chances are that Jacques would reply, 'What! Pass the ball to Henri! No! No! No! In that case Henri might make the basket.'"

Of course, we have instances of the same lack of team play and exalted individualism in America in both football and basketball, but no team so afflicted can have any success. Whether it is a neighborhood, high school or college team, remember this: The idea is to get the best 11 players, with each individual playing to benefit the team.

Let me cite an experience I had with one of the candidates for our team. We gather about 300 candidates together at the opening of practice in the fall. Most of them are highly individualistic. If you mentioned to them the idea of cooperation, they might say "baloney."

Many of them have very good opinions of themselves, and if the coach doesn't think they are any good, they have the clippings from their hometown newspapers, which tell otherwise. Many of these lads were the stars in their high school days who carried the ball or threw the forward pass. This specialty is all well and good, but the college coach cannot use them unless they can cooperate with their teammates.

The Four Horsemen averaged only 158 pounds in weight, but in spite of their lack of bulk, they made a wonderful record in football. If you were to ask me today what stands out in my mind regarding these four boys, I would say their resiliency of mind and spirit of cooperation.

As a matter of fact, I had a fifth-string backfield that year which averaged 185 pounds and were tough and fast. The reason they sat on the bench that fall was due to the fact that they were four individuals suffering from "Charley horse between the ears," and refused to work together.

I remember way back when we opened our season against Kalamazoo College. There was a young sophomore back-then we decided to start with the varsity that day because of his impressive showing in practice scrimmage. What happened? Three times in the first half, the quarterbacks called his number, and three times this lad made long runs for touchdowns: 60, 70, and 80 yards in length. Each time, so well did his teammates block and clear the path for him that not a single Kalamazoo tackler got in his way, and as old as I am,

I could probably have made the runs myself.

The next day I picked up our local paper to see if our local sports scribe would give credit where credit was justly due. Would he say that the feature of the play was the superb team play, the fine blocking and tackling? But no, this chap knew his readers and he gave them what he thought they wanted. He had a big streamer headline which read: "New Star Looms on the Horizon of Fame," and he nicknamed the boy the "Kokomo Flash." On Monday he had several full-length pictures of the lad in his paper and several columns dealing with his life history and so forth.

Nothing like this had ever happened to the young sophomore before and therefore, having no immunity, he soon was suffering from a bad case of swelled head. We gave him the usual serum treatment, which is ridicule from teammates and student body. This generally reduces the fever and the swelling.

Two weeks later, we started for West Point to play Army. Thinking the Kokomo Flash had entirely recovered from his malady, we decided to play him again at halfback. I remember the afternoon of the game well. The boy's father and mother were there to see the boy perform, and I think there were also a couple of aunts.

And what about the game? Well, after about 10 minutes, during which time this young chap posed around, evidently wondering how he looked from the grandstand, we took him out of the game and put back in his place a little third-string halfback who was anxious to go out there and do his bit for the team. We nosed out the Army luckily and left for home.

Monday afternoon, the day's classes being over, we had our next practice. The Kokomo Flash was sulking over in the corner and I didn't pay any attention to him. Tuesday afternoon he was still sulking, so I continued to ignore him.

... little Joe Brandy, the quarterback, who weighs about 135 pounds when he has all his keys in his pocket.

Wednesday afternoon he come over to me and said: "Coach, I think I'll turn in my suit."

"Well," I replied in a quite friendly tone, "I was just thinking of asking you for it."

"The rawest and most unfair deal I ever got in my life was the way you treated me in front of my folks last Saturday," he said.

"Don't you know why I took you out of that game?"

He didn't seem to understand, so I said, "I'll refresh your memory. We received the kick-off and made two first downs. Then the Army defense stiffened, and on fourth down George Gipp went back into kick formation and sent a long spiral soaring 60 yards down the field. Nine of your teammates ran down that field just as fast as they could in order that the Army return man, catching the punt, could not bring it back an inch. All except you. You jogged down the field very easily, apparently saving yourself for later on when you were going to carry the ball and make a long run.

"But we overlooked that. A little bit later we had the ball, and again the Army held us and George Gipp sent another long spiral up the field. Again, nine of your teammates gave all they had as they sprinted down the field covering the kick, all but you, the fancy prima donna. You gamboled up the greensward very leisurely, still saving yourself for later on when they were going to call your number and you were going to make a long run. Were you hoping to get your name in the headlines of the New York papers? We also overlooked that.

"Just a few minutes after that, the Army fumbled on the 20-yard line and we recovered the ball. As we lined up, just 20 yards from a touchdown, little Joe Brandy the quarterback, who weighs about 135 pounds when he has all his keys in his pocket, turned around to you boys and said: 'Let's dig in and go. Here's our chance.'

"He barked out the numbers, calling for a play where the ball goes to you and you go around right end. The ball came to you and you started around right end but just ahead of you ran George Gipp, the other halfback, your teammate. On this play it was his assignment to take the Army left end out of the play and keep him out, and he did. As a result, you weaved and wriggled for 11 yards before you were stopped. It was first down on the Army nine-yard line. The stands echoed to the cheers of the crowd mentioning just your name. Joe Brandy turned around and called for the same play. That is, the same play except that the ball goes to Gipp and he runs around the other end.

"On this play it was your duty, your quota, to do for him what he had done for you, namely take the Army right end out of the play and keep him out. But what did you do? You didn't even annoy him, and as a result Gipp was thrown for a four-yard loss. As you lined up, quick as a flash Brandy called for the same play over again. It was your turn to do your bit for the team. But no, again you went out and leaned weakly against the Army end who tossed you aside and threw Gipp for another loss. So, I took you out."

The lad had good stuff in him, came from good stock, and he stayed out all the rest of that year. The following year he became a regular and was picked by quite a few experts as an All-Western halfback. He had imbibed the spirit of team play, learned the lesson that in organization no one man can stand out in the limelight and take all the applause. There must be somebody to do the chores.

Since that time, I conceived the idea of putting up signs in the locker room to instill this sort of teamwork in the boys.

These signs were placed at vantage points

where they had to read them every day, whether they wanted to or not. You ask what was on these signs? Well, some of them read: "The other team is good but we are better if we will fight together."

"Be a good loser, don't beef. But don't lose."

 I don't want the guy who'll die for Notre Dame. I want men who'll fight to keep it alive."

"I don't expect gratitude, but an ingrate I can never forgive."

But the sign which I like best, because it has particular application to the episode I just mentioned, is the one which reads: "Success is based on what the team does, not on how you look."

Once in a while, I still have to hang up that sign in some individual locker, and whenever I do, the lad involved will generally come to me with an air of reproach saying, "You've got me all wrong, Coach."

I'll say, "What, was that hanging up in your locker? I beg your pardon."

But it has an effect just the same.

I have kept other stars on the bench over the years. Whenever I find any young fellow who is a chronic whiner and disturber, who insists on blaming his own shortcomings on his coaches and teammates — never on himself — he is taking the shortest way out.

The next day that young chap comes out for practice, there is no suit in his locker. I hope the shock has done him good. No community, no government, no fraternal organization, no American Legion Post, no business organization — no matter how fine the individual personnel — can get very far, can get anything done, without the spirit of cooperation.

We need leaders, in all honor to those who are real leaders, but we'll mellow just a little the halo and bouquets we confer on our big stars.

SECTION 3: ROCKNE ON ROCKNE

As Stonewall Jackson once said, "The object in warfare is to 'get there first with the mostest men.'"

42

FOOTBALL AND WARFARE

There is, of course, an analogy between football and warfare.

Football is a complex game and carries all the complexities of a modern war. Football is a whole war in itself. We can consider the line on offensive as either artillery smashing holes in the defense, or infantry protecting the backfield which, in its maneuvering, may either be the cavalry for end runs, tanks for line plunges, or airplanes in the case of a forward pass.

On the defense, the line may be either artillery to break up the offensive team's formations, or individual bayonet men when they are able to spear the ballcarrier by themselves. The backfield members would be likened to cavalry against running plays, although they can be changed to anti-aircraft gunners in case the enemy launches a forward-pass attack.

The quarterback on the offensive, of course, is the chief of staff who decides whether or not the play will be a flank movement, a thrust, a feint which hides the real thrust to be aimed at some other point, or an airplane attack aimed at the defensive team's base of supplies by means of a forward pass.

Or will he change the scene of battle by means of a punt?

The coaches on the sidelines can be likened to the generals of the armies. The commissary department is the boys with the water buckets. Sitting in the stands are the various strategy boards who can be likened to Congress. They will fire the generals as their whims and the forces of war may indicate. There is a similarity between football and warfare.

351

The common sense rules of the Rules Committee will hold pretty well in football. As Stonewall Jackson once said, "The object in warfare is to 'get there first with the mostest men.'"

The same holds true in football. However, there is one big difference. In warfare, men are playing a serious game. It is a matter of life and death; the safety of country and homes may be jeopardized. When a man is killed, he is killed. Human lives are in danger. Under these conditions, the chief of staff and the general can take no unnecessary chances. The game must be played very safe, and it is certainly anything but fun. We have all learned that.

Football should be fun, and it is not perilous. If you are knocked down, you can get up again. If the enemy scores a touchdown against you, you still have a chance to come back and score two touchdowns.

But, most of all, it is good, clean, serious fun. Whereas the boys go out and give the best of themselves in their desire to win, yet in the proper environment they learn to show those forms of generosity.

Section 3: Rockne on Rockne

Sportsmanship combines dignity and humility.

43

SPORTSMANSHIP

Sportsmanship is an important part of football.

I was talking to a golfer and a tennis enthusiast the other day, and both were rather joshing me. They said there was more sportsmanship shown in golf and tennis than in football, because there was very little wrangling and ill-feeling created in them.

Golf belongs to what might be called the "counting" type of competition, where it is a matter of counting strokes to see whether or not one man beats another. It is true, one must be a gentleman so as to count all the strokes, but neither one man nor the other can play his opponent's weaknesses or interfere with him by means of bodily contact. The struggle in golf is largely within oneself.

The game of tennis belongs to another class of competition. Here, too, you count strokes, but it is possible for one player to work on, or play on, the weaknesses of his opponent. Furthermore, in the game of tennis there are decisions as to bounds. Sometimes tempers are frayed, so there is a mild test of sportsmanship here. A good sportsman playing tennis will concede close decisions to his opponent. His temper, though, will be surely tried if his opponent keeps playing his weakness with telling effect.

In my opinion, playing football is the most difficult test of sportsmanship. A young man has to stand up to sixty minutes of grueling attack in the bodily-contact type of game such as football. If he is up against a team of opponents who are smarter and physically superior, an opponent who is continuously knocking him down, it takes a tremendous amount of restraint and emotional control for a young man to stay in there and keep playing the game according to "Hoyle."

The hard, physical contact games put pressure on a man. It will severely test his sportsmanship. You will never see any occasions of physical combat between competitors at a track meet, a golf tournament, or a tennis tournament. Indeed, you see it rarely in college football or hockey, but when you consider the tremendous strain under which the contestants play, when you consider the hundreds of thousands of boys who play these games, and how rare are the occurrences of muckerism, it is remarkable.

I know that when I play golf, tennis or squash, I have no trouble being a good loser or a good winner. The contest is largely within me. But I can remember when I played football, it was awfully hard at times to control my temper and to resist the temptation of doing something muckerish, particularly when the game was not going our way. I do feel that in playing football I was subjected to a real test of sportsmanship, and in the other sports not so much.

Real sportsmanship is when playing on your ground, the ideal student takes much pride in showing the other team every consideration, every form of thoughtful hospitality, as though they were guests in his own home. If he does these things, he need have no fear as to what people will think of him.

Playing football, you must be fair, be smart, and be brave. You all know what it is to be fair, and no boy is respected any more than the boy who stresses this. To be smart, study football the same as you would chess or your other classes, so that you will always have the situation well in hand and you will do the right thing at the right time. And be brave.

To be brave means to have mental and moral courage. Just what this is, is sometimes hard to say, but I heard one man define it as, "being afraid to do a thing and yet doing it."

Sportsmanship combines dignity and humility. The boys should play the game and get a lot of fun out of it. Don't criticize one another and look for faults. All of us have plenty of faults. Let's get more fun and more team play by looking for the good points of our teammates. Let's have in mind trying to beat the other team if we can, but let's do it fairly and honestly. Let's develop a fine sense of fair play. Let's respect the rules of the game and the rights of the opponents. Let's be as fair as we can in every way.

Don't forget that eleven wide-awake boys who have their heads up, using their eyes to see and with their minds active, are pretty hard to beat. Eleven smart boys, everything else being equal, will decisively beat eleven boys who are dull mentally and who do not use their eyes. Everything else being equal, a football game is largely a contest of wits.

A smart team is a team that is not fooled, but plays good sound football all the time. They take no unnecessary chances on offense, and they never relax mentally on defense. The victory goes not only to the strong and brave, but to the smart team.

Let's have no swell-heads or egotists. Play the game like gentlemen and try to win like a gentleman.

In the words of President Roosevelt: "Don't fool, don't flinch, and when you hit the line, hit it hard."

To the cricket field of old England, the world owes a tardily-acknowledged debt, for on them was born and nurtured the modern idea of sportsmanship.

Sportsmanship is more than a word to be

bandied about by college yell leaders and newspapermen. It is an attitude towards the other fellow. It is a philosophy of living, if a football coach may be allowed so scholarly an expression. It is, I am sure, one of the really big things of our day. And it all started in England.

Of course, the ancient Greeks had their athletic competitions, but their games would mean little to moderns had not English sport traditions prepared men for the Olympic revival. During the Middle Ages, people forgot how to play. They said it with lances in those days when steel or brass trousers and vests were in style.

Then, a few hundred years ago, English school boys developed the notion of playing games just for fun. The old chivalric idea of doing your best and letting the other fellow do the same was transferred to the cricket fields of Eton and Harrow, Oxford and Cambridge. And "play cricket" became the English expression for playing hard, and accepting defeat without humiliation or victory without gloating.

The athletic competition idea in recent years has taken vigorous root in the New World. Thanks to such straight-shooting athletic mentors as Walter Camp of Yale, "Grand Old Man" Stagg of Chicago, and George Huff of Illinois, the United States has built up a fine set of sport traditions. And, so have Japan, and India, and Australia and France, and almost every other nation of the world.

Sportsmanship is simply a corollary of the Golden Rule. You want to play your best; hence, you take no advantage that will prevent the other fellow from doing the same. You respect him, as you want him to respect you. You give and take on a fifty-fifty basis. You play the game, and when it is over, there are no whines nor excuses. You both have done your best.

We teach sportsmanship in football. When our team went up against Northwestern University in Dyche Stadium at Evanston, Illinois, one Notre Dame man had an injured muscle in his side. The Northwestern trainer came around and offered him the use of a protective appliance — offered it to a player of the rival team! Not only that, but just before the kick-off, the Northwestern man who was to play opposite our fellow came up and said: "They tell me you have a sore spot. Where is it?" Our man showed him.

Did the Northwestern player take advantage of his information? He did not. Our chap played forty-five minutes, and his sore spot was never touched. That is sportsmanship.

We need such sportsmanship everywhere and every day. We need it because there are ill-tempered men and women in homes and offices. We need it because there are road hogs on the highways and political meddlers in public positions. We need it because of bootleggers and other social impedimenta. Sportsmanship not only provides a principle of action, but a scale of values for generous judgement.

As the fine spirit of sportsmanship develops in athletic competitions, men bring it into other relationships. They introduce it into domestic situations. They apply it in meetings of boards of directors, where unfair advantages could be taken. They are beginning to use it in national politics. May we hope someday it will be extended to the field of international relations. For probably what the world most needs today is a spirit of sportsmanship among nations.

When one suggests such a possibility, he cannot not be accused of being visionary. Already in tennis, golf, soccer, yachting, and track competition, we see young, spirited men

Rockne of Ages

*... I look through the eyes of a football coach and
speak the words of the gridiron ...*

competing in international games. The sportsmanship engendered in such contests cannot but have repercussions in other activities that cross and re-cross national boundaries.

At the last Olympic contests at Amsterdam, I saw an incident that stands out in my mind. And yet it is typical of many. The great English athlete Lowe ran half-mile in record time. With a beautiful, dazzling burst of speed, he left the field almost literally standing still, and flashed into the tape several lengths ahead of his rivals.

Winners of the race were announced, and from the great pole floated the English flag. Below it was the Swedish, and below that the German, second and third winners respectively. The applause was like the roar of a tremendous salute from a fleet of battleships.

Where were the athletes? There they went across the field, Lowe in fifth-center with his arms affectionately around the men he had just beaten. They were chatting companionably, the English, the Swedish runner, and the German. Then the 40,000 people cheered again. This time it was louder than before. It was an impressive sight, for just ten years before, had these boys been of military age, two of them would in all probability have been fighting each other with bayonets, shrapnel and poison gas in the slime and stench of the trenches.

In 1925, Shimidzu was captain of the Japanese Cup tennis team. France and Japan had reached the final round, which would decide which country would compete with the United States. Quite unexpectedly, Lacoste, French ace, was defeated in the first match by Harada of Japan, and Cochet was barely able to escape defeat from Tawara.

Borotra, hero of the French courts, who could probably have saved the day for France, arrived on the second day of the matches.

Though he was not officially nominated, and hence ineligible, Shimidzu earnestly suggested he play the following afternoon anyway. It was a beau geste of sportsmanship that is still remembered in the tennis world.

And, so it goes, wherever men get together in athletic rivalry, there you will find sportsmanship. Who can measure the influence of grizzled old Sir Thomas Lipton in promoting amity between England and the United States by his dogged persistence in attempting to regain the America's Cup? Bobby Jones, with his steady hand, has been almost as effective an "ambassador of goodwill" in Europe as Lindbergh.

The world needs sportsmanship. The rules of fair play and clean play must be read into international politics and economic relations, if universal peace is to come and to stay.

It used to be said that music was the international language. That is still true, I suppose, but there is another international language that all of us should master. It is the fine language of sportsmanship, first developed in England and since exported even to surprisingly remote corners of the earth. It is a natural Esperanto, for all men soon learn to understand it, regardless of the color of their skin, the length of their bodies, or their political parties.

Opinions will vary as to the game that best lends itself to promoting international sportsmanship. Some will vote for tennis, some for yachting, and others for golf. Baseball and track, too, have their devotee, but I cast my ballot for football — and, of course, the kind that is played in the United States. Years of experience with football of the rough-and-tumble variety has convinced me it is unsurpassed for bringing out the fine qualities of a young fellow.

Some soccer is played in the United States, and our soccer teams take part in international matches. I wish that our overseas cousins would develop football elevens similarly to meet our American teams on the gridiron.

So, I would respectfully suggest football as a substitute for bloodshed. I believe my professional friends would classify it under the high-flown title of a "moral equivalent for war." Let it go at that, providing we mean the same thing.

In football, young men can give expression to that fundamental urge for combat that arises from an exuberance of red blood and animal spirits. Man has it in him, and if he doesn't get it out of his system one way, he will another. Some peoples, in times past, have expressed it in war.

In football, more than any other sport unless it be boxing, one sees conflict in its essential elements. In pugilism, it is one man against another, a personal encounter. But in football you have a socialized clash. Here are eleven men, organized to a high degree of co-ordinated efficiency, with each unit trained to physical perfection and schooled to meet situations.

The signals are given. There is a clump-clump of cleated shoes, the swish of grating drill breeches. The ball is snapped, and the lines charge. Bang! It is every man for himself. Up to that point, each player has been a part of a mobile machine, a unit in the social group. Then for an instant — or several instants if he is lucky — he emerges and is in an individual striving against, giving his best to out-rival the man who tries to stop him.

That is the picture of society, too, and I don't care whether you are thinking of an old-fashioned debating club, a Rotary club, a national government, a League of Nations, or mankind at large. Football epitomizes better than any other sport the give-and-take process of civilization. That is why I am so strong for football. It trains boys to become men. It puts in the back part of a fellow's head some never-to-be-forgotten ideas of how a gentleman can give his best to overcome an opponent, and still be a gentleman.

A man who can be a gentleman on a football field can be a gentleman anywhere, and what is more to the point, will. If I had my way, I would teach young men of all countries to reach for a football instead of a hand grenade.

Yes, I would like to see international football. It would do a lot to perpetuate and increase that fine old English spirit of sportsmanship among young fellows of the world. And they're the chaps who really count, you know. It would give them lessons in fair dealing and respect for others they wouldn't forget when it comes their turn to run affairs.

I look through the eyes of a football coach and speak the words of the gridiron when I say what is most needed in business and politics, national or international, is more sportsmanship. The most encouraging thing on the horizon is the developing spirit of fair play among young men.

Our fathers didn't know of international sports on the scale we do. The movement is growing. That is why I am an optimist.

SECTION 3: ROCKNE ON ROCKNE

... ALL SPORTS FOR ALL!

44

NON SCHOLARSHIP

*"I think it would be a wonderful thing if a coach could just forget
all about the high-school and prep school wonders of the world
and develop a team from among the students of his institution who
came to his school because they liked it best and not because any
attractive offers made for athletic ability in various lines of sports."*

From Interview with Knute Rockne

L et the stadiums keep on getting bigger and let the crowds grow with them. Let the competition grow keener.

But someday I hope that scholarships for college football, baseball, basketball and all other kind of players will be a thing of the past.

I don't know who is going to lead the way in this. A coach can't, because he must have a winner or loser in his job. Maybe the college presidents will get together sometime and lead the way.

I think it would be a wonderful thing if coaches could just forget all about the high school and prep school wonders of the world and develop a team from among the students of his institution who came to his institution because they liked it best and not because of any attractive offers made for athletic ability in various lines of sport.

All sports for all.

That's my opinion of the height of perfection, in so far as college students are concerned. Instead of the specialized football or baseball player, I think it would be wonderful if every student could develop in many kinds of sport.

At Notre Dame we are developing not only football players, I am glad to say, but are paying attention to handball, a great and growing sport, and to golf and tennis. Ninety per cent of our students are taking part in some sort of sport, and we have plenty of interclass and interdormitory competition.

And as another thought in this cutting down of scholarships, I would be in favor of listing every student on the books as to who he was and just what assistance, if any, he was getting, so there would be nothing underhand about it.

Scouting is the pitting of brains of one man against those of another. It is the science of observation and improving from such observations.

You, newspaper men, read other papers, don't you? And when you see the other fellow has a new trend of thought on a story you try to beat him out the next time. Automobile dealers look at other dealers' windows and at their new models and benefit thereby.

So why shouldn't football coaches or basketball coaches see other teams play and get a line on their news ideas? I can see nothing wrong with scouting.

I'm no wizard or magician or anything else. That talk in there was just keeping up the emotional side of the game. College athletes, in order to win, have to be right physically and mentally and emotionally, and the last is just

as important as the other two.

Coaching a football team is principally knowing a good system and imparting it to your men. Ours is the Notre Dame system, and is followed at Villanova by Harry Stuhldreher and by others of my men who have gone out from our school. Then there is the Glenn Warner system, the Howard Jones system, the Bezdek "spinner," and others.

Our followers go out and take our system with them, putting in their own ideas as well, until in time, you get cross-sections of this and that system. The Penn, Georgetown and Pitt systems are offshoots of the Warner system.

Each coach thinks his system is the best or he wouldn't follow it. Regardless of what may be said, a coach soon loses his popularity if his teams are beaten continually. In every line of college sport, he must please his athletes, student body, faculty, alumni and townspeople. If he falls down in any one of these places he is doomed.

Of the five, I think the alumni are the hardest to please. They work at some other business throughout the week and on Saturday go out to see their team in action. They want recreation and enjoyment and can't have it in defeat. They insist on victories and soon get out their hammers if a bad season comes along."

The word "gigantic" can scarcely apply to the college sports other than football. Basketball is growing, but there need be no discussion of it ever reaching the magnitude of football, because it won't. Football is the great college game because college men play it best.

In baseball, the professional big leaguers are not the stars, but professional football is a no-better brand than college football. Football owes its prominence, I think, because it offers the chance for bodily-contact.

Despite our 1929 civilization, all men

love to revert to primitive type, either openly or in their hearts. They love to see the clashing of bodies out on the gridiron. Basketball does not have that element, because when the bodily-contact occurs the referee calls a foul. Foul after foul slows up the game. Baseball does not have the primitive side. Neither does rowing or track.

Hence the great popularity of football.

THE MODERN TREND OF FOOTBALL

I am not so old that I cannot remember "way back" when we used kerosene lamps to see after the sun set, when we took a bath on Saturday night in the old washtub, and when we got our heat from the old baseburner.

I can remember riding on the old cable cars in Chicago. And when automobiles first came out and chugged their way painfully down the boulevard, the other lads and myself would greet the driver with raucous shouts of: "Get a horse! Get a horse!"

Today, modern invention has brought so many changes that we seem to be in a constant state of flux. Two of the improvements which will no doubt make remarkable advances in the next ten years are aviation and television radio. To say that these will never come about would be just as sensible as our childish jibes that we used to hurl at the first automobile.

There is no question, but that in a few years we will be able to travel from Chicago to any part of the United States in 15 hours. Within a year or so a man will be able to sit down at home at his radio and not only hear an account of the game, but see it by means of television.

What will be the effect of these inventions on the game of football?

Rapid transit strides made possible by aviation will increase intersectional games, bringing more color into the various college schedules.

I don't believe that television radio will affect the crowds any more than radio does today. There are some of certain temperaments who will be content to sit at home and get the account of the game that way. But the real dyed-in-the-wool fan will want to be out there in the throng, getting the thrill and the feel of the multitude.

No doubt other modern inventions will come about in this same period. Anyone who lets precedent govern his thoughts along this line will be in for many a shock.

HAS FOOTBALL KEPT PACE?

Football coaches have been hampered in their creative genius, in their perfecting of new theories by "Old Man Precedent."

I remember when we first went east to play West Point in 1913. There were two things I inquired about from a certain Eastern coach.

I said to him: "Why is it an Eastern team always keeps a safety back 50 yards against any formation, while if the opponent took punt formation two men go back approximately 50 yards?"

His reply was that it had always been so. In other words, precedent prevented certain Eastern coaches from making adequate use of their safety man.

I believe the reason many high school coaches made more use of the forward pass during its infancy than the college coaches did was because high school coaches were not hampered by "Old Foggy Precedent."

The important innovations in football during the last decade have been the spinner attack of Hugo Bezdek; the double wing-back formation of Glenn Warner; the ingenious spinner attack as devised by Wally Steffen of Carnegie Tech; and the smart use made of the forward-passing game at Michigan and other schools.

We also have the huddle as introduced by Bob Zuppke; the novel cutback features of Howard Jones of Southern California; the clever interchanging of duties by the wing back and flanking end as used by Clarence Spears at Minnesota; and the lateral and forward-passing tricks employed by Ray Morrison of Southern Methodist University.

There have been, no doubt, other innovations, but those are just a few that I mention offhand. Certainly, none of these coaches, in putting on their new ideas, allowed themselves to be influenced by precedent.

IN FAVOR OF SPRING GAMES

The five or six weeks of spring football receives practically no publicity. There are no trips away from home, and no absences from classes. There is no student interest, beyond that of the boys taking part in the practice.

The coach gets a line on his material. And with five, or six weeks' time on his hands, he is able to give every boy on a very large squad a chance to show what he can do. This is impossible in the fall as there is not time enough to give anyone other than the first string a chance. So, spring practice makes for democracy and a fair chance for every boy.

In fact, I would be in favor of some spring games between schools, allowing only those boys to play who had not earned their letters, or who had not been members of the first string previously. This would provide a chance for the ordinary boy to represent his school in contests, whereas in the fall only the best, of course, will have the honor of representing their institution.

Perhaps this won't be possible, however, until the word "overemphasis" will have been laid away among the moth balls where it belongs. From present indications that won't happen for several years, but I believe it should come about eventually.

Just how much can be accomplished in spring football practice is entirely up to the energy, personality, and inventiveness of the coach. At Notre Dame we practically do all of our coaching and scrimmaging in the spring. In the fall it is merely a matter of conditioning and polishing up, keeping the team fit mentally and physically.

SOME PLAYS TO DEVELOP

Personally, I believe that there are fertile fields to be explored within the next 10 years, particularly regarding offensive football. I don't believe that the American teams have utilized the lateral pass to the full extent of its possibilities. I believe that our return of a kickoff is still in an imperfect state.

As I see some of these teams using a spinner attack with one man spinning, a thought has occurred to me: Why not have two men spinning, one with the ball and one without it, with the third man faking for it?

I also see in my dreams sometimes the prep school star entering college with a technique so highly developed that he can throw accurately 60 yards with either hand and can cover up where he is looking by assuming the cross-eyed expression made famous by Ben Turpin in the movies.

Then there is a possibility of deploying a man out 10 or 15 yards from a double wing-

The coach gets a line on his material.

back formation, using him sometimes in motion and sometimes just as a decoy from the field. This might open an avenue of offense which would be productive of much deception and sufficient power.

But I will not bore you with any more detail. Suffice to say that for the man with initiative and creative ability there is still a great field ahead.

What the public likes to see is more open stuff, more football that is different, and yet where the decoying and timing is so fine and the play so open and apparent that the average spectator is able to see and appreciate just what is going on.

Warner's attack, as shown in New York against the 1928 Army team, was the sensation of the East. But Warner, Stagg, Yost and others of the old guard who have given so much to football are nearing the close of their careers, and it will be up to the younger men to blaze the trail with new ideas, new theories, and colorful schemes that will enable our great American game of football to keep pace with this wonderful mechanical age of ours.

A STUDY IN CULTURE

Football and all athletics should be a part of culture, the culture that makes the whole man, not the part-time thinker. Ancient Greece was a cradle of culture, and ancient

Greece was a nation of athletes.

Boys must have an outlet for animal spirits. Their education must contain training in clean contests, otherwise, they will be lost in a world that thrives on competition and in which those who cannot compete cannot hope to thrive.

Football, as the leading American amateur pastime, provides participants, students and other spectators with the most colorful, the most skillful, and the most beneficial of all athletic contests, which is why it stirs the pulse, captures the imagination, and at the same time builds character without which culture is valueless.

But while the gridiron game is essentially amateur, professional football has its thrills — and I'm one champion of amateur sport who will never deny it.

I did not see Benny Friedman play with Michigan, so I took advantage of a chance to see this famed quarterback play pro football against the Chicago Bears.

It was an afternoon of thrills at the extraordinary dexterity of his passing. Four yards, 10 yards, 40 yards, harassed and pounded, he threw the ball from all angles, standing or running at terrific speed, hitting his target right on the button.

There are those who say Friedman is the greatest passer of all time. He could hit a dime at 40 yards. Besides being a great passer, he hit the line, tackled, blocked and did everything. He was not a mere specialty man because he could do all of what a fine football player should be able to do.

In grading thrills of gridiron action an experienced observer has difficulties. But I sat in the stands in Atlanta one afternoon and saw a magnificent Notre Dame team that seemed headed for its annual victory over Georgia Tech suddenly recoil before the furious pounding of one man — Henry R. Pund, center.

Nobody could stop him. Notre Dame fought like tigers, but this man was a tiger-tamer. I counted 20 scoring plays that this man ruined. With this giant dervish shattering them it was a sight for the gods. We were hopelessly beaten, but I had the thrill of my life to see great fighters go down in defeat before a greater fighter.

Endlessly, the sights and sounds of the most exciting of all games, with the blare of bands, the waving pennants, the cheering crowds, convey the lesson to anyone that calls on me in the name of culture should remember. Football is clean sport, which is as much a part of culture as clean literature.

THE VALUE OF FOOTBALL

The president of an Eastern college has been quoted as saying that the system of football is all wrong, and that since neither the player nor spectators derive any benefit from the game it should be abolished. He contends that players are mere automatons moving at the will of the coach, that no mental effort on their part is involved.

He is entirely wrong. Every man on the Notre Dame squad knows that his resourcefulness is relied upon and he does not have to wait for me to press a button before he moves.

Out there, every man must think of the one thing he is playing. The thought of his best girl or the next dance must never enter his mind while he is in the game. On the field, a man learns things which the classroom sometimes fails to supply. He learns the great lesson of fair play and he is taught to have respect for the other man's ideas. He learns also the lesson of humility.

(FROM A SPEECH CAUGHT ON FILM)

"You tackles are not stopping them. They're coming through you, through you, I say, and you've got to stop them!

You ends are not getting down that field fast enough. You've got to move. You've got to hit them and hit them hard. We want that ball, I tell you, because when we get that ball, we begin our drive they cannot stop. You hear me?

They cannot stop us, men. So, get out there now and play like demons, play until you drop and never give up. I want you to always fight, fight, fight!

From "Abolish Athletic Scholarships"

By C. William Duncan

Interview with Knute Rockne published in The Seattle Times, February 24, 1929

What does the student body get from football?

I hold that the men in the stands learn to appreciate fair play. Men who watch a contest played fairly and squarely develop a high standard of sportsmanship, and that is a mighty fine thing. You won't find any bigotry, intolerance or narrow-mindedness where you find clean sportsmanship. Cheering the team on to victory is another fine thing. It adds color to college life.

I think the college president is mistaken when he says that football should be abolished. Football, due to its popularity, pays for all the other college sports.

If we were to abolish football, we must abolish all other athletics. Any curriculum which does not include athletics is unbalanced. The president paradoxes his argument for the abolishment of football... when he said that a man who is physically fit may go wrong, but he can always come back.

We have, here, much for which other schools envy us. We have had a successful season.

But if we are to keep Notre Dame what she is, the greatest university in America, we must work hard. We are competing with great institutions and should we allow ourselves to become self-satisfied, "dry rot" will set in and we will be lost. There are many of us who are too self-satisfied.

We have too large a percentage of students who do nothing but criticize. In the jungle there are two beasts: One is the killer who slays, eats what he wants, and goes his way; the other is the jackal who follows him and eats what is left and then probably criticizes the killer for not leaving enough.

All of us have our faults and it is easy for anyone to criticize the fellows who are trying to do something. But instead of doing this, why not look for the good points in the other man?

If you have any ability at all, stop moaning and knocking. Get out and do things. If you can run, go out to the track. If you can sing, get in the Glee Club. If you can argue, go out for debating. If you can write, get on the Daily or Scholastic.

Do something and you won't have to worry about "dry rot" setting in.

The Greeks Had a Way

Back in the pagan days of Greece, Plato, the philosopher, remarked that the first aim in the education of a young man should be, "Know thyself."

Every year hundreds of thousands of young men receive their diplomas from their colleges and go out to face the world. I wonder just how many of these lads know themselves.

With the hundred-and-one experiments in education going, or in many of our colleges, many of them freakish, impractical and purely theoretical, we are swinging away from the old-fashioned ideas of education.

The three words which are seldom mentioned in educational circles are courage, competition and personality. Just why this is so, I do not know.

The young-boy graduate needs, above all, courage to face the tough problems of life. Except in civil service and in some teaching circles, all life is competition, and yet many of our young men have been taught by teachers who shun competition. Only the boys who have worked their way through school — have competed in athletic contests, political contests on the campus, or have competed on various scholastic journals — understand, fully, the meaning of the word.

And as for personality that goes along with confidence, I wonder just how many of these young men have had experience of the kind that build up confidence? Wasn't the old Greek system of education superior to ours? Theirs was based on a premise that is fundamentally sound: "Know thyself."

Football Misunderstood

The Rules Committee has done well fostering the development of the game. In my opinion, and that of all the coaches to whom I have spoken to, changes in rules have been and should be limited to just the details.

There are always a lot of fanatics who want to introduce sets of rules to make the game more like soccer, or more like rugby, or more like twiddled-winks, bobbing up each fall. But none of the rules have been of that classification.

Football is a good game now, a healthful, sportsman-like game, and undue tampering with its rules can do nothing but harm.

I don't like to lose. And that is not so much because it's just a football game, because defeat means failure to reach your objective. I don't want a football player who doesn't take defeat to heart, who laughs it off with the thought, "Well, there's another one next Saturday."

The trouble in American life today, in business as well as in sports, is that too many people are afraid of competition. The result is that in some circles people have come to sneer at success if it costs hard work and training and sacrifice. That's one of the chief reasons for the sentiment against intercollegiate football; one of the reasons why these people want to cut the schedules, do away with even voluntary spring practice and give us intramural sports in the colleges to the exclusion of everything else.

If they are not careful, they will have this nation "softening up." The kids are all right, yet, in spite of the automobile and sorority teas and weekend parties in the city.

The game will be free from attacks for now. Outbursts will not occur until December. At that time "Mr. Pop Off" and "Mr. All Off," having no other means of breaking into print, will make their annual attack against the brutal, dehumanizing game of football. As one of these chaps once said, "It's a terrible game the way these boys bump each other and everything."

I attended a pacifist meeting this year at one of the great Midwest universities. During that meeting I analyzed the crowd as well and as fairly as I could. I found that, almost without exception, they were physically below normal. I questioned about a half-dozen of the chaps regarding football, and I found they were just as anti-football as they were anti-military.

The thought has occurred to me since that the resentment of these men against the soldier, the resentment of these men against football, was a natural thing. It is a result of their inferiority complex. These men were lacking in the qualities of courage, physique, and loyalty that go to make up a football player or soldier, hence their natural resentment against both. However, these people are a small minority.

The wonderful programs now being sponsored by our high schools and colleges throughout the United States assure the virility and physical fitness of our youth. We shall always have the objectors, the reformers and the pseudo-intelligentsia. At times they get somewhat annoying.

However, we might all take the point of view taken by James "Champ" Clark when that statesman was assailed by some crazy simpleton. Rising to his feet with ease and dignity, he merely flicked an imaginary particle from his coat as he said: "Shoo-fly."

THE LEGENDS

These accidents will happen in the best of all possible worlds. Indeed, the football epic of the Four Horsemen is the story of an accident.

... sportswriter Grantland Rice rose to lyric heights ... by naming them "The Four Horsemen."

45

THE FOUR HORSEMEN

A sleepy-eyed lad who looked as though he was born to be a tester in an alarm clock factory loafed about the backfield in the freshmen lineup for practice.

With him in the backfield was his companion halfback, a youngster who appeared to be half-puzzled by everything going on around him.

Between them was a small wiry boy with a sharp handsome face and a clear commanding voice. These assets seemed the best the youngster had, for in his first plays during that practice game he made as many mistakes as he called signals, and he called a lot. As a rule, rookie quarterbacks call a lot of signals.

It was not an inspiring practice to watch. Even the likely looking youngster at fullback who could run like a streak ran quite as often into the hands of tackles as through holes in the line.

After watching this backfield performance for an entire quarter, I shook my head. "Not so hot," I thought, especially when the entire four were smeared by a clumsy but willing scrub tackle — who weighed about as much as the entire quartet — who pounded through like an ice wagon to block a kick.

"Not so hot," I repeated, preparing to exercise the virtue of patience and wait optimistically for the season's developments. This freshman bunch could be whipped into a combination of average players, but not much more. That was the sum of the dream I had of them that day.

Thankfully, it didn't come true.

Three years later, this trio, along with an addition, took the field to the cheers of 50,000 people at the Polo Grounds and dazzled into defeat the strongest Army eleven ever sent against anybody. The next morning, sportswriter Grantland Rice rose to lyric heights in celebrating their speed, rhythm and precision, winding up a litany of hallelujahs by naming them "The Four Horsemen."

Harry Stuhldreher, the quarterback, hailed from Massillon, Ohio; Don Miller, halfback, came from Defiance, Ohio; Jimmy Crowley, the other halfback, hailed from Green Bay, Wisconsin; and Elmer Layden, the dashing, slashing fullback, had his home in Davenport, Iowa.

How it came to pass that four young men so eminently qualified by temperament, physique and instinctive pacing to complement one another perfectly and, thus, produce the best coordinated and most picturesque backfield in the recent history of football is one of the inscrutable achievements of coincidence of which I know nothing that is a more satisfying mouthful of words.

These men, and the others of the freshman squad in 1921, were soundly beaten by such teams like Lake Forest Academy and the Michigan State freshmen.

Of the lot, Stuhldreher had the most promise. He sounded like a leader on the field. He was a good and fearless blocker, and as he gained football knowledge, he showed signs of smartness in emergencies.

Layden had speed — he could run a 100-yard dash within 10 seconds at a track meet. But speed and some kicking ability seemed to be all his football wares.

Jimmy Crowley was only less humorous in play than in appearance. He looked dull and always resembled a lad about to get out of or into bed. He showed very little potential as a freshman, certainly none of the nimble wit that made him as celebrated for repartee as for broken-field running.

Don Miller traveled that first year on the reputation and recommendation of his brother, "Red" Miller, the great Notre Dame halfback who made such havoc when his team beat Michigan in 1909. Red had sung the praises of another Miller, Jerry, who made a fine high school record but couldn't add to his poundage of 135. Unfortunately, he also grew quite deaf and so was disqualified for the tough going of big-league football. Don also ran track in his freshman year, surprised me when he came out for spring practice and with his fleetness and daring sized up as a halfback to cheer the heart of any coach.

In the fall of 1922, Notre Dame had lost all its veteran backs except Paul Castner at fullback and Frank Thomas at quarterback, one of those decimations by graduation that give coaches gray hair or, as in my case, remove what little hair they have.

This 1922 squad, the first on which the Four Horsemen got their chance, romped through its preliminary games against Kalamazoo, St. Louis, Purdue and DePaul. With the first big game looming against Georgia Tech, Stuhldreher was promoted to alternate as quarterback with Thomas. Crowley and Layden were assigned to alternate as left halfbacks, while Castner, the veteran, remained at fullback, and Don Miller received the right halfback berth.

Crowley won his place only by a surprising performance against Purdue, when the sleepy one astonished Purdue a great deal — and me a great deal more — with the liveliest exhibition of cutting, jumping, sidestepping, change of pace and determined ball-toting

... Stuhldreher could read through another team's strategy without a key to the code ...

that I had seen in many a day.

The Georgia Tech game of 1922 found the Four Horsemen ready to demonstrate. The experienced Castner guided them through their green patches, but practice had displayed their unusual gift for synchronization. They showed it against Georgia Tech for the first time and were largely instrumental in turning in a 13 — 3 victory.

HARRY STUHLDREHER

Yet in that same game, Stuhldreher, who had appeared most promising of the bunch, made the biggest mistake of his career, one that stamped him still an apprentice quarterback. When our team reached the five-yard line, Stuhldreher passed on second down over the goal line for a touchback and it became Tech's ball on our 20-yard line.

Never again did Stuhldreher make a tactical error while running the team as quarterback. I have in mind the uproar that followed his spectacular, or what seemed to be a spectacular error during the Tournament of Roses game against Stanford on New Year's Day in 1925.

Notre Dame was ahead, yet Stuhldreher passed straight into the hands of a Stanford player. The fact is that Stuhldreher had badly hurt his foot. We didn't know until the game was over that he had broken a bone and was suffering tremendously throughout the game.

Even this circumstance, of course, could not excuse passing on second down with his team leading. But Ed Hunsinger, our right end, had told Stuhldreher in a huddle that the Stanford safety did not follow him deep into the scoring zone on Notre Dame's offensive plays. Knowing this, Stuhldreher was ready to open up. On second down he called for a forward pass to Hunsinger.

Sure enough, on the play Hunsinger got to clear away from the Stanford safety, who failed to follow him deep enough. He was clear in the open, ready to race for a touchdown on receipt of the ball. A 45-yard pass would have done the trick, and a 45-yard pass straight to the target was easy enough for Stuhldreher, but not this time. As the plucky little quarterback squared himself to shoot, bringing down the foot with the broken bone to take his stance, excruciating pain shot through him, so that instead of his usual vigor the ball sailed a measly 20 yards.

Yet Stuhldreher's tactics were sound for such a good ball thrower. For even if Hunsinger had failed to catch the ball and it had been intercepted, a 45-yard pass would have been as useful as a punt. If Hunsinger had caught it, it was a sure touchdown. The worst thing that could have happened would have been an incomplete pass, which would have cost us a down. As the play took place on third down, an incomplete pass would not have hurt because Layden was there to kick the ball on the next play. And Layden was a kicker.

Against Army in 1924, Stuhldreher found their ends were smashing in close. As a result, he sent Crowley and Miller circling the ends. In the very next game, against Princeton, he found the tackle and end on each side were very wide, so he confined his tactics all day to sharp thrusts by Layden through the thinned-out line and cutbacks by Crowley and Miller.

In the game following that, against Georgia Tech, he made gains back to our weak side because Georgia Tech had over-shifted to our strong side, thus leaving the weak side unguarded.

And in the game against Wisconsin, fairly strong that year, Stuhldreher repeatedly found a gap between tackle and end that netted neat gains. To prove his versatility conclusively, when Nebraska's line in the next

game was exceedingly tough before a fast plowing backfield, Stuhldreher wasted little time or strength on line drives. He opened up a passing attack and completed 10 before the final whistle, the score being 34 — 7.

JIMMY CROWLEY

This diversity of attack caused a well-known football writer to wonder what the Four Horsemen could do with a kicking game. As if in a direct response, they put one on in their last appearance for Notre Dame, in the Tournament of Roses game against Stanford.

The entire team had wilted in the heat. The boys were unable to move. They had to rely on Layden's punting, not their usual game. Layden, however, got off a pair of punts of around 80 yards which were quite useful. Stanford lost the game despite its hard, smashing play, and Pop Warner was disappointed, making much of the fact that Stanford had made more first downs than Notre Dame.

To this comment, Crowley, as a spontaneous spokesman for the Four Horsemen, pointed out that the score was 27 — 10, adding, "Next year in the major leagues they aren't going to count runs that come over the plate. They'll just count the men left on bases."

Pop Warner, like the grand old sport he is, admitted Crowley had the laugh, and that the only payoff in football was the ball over the line and not down close to it.

Crowley was always quick at a comeback. After one big Eastern game, an official who had penalized Notre Dame all afternoon, to the neglect of the Eastern team that he rarely looked at, met Crowley, and they trudged side-by-side into the dressing room.

... Crowley was the nerviest back I've known ...

The official said to Crowley, "You were lucky to win today."

"Yes, Cyclops," said Crowley. "After watching you officiate, you don't even begin to know how lucky we were."

Crowley was the comedian of the outfit, but not at first. You never saw a more serious bunch of football players than the Four Horsemen before they had really made good, or a livelier group afterward.

One afternoon, Crowley had come back from vacation and stopped at my office. This was after fame had perched on his sloping shoulders.

"Ran into a grand high school player in Green Bay, Coach," he said.

"Good, is he?" I asked.

"Awful good," he said.

"You really mean that, Jim?" I said.

"He's awful good," said Crowley.

"You mean, as good as you?" I asked.

"Well," said Jim, edging toward the door. "Perhaps not that good . . . but awful good."

The official debut of Crowley and his other Horsemen as big-leaguers was actually against Carnegie Tech. Castner, the veteran fullback who had been their bellwether in the early games, was so seriously injured in the game against Butler — a broken hip in a flying fall — that he was out for the season.

I moved Layden from left halfback, where he had been alternating with Crowley, to fullback. These boys surprised the football fans of Pittsburgh with their perfect timing, as they functioned for the first time as a unit backfield. Layden amazed me by his terrific speed as fullback. He adopted a straight-line drive that made him one of the most unusual fullbacks in football.

They won. This victory, however, didn't thrill me as much as the defeat they suffered the very next game against Nebraska. The Cornhuskers had one of the heaviest teams in their history, and they are known for very active heft. They pushed the relatively little Four Horsemen team all over the field.

... Examine their records closely and you'll find the Four Horsemen stand unique as a continuing combination in the backfield ...

At the half, the score was 14 — 0, and it would have been another touchdown if the lightweight boys from South Bend hadn't held the big Cornhuskers on their one-yard line for four straight downs. They emerged from that battering a sadly crumpled team.

But they came out fighting mad for the second half, whacked across a touchdown in the third quarter, and carried the ball to Nebraska's one-yard line toward the end of the final period. Stuhldreher called for a pass, and Layden spurted ahead to a corner of the field, where he was all set to receive and down the ball for six more points. But Stuhldreher, always aware, this time was not alert enough. Sam Weir, the huge 250-pound Nebraska tackle, crashed through the line and flattened the 150-pound Notre Dame quarterback.

Our college alumni in Lincoln had a banquet ready for the Four Horsemen team that night. But Crowley, who came through the drumming bruised and bandaged, put it this way, "We need a thermometer more than a feed."

They went to bed to nurse their sore spots.

The Four Horsemen once were blamed for a breach of football etiquette in which they were in no way involved. This was against Wisconsin in 1924.

We had the game well in hand, so in the second half the Horsemen were taken out and sent to the showers. In the final two minutes of play, a substitute halfback went in for Crowley. After running a touchdown, he strutted his stuff, and as he crossed the line for the score, he thumbed his nose at a Wisconsin player pursuing him. He was instantly yanked from the game.

Many thought Crowley had made the vulgar gesture, but that was never Crowley's idea of wit. His style of thought and good-humored balance of character was of the sterling stuff that wears better in adversity than in success.

Against Princeton, he and his three teammates were at their best. But Crowley faltered once. He had taken the ball, skirted Princeton's shock troops, and began one of the rhythmic runs of the Four Horsemen. Jacob Slagle of Princeton ripped up the field to meet him. Crowley veered and Slagle caught him from behind.

In the dressing room between halves, sleepy-eyed Jim was apologetic. "I made a mistake," he said. "I didn't know Slagle was that fast. I should have cut back."

"That wasn't the mistake you made," I said. "That wasn't it."

"Yes, it was," he said. "I admit it. A mistake."

"No," I said. "Slagle didn't know who you were. If you had shown him those New York clippings you've been saving, telling how good you were, he wouldn't have dared come near you."

Crowley laughed at this comment louder than anybody. Perhaps he knew what all the team knew, that the Four Horsemen, great though they were, received a measure of praise that they should have shared with the stalwart linesmen — whom we called the Seven Mules.

This taunting caused a few timely jabs from some of the Mules. Adam Walsh, our center (and) a tower of strength for the Horsemen to play behind, watched them try unsuccessfully to get started on one of their famous runs against Lombard with a second-string line to screen them.

There was nothing doing, so I shot in Walsh and the other six Mules.

"What seems to be the matter, boys?" said Walsh as he took the ball to snap back for the first scrimmage. "It seems you need a little help."

This banter helped to check the rising tide of self-esteem, which only the rarest of young athletes can stem in the face of wholesale flattery. One of the Horsemen suffered just a trifle from a swelled head, which was cured in short order. This particular Horseman came to the squad manager and asked for a clean pair of stockings and a new belt.

The manager said, "OK, but turn in your old ones."

"What for?" said the Horseman.

Edgar "Rip" Miller, one of the Seven Mules, standing within earshot among five of the other six, rebuked the manager. "What do you mean, talking that way?" he said. "Don't you know who this is? This is one of the Four Horsemen."

"No-o?" said the manager, in mock awe.

"Ye-es," said Rip in more mock awe.

As the Horseman walked away confused, manager and players stood staring while the players nudged one another murmuring reverently, "He's one of the Four Horsemen." The lad was cured. Next morning, he went back to the manager and said his old stockings and belt would do.

Those Horsemen were pretty good themselves at concerted kidding. Against Army in 1924, they had been warned in practice of the prowess of Ed Garbisch, the great Army All-American center. When they met him, he punctuated some of their attempts to get away. They in turn found a way to agitate Garbisch.

On subsequent plays, when the drive was against him and he was smeared, one Horseman would politely inquire of another so that Garbisch, picking himself up from the ground, could overhear, "Is that the great Mr. Garbisch?"

To which another would solemnly reply, "Yes, that's the great Mr. Garbisch."

When on another smash the All-American center was floored, Crowley would ask of Miller in amazement, "You don't mean to say that's the great Mr. Garbisch?"

And Miller would retort, "If the number's correct, it's none other than Mr. Garbisch in person."

It didn't help Garbisch's game much.

Quick to block and abuse opponents, the Horsemen, through their most articulate member, did not spare themselves when they failed.

I tried to make Jimmy Crowley a triple-threat man. He could pass and run in great shape, but his kicking was good for just about forty yards. This was, perhaps, due to an unusual fault. He would take three steps with the ball — and that made his kicking dangerous, as he held the ball too long and there was risk of the defense breaking through

... Layden pierced a line through sheer speed, cutting it like a knife ...

and blocking it. He practiced for weeks to kick almost simultaneously with receipt of the ball.

When Layden got injured slightly in the Princeton game, Crowley was assigned to do the punting. On the first try, his old bad habit returned subconsciously and he took three steps. A fast-charging Princeton tackle broke through and blocked the kick, which rolled over our goal line for a safety and two points for the Tigers.

After the game was over, a teammate chided Crowley, "I see you're a triple-threat man this year."

"Yes," snapped Crowley. "Trip, stumble, or fumble."

While this teasing on the part of their squad mates lasted, the Horsemen took the best means to offset it by joining in the chorus.

On the only day in a great season that they weren't able to shine — against Northwestern at Soldier Field in Chicago — they expected razzing. Northwestern was an inspired team, while the Four Horsemen were off-key, off-color, stale, and plainly unable to get anywhere. We beat Northwestern, but only after a heart-catching, nip-and-tuck game.

On the train returning to South Bend, a gentleman who had too much to drink barged into the car containing the squad. The conductor requested his ticket. The drunk brushed him aside. "Where are you going?" the conductor demanded. "New York, Toledo or Cleveland?"

"I don't know," sighed the inebriate. "I guess I'm not going anywhere."

Jimmy Crowley turned to his teammates and remarked, "Must be one of the Four Horsemen."

ELMER LAYDEN

Layden, a quiet member of the quartet, was their star on defense. His ability to intercept passes was uncanny, and it never had more value than in our Tournament of Roses game with Stanford on New Year's Day, 1925.

Pop Warner, greatest originator of smart

plays, had a forward pass play that enabled him to win a tie for the Coast championship even without the help of Ernie Nevers, his All-American fullback, who had been injured most of the season.

Nevers was in the lineup against us, and what a game he played. Twice after Stanford had advanced to about our 30-yard line, they called for this dangerous pass out into the flat zone, and both times, Layden, jumping high in the air, tipped and caught the ball and ran for touchdowns.

Each of these Horsemen shone individually on his day. As Layden's was against Stanford, so Miller's was against Princeton. His long runs for touchdowns were a feature during his three years of play. But he was a much better defensive player than he has been given credit for being.

DON MILLER

In this Princeton game of 1923, Miller had just gone off right tackle for what looked like a good gain when he fumbled the ball, which went rolling along the ground. Quick as a flash, a Princeton back trained in the alert Bill Roper way of stooping at full speed and picking up a loose ball, scooped it up. The next thing we saw was this Princeton halfback, with two interferers in front, speeding down the field.

The goal line was 75 yards away — and no one between the runners and the goal line but Don Miller.

Wasting no time after his error, Miller had recovered poise and was racing across field to cut off the Princeton men. The stands were in an uproar. It seemed impossible that Miller could overtake them, or if he could, then he would have to offer much resistance against three men.

... Miller was the most dangerous of the quartet ...

goal line, Clem Crowe had time to rush up and tackle the ballcarrier from behind. The touchdown was not scored, and so Miller redeemed his fumble by as heady a piece of work as any I have ever seen.

Crowley was the nerviest back I've known. He would throw himself anywhere. Also, since I'm using superlatives where they belong, he was the greatest interferer for his weight I have ever seen and a particularly effective ballcarrier on the critical third down.

Examine their records closely and you'll find the Four Horsemen stand unique as a continuing combination in the backfield. They lost but two games out of 30 — both of these to the heavier Nebraska team in 1922 and 1923.

In the 1923 game, their speed was seriously handicapped by the condition of the field. Nebraska had just built a new stadium and had been unable to grow grass on the gridiron. The clay field was hard-baked, so in order to prevent unnecessary bruises to the players, this field had been plowed to make it soft. A well-intentioned procedure, but it applied four-wheel brakes to the Horsemen.

But these lads of the colorful cavalry of Notre Dame need no alibi. The record was good enough. And the same is true of their scholastic records. They retain their interest in football while attaining success in business.

All are coaching the game. Stuhldreher, the quarterback, coaches Villanova University; Don Miller, the Ohio State backfield; Jimmy Crowley, Michigan State College; and Elmer Layden, between spells at the practice of law in Pittsburgh, coaches Duquesne University. While Adam Walsh, headman of the Seven Mules that bore the brunt for the charge of the light brigade of the Four Horsemen, is an engineer and coaches the Yale line.

Pressing his speed, he ran in front and to one side of the two interferers, crowding them toward the sideline. He feinted in and out to slow up the Princeton cavalcade, and did this so calculatingly that by the time they were within 20 yards or so of the Notre Dame

Their fame was a bit embarrassing. At their

... these lads of the colorful cavalry of Notre Dame need no alibi ... The record was good enough ... same is true of their scholastic records ...

heyday, I was hounded by newsmen and sob sisters trying to get collective and individual interviews, genealogies, and prophecies with, by, and for them. One determined lady pursued them by mail, telegraph, telephone, and foot for stories to appear in an obscure journal. Finally, she caught up with Crowley.

"Who on earth is she?" he was asked.

"Oh," he said blandly, "she's the third Horsewoman."

And biblical students of the Apocalypse would recall that the third horseman personified pestilence.

An accident of Blasco Ibañez's best-selling popularity inspired their name. Serendipity brought them together. But it was no accident that made them collectively and individually fine players. That was design and hard work. The Four Horsemen have the right to ride with the gridiron great.

Carideo ... the kind of quarterback who inspires confidence and respect ...

46

FRANK CARIDEO

Frank Carideo, an All-American quarterback, was generally regarded as one of the smartest field pilots to ever play the game.

When he came to Notre Dame from Mount Vernon, New York, his high school reputation was good, but in his first appearances with the scrubs, there seemed nothing to foretell that within three years he'd become the country's outstanding player for his position.

Carideo, with other aspirants for the job of field general, was given a thorough drilling by the coaches. He had a few flaws, principally being too conservative in his choice of plays. These are corrected. He may be occupied for an entire afternoon, or for two afternoons, doing nothing but passing the ball back to a carrier until deftness of motion becomes automatic.

Finally, he is picked to go in with a scrub freshman team for a practice game against the regulars. He doesn't know that a test has been devised, as it always is, for promising players. The center Ed "Iago" Agnew is in my confidence.

Carideo, aspiring quarterback, goes in to run the second scrub. He's told that he's boss on the field, absolute boss, warned that the coach will watch every play and intervene only when he makes a glaring mistake. Carideo doesn't know that it has already been predetermined for him to make a few of those obvious mistakes.

Play begins.

Carideo's team receives the kickoff, which is brought back to the 15-yard line. The logical thing to do is to punt.

Probably, Carideo has this in mind. But the Mephistopheles center, Iago, suggests a running play. Carideo falls for it and calls for the run. Our arch-conspirator then makes a pass so poorly that it can't be caught, and of course it's fumbled. No need to tell Carideo that he was in the danger zone where, the conditions as they were, the thing for him to do was to get out of there quickly and safely by punting.

A little bit later one of Carideo's halfbacks is tackled near the sideline. Carideo's next play should be to take the ball out of bounds or run it back into the center of the field. But now Iago suggests punt. Carideo calls for a punt. The ball is passed over toward the sideline, so that the kicker is lucky to catch the ball at all, and when he does he's facing in the wrong direction (the bad pass having pulled him completely out of position). The kicked ball goes out of bounds almost immediately.

No need for me to tell Carideo that he should never call a punt when close to the sidelines. That advice would have meant nothing to him, but with the experience of this mistake seared into his soul, rest assured he would never repeat it.

Remember, all the time this is going on I am acting as timekeeper of the game, and so I can lengthen or shorten the periods as I wish.

In this particular scrimmage, Carideo's team scored early in the first period and then threatened a score near the end of the same period. They reached the five-yard line. Carideo calls for a play and our ever-ready center Iago turns around and calls: "Check!"

Carideo repeats the play.

Iago then turns to Carideo regarding his choice of play, and says, "No, no, Frank!"

Then he goes back and whispers to Carideo, "Shoot the play right over me and we'll go all the way for a touchdown."

The play doesn't gain an inch.

Again the same heckling delay and advice by the center continues. In the midst of this, I fired the gun to announce the end of the half. Carideo's chance for a score had been lost through indecision and unnecessary delay when seconds were mighty precious.

In-between halves, Carideo asked me, "What would you do under the same situation?"

I take him to one side and tell him next time tell the center to mind his own business, listen to the play, pass the ball, and get his size 12 shoes out of the way so they won't interfere with the ballcarrier. Keep in touch with time left to play, so you can hustle your plays as quickly as necessary.

In the next series of plays, our center and Carideo are still working on the same organization. We allow Carideo to make just two mistakes purposely.

The first time he gets down to the goal line, our veteran center will suggest a forward pass on first down. Carideo calls for the forward pass, and if the defense intercepts the pass and goes over the goal line for a touchback, great! He has made one of the most common errors a quarterback can make and one that he will never repeat.

The next mistake we purposely plan is to have him wait until fourth down to kick when deep in his own territory. Again, Iago the center makes a bad pass, the kicker is unable to get the ball.

Results: Opponents get the ball next to Carideo's goal line. No need for me to discuss these mistakes with Carideo because they are self-evident. We now have the working basis for quarterback play and the center, who by his timely misplays and bad suggestions, has helped to educate Carideo.

SECTION 3: ROCKNE ON ROCKNE

Carideo ... would visit me at my home ... on Saint Vincent Street
... we would go over the mistakes made in practice ...

Iago now retires from the scene with the satisfaction that he was part of the education process. Carideo would do most of the talking when we would meet to review the day's events. I gave him a little theory, which he takes in spoonfuls — homeopathic doses, as it were, so as to make sure that every drop is fully assimilated. I could tell him a vast amount of football just then, but he would only get mental indigestion. I remind him of the fundamentals of quarterback play, which, with the other lessons he's learned, will lead him through the secret byways and labyrinths to attain field generalship.

One or two more practice games, and only then Carideo is ready to study the strategy map and learn all the many do's and don'ts for a quarterback. He begins to develop his powers of observation so he can recognize a defense when he sees it. He begins to get a sense of values and personnel, both as regards offensive players and defense. He studies to recognize when to hustle the play and when to slow it up. He reasons when to gamble and when to play it safe. He begins to use plays in logical sequence, one play being used to make the successive play good.

Carideo learns how to pick out a weak spot

and how to avoid strong parts of the defense. He learns when to use "Loose-Hipped Harry," who either gains 20 yards or loses five; when to use "One-Yard Elmer," who never gains much but always is good for a yard; when to use "Plugging Pete," who never gains much, but whose off-tackle drive is generally good for three yards.

As Carideo develops, all through experience and a kindly word of advice now and then, he begins to map out plans for campaigns against certain teams and certain defenses, always trying to outguess them, never wasting any energy, and saving up for the goal line and special scoring plays he has carried all the time undercover.

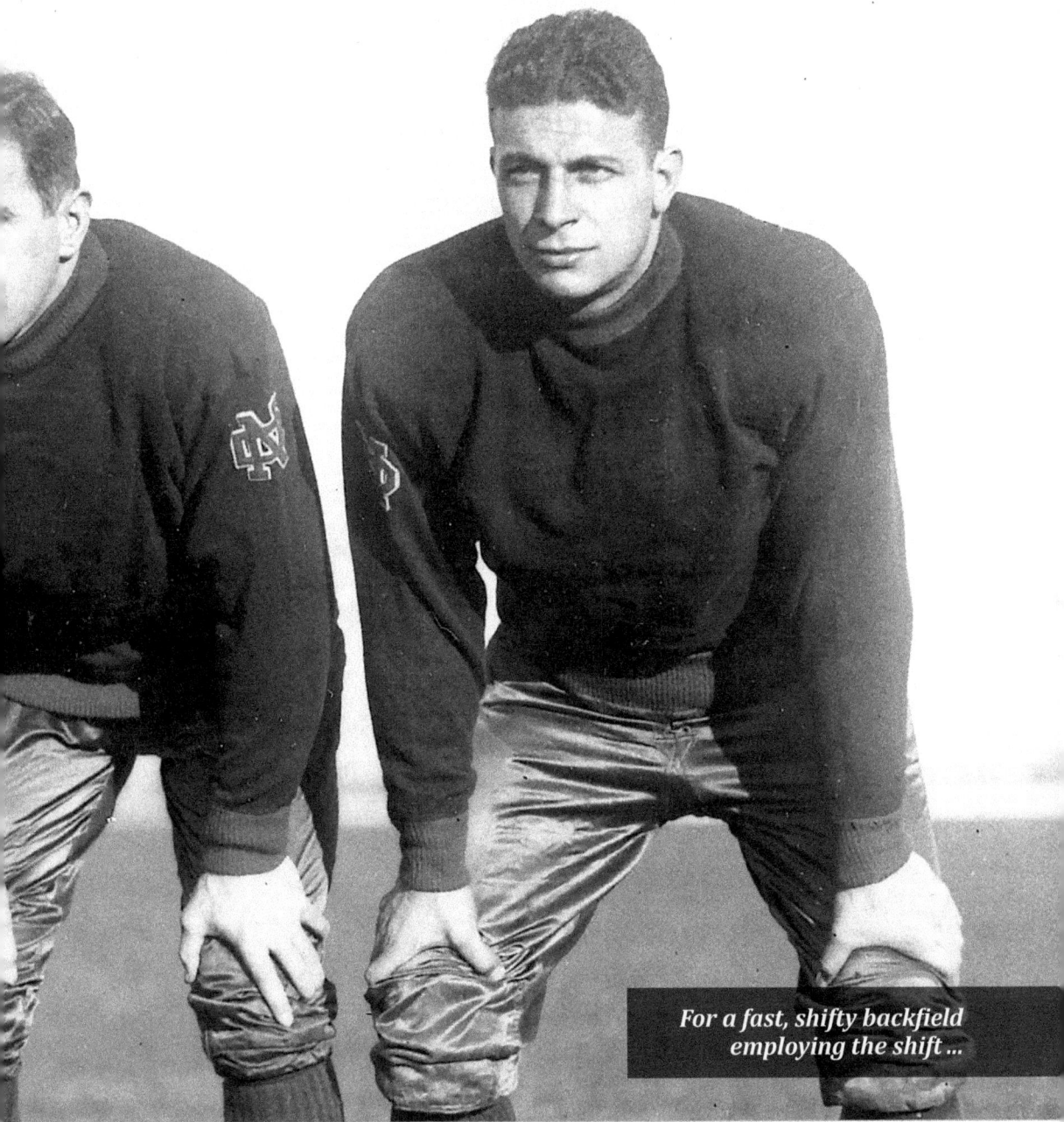

For a fast, shifty backfield employing the shift ...

That is the development of a quarterback, and we try to train every player on the team to think along the same lines so that every player can play smart football. It's, elementally, the system of trial and error. I don't know of any other that can be successful in the intensive training necessitated by the short football practice season.

If it is asked, as it probably will be, whether or not a keen-eyed coach can pick a player of character at first glance, the answer is that a coach with such excellent sight would be more of a marvel than any player. The only man who can pick men by taking a look at them is a night clerk, who's suspicious by nature of men without baggage.

"Most freshmen regard the football coach as if he's a deity on duty for the season. This boy's manner toward me was almost indifferent."

Good Luck from Gipp

47

GEORGE GIPP

"Gipp was Nature's pet and, as with many of
her pets, Nature also punished him."

Knute Rockne

George Gipp was a great football player.

He was unequaled in the game by anyone, except perhaps Jim Thorpe. Gipp was Nature's pet and, as with many of her pets, Nature also punished him.

Gipp had everything to make a man great: splendid physique (6 feet 2 inches tall and 185 pounds, all bone and muscle), balanced temperament, a brilliant mind. He became great at the art he loved most — football. If his untimely end held a touch of tragedy, it was not because of any lack of mental or moral assets on his part, but because Nature, which had given to him so generously, denied him at the very peak of his career when he was to be crowned the outstanding All-American halfback.

I first met Gipp on a nearly empty practice field in the autumn of 1916. A tall lad in everyday campus clothes was booting a football to a boy in a playing suit who then kicked it back. The uniformed lad was a candidate for the freshman team. Their casual play seemed nothing more than a common duet of punts between a football aspirant and some hall friend or roommate who had come out to oblige.

For about 10 minutes I watched him. His kicks were far and placed evidently where he wanted them to go to give the other player catching practice. Here, I thought, was somebody worth examining. When he walked from the field as if bored, I stopped him.

"What's your name?" I asked.

Most freshmen regard the football coach as if he's a deity on duty for the season. This boy's manner toward me was almost indifferent.

"Gipp," he said, "George Gipp. I come from Calumet, Michigan."

"Played high school football?" I asked.

"No," he said. "Don't particularly care for football. Baseball's my dish."

"What led you to come to Notre Dame?" I asked.

"Friends of mine are here," he said.

"Put on a football suit tomorrow," I suggested, "and come out with the freshmen scrubs. I think you'll make a football player."

The lad with Gipp stared wide-eyed. "Why, he's been kicking those punts and drops with ordinary low shoes," he said. "What'll he do with football boots?"

That question was soon answered. Gipp romped through the freshman line on the very first play of a scrub game, the first time he had ever carried a football in competition under a coach's eye. I learned that he had gone out for the Brownson Hall team, the usual thing for boys to do at Notre Dame, as every student physically capable of doing so is expected to enroll in his hall squad. But Gipp was not interested and had quit that team.

After a month of knocking about with the freshmen, in which I observed him four or five times and watched how naturally he acquired running, kicking and tackling techniques, we sent Gipp into his first game. It was against Western State Normal, tough competition for any bunch of freshmen.

The game was tied up in the last three minutes. Gipp had been doing a good deal of ball-carrying, showing a lot of what he had learned and a lot he needed to learn — principally cutting back and interfering.

In one of those frown-faced huddles (dear to all freshmen teams), Gipp insisted that he be allowed to try for a kick to win three points and the game. His quarterback and captain argued against it. The quarterback called for a punt, as a matter of fact, to get the ball out of his own territory and make sure of a draw when a win seemed impossible.

Gipp took the ball and fell back to his own 38-yard line. With effortless grace he dropped the ball, booted it and sent it soaring high and away, parting the square of space above the crossbar. A perfect bid for the three points that won the game.

This Frank Merriwell finish, disregarding signals to win a game, was so poetically right that I thought Gipp too good to be true. He himself seemed to have no thought about the matter. Where another boy would be flushed in triumph, this youngster took congratulations calmly. Even when I asked him to come out in the next practice between varsity and scrubs, he showed no emotion.

"All right," he said. "If you think I can do any good."

SECTION 3: ROCKNE ON ROCKNE

... Gipp, going behind a phalanx of Nebraska players, flipped the ball to 'Bergman just as he'd toss a cigarette ...

The varsity knew Gipp was going to be sent in against them and were primed to stop him. They didn't.

48

PRIMED FOR GREATNESS

In this game, the scrubs were to represent the Army. Good scrub players had been schooled to imitate the styles of various Army stars, but I had found no one on either varsity or scrub squads who could give an imitation of Elmer Oliphant, the ground-gaining Army master. This void was why I wanted Gipp.

For three days, I took him personally in hand, making him vary his pace, break his runs, and cut back and dodge. He was extremely patient, even during the dull repetition in slow-motion of every part of a long broken-field run. Next, he was initiated into Oliphant's veering style of ball-carrying.

The varsity knew Gipp was going to be sent in against them and were primed to stop him. They didn't. Gipp gave a perfect imitation of Oliphant and ran wide around end, passing the secondary defense with ease and scoring a touchdown. The only drawback was that in the actual game with Army, Oliphant gave a perfect imitation of Gipp and also made an end run for a touchdown.

Becoming a hero of campus talk during his freshman year is enough to inflate any youngster's head. But Gipp had the superb personal policy of being indifferent to everything. Even on my short acquaintance with him, this demeanor caused me to marvel. The explanation came, quite dramatically, later.

Gipp reported to me that he would have to work his way through school. There were a few jobs of the white-collar type available. Those who had them to offer would have been glad

I became head coach in 1918 and made it my firm rule to handle the boys without in the least putting anybody in a spot where I might be suspected of favoritism ...

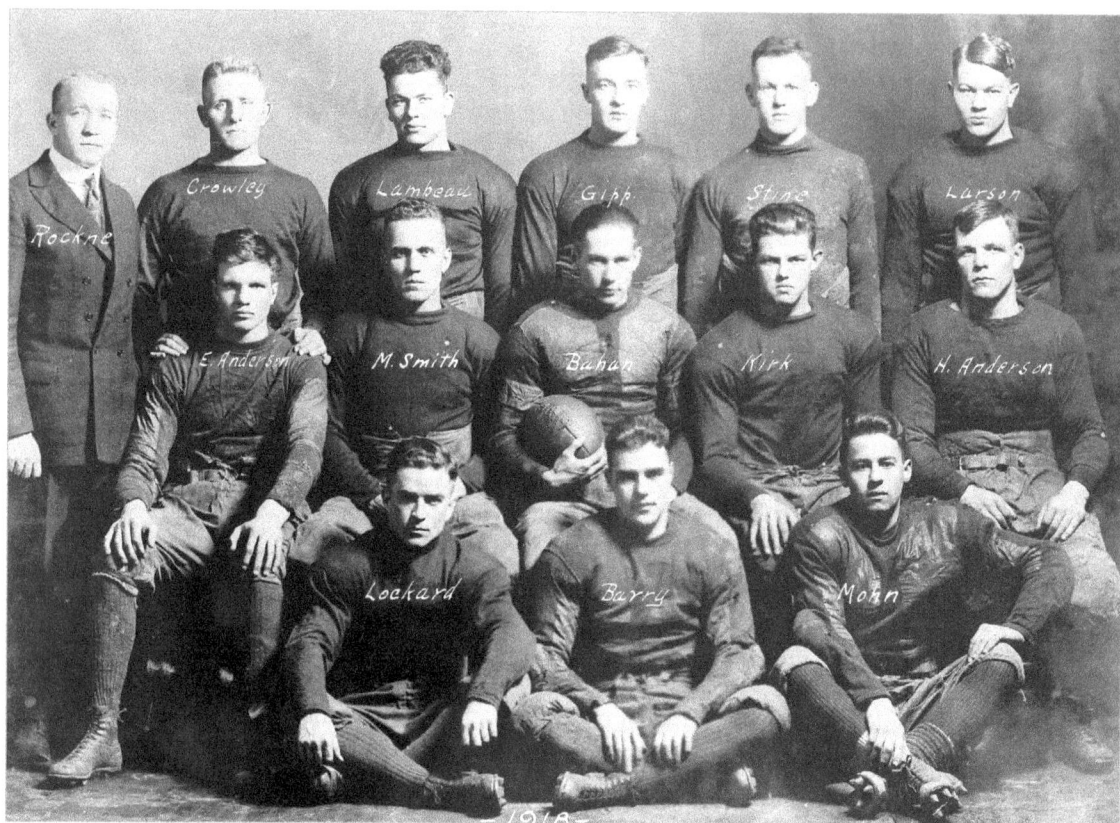

to hire a boy who, in his freshman year, was already an accepted football hero in a school that had no small reputation for football heroes.

Gipp made his own choice.

"I want to wait on tables," he said.

He became a hash-slinger, and a most efficient one at that. Visitors to the refectory were surprised to have Gipp pointed out to them — after his fame spread beyond the Midwest — wearing a white waiter's coat and passing out bowls of soup and plates of stew. But the two tables in his charge (waiters nearest the kitchen had to cover two tables) were always promptly served and just as promptly cleared. He took the job seriously because it paid for his room and board.

My fear for Gipp was that Nature had made him such a fine athlete that, over-gifted, he would not appreciate nor respect his talents. He lived quietly, had few companions, apparently cared nothing for female company, of which there's none on the Notre Dame campus. He skipped the study room more

... Gipp, while having an opportunity to show that his greatness was growing, was not given too many chances to shine.

frequently than I liked to see him do, but a check-up on his habits showed him with fewer than the usual faults of star athletes.

During his first summer, he surpassed everybody as an outfielder and hitter in freshman baseball. There, as in football, he quickly showed a tendency to dominate quietly but effectively. He had a keen sense of strategy. I didn't see this game, but I was told that once when he was sent in with orders to bunt, he slugged the ball for a home run and explained that the afternoon was much too hot to be running around bases. He had a fine throwing arm, shooting the ball from boundary to plate on one hop.

What I hoped would be the hallmark of quality in the athlete who seemed too good to be true — namely, humor — was lacking in his early months at school. He was pleasant without being cheerful, affable without being congenial. He appeared just too sure of himself.

In his first year of gridiron play, we held him under leash. We had plenty of stars, and as he was only 20 and the war was on, it was my policy to save him for the 1918 season. At that time, it looked as if all our first-string men would join the service, which is exactly what happened.

After a brief season that did not officially

count as a scholastic year in 1918, Gipp, while having an opportunity to show that his greatness was growing, was not given too many chances to shine. I became head coach in 1918 and made it my firm rule to handle the boys without in the least putting anybody in a spot where I might be suspected of favoritism.

Gipp joined the Students' Army Training Corps, which some cynics irreverently called "Safe at the College." When Gipp returned to school after the holidays, he switched his course from arts to law, which meant nothing to me so long as he studied.

I believed 1919 would be a great year for Gipp. During early spring practice, he displayed uncanny accuracy in kicking and blocking. I should have mentioned that he had shown the football intuition that no coach or system can teach in the first major game in which he had appeared for long — against Army at West Point in 1917.

We had the Army beaten 7 — 2 as we came to the last few minutes of play. The cadets cut loose and marched to the tune of several first downs, planting the ball on our 20-yard line. There they were held, but advanced for the fourth and final down to our eight-yard line with the score still at 7 — 2.

Gipp knew the score. Army's quarterback barked signals and they lined up for a place kick.

Gipp instantly yelled out, "Look out for a pass!"

He was right. Army didn't kick. They gambled for six points instead of an almost certain three. Six points would have won the game. But Gipp warned our defense in time. Receivers were covered, and he himself knocked the pass down and saved the game.

That was quick thinking. It defined him, as far as I was concerned. I knew there'd be nothing to stop this man being the outstanding star of his next full season. Nothing, that is, except Gipp.

SECTION 3: ROCKNE ON ROCKNE

The lad had brilliance and a sense of dramatic opportunism of doing the right, best thing at exactly the given moment.

49
TESTING THE BOUNDARIES

On a bright spring morning of 1919, I received the news — the news that puts a coach beside himself, that his star has been fired from school. Gipp was kicked out for missing too many classes. It seemed too late to do anything except scold him, and that was profitless.

Yet when I confronted him on his remissness and told him that he had put the finish to, not on, a brilliant athletic career, he quietly asked me why he couldn't have an oral examination. Even some townsmen of South Bend appealed to the school authorities to give Gipp another chance. Gipp claimed to have been ill, and he got permission for the exam on that account.

Gipp went into that examination room with nearly the whole school and city awaiting the outcome. Some of his inquisitors were no football fans. They were prepared to stop his scholastic run with tough questions and recollections from the books. His professors knew that Gipp was not a diligent student. He made no notes. But he astonished everybody by what he knew when it came to cross-examination.

He passed back into school, and there was general rejoicing. Not, however, by Gipp. As usual, he calmly accepted victory, and it was observed that he was more regular in attending class.

Gipp was really a master showman with a mind alert to catch every effective detail of a show. Secretly, although he gave no outward sign, he loved the dramatic. To him it was striking fun to be fired from school because he wouldn't study, only to be returned when it was discovered, under fire, that he knew quite as much as the most unwearyingly plodders.

The lad had brilliance and a sense of dramatic opportunism of doing the right, best thing at exactly the given moment. That made me wonder, at times, what self-dramatizing leaders of men must have been among his forebears. Even Gipp's voice was a warm, vibrant baritone, full of life. Yet his ancestry, so far as I knew, was Puritan. His father was a Congregational minister.

This detail mentioned by him when he applied for a change of room at the University led to one of his crisp comebacks. A dormitory mate in Sorin Hall chiding Gipp as a meek, heretical lamb among orthodox wolves was surprised when Gipp pointed to a line of showers next to his room door.

"I'm the holy one around here," he said. "Cleanliness is always next to godliness."

This hallmark of humor which developed in what might be called his manners, step-by-step with the development of his athletic prowess, first stamped him — at least in my sight — as the solid gold article called greatness. He displayed it first on the gridiron during the opening game of the 1919 season against Kalamazoo.

Not desiring to pile up a score against Kalamazoo and urgently wishing to give Gipp and the rest of the boys a strict test, I asked the officials to impose penalties without hesitation, even at times without reason.

Gipp shone in the first period with an 80-yard run. As the stands cheered the star's first touchdown of the season, the grim officials called back the ball, ruling one of our linesmen offside. Within 10 minutes, Gipp broke through the entire Kalamazoo defense for a 68-yard run to a touchdown. Once more a grim field judge ruled a guard offside.

Gipp was mad clear through. He said nothing. Even during the intermission, he made no bleat to me. That was one more striking piece of evidence that the boy had real, unmistakable class.

During the third period he hung back for a while, as we were ahead and it was always his whim to loaf when an opposing team was obviously weaker. But he caught a punt and couldn't resist the temptation to show his stuff as the crowd yelled, "Gipp! Gipp!" He tore off 70 yards and another touchdown. But the judge's whistle had blown just before Gipp crossed the line. Another penalty for holding.

Gipp strode by the official and quickly remarked, "Next time give me one whistle to stop and two to keep going."

Only against pushovers was he lazy and deliberate, reducing his efforts to a minimum when an easy game was on ice.

The high, dramatic moments of the major battles found him daring, hard-hitting, almost vicious in his attack. What made him a marvel was that no matter how outwardly eager he appeared, he was always internally cold.

SECTION 3: ROCKNE ON ROCKNE

The teams lined up... Fred Larson, at center for us, awaited signals when Gipp called sharply, "Pass me the ball!"

50

ULTIMATE GAMESMAN

I n the Army game of 1919, the cadets had us at a disadvantage of 9 — 0 and it looked as if they were going to hold it. Toward the end of the first half, the Notre Dame quarterback, Joe Brandy, opened up a passing attack — Gipp throwing. This attack culminated with a cannonball pass from Gipp to Pete Bahan on the Army's one-yard line.

The teams lined up. Fred Larson, at center for us, awaited signals when Gipp called sharply, "Pass me the ball!"

Gipp had had a flash of the head linesman lifting his horn to blow the end of the half. While both teams looked on in surprise, he grabbed the ball from Larson and dove over the goal line for a touchdown. The instant Gipp caught the ball the linesman's horn sounded, but the half wasn't over until the ball was dead, and the ball wasn't dead until the touchdown was made. I've never seen a quicker piece of thinking on the part of a player.

Nor have I ever seen a better balance of versatility — of slow acting as the result of quick thinking — than in perhaps the most grueling game Notre Dame ever played with its toughest western opponent, Nebraska. This was in 1919. In the opening scrimmages that season, we had seven men badly hurt, but they got well enough to go with the squad to Lincoln.

Before 10 seconds of the game had passed, Gipp, going behind a phalanx of Nebraska players, flipped the ball to Arthur "Dutch" Bergman just as he'd toss a cigarette.

Bergman caught a pass from Gipp, and with a clear field ahead, ran for a touchdown. War was declared, and that game became grim and bruising.

409

Nebraska scored. We went into the second half with a one-point edge as they had failed to make the point after goal. We scored again. But the battering our men were getting had its effect. All available Notre Dame subs were used up by the beginning of the final period. The Nebraska bench was loaded with fresh players eager to go in.

The Cornhuskers realized they had us on the run, although we led by 14 — 6. They came on stronger than ever as the fourth period opened, threw us back, and kicked a goal for three points. The score was 14 — 9 with 12 minutes to go and the Notre Dame men were dragging their legs, worn out, and no replacements.

Gipp took command, and the ball.

"Let's stall," he told his quarterback.

So, they stood talking while the watch ran on. A minute was killed. The referee came up, penalized us five yards.

"Why?" said Gipp in indignant surprise. "I thought time was out."

"Think again," said the referee.

In subsequent plays, when the rest of the backfield shifted one way, Gipp would shift the other and they'd have to do it all over again — all while the watch was running, eating up seconds. He was cautioned by the referee.

Gipp pulled another trick. Carrying the ball, he'd let himself be tackled and when he went down, he held the other player in a hug and shouted, "Let me up!"

He took 15 to 20 seconds before he'd let them pull him up. The crowd roared impatiently. The players chafed, seeing precious minutes eaten up by dilatory tactics. Gipp taunted them by kicking the ball cleverly out of bounds. He urged our quarterback to stutter signals to make them last longer.

In brief, he killed minute after minute un-til the whistle blew and we won.

Nebraska's chagrined coach, good old Henry Schulte, said to Gipp, "What course do you take at Notre Dame?"

"Plumbing," laughed Gipp.

Gipp delighted in improvising strategy. Nebraska had tasted that technique before, in 1918, when our first- and second-string quarterbacks were knocked out. Gipp switched to the quarterback position and shouted signals with glorious abandon. He alternated energy with leisureliness.

Against Purdue in 1919, on the first play of the second quarter, he ran 90 yards for a touchdown. Content with that burst of energy, he was called on to run again, but said, so that the Purdue men could overhear, "Oh, no. Let's pass."

And he passed them dizzy.

Before I forget the Nebraska game in 1918, Gipp took a fancy that another player should make the touchdown. He gave him the ball and the line opened holes. But Nebraska stiffened and was holding us. Gipp passed word to the other halfback to follow him on a line plunge at Nebraska's 10-yard mark. Gipp carried the player hanging on to his belt across the goal line, but a keen field judge disallowed the score and penalized Notre Dame 15 yards. He had seen the player towed by Gipp's belt.

In game after game, Gipp showed the same resourcefulness. Sometimes it succeeded, less often it failed. But his ingenuity and initiative never failed. Nor did his courage.

Against Indiana in the game of 1920, we were a beaten team. We thought it would be an easy win. It wasn't. Gipp's shoulder was dislocated. I took him out. The Hoosiers led us 10 — 0 and the game had only minutes to go. The ball went down in a fury of old Notre Dame fighting spirit to Indiana's seven-yard line.

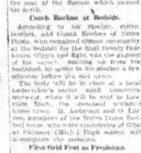

The third quarter ended and, by the rules, I could substitute anyone I wanted. Gipp, the cripple, came to me and insisted upon going in. Reluctantly, I consented. He charged on the field and the stands rose to their feet. Rarely have I seen a more thrilling sight than those stands, filled with thousands veiled in the twilight, screaming the name of one man, "Gipp!"

Of course, he was marked. The Indiana men, their first victory over us in 30 years smelling sweet in their nostrils, weren't going to let a crippled hero beat them.

But Gipp had something to say about that. He tried once, disdaining runs, passing. With a banged-up shoulder he smashed the line —

and failed. Indiana roared. He tried again. Taking the ball, he crouched into a self-driven battering ram. Smash, and over he went!

But I'm stressing too much the picturesque and dramatic offensive plays that brought George Gipp into the limelight, in which he knew how to comport himself without the slightest increase in self-esteem or the most remote hint of condescension toward humbler members of the combination on which he played.

Gipp was a master of defense. I can say of him what cannot, I believe, be said of any other football player, certainly not of any other Notre Dame player — that not a single forward pass was ever completed in territory defended by George Gipp. He had the timing of a tiger in pouncing on its prey. He simply never missed.

A great player, what everybody who knew him in and out of school called "a great guy," Gipp had a weakness. Before I learned firsthand what it was, I had seen a striking show of it in a football game.

Those who saw the Army — Notre Dame game in 1920 may remember that at a point when the Army led us by 17 — 14 near the end of the first half, Gipp did a strange thing. The quarterback called for a kick, and our men set in motion for formation. Gipp was to kick, and the position sent him behind his own goal line.

As even a neophyte knows, when behind your own goal line there is only one orthodox thing to do, and that is kick. The Army, a cit-adel of orthodox football, knew the kick was coming, and they were pressing to receive it to keep their score ahead of Notre Dame's.

But Gipp was not orthodox. Passing another player, Roger Kiley, on his way to receive the ball he warned him, "When I get the ball, tear ahead. I'll pass it."

Gipp took the snap-back, poised to kick. Army charged. Before a finger could touch him, he had sidestepped and thrown the ball 45 yards to Kiley in a field as free as the ocean. But Kiley, for the first and only time in his career, dropped the ball.

That was gambling, absolute gambling. Gipp made amends for a mistake he hadn't committed by ripping the Army line to pieces in the second half and putting his team in front for the final count of 27-17, but he had proved to me that he was a gambler.

DEATH TAKES GIPP AFTER HARD FIGHT

[BY ASSOCIATED PRESS TO GAZETTE TIMES.]

SOUTH BEND, IND., Dec. 14.— George Gipp, Notre Dame football player, died at 3:23 o'clock this morning from streptococcic throat disease.

Gipp, whose splendid playing won him country-wide recognition and made him a choice for a position on an All-American eleven, had been ill since the Notre Dame-Northwestern game, November 20.

Pneumonia also helped weaken the athlete. Specialists called from Chicago succeeded in ridding his system of pneumonia, however, but Gipp did not have the stamina left to ward off the poison resulting from the throat affection.

During the final hours of his fight for life Gipp was rational and was said too show remarkable grit as he gradually grew weaker, refusing to give in to the inevitable. His mother, brother and sister were at the bedside when he died.

Gipp first jumped into the spotlight as an unusual football player when Notre Dame clashed with the Army in 1919, when his kicking, forward passing, field running and generalship won him the plaudits of the Eastern football critics.

One ray of happiness was brought into the athlete's few remaining hours when he was informed that he had been selected as a player on a mythical all-American eleven. During his illness he also was informed that he had been offered a contract by the Chicago National League baseball club. Gipp's ability as a baseball player was on a par with that in football.

Gipp was aged 24. His home was in Laurium, Mich. He was a senior at Notre Dame, being a law student.

Hundreds of admirers of Gipp viewed the remains, which lay in state tonight. The student body of Notre Dame will accompany the body to the train tomorrow morning, when the deceased will be shipped to Laurium, Mich., for burial. Several members of the Notre Dame football team will attend the funeral.

Jack Chevigny was badly battered, but he answered with a touchdown.

51

WIN ONE FOR THE GIPPER

I learned later, after his death, that this was so. I had often wondered why George Gipp, not a rich boy, always had sufficient funds. He was an expert card player, an expert billiard player, expert as he would have been in almost anything he took up. It was his pastime to go to rendezvous with visiting gentlemen of the trade and beat them at their own games.

Superficially, it never affected Gipp's training, for his physical condition seemed splendid always. He could sprint a hundred yards in 10.2 seconds any and every day. Listed as halfback, he also played fullback and quarterback. In his three seasons (1918, 1919, 1920) he rushed for 2,341 yards and passed for 1,789. His average return on punts was 14 yards, and his kick returns averaged 22 yards.

The lad never knew how personally popular he was among and above a popular team. When Grantland Rice and other prominent sportswriters went for the first time to West Point to report an Army — Notre Dame game and to view this wonder-man, Gipp, their staccato praise the next day meant little to him. An ordinarily self-appreciative player would have bought every newspaper in sight and read the clippings until he'd memorized them backwards. Gipp didn't even read them once. So far as I'm aware, he never posed for a photograph. The only photo I have of him is one snapped on the playing field.

George Gipp seemed indestructible on the football field. But on a damp, freezing afternoon he contracted an infected sore throat around the time of our game with Northwestern. The whole city of South Bend joined the university in anxiety over Gipp. His condition worsened

*Slashing through the Army line for a touchdown,
he yelled out, "That's one for the Gipper!"*

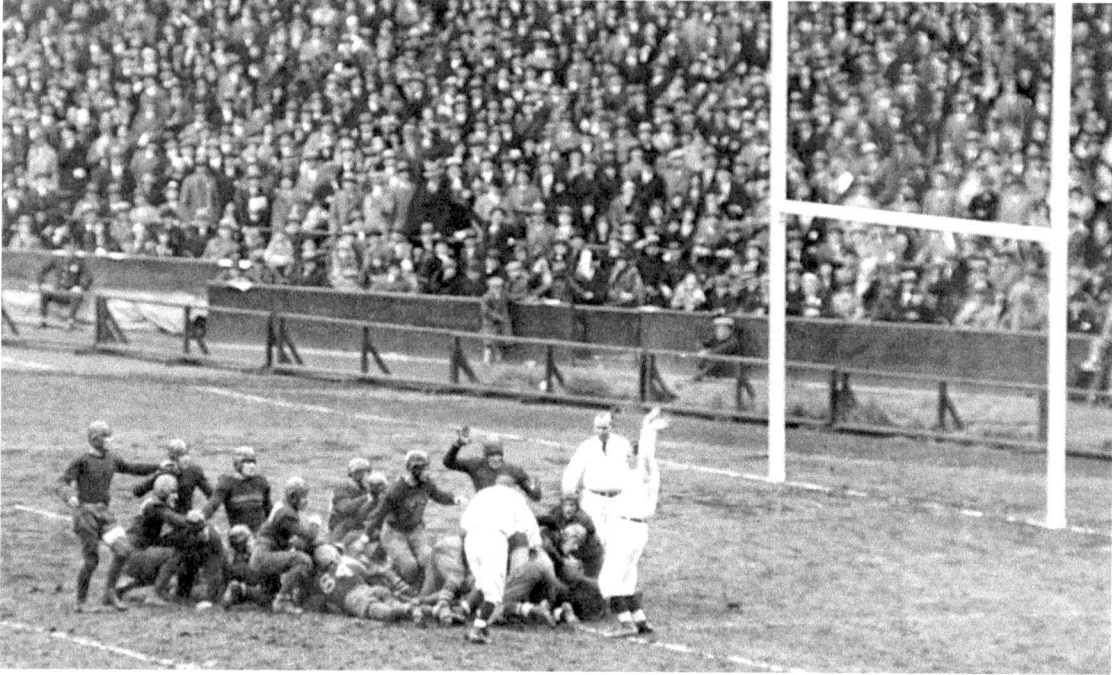

and he had to be hospitalized.

"It's pretty tough to go," said someone at the bedside.

"What's tough about it?" Gipp smiled up at us feebly. "I've no complaint."

He turned to me.

A few minutes later he motioned me forward. I leaned over his bed and he said to me, "I've got to go, Rock. It's all-right. I'm not afraid."

His eyes brightened in a frame of pallor.

"Some time, Rock," he said, "when the team's up against it, when things are wrong and the breaks are beating the boys, tell them to go in there with all they've got and win just one for the Gipper. I don't know where I'll be then, Rock. But I'll know about it, and I'll be happy."

It became national news when Gipp died, but that was only the measure of his athletic celebrity. What was never in the news was his utter gameness.

Gipp had scaled the glamorous heights of all boyhood dreams by shining as a national football hero. The White Sox had just bid for his baseball service on graduation. Walter Camp had just named him All-American fullback. There is controversy and recent investigation of the "Win one..." story. This does not look like the one that is debunked.

The 1928 team was having a tough season, cracked by Wisconsin in its second game and shortly after we were beaten by Georgia Tech. Then came Army, Gipp's old love and hate. The cadets had spread ruin almost everywhere that year. And they were out to give Notre Dame the beating of years.

The Army game was played in Yankee Stadium as 80,000 people looked on. Two dogged foes fighting their hearts out.

At the half we were even, 0 — 0. For the first time since Gipp's death, I told the boys what he had said. These lads on that 1928 team had never met Gipp, had never seen him. But Gipp is a legend at Notre Dame. Every football writer said that Notre Dame would be beaten badly. It looked as if we were weakening. But the boys came out for the second half exalted, inspired, overpowering.

Army scored 6 points. Jack Chevigny was badly battered, but he answered with a touchdown. Slashing through the Army line for a touchdown, he yelled out, "That's one for the Gipper!"

It was a fierce battle. With three minutes to play, the score stood 6-6. We had the ball on the Army 20-yard line. It was third down, five yards to go.

It was time to gamble. I called for Johnny O'Brien, "All right, Johnny. Out you go!"

When Carideo saw O'Brien enter the game, he knew exactly the play to call. They had a specialty in which he excelled, a particularly pet play which he and Butch Niemic had worked on often in practice. On the crack of the whip, O'Brien started down the field, veered to the left and then suddenly cut towards the right-hand corner of the field. Niemic took the ball, rolled out, and threw a long pass to O'Brien. He juggled it, but managed to catch the pass as he was falling over the goal line.

The final score was Notre Dame 12, Army 6.

... this lad the newspaper writers dubbed 'One Play O'Brien...' Johnny was never given much playing time... He gave unselfishly to the effort of the team ...

Willie Heston ... probably the greatest halfback in the old game ...

52

BIG-LEAGUERS

Looking back over my career in football, it's studded with the thrills that ensue from the drama of the gridiron to exhilarate onlookers, and to give the young and their elders the something heroic in times of peace that stirs men quite as much.

And, to quite as important a cultural purpose, as the heroics of war.

As I sat deep in thought, musing over the contents of the letter from a football fan, I was taken back to a snow-covered field in Chicago many years ago. I saw a bullet-like form catapult through the Chicago line and break loose with a clear field except for a small figure which moved rapidly to meet him. The small man sprang to tackle, but the ballcarrier hurdled clear over him, and landing on the other side continued his course down the snow-covered field. It looked like a sure touchdown.

Quick as a flash, the tackler who had been hurdled recovered himself, and in 15 yards had tackled the ball-muffler down from behind. The hearts of the spectators went up in their mouths several times while this play was taking place.

This was one of these thrills which one experiences so rarely. It was football. The ballcarrier was Willie Heston, probably the greatest halfback in the old game. The quarterback was Walter Eckersall, easily the greatest quarterback of the old game. Both would have been just as immense in the modern game.

I can see Eckersall's high punts scoring 50 or 60 yards down the field as though it were yesterday. I have never seen a faster man on the football field. Very few sprinters can carry a football suit — Eckersall was one of the few.

As for Heston, he could do anything. Speed, power and deception, he had it all. Never was there a faster buck off the mark. And he ran so low he was impossible to handle.

The first time I saw Pete Hauser was when Haskell played Chicago in 1904. And what an exhibition of hurdling, diving and sidestepping he gave! The next time I saw him was in 1907 when he was playing with Carlisle.

I am not sure, but I believe he then used the name "Waseka." His natural skills were made honed by the experience of several seasons. Although he was a little heavier, his speed was unaffected. Never written up to any great extent, I believe Pete Houser was one of the greatest backs on the gridiron for all time.

And then there was Edward "Ted" Coy of Yale, who probably hit the line as hard as any human. What a riot of color he flashed during his brief career.

A great Army backfield led by Light Horse Harry Wilson pulled a game out of the fire in the classic between Army and Navy when they met at Soldiers Field, Chicago, in 1926.

The Army had been out-charged, outmaneuvered and outplayed by a relentless Navy team. As dusk gathered over the field the score stood 20-13 in favor of Navy.

With defeat staring them in the face, this great Army backfield moved up the field. At the crucial moment, the Army quarterback called for a cutback by Wilson — his favorite play.

There was no hole there, but Wilson made one. He just handcuffed the two Navy linemen who tried to hang on to him. Into the open he sprang. He slapped his hip into the Navy linebacker, sidestepped the Navy safety, reversed his field, up and over the goal line.

Murrell kicked and the score was tied 20-20. It was a game of thrills.

I saw Edward "Eddie" Mahan of Harvard play only one time. He was one of the finest of the fine. His punts averaged well over 50 yards, his open field running was a delight, his poise and ease of movement gave the spectators confidence that Mahan could do anything.

Well-fortified, he was surrounded by such stars as Huntington "Tack" Hardwick, Stanley "Bags" Pennock, Frederick "Beebo" Bradlee, Justin Logan, and others. But standing out clear from this great array of talent was Mahan, one of the smoothest and easiest performers the game has ever seen.

Of course, the obvious thrill in football is the long run with the herd of opponents in full cry. I saw the first real thriller of this kind when Notre Dame played the Army in November, 1915.

The great Army halfback, Elmer Oliphant, had just made a fair catch on his own 48-yard line. This allowed him the privilege of a free kick. With his quarterback holding the ball, Oliphant sent the ball straight and true for the goal posts. It looked as if it were surely going over when it suddenly dropped in a downward arc, struck the crossbar and bounded back in the field of play. This made it a touchback and the ball was brought out 20 yards and given to Notre Dame.

Three inches higher and Oliphant's kick would have won the game for Army.

On the next play, Alfred "Big Dutch" Bergman gained 18 yards, ran out of bounds, fell over a bench and was severely injured. It did not seem that he could continue.

But Bergman, besides being a great

halfback, had the most remarkable powers of recuperation I have ever seen. With 30 seconds left to play, Notre Dame's quarterback, Jimmy Phalen, now coach at the University of Washington, called for a forward pass, and Stan Cofall flicked a 15-yard pass to Bergman, who caught it, dodged a linebacker, and outran the safety over the goal line — a run of 40 yards.

Rooters on both sides were flabbergasted. It was minutes, I know, before I realized exactly what I had witnessed. Bergman was a useful back to have because he was ready to break loose for a touchdown at any time. So, for that matter, was Oliphant, who ranks with the truly great at the game.

Without a doubt, George Gipp is the greatest back in Notre Dame's history. Some folks will say he was not in shape. I remember well, the Army-Notre Dame game of 1920.

The last quarter opened with Notre Dame trailing by 17 — 14. Both teams were heavy in their tracks from the intense pace of the contest.

Gipp had been playing since the opening whistle. Like a tall, thoroughbred racehorse, he knifed, sliced, twisted, ran, and plunged over and around the Army team for two clear touchdowns. And no one who saw that great drive in the gathering dusk on the plains but was inspired by the tremendous physical vigor and condition of the athlete who led it.

Then came Aubrey Devine and Gordon Locke of Iowa, Harry Kipke of Michigan, George "Tank" McLaren of Pittsburgh, Ernest "Ernie" Nevers of Stanford, Joe Guyon of Georgia Tech, and Marvin "Mal" Stevens of Yale — all remarkable young athletes who thrilled spectators clear to the peripheral circulation.

Until a certain afternoon in 1924, when Notre Dame played the Army, the Notre Dame backfield was just Harry Stuhldreher, Jim Crowley, Elmer Layden and Don Miller.

The morning after that game they became the Four Horsemen. Grantland Rice's name stuck with them and their fame became indelibly fixed in football history.

Behind a light, clever, stubborn line, these four backs swept their way to an undefeated season. Their exploits are too recent to be discussed here. But thrills they created and thrills they made, and it will be a long time before they are forgotten.

Then there came Harold "Red" Grange of Illinois, who, in the Michigan game of 1924, startled 75,000 people with feats one might have read about in the old Frank Merriwell series, but which had certainly never before been witnessed by mortal eye.

During the next two years, there were times when Grange was stopped, and stopped cold, but when he had his day — what a day!

Sheer beauty of play was never better illustrated, I think, than in two Notre Dame scoring plays in 1926 — Christie Flanagan against Army, and Arthur "Pary" Parisien against Southern California.

In the Army game, there never were two teams more evenly matched. As the first half drew to a close it was evident to the expert eye that these two teams might play for days without a score.

However, Harry O'Boyle was puncturing the line for short, sure gains, which was annoying them. John "Cap" McEwan, the Army coach, was using a unique defense to nullify the technique of the Notre Dame ends in blocking tackles. He dropped the Army tackles back three yards. This stopped Flanagan's wide runs, but it left them vulnerable to O'Boyle's plunges.

... Then there came Harold "Red" Grange of Illinois ... with feats one might have read about in the old Frank Merriwell series ...

In the second half, Army kicked off to Notre Dame. It became our ball on our 30-yard line.

The first play was a plunge for O'Boyle, for no gain. Our right end told our quarterback, Gene Edwards, in a huddle that the Army tackle was up on the line of scrimmage and not three yards back as in the first half.

Quick as a flash, Edwards called for Flanagan's favorite off-tackle play. John

Wallace blocked Army's tackle in alone. Tom Hearden took the Army end out of the play. Our right guard and quarterback deflected Harold "Brick" Muller.

Like a streak through this opening went Flanagan. He reversed his field through the secondary, tertiary, and quaternary defensemen who were picked up by John Voedisch, Fred Miller and Clipper Smith, who had gone through ahead of him clearing an open path.

It was a perfect play. Nobody laid a hand on Flanagan as he ran his 70 yards for a touchdown.

The Army learned something from that play. The very next game we played against Army, Christian "Red" Cagle, in an identical play, ran 45 yards against us for a touchdown. That likewise, gave me a thrill — not of exhilaration, but of exacerbation- for our tactics were perfectly reproduced by Mr. Cagle and company.

Parisien the little Frenchman was backed up by nine Irishmen and a German, none of whom know when they're beaten.

53

PARISIEN MELODRAMA

"I turned to Art Parisien, a little French quarterback who'd been injured during the year and hadn't played since..."

Knute Rockne

Melodramatic intrusion of a planned and practiced play at a time and place not planned, nor practiced, gave Parisien his greatest moment of gridiron glory.

In the gorgeous setting of the Southern California stadium, we, as guests, had, I thought, our hosts comfortably in the bag. The score was 7 — 6 in Notre Dame's favor, and I sat on the bench murmuring "tempus fugit" and hoping it would "fugit" a little quicker.

Suddenly, the wind veered from behind us and came off the Graham McNamee mountains laden with the aroma of citrus groves. It stirred and stimulated the nostrils of the Los Angeles lads, who awoke sharply to a realization of what was expected of them.

"Dynamite Don" Williams went right through our line for a touchdown. Our regular guards had been exhausted from the heat and a smart Southern California quarterback picked on the subs. The kick failed. The score was 12 — 7 in favor of Southern California.

We received the kickoff. It went for a touchback and was our ball on our 20-yard line.

Heat had taken further toll. Flanagan and a regular quarterback had left the game before

425

this. Notre Dame tried three plays and failed. John Niemiec punted 60 yards down the field. During those three plays, I saw what I was hoping I wouldn't see. I saw 10 Notre Dame players still trying, giving the best of themselves, and doggedly digging in.

But the substitute quarterback had an air of resignation. Hope as regards this game had left him.

The Southern California team, who had taken Williams out, tried two plays then kicked the ball back to us as though to say, "There it is, what you are going to do with it?"

I turned to Art Parisien, a little French quarterback who'd been injured during the year and hadn't played since.

"Art, how do you feel?"

"Great."

"Well," I said, "do you think if you went in there you might play those two left-handed passes of yours, numbers 83 and 84, and maybe pull this game out of the fire yet?"

Before I'd finished talking, he had his headgear on and, as he ran from the bench for the field, he called back to me.

"Coach, it's a cinch."

This was not egotism, just self-confidence. Parisien took the ball on our 30-yard line. Time left to play was just a little over a minute.

The crowd was apathetic and some were leaving. Apparently, it was all over.

On the first play, Parisien pulled a tricky spinner and skipped through center for eight yards. He called for timeout. You could see his youthful eagerness imbuing his 10 teammates.

On the next play, out of a whirling mass of players, came Art Parisien sprinting with the ball. Turning quick as a flash, he flicked a left-handed pass 30 yards to Niemiec, who was tackled and floored by Jeff Cravath, ever-alert California center.

Next came a tearing wide-end run by Niemiec that didn't gain any; it was a maneuver for position for the following play.

Our acting captain called to the field judge.

"How much time?"

"Thirty seconds," called the field judge.

Parisien's staccato bark rang out. The ball was passed. And again, out of a mass of players, Parisien sprinted. Again, his left hand flicked a pass of 30 yards to the nimble Niemiec, who crossed Southern California's goal line for the winning touchdown.

Eighty thousand people sat in that warm afternoon air, frozen with the thrill of that play. No sweeter balm has ever come to a coach's heart.

Section 3: Rockne on Rockne

SECTION 4
THE INVESTIGATION

ockne's Fatal Crash!

VITIES

KANSAS CITY

HUNTERS TOOK
LARGE PARTS OF
EFORE BODIES
EMOVED

RUPTURED WING
FOUND HALF MILE
FROM WRECK

GLED

The Department of Commerce's policy of keeping plane crash investigations secret began to succumb to the frequent demands of the country's watchdog press.

54

PUBLIC DEMAND

"First reports were that the plane exploded."

The magnitude of that single line of seven words documented on page 16 of the Aeronautics Branch of the U.S. Department of Commerce's official investigation report into the crash of Transcontinental & Western Air Flight 5 that killed Knute Rockne and seven others cannot be understated.

Just a few hours after the crash occurred at about 10:45 a.m. on the morning of March 31, 1931, newspapers across the country ran their first, on-the-spot breaking news stories. All quoted young Edward Baker saying he heard the Fokker F-10A "explode in the air" and "spin in flames" as it crashed to the ground in a pasture on his father's rural Kansas ranch.

Just as news of the crash began pinging teletype and telegraph wire services, news reporters and photographers throughout Kansas grabbed equipment, hopped in cars or on charter planes, and headed to the remote site at the edge of the state's rugged Flint Hills to interview witnesses and get the first details of the tragedy. Edward Baker, his brother Arthur Baker, Clarence H. McCracken, R.C. Blackburn, Easter Heathman, and members of the Heathman family all gave emotional eyewitness accounts that made up the first descriptions reported within a few hours of the Rockne crash by newspapers and radio stations across the country. Those first recollections were raw, vivid, and in all probability, freshly accurate.

"Looking up, the youth saw an airplane burst into flames and rocket toward the earth," the Sedalia (Mo.) Democrat reported Edward Baker's account published in the afternoon edition on March 31, 1931.

The Department of Commerce's lead investigator in Kansas City, Leonard Jurden, wasn't notified of the accident until 12:15 p.m. when newspapers called him to identify the plane. Jurden left Kansas City at about 2:30 p.m. and drove to the site with T&WA officials R.M. Jacobs, John Collins and R.S. Bridges. By the time Jurden arrived in Cottonwood Falls (where the bodies were taken) at about 7 p.m., souvenir scavengers were long gone after they had ravaged the crash site and taken off with significant chunks of the airliner that contained vital clues as to what may have caused the plane to come down.

The following day, that "explosion" was scaled down into second-day versions by witnesses who recounted hearing a "sputtering" engine that "backfired" in the clouds. Follow-up accounts reported no signs of fire, just a severed wing floating "like a feather" from the sky that landed separately from the rest of the wreckage. First-day details of a fiery plane spinning down from the sky washed out into second-day conjectures of ice forming on the wings.

Whether the Department of Commerce investigators coerced witnesses into backing off from their initial explosive descriptions can never be known. It was public knowledge that the Aeronautics Branch of the Department of Commerce, the federal government's regulating branch of air travel and the forerunner to the Federal Aviation Administration (FAA), had already spent five years fighting both press and public pressure to keep crash investigations confidential.

Herbert Hoover took charge of the Department of Commerce in 1926. The President quickly moved forward with the realization that commercial aviation would only prosper if the federal government managed the

... the period's nationally renowned columnist Ernie Pyle ...

licensing of pilots and oversaw the safety of aircraft operation.

Hoover's policy infused quick progression into the commercial aviation industry under the leadership of two directors — William P. MacCracken and Col. Clarence Young. By 1930, 417,500 passengers were taking to the air, more than double the previous year's airline travel numbers of 173,300.

Commercial progress put the young industry under a public microscope. Since its inception under the Air Commerce Act of 1926, the Aeronautics Branch's policy of keeping findings of airplane crashes sealed brought relentless pressure from the national press. With more planes taking to the air, more accidents occurred — some due to manufacturing designs in experimental stages, others due to growing pains of an industry emerging from its infancy.

Every plane crash in the early days of aviation travel was a learning experience for a young Aeronautics Branch of the Department Commerce. Each crash presented a new set of circumstances for an agency crawling through its own infancy of conducting investigations.

Mounting pressure from the country's leading newspapers — The New York Times, Washington Daily News, Chicago Daily Tribune, and even the period's nationally renowned columnist Ernie Pyle — exerted First Amendment influence to force the Department of Commerce to make crash findings public. Pyle led the charge through his widely-read aviation column that appeared in syndication for the Scripps-Howard newspapers from 1928 to 1932.

The constant public push for transparency created a boiling pot of hostility between the press and the federal government. With more and more people choosing air travel, the general public demanded to know how safe passengers would be on a plane. The Department of Commerce's policy of keeping plane crash investigations secret began to succumb to the frequent demands of the country's watchdog press.

But the crash of T&WA Flight 5 was unprecedented. Not only was the crash the first high-profile airline tragedy to fall under the DOC's investigation jurisdiction, Rockne's death made it impossible for the Aeronautics Branch to conceal its findings in the cause. There had been a throng of airline crashes in previous years, but this one was special. If Knute Rockne could die in a plane crash, anyone could. The nation demanded answers. The Aeronautics Branch had no choice but to cave to the public's right to know and the media's right to publish for the sake of future aviation safety.

"The press, as well as people in all walks of life have looked toward the Dept. for an explanation of the catastrophy (sic)," DOC Aeronautics Branch officials acknowledged in an undated five-page statement that was included with the accident investigation's official report.

Faced with an airline crash that resulted in the death of a beloved American icon, the DOC had no choice but to break policy and go public. Filed April 15, 1931, the DOC report also cited an editorial from the New York Times.

"For the first time," the DOC stated, "the Department now makes public an air accident finding."

But some reports needed to be tempered. An "explosion" in the air? The plane tumbled from the sky "in flames?" The last thing the federal government needed was public hysteria knocking down the doors of Washington over the possibility of a bomb being planted on the plane that killed the beloved Rockne.

Fokker's aloof disposition bordered on heartlessness.

55

ANTHONY FOKKER

The Flying Dutchman had nothing on the real Anthony Fokker.

Born Anton Herman Gerard "Anthony" Fokker on April 6, 1890, in the Dutch East Indies of what is now Indonesia, Anthony Fokker was 4 years old when his family returned to their native Netherlands to settle in Haarlem so Fokker and his older sister, Toos, could grow up with a traditional Dutch upbringing.

School was of little interest to Fokker. Yet, the Dutch teen who dropped out before he could complete high school possessed a keen natural sense for mechanics. Model trains and steam engines were his toys. Young Anthony loved nothing more than experimenting with designs of the earliest model airplanes.

Roughly around the same time Knute Rockne and Gus Dorais were perfecting their forward passing routes during summer workouts at Cedar Point in Sandusky, Ohio, Fokker was 4,000 miles across the Atlantic Ocean perfecting a wheel that would not puncture. Although the idea had already been patented, it was Fokker who first installed a perimeter of a rubber wheel with a series of puncture-proof metal plates.

Fokker took a job as director of a Dutch manufacturing company. When World War I broke out, the German government moved in to take control of the factory. Staying on as the company's director and main design engineer, Fokker began designing aircraft for the Imperial German Army Air Service.

Among his most notable products included the Fokker Eindecker and the Fokker Dr. I, a triplane that gained instant worldwide fame for being the sophisticated war machine flown by German flying ace Manfred von Richtofen, famously known as the Red Baron. Fokker's company was responsible for delivering more than 700 military planes to the German air force, the German navy, and Austria and Hungary.

Fokker designed and manufactured the world's most renowned flying military bombers of the time period commanded by the likes of the Red Baron. He was also a skilled pilot who demonstrated his aircraft to Germany's highest-ranking leaders. Fokker worked closely with accomplished fighter pilot, Otto Parschau, to bring the Eindecker into military use. On one occasion both Fokker and Parschau demonstrated the aircraft, prompting flying ace Max Immelman to comment in a letter:

"Fokker, especially, amazed us with his skill."

Fokker's renown as an aviation pioneer who was equally skilled as a pilot on the same level as The Red Baron was immortalized in folklore. "The Flying Dutchman," a World War I flying ace based on Fokker who piloted the same skies with the Red Baron while cultivating his own magnanimous legend, was immortalized as the hero of films such as "Von Richthofen and Brown" and "Young Indiana Jones Chronicles: Attack of the Hawkmen."

When it came to business dealings, however, Fokker was a flawed man. His factory floor was filled with several prototypes in development and production at the same time, but he struggled to fulfill war contracts because he failed to reinvest his wartime profits. Fokker was not a formally educated engineer, which may have led to his distrust for qualified educated engineers and his resentment toward frequent German insistence that he conduct stringent structural tests to ensure that German-used aircraft were fit for combat.

Fokker's aloof disposition bordered on heartlessness. His nasty temper and insensitive disregard for a colleague's life flared up on June 27, 1916, when designer Martin Kreuzer crashed a prototype Fokker D.I. aircraft. As Kreuzer lay mortally injured gasping his last few breaths, Fokker proceeded to give a verbal report on the jammed rudder that caused the crash while wailing obscenities toward the dying pilot.

Fellow designer Reinhold Platz, who witnessed the incident, recounted later that Fokker "... hurried to the scene and shouted reproaches at the mortally injured man."

Fokker could also be charismatic with service pilots and charming to senior officers. His charm served him well when his newly delivered Fokker Dr.I triplanes suddenly began experiencing a string of fatal accidents in 1917. Still, that charm couldn't keep his Fokker Dr.I triplane from being temporarily grounded as too dangerous to fly.

The problem arose when the triplane's top wings ripped away under aerobatic conditions. In one instance, the Red Baron's brother, Lothar von Richthofen, miraculously survived a crash caused by a severed wing. Fokker proved to Germany's high command that the cause of the crashes was not due to the triplane's basic design, but the German military concluded that the plane's problems were due to shoddy workmanship under poor supervision and lax quality control at the Fokker factory.

Fokker received a stern warning, but the scenario repeated itself with the introduction of the E.V/D VIII monoplane in mid-1918. When a high-level German inquiry revealed more production and workmanship issues, German authorities threatened to file criminal charges against Fokker.

Instead of facing potential criminal charges, Fokker left Germany and returned to the Netherlands shortly after World War I came to an end. He blamed overzealous German Air Force inspectors for requiring what he considered to be an ill-conceived design change.

"When the first D-8 [sic] was submitted to the engineering division to be sand-load tested, the wings proved to be sufficiently strong, but the regulations called for a proportionate strength in the rear spar compared to the front spar," Fokker wrote in his responding report. "Complying with the government's edict, we strengthened the rear spar and started to produce in quantity...[8]"

Fokker's troubles only mounted.

The D.VIII's wing continued to collapse at high speed. Fokker recalled the plane for further testing. After discovering that the reinforced rear spar caused the wings to flex unevenly at high speeds and increase the angle of attack at the wings' tips which caused the wing to shear apart under increased loads, Fokker resolved the problem by restoring the rear spar to his original specifications.

At the end of World War I, the German Revolution swept through the Netherlands. Fokker escaped to the United States and immediately established the North American branch of his company, the Atlantic Aircraft Corporation, with facilities in New York and New Jersey. Upon arrival in the U.S., Fokker quickly began operations to develop the Fokker F-VII airplane.

Designed in 1924 by Walter Rethel as a single-engine transport aircraft, five aircrafts of the F.VII model were built for the Dutch airline KLM. One of the planes — the registered H-NACC — would be used in the first flight from the Netherlands to the Dutch East Indies. Lt. Commander Richard E. Byrd and Machinist Floyd Bennett also flew a Fokker F-VII during aviation history's first flight to the North Pole

In America, Fokker quickly became the world's largest aircraft manufacturer. The U.S. Army and Navy lined up to acquire his aircraft. Large carriers such as Pan American and T&WA used Fokker's planes to transport passengers during the dawn of commercial aviation.

When word reached Fokker about the inaugural Ford Reliability Tour, proposed by the Ford Motor Company to develop competition for transport aircraft, Fokker instructed his company's head designer, Reinhold Platz, to convert a single-engine F.VII A airliner to a trimotor craft powered by 200-horsepower Wright Whirlwind radial engines.

The result, dubbed the Fokker F.VII A/3M, won the Ford Reliability Tour with a structure that consisted of a fabric-covered steel-tube fuselage and a plywood-skinned wooden wing. Fokker further modified the design into the Fokker F.VII B/3M with a slightly-increased wing area over the A/3M and a power increase to 220-horsepower per engine.

Out of the Fokker F.VII B/3M was born the Fokker F-10, a larger version of the B/3M built to carry 12 passengers in an enclosed cabin. The Fokker F-10, popularly known as the Fokker Trimotor, dominated the American market in the late 1920s and was the aircraft of choice for the world's largest airlines in Europe and the U.S.

More problems hit Fokker's American operations in 1927. Richard Byrd was planning to use a Fokker three-engine plane to be the first aviator to fly non-stop across the Atlantic Ocean, but the plane sustained damage during a test flight. Charles Lindbergh wound up flying the "Spirit of St. Louis," a single-engine monoplane designed by Donald A. Hall of Ryan Airlines, across the Atlantic for the first non-stop trans-Atlantic flight. That fatal test flight cost Fokker a place in aviation history books.

The Fokker aeronautics empire rebounded two years later when the "Question Mark," a modified Atlantic-Fokker C-2 transport plane used by the United States Army Air Corps commanded by Major Carl A. Spaatz, set new world records for flight endurance. During a non-stop flight that spanned 150 hours between January 1 and January 7, 1929, Fokker's Question Mark established world records for sustained flight, refueled flight, and distance before landing near Los Angeles, California.

Then, the Fokker F-10 Flight 599 crashed on March 31, 1931, killing Knute Rockne, five other passengers and both pilots. The aeronautics manufacturing empire Anthony Fokker had spent more than two decades building came to a grinding halt.

SECTION 4: THE INVESTIGATION

"I don't know who signed the plane off, but they took the airplane. Nobody was safe in that aircraft." —
Mechanic E.C. Red Long

56

NON-GROUNDED

Three days prior to the crash, Anthony Fokker "personally inspected this plane" and signed off on the air ship's safety, DOC investigators stated in the Aeronautics Branch of the U.S. Department of Commerce's official accident investigation report.

Fokker approval on his product's safety condition was business as usual. The Fokker F-10A Super Trimotor wooden-structured, wooden-winged aircraft operated with a payload of 12 passengers with three 425-horsepower Pratt & Whitney Wasp engines that could hit 154 miles an hour at top speed. Like all aircraft designed by the famous airship designer, the Fokker F-10A was said to be among the safest planes in the world during the late 1920s.

The military begged to differ.

Three months prior to the Rockne crash, the Fokker F-10 came under intense military scrutiny in the wake of extensive testing at Wright Field in Dayton, Ohio. U.S. Army and Department of Commerce engineers revealed a suspect wooden wing structure that, when reaching a speed of 80 miles per hour, caused the plane to "fly like a duck."

"The plywood-covering checks in very good shape," wrote Dillard Hamilton, a National Parks Airways inspector, in a letter to Gilbert G. Budwig, director of air regulation for the Aeronautics Branch. "But I always worry about the spars and internal bracing. That is covered up where one cannot check."

Hamilton noted that a representative from Fokker's factory suggested adjusting the F-10's "allerons," or control surfaces on the wing, to "relieve tail heaviness." But Hamilton remained concerned that an adjustment — which entailed rigging the angle of alignment — might cause the pilot to lose control during a turn in bad weather.

Budwig replied: "We are not familiar with the factory recommendation... and do not believe that such rigging will correct tail heaviness. In view of the turning characteristics which you describe, it would be advisable to rig the allerons in the normal manner."

Further concerns arose when U.S. Navy officials summarily rejected the Fokker F-10A on two separate occasions during additional military testing in early 1931. The Navy's rejections prompted the Aeronautics Branch to announce intentions to ground the Fokker F-10A after Rear Admiral William A. Moffett, chief of the Navy Bureau of Aeronautics, made it known that a trial board ruled the F-10 "unstable" following a flight test at the Anacostia naval air station on January 15, 1931.

But the Aeronautics Branch of the Department of Commerce took no immediate action. The Fokker F-10 remained in the air.

"Six passengers were manifested, only half filling the 12-place cabin..." retired U.S. Air Force Lt. Colonel Boardman C. Reed wrote in the January 1989 issue of "Vintage Airplane" magazine, "but one had a change of plans at the last minute. Knute Rockne took his place."

Rockne was traveling on the overnight train to Kansas City when the Transcontinental Western Air Express Fokker F-10AF-1 NC 999E flew into Kansas City from Los Angeles. The plane was scheduled to be turned back to retrace its route to Los Angeles as "Flight 5" the next morning, March 31.

T&WA mechanic E.C. "Red" Long thought better of putting the plane in the air on his signature. Long had inspected the plane a few days before and found "... the wing panels were all loose on the wing. They were coming loose and it would take days to fix it, and I said the airplane wasn't fit to fly."

Long refused to sign the log. But an unknown T&WA supervisor pulled rank on the mechanic by claiming the company needed the plane in service.

"I don't know who signed the plane off, but they took the airplane," Long told DOC investigators. "Nobody was safe in that aircraft."

That morning, T&WA Flight 5 was supposed to depart Kansas City Municipal Airport at 8:30 a.m. The plane remained on the ground for 45 minutes to wait for a late shipment of mail. According to the investigation report, "... the airline removed four seats from the rear of the plane and replaced it by a mail bin." The late-addition mail bin was filled with 28 pouches that weighed 95 pounds.

"Would that have any effect in balancing?" one investigator asked in the DOC official crash investigation report. "If Govt. or private inquiry shows that the airline was negligent, what penalty can the govt. inflict on the airline?"

T&WA employees would not have protested if Flight 5 had stayed grounded under mechanic Red Long's order. In the wake of drastic salary cuts outlined in the DOC investigation, pilots and mechanics were ready to walk off the job with morale among all employees "shot" after the company cut the pay of pilots "about 30%" with "no warning or notice," lead investigator Leonard Jurden wrote in a letter to Gilbert Budwig.

"Due to this condition and then the accident, morale sagged even lower and nerves ragged," Jurden noted.

Red flags all over Kansas City Municipal

Airport that March 31, 1931 morning begged the question: Why was Fokker F-10A Flight 5 allowed to take off?

The T&WA flight mechanic had refused to sign off on the plane's structural safety. A last-minute ticket transfer had put Knute Rockne aboard as a passenger... meaning, the T&WA supervisor who overruled Red Long at the last minute knew that one of the most beloved sports figures in the country was potentially in danger of traveling on a plane that had already been determined by the military and T&WA to be structurally unsafe.

Then, takeoff was delayed for 45 minutes to await the arrival of a late mail shipment. Four passenger seats were removed to make space for a bin filled with 95 pounds of mail.

Weather conditions were cold, cloudy and iffy. And T&WA employees were ready to walk off the job over sudden salary cuts.

Somebody wanted that plane carrying Knute Rockne in the air.

1930 as compared to that of 1928. Indisputably, some of that was caused by fool's luck. We started to specialize in the construction of Airports. It was a new venture; we were in virgin territory; no manuals itemizing Airport Construction Costs were available, because few Airports had been built; we had to purchase thousands of dollars worth of tractor and shovel equipment, and no men with a knowledge adapted to our particular type of construction work were available. Accordingly, we had to train our own after first finding out ourselves, and so the list of obstacles continues, but why bring up any more of that now. We filled our canteens, strapped on light marching orders, and here we are, just beginning to see daylight, for which all thanks are duly rendered.

Perhaps one of the most enjoyable concomitant conditions opened up by the path of endeavor has been the setting up and establishing of friendships and business contacts with men and companies directly or indirectly connected with our work. Business, to most people, is a humdrum occupation, unless some alleviating factor is found. To our way of thinking, profit, represented solely by dollars and cents, is a tasteless reward for work and sweat, unless it is accompanied by a warm handshake or a hearty greeting now and then.

Recognizing the fact that we were engaged in a new type of business, we established a modern method of advertising for contact and promotion work. It was our belief that to successfully build airports we must first become "airminded," and so be able to talk the language of the aviation industry. With that thought in mind, a Fleet Biplane was purchased and given a distinctive paint job with the company's name prominently displayed. The plane soon became a familiar sight at all established airports in New England. With it came an open door to a good many potential promoters of future airports. Recently a spectacular Gee Bee Sportser was added to our aviation equipment and entered in air races and state air tours. Our business horizon broadened, so that now we are visualizing construction work in the North during the summer months and southern work during the winter. It is easy enough for a man to dream dreams, and we find it something of an interesting gamble watching to see if our own dreams actually materialize.

Speaking of dreams, and if I may be pardoned for inserting a personal touch into this account, I at present am considering entering the Marine Corps Reserve, and am wondering, in the event that I do, how many of my old friends will be encountered. Until then—so long.

Very truly yours,
(Sgd) RAYMOND B. NOTT.

THE PILOT WHO PASSED WITH ROCKNE

Robert G. "Joe-Pete" Fry, ex-master sergeant and naval aviation pilot, was the name of the man who was flying the Western Air Express passenger plane that crashed in Kansas on the 31st of March, killing the famous Knute Rockne and seven others besides himself.

shock to Brown Field and to Marine Aviation everywhere as he was recognized as one of the ablest pilots ever produced from the enlisted ranks. Fry learned to fly in Guam back in 1923 and flew all over the country while stationed at Brown Field, going to China in 1927, where his flying during the Chinese revolution won him more honors.

Ice-clogged controls, a lost propeller, or any of the 100 other probable causes, makes it just one of those things that happen when the master pilot calls to Valhalla those who fly.

The late Robert G. "Joe-Pete" Fry.

Affectionately and ever known as just plain "Joe-Pete," Fry endeared himself to the hearts of officers and men alike while in the service and was recognized as one of the ablest pilots in commercial aviation at the time of his death.

QUARTERMASTER'S SCHOOL, PHILADELPHIA, PA.
By Joseph Schroeder, Jr.

This will introduce the new class attending the Quartermaster's School of Administration at the Philadelphia Depot of Supplies, which began March 2nd and will graduate July 31st—we hope.

For those who may not know it, let me say that this is a regular school. In fact, it will remind you of the good old school days. Remember?

To get down to facts, the object of the school is to teach Quartermaster's Department Administration in all its phases and, any man who graduates from one of the classes, has a distinct advantage over the man who steps into a Quartermaster's office and attempts to gain his knowledge by experience and letters of correction from Headquarters. These letters are a source of distaste to any Quartermaster officer and, from the number of applications received in Headquarters for graduates of the last class, these officers seem to believe that this schooling does tend to eliminate some of the errors.

The studies cover arithmetic, spelling, typing and all chapters of the Marine Corps Manual pertaining to the Quartermaster's Department. In addition,

tical experience is given, such as, keeping a property account, making out vouchers of all kinds and the technical points involved in every-day routine in the Quartermaster's Department. It would seem that five months is quite a short time in which to assimilate this knowledge, but that is where we introduce our instructor, Quartermaster Sergeant Hayes Rainier.

Quartermaster Sergeant Rainier is most certainly qualified for this work in every respect. He has a most excellent record with the Corps and has a thorough knowledge, not only of the Quartermaster's Department Administration, but human nature as well. His is a position of responsibility, of which few are aware. He is charged with not only giving instruction, but he must be certain that this instruction is correct in every detail. Headquarters relies upon him to turn out men with the ability to do things as they should be done and I am sure he has succeeded admirably.

The entire class is looking forward to making the highest marks attainable and have made an excellent start toward that end. Anyone walking into the squadroom at night could easily discern the reason. You would find, in one corner, a number of fellows grouped around a bunk, hot on the trail of the solution of a particularly tricky problem in arithmetic or arguing the fine points of interpretation of some article of the Manual. Interest, such as this, shows that the men are really in earnest regarding their work.

The roster of the class includes such famous personages as Sergeant Clausen, NCO in charge, recently of Parris Island; Sergeant Arthur J. "Shamrock" Kelly, of Quantico fame; Sergeant Johnny Mastny late of the Wyoming guard; Corporal Willie Cramer—the "kid"—also from Parris Island; Corporal Rodriguez of Nicaraguan repute and many others too numerous to mention in these columns.

While every man is serious regarding his studies, humor and wit is plentiful, either by direct intention or unconsciously. Corporal Rodriguez found, after receiving an invoice on some furniture, that he has one too many typewriters on his property account (fictitious) and is trying to give it away to avoid a correction. Sergeant Kelly was willing to take the typewriter off his hands, but says "the muzzler's mate only has it on paper." We haven't been able to find out just what a "muzzler's mate" is, and if anyone else beside Kelly knows, we would appreciate a definition. Sergeant Starr is going in for light opera and is practicing on the refrain "Carry me back to San Diego." Sergeant Mastny is always optimistic. He's never downhearted about anything like an inspection. He always says "well we can do it if we have to." Sergeant Clausen is the liberty hound of the class, I hardly believe he knows the location of his bunk. And Willie Cramer—well, when Willie yells "where's the Xyards," look out—Blackjack Willie likes to practice at the other boys' expense.

Since most of the fellows came to this class from various posts of the Marine Corps, I know it won't be amiss to mention that they all send greetings to the buddies they left behind and we'll all see you again soon, as Quartermaster Sergeants—IF.

It's unclear whether Fry knew that the plane had been grounded by Red Long ...

57

JOE-PETE

There wasn't a better pilot in 1931 to fly the Fokker F-10A Flight 5 under any conditions than Joe-Pete.

Master Sgt. Robert G. "Joe-Pete" Fry was a tall, 32-year-old former Marine fighter pilot who earned his wings in Guam in 1923 and was a fully designated Naval Aviation Pilot (NAP) by 1924. Over the next three years, Fry flew all over the United States from his station at Brown Field in Quantico, Virginia. In 1927, he was shipped out to China to fly with the 3rd Marine Expeditionary Force.

Joe-Pete's masterful knack for negotiating treacherous weather conditions in the sky was tested profoundly while flying Boeing FB-1 fighters with Fighting Squadron #10 out of Camp MacMurray at Hsin Ho, China in 1928.

Fry was flying a reconnaissance mission over hostile territory when he encountered a nasty major sand-wind storm and got lost. After skillfully maneuvering a miraculous forced landing safely to the ground, he suddenly found himself swarmed by Chinese rebels.

The Chinese suspected Joe-Pete to be a foreign spy, a captured prisoner of war who should be met with slow torture and a fatal bullet. But Joe-Pete not only carried masterful flight skills, he possessed an extraordinary wit that allowed him to keep calm under the most intense pressure. Using those wits, Joe-Pete convinced his captors that he was just a lost pilot with no interest in the Chinese Civil War.

The Chinese rebels bought the explanation. Fry was released back to the skies, and he returned safely to his base at Camp MacMurray.

Fry returned to the United States in April 1930. He was hired by Western Air Express with high Marine Corps' recommendations lauding his skills as "one of the ablest pilots produced from the enlisted ranks." With his China fighter-pilot pal Harlan Hull, who was also hired by Western Air Express, Fry remained in the Marine Corps Reserves while flying for Western Air Express — which would later merge with Transcontinental to form Transcontinental & Western Air (T&WA).

Fry settled into a daily route, flying a regular schedule between Kansas City and Los Angeles that allowed him to maintain residences in both cities. Before flying on March 31, 1931, Joe-Pete had logged an impressive total of 1,263 hours and 33 minutes as a pilot, and 227 hours and 57 minutes as a co-pilot. His Co-pilot Herman J. Mathias, also had 219 hours and 23 minutes under his belt. Over the previous 90 days Fry had logged 191 hours and 36 minutes, flying 2,511 of those miles at night. Mathias' previous 90-day log showed 112 hours and 29 minutes.

Fry flew the Fokker F-10A plane to Los Angeles from Kansas City on March 30. He departed routinely at the regularly scheduled 8:15 a.m. takeoff time, and returned to Kansas City without incident to repeat the flight on March 31.

It's unclear whether Fry knew that the plane had been grounded by Red Long before it was cleared for flight. With the takeoff time delayed to wait for a late mail shipment to arrive, Fry kept his eye on the weather reports. Kansas City skies were overcast with very light snow falling at times and mild winds from the north at two-to-three miles per hour. Fry figured he would catch clear weather over Salina by about 10:15 a.m. Wichita, the first stop, reported clear, hazy weather with temperatures at 37 degrees and winds out of the northwest at 10 miles per hour.

Bad weather didn't concern Joe-Pete in the least. He'd flown through bad weather on countless occasions. If he could navigate through a nasty, windy sandstorm over China and negotiate a landing that few on the planet could have survived, he could get the plane from Kansas City to Los Angeles.

Bad weather was nothing new to Joe-Pete, just part of the job. T&WA's most skilled pilot was much more concerned about having his pay cut by 30 percent.

SECTION 4: THE INVESTIGATION

At 10:22, flying 25 miles northeast of Cassoday, Kansas, the NAT plane flew close enough to the Fokker F-10 for the pilots to wave at each other.

58

IN FLIGHT

At 9:15 a.m., T&WA Flight 5 departed Kansas City Municipal Airport following a 45-minute delay. On board, according to the flight's log, were Knute Rockne and five other passengers.

T&WA operations supervisor Jack Frye watched from his office window as Robert Fry expertly navigated a smooth 600-yard crosswind takeoff before the dark red and silver Fokker F-10AF-1, NC-999E disappeared above the low-lying ceiling of clouds in less than a minute.

Fifteen minutes after Flight 5 departed, Paul E. Johnson, an airmail pilot flying for National Air Transport, took off from the same runway in Kansas City and headed towards Coffeeville, Arkansas. Johnson flew on "good weather reports given," despite Kansas City weather that showed a 500-foot cloud ceiling.

"Had to go up the Missouri River and out through the valley south of the Kaw River, and continuous north or regular course down Emporia because of the weather conditions," Johnson wrote in his flight report contained in the Aeronautics Branch's investigation report.

"Low ceiling and misty rain between Kansas City and Emporia, with alternate icy pick-ups and holes with good weather for four or five miles," Johnson noted. "Took... 40 minutes to get to Emporia, where... ran into low drifts of fog, snow-covered ground, and had to fly under drifts. Ran into wall of fog west of Emporia about 10 miles and started to turn towards the northwest where the weather appeared to be clearing. Started to pick up ice very rapidly and was flying just over the tree tops. Afraid to turn around and come back to Kansas City because

449

of the Fokker, which I assumed to be in the rear of my ship."

At 9:52 a.m., a cold front knifed into a warming zone over the red Flint Hills. Fry was in radio contact with Kansas City flying 10 miles southwest of Ottawa, 40 minutes out of Kansas City, when the weather suddenly grew heavier.

T&WA radio operator G.A. O'Reily in Wichita contacted Flight 5 to get an update.

"I can't talk now, too busy," Co-pilot Herman J. Mathias responded.

"What are you going to do?" O'Reily asked.

"I don't know," Mathias replied.

At 10:22, flying 25 miles northeast of Cassoday, Kansas, the NAT plane flew close enough to the Fokker F-10 for the pilots to wave at each other. Johnson overtook and passed above Flight 5. The Fokker Trimotor may have been capable of a top-end speed of 154 mph, but the plane drudged slowly at its optimum maneuvering speed of 102-103 mph, well below its 126 mph cruising capabilities.

"I then turned northwest after the second drift, intending to turn around to the right," Johnson told investigators later. "That was the last time I saw the F-10. It was turning, too, to the northwest."

Mathias radioed the T&WA station in Wichita: Flight 5 was on course 35 miles north of the Cassoday beacon light near Emporia.

O'Reily responded: "The sun is shining in Wichita."

Mathias' voice came back muddy through static: "The weather is getting tough. We've been forced too low by clouds. We're going to turn around and go back to Kansas City."

A few minutes later, Mathias radioed back: Flight 5 is going to try once more to get through the bad weather. The co-pilot told O'Reily to stand by.

Mrs. E.S. Chartier, a weather observer in Emporia, Kansas, reported general weather conditions as "improved quite an extent" from an earlier forecast. The cloud ceiling had risen, first to 1,200 feet, then to 1,500 feet. A higher ceiling was expected by noon.

At 10:40 a.m., Mrs. Chartier broadcast a "peculiar depressing condition" in the air, a "cyclonic atmosphere," a dark funnel-shaped cloud in the southwest.

The NAT plane headed west and started climbing in altitude. At 800 feet the plane encountered a 50-foot space between fog and low clouds. Johnson turned the plane south, then southwest toward Cassoday where good weather was being reported. Johnson's plane picked up ice very rapidly. No way it could fly higher than 1,500 feet.

"Ice on struts, allerons bowed," Johnson reported. "Air speed indicator iced up." Johnson flew relying on the turn indicator, climb indicator and tachometer. Ice was too heavy for the plane to gain more altitude. The NAT plane's motor flew wide open until Johnson "broke out of everything 15 miles straight east of Wichita."

Johnson landed the NAT plane safely in Wichita.

At 10:45, Fry and Mathias were unable to radio their position. In Wichita, O'Reily radioed weather conditions: "Practically clear and unlimited visibility seven miles, wind northwest... few clouds northeast."

"We've headed back but it's getting tighter," Mathias said. "Think we'll come on to Wichita, it looks pretty bad."

"Can you get through? O'Reily asked.

There was no response. O'Reily repeated his question.

"Don't know yet. Don't know yet," Mathias replied.

Those were the last words Wichita air traffic control received from Flight 5.

Section 4: The Investigation

... much of the plane had been snatched up by souvenir hunters and hauled away.

59

A CORONER'S JURY

Leonard Jurden, T&WA district agent H.G. Edgerton of Wichita, T&WA President Harris Hanshue, and Anthony Fokker were among the first investigative authorities called to analyze the carnage and determine the cause of the crash.

Their first stop was Cottonwood Falls, where the bodies of Rockne and the seven other victims had been taken. By the time they arrived on the scene, much of the plane — large pieces of wing, fuselage, and other significant parts that might have revealed the actual cause of the crash — had been snatched up by souvenir hunters and hauled away.

"Department investigators learned from eyewitnesses that the airplane was flying at an altitude between 500-600 feet apparently in a northeast direction, the assumption being that the pilot turned north of his course to avoid an unfavorable weather condition," Jurden wrote in the investigation report.

Two days after the crash, a coroner's jury convened in Cottonwood Falls to hear testimony by farmers who witnessed the catastrophe. Professional aviation experts were also called in to offer circumstantial theories in an effort to determine the cause.

Four farmers testified at the coroner's jury — Edward Baker; his brother, Arthur Baker; R.C. Blackburn; and Clarence H. McCracken. All gave similar eyewitness accounts. Edward Baker's statement in the accident investigation report coincided with his brother's account, but his recollection two days later slightly varied from the "terrific explosion" he heard in the clouds that was recounted to newspaper reporters at the scene of the crash.

Edward Baker explained to DOC investigators that he and his brother, Arthur, were about one and one-half miles away from the scene when they heard a plane in the clouds twice — five minutes apart. The first plane was likely the NAT plane piloted by Paul Johnson. The second time, Edward Baker said, the plane sounded as if the pilot had gunned the motor and shut it off with some backfire — and then the crash happened. Edward Baker told Jurden he saw only the wing fall, "... but not the main part of the plane."

McCracken recalled feeding cattle on Steward Baker's farm at the time. "The engine sounded all right until it was falling," he said. The plane emerged from the clouds "very fast," almost straight down. McCracken maintained that when the plane came out of the clouds, one motor seemed to be sputtering. A hill obscured McCracken's view of the plane hitting the ground.

"A few seconds after the ship came out of the clouds, I saw part of the wing come down, drifting slowly," McCracken said. "When the ship came out of the clouds it seemed to me to be going end over end. After the plane hit and (the) wing came down, there were objects that came floating down."

"I heard the plane flying above the clouds, hanging low over the ground," R.C. Blackburn testified. "The motor was sputtering... Suddenly the plane shot out of the clouds, it was tipping to one side and headed straight for the earth. A moment later I saw part of the wing floating down."

"It might have been backfiring, then we heard a sound which may have been the crash," Edward Baker said. "I said the plane must have exploded. Just after the plane fell, we saw the wing come down."

Blackburn remembered arriving at the site and scouring the wreckage. The break in the wing "appeared a little ragged and splintered, but went square across. An unbroken light on the top side, number side up." He also spotted a bag of mail under the wing and "three more sacks" between the wing and the plane.

L.E. Mann told the jury he rode to the site with Wallace Evans, Blackburn, and three others, including Dr. A.E. Titus. All helped remove the bodies. Mann said an hour had passed before he was able to get a good look at the wing. "U-shaped pieces of ice lying around the wing, about 6 inches long," he recounted.

Anthony Fokker flew over the scene on April 2nd with Jack Frye, T&WA's operations supervisor. He picked up a small piece of the wing left behind and part of the bottom flange of the spar, "which showed a break under tension...

"Material and glue joints, all perfect," Fokker insisted. He pointed out that he had analyzed some middle pieces of the spar directly above the fuselage, and a part of the wing that had been brought back to the spot where the plane had crashed.

Fokker concluded that the break was not caused by propeller failure, which countered DOC investigators' original findings. The right engine, Fokker said, struck the ground first, showing that the plane fell sideways and backwards. He suggested that the plane crashed at an "excessive speed" following a prolonged dive. Figuring the pilot lost control temporarily, or that everyone "was thrown forward including luggage and mail... If the luggage and mail sacks in the compartment were not properly secured or strapped down, a shifting load might fall forward into the pilot's cockpit, crash through roof or windows, or fall forward on the steering column, causing it

Fokker Lays Crash to Ice as Jury Fails to Fix Blame

By Associated Press.

COTTONWOOD FALLS, Kan., April 2.—A coroner's jury having failed to determine the cause of an airplane crash which sent Knute Rockne and seven others to their deaths, interest turned to-day toward an inspection by Anthony Fokker, designer of the craft. Flying here from Los Angeles, Calif., Fokker expressed the belief that "the flight should not have been undertaken in existing weather conditions" and that adverse flying conditions and the human element rather than a structural failure was responsible.

He said, however, that he would withhold a definite statement until he had viewed the wreckage of the Transcontinental and Western air express liner and had talked with witnesses.

The short verdict, "the deceased came to their deaths in an airplane fall, cause undetermined," closed the state's investigation after cowboys, who were the first to reach the scene, and aviation experts had testified.

Mystery in $55,000 Check.

Guards patrolled the forlorn scene of the mishap, near Bazaar, Kan., while authorities sought to substantiate reports that H. J. Christen, Chicago, one of the victims, had cashed a $55,000 check shortly before he boarded the ill-fated liner. No such sum was found by authorities at the scene. From Chicago came word that Murray Miller, Christen's attorney, doubted Christen had the money on his person during the flight. Miller believed Christen might have deposited the money in another bank before leaving Chicago.

Fokker came here at the request of interested aircraft officials. The Fokker corporation is a subsidiary of General Aviation, which owns a large interest in the T. & W. A. E.

Sees "Human Element."

The designer said he had his own opinion of the crash.

"Ice, forming on the wings, may have played a part," he said. "In my opinion the ship was placed in a violent maneuver and the wing was torn off as a result. I would put the human element very strongly into the cause of the crash."

Three hundred ships of the type, he added, have been built in conformity with his designs, and there has been no accident of major importance involving them where the cause appeared to be wing failure.

Jack Trye, vice president in charge of the air line's operations, said he favored a theory that "ice forming on instruments caused the pilot to become confused."

Played With 'Rock'; Buried Day of Crash

By Associated Press.

ELMIRA, N. Y., April 2.—James Watkins, who played the other end with Knute Rockne on the Notre Dame football team in 1911, was being buried here the same day that Rockne was killed in Kansas.

Watkins, a 43-year-old engineer for a gas drilling company, died Saturday and was buried Tuesday. He was a native of Indiana and engineered gas well development in Mexico and South America before coming here last September from Wellsville, N. Y.

CONSERVATIVE HEAD QUITS.

By Associated Press.

LONDON, April 2.—Neville Chamberlain, chairman of the conservative party organization, retired Wednesday and was succeeded by Lord Stonehaven, former governor general of Australia.

A clip from the South Bend Tribune on April 2, 1931, reporting that a Coroner's Jury failed to reach a conclusion as to the cause of the crash.

to jam and (the) pilot unable to recover."

Otherwise, the plane's designer theorized that "... pilot may have lost control on account of inexperience in blind flying, through failure or faulty indication of navigation instruments, or through excessive ice formation on the airplane."

Four pilots gave their own expert opinions to Aeronautics Branch investigator Fred H. Grieme. Each theoretically agreed with Fokker that weather caused Fry to lose control of the plane. Each also shared the theory that Fry appeared to get caught in bad weather, tried to pull through it, and fell into a spin resulting in losing the wing.

But one co-pilot knew Fry too well to agree with the four theorists. The co-pilot, only documented by his last name, "Herford," had flown with Fry on several occasions. He steadfastly insisted that Fry was not to blame. "He was considered as one of the best blind flyers in the (T&WA) company, and he always pulled through the fogs and clouds on leaving (Los Angeles)," Herford maintained.

Grieme wrote in the DOC accident investigation report that "Co-pilot Herford... did not think Fry would get into trouble flying blind and was sure that something unusual had happened."

Section 4: The Investigation

D   5823X907   PLANE WRECK   DDA
WRECK OF PLANE IN WHICH ROCKNE WAS KILLED

BAZAAR, Kansas—A view of the wreckage of the
Transcontinental and Western plane which exploded
in the air and fell in a spin in a pasture near
here, killing Knute Rockne, famous Notre Dame football coach, and seven others. A coroner's jury
found that the plane was wrecked by "causes unknown".
5823X907   PLANE WRECK

60

OFFICIAL INCONCLUSIONS

Investigators initially determined that weather moisture was a factor after finding that the plane's plywood outer skin was bonded to the ribs and spars with water-based aliphatic resin glue. Flying through rain caused the bond to deteriorate, causing sections of the plywood to suddenly separate in flight and sever the wing.

That was one theory.

The Department of Commerce issued a release blaming the crash on a broken propeller on the right engine. Ice, the investigators surmised, had formed on the propeller hub, which may have broken loose and struck one of the propeller blades. The propeller blade broke, created an unbalanced condition, and produced sufficient vibration to cause not only the hub and remaining blades to leave the engine, but also accounted for the in-flight wing separation... this analysis was determined after investigators dug the engine out of the ground, but couldn't find the engine's propeller hub or blades.

On April 8, the Department of Commerce issued a second press release that contradicted the first.

The cause of the crash was not due to broken propeller, the second release stated. The propeller and the hub were eventually located "...underground beneath the place where the engine, to which it had been attached, was dug out of the earth."

Investigators constructed a new theory: Ice formed on the aircraft and rendered the pilot's instruments inoperative while flying in the clouds, which caused the pilot to become dis-

Undated 5-page Statement from Dept. of Commerce, Aeronautics Branch.
...The press, as well as people in all walks of life have looked toward
the Dept. for an explanation of the catastrophy. Dept. charged with
investigation of accidents to civil aircraft, and yet is without authority to hold formal hearings, subpoena witnesses, require testimony under
oath, or to insist upon preserving the crashed airplane for inspection.
Problems involved are apparent. Findings of dept. are secured informally.
Not infrequently, satisfactory evidence of the cause of the accident does
not exist. Dept investigation is made for the purpose of attempting to
determine the cause from an operating point of view in order that rem-
edies may be considered, and, if indicated, applied against future operations. No attempt is made to determine legal responsibility because it
is not with in the province of the Dept. to do so.
...investigators have been obliged to draw upon their flying knowledge
and experience to set up certain assumptions in arriving at conclusions
with refrence to this particular accident. Therefore, the assignment of
causes as shown are to a substantial extent premised upon opinion and
conjecture. The following statement is not to be construed as an official finding of the Department..
...Dept. investigators learned from eye-witnesses that the airplane was
flying at an altitude between 500-600 feet apparently in a northeast
direction, the assumption being that the pilot turned north of his course
to avoid an unfavorable weather condition. At approximately 10:35 A.M.
the airplane radioed Wichita radio station to learn the weather at that
point. Wichita indicated satisfactory flying weather and inquired of the
pilots whether or not they would get through. Pilots did not respond.

... much of the plane had been snatched up by souvenir hunters and hauled away.

oriented and the aircraft to spiral into a deep dive. When the pilot reoriented himself, he overstressed the wing by trying to correct the unusual aircraft altitude too rapidly, which caused the wing to separate.

The Department of Commerce's revised theory appeared to be little more than conjecture put out by investigators who didn't really know what caused the crash but were desperate to toss theories against the wall to see which one stuck. Newspaper columnist Ernie Pyle blasted the investigation for looking more like a federal goose chase conducted by incompetents who were chasing their own tail.

"Do you know the old expression, 'eating crow?'" Pyle wrote in his syndicated column on April 8. "Well, the Department of Commerce is eating crow today on the Rockne crash. And since I was thoroughly sold on the Department's original explanation of the accident, I have or-

dered a nice plateful of crow for my own lunch."

The New York Times cut deeper into the Department of Commerce's haphazard findings. The Times slammed the DOC for rushing to judgment to appease a public left just as confused by the investigation's second official conclusion as the first.

"This was the first time the Commerce Department had made public the findings of its inspectors," the Times editorialized on April 8. "Officials indicated the reversal of policy was prompted by the tremendous public interest aroused by the sudden death of one of the greatest football figures in history."

Blackburn and the Bakers agreed there was no ice on the plane. Department of Commerce inspector Leonard Jurden testified to pilot Robert Fry, a former U.S. Marine Corps pilot with 4,500 hours of flight experience under his belt, as being "wholly competent." Jack Frye, vice

Section 4: The Investigation

Letter from Arnold Elson of N.Y.City 4/1/31

As<u>ks</u> for information, plans of plane, explanation of probable cause of crash, and what will the gov't do to make sure "no other planes have the same defaults in their structures". He understands that the air-line removed four seats from the rear of the plane and replaced it by a mail bin. Would that have any effect in balancing? If Govt. or pri-vate inquiry shows that the airline was negligent, what penalty can the govt. inflict on the airline?

Answer to above from E.McD Kintz, Chief, Enforcement Section.   4/4/31

Says "The Dept. makes public its findings on accident investigations only in statistical form". Says that there is no proof in Dept.'s poss-ession of the accident's having been the result of structural defect. Assures Elson that Dept will make every effort to regulate airline op-eration so as to prevent accidents of any nature or cause.

Details of Aircraft maintenance from W.H.Simmons to Clifford Mutchler, Asst. to V.P. in Chg. of Operations, T.W.A., March 31, 1931

Plane # 116 Mfg. # 1063   Plane commissioned 10/29/29   1887:37 on it.
Not major overhauled. Wasp Engines :

	T W A#	Mfg. #	Time since O.H.	Total Time
L	178	1354	339:40	1894:26
C	174	1906	176:56	577:18
R	171	1598	176:56	1038:36

Pilot: Robert G. Fry Time last 90 days 191:36 as pilot.
                       Nite Miles   2511 as pilot
Co*Pilot: H. Mathias Time last 90 days 112:29 as co-pilot
                       Nite Miles   0

	Total Time with W.A.E. and T & W.A.		Pilot
	As pilot	as Co-pilot	Nite Miles
Robert G. Fry	1263:33	227:57	22964
H. Mathias	0	219:23 (W.A.E.)	0

Propellor time same as engine time since overhaul.

2 propellors installed & Engine changed Ship 116, Jan. 31, 1931
Center Hub # 10977 (c) blades #'s 17073-17074-17075 Etched-Checked-Bal-
Right Hub # 8837 (c) blades #'s 17689-18618-18522   anced 1/31/30

Statement from Ray E. Spengler, April 4, 1931 Chief Mech. TWA, KC.

He arrived at scene about 6:30, and did not leave the wreckage until April 3 about 4 P.M. after all debris had been removed. Found all engines, and accounted for four of nine blades. Sheriff asked to locate the remaining five blades. Three returned in evening of April 2nd. Re-maining two returned April 3 about noon. All people who returned them said they were taken from the scene of the accident

Manifest for Plane # 116, Flight 3, 3/31/31, Western Division, (Alameda, Glendale, Los Angles, Kingman, Winslow, Albuquerque, AMarillo, Wichita, Kansas City.) "On" at Kansas City Passengers 915 # Baggage 146 # Mail 63-6 #. Total 1125-6#.

"... the airlines removed four seats from the rear of the plane and replaced it with a mail bin ..."

Grieme wrote in the DOC accident investigation report that "Co-pilot Herford... did not think Fry would get into trouble flying blind and was sure that something unusual had happened."

president of T&WA operations, admitted to the jury that he couldn't make a determination until he had conducted a further investigation. T&WA field manager A.L. Sondine said the plane had been inspected twice and "reported in good condition" on two occasions immediately preceding the fatal crash.

Passengers on the plane weighed in at a combined 915 pounds. Baggage added 146 pounds. There was a discrepancy in the weight of the mail, originally listed at 63.6 pounds but raised to nearly 95 pounds after the late shipment arrived.

Mail sacks were found on the ground between the broken wing and the main fuselage. Two more bags were found 50 yards away in the southeast direction of where the broken wing lay. The smallest sack — labeled from Kansas City to Wichita — was retrieved from underneath the broken wing when investigators lifted about an 18-foot section of the wing, indicating that wing failure occurred near stations 8-11 where the engine attachment points were located on the one-piece wooden wing.

Edward Baker testified, "... a good-sized piece of wood came down after the wing, a little south and east of the main plane."

Was that piece a lighter piece of the wing, perhaps blown higher into the air by an explosion?

Fokker stood by his initial determination, "...the human element. In my opinion. The ship was placed in a violent maneuver and the wing was torn off as a result... Three hundred ships like the one which crashed have been built in conformity with the same design. There has been no accident of major importance to them where the cause appeared to be a structural failure of a wing."

But the words of Fry's former co-pilot, Herford, overwhelmed the others' hypothetical criticisms of Joe-Pete Fry's flying skills. Herford's contention that Fry "...was considered as one of the best blind flyers in the company, and he always pulled through the fogs and clouds on leaving (Los Angeles)," spoke the loudest.

Grieme noted in the DOC report that "Co-pilot Herford... did not think Fry would get into trouble flying blind and was sure that something unusual had happened."

The coroner's jury found the cause of the crash to be "undetermined."

The Department of Commerce's official findings were also "inconclusive."

Section 4: The Investigation

25c

UNCENSORED!

TRUTH ABOUT

ROCKNE'S
STRANGE
DEATH!

Not a Broken Propeller
Not Ice on the Wing

At Last—Inside Story
of the Fatal Crash!

61

UNCENSORED!

Something unusual did happen, according to a booklet published less than two months after the crash.

"UNCENSORED! TRUTH ABOUT ROCKNE'S STRANGE DEATH... Not a Broken Propeller, Not Ice on the Wing... At Last — Inside Story of the Fatal Crash" immediately raised questions over the likely possibility that the plane carrying Knute Rockne was sabotaged. "UNCENSORED! shredded the Department of Commerce's findings as nothing more than hypothetical "conjecture."

The book, published by Graphics Arts, Corporation in Minneapolis, Minnesota, is a collector's item today.

"Considering the purpose of the investigation and the frequent lack of direct information, investigators have been obliged to draw on their flying knowledge and experience to set up certain assumptions in arriving at conclusions with reference to this particular accident," "UNCENSORED!" claimed. "Therefore, the assignment of causes as shown are to a substantial extent premised upon opinion and conjecture."

In addition to printing investigators' official findings, "UNCENSORED!" delved deeply into coverage of specifics of the Fokker Trimotor plane and details of the pilots' final radio communications with air traffic controllers at Wichita Airport. The book also addressed contradictions between newspaper and eyewitness accounts.

"None have yet dared to tell the truth about the horrible tragedy that destroyed the greatest

... the fatal crash of a Boeing 247 airplane near Chesterton, Indiana hit too close to home to the Rockne crash for any bomb theorists to ignore.

and most beloved man in the history of American sport," the book's authors claimed. "Has the truth been suppressed for selfish and cowardly reasons?"

The writers cited airline officials' conclusions that the Fokker Trimotor plane carrying Rockne was less than two years old and in nearly new mechanical condition with a "comparatively small number of flying hours chalked against it."

"In conclusion," the book contended, "it would seem that the airplane involved had been operated entirely in accordance with the Air Commerce Regulations; that the daily inspections were satisfactorily concluded;

that the airplane was, to the best of everyone's knowledge, thoroughly airworthy; and also, that no blame can be attached to the pilots."

"UNCENSORED!" also reveals, "Digging deep into the ground, the missing propeller blades were found!"

Finding the propellers and the split hub cap buried under the debris lent credence to the theory that the pilot, in his futile attempts to pull the plane out of a steep dive without the benefit of certain flight instruments rendered inoperative due to ice collected on the plane's outer shell, had "wrenched away the wing."

But Aeronautics Branch investigators found no traces of ice on the plane. Fokker, himself, admitted that of all of his 300 planes of the same type, none ever experienced an accident caused by a wing that failed. Fokker's wings were noted for tremendous durability, built to withstand loads 11 times greater than a load imposed on a wing under flying conditions detailed in the DOC's findings.

Pilot Robert Fry's flight skills were also regarded as tops among his peers at the time. Veteran fliers, including Army and transport pilots, went public refusing to believe that an experienced pilot of Fry's caliber would go into a nose dive and rip off a wing. Besides, they reasoned, eyewitnesses said the plane had been flying low under the clouds, not high enough for the plane to go into a nose dive.

Considering the supreme condition of the plane, and considering the plane's low-flying altitude seen moments before the crash, a clue to the actual cause of the crash may have been implied in an artist's rendering published in "CENSORED!" The sketch shows the left wing breaking off in the air and falling to the ground before landing about a half-mile from the bulk of the wreckage.

What could cause the wing to sever?

"Some of the theories advanced that the wing gave way of its own accord or because of an unusual load are ridiculous," said one Army air service pilot quoted in "UNCENSORED!" "But it's not ridiculous to consider that time after time we have had examples of sabotage, and that this might have happened to the Rockne plane, for reasons unknown."

The pilot described acts of sabotage he had seen on various aircraft. A mechanic working on a giant dirigible at Goodrich had been caught spitting on points where rivets were fastened to the framework knowing that the rivets would loosen — after they had passed inspection. Had the mechanic's acts not been

discovered, "...the dirigible would have been wrecked on its first voyage," the pilot said.

"Airplanes in the Army and Navy have been tampered with to our definite knowledge, not once but many times," the pilot admitted. "Case after case is on the records" of gas lines sawed through, struts weakened, and other parts such as cotter pins removed from tail controls — all so parts would break and cause a plane to crash in what would seemingly appear to be a tragic accident.

"A bolt sawed half through, then covered with black gum; a hidden wire nicked with pliers — all those things are possible," the pilot insisted.

"UNCENSORED!" failed to mention eyewitness Edward Baker by name. But the book clearly confirmed the teen farmer's account of hearing what sounded like a bomb exploding on the plane in midair, a confirmation that was further magnified two years later in shocking headlines first printed by the South Bend News-Times in January 1933.

According to the South Bend News-Times, an "unimpeachable source" revealed that the United States Secret Service had investigated the possibility of a bomb planted on the plane — a bomb that may have been intended for a Notre Dame priest, Father John Reynolds, set by Al Capone's gang after Father Reynolds testified in the murder trial of Capone henchman Leo Brothers. The source also maintained that Secret Service knew the identification of the mobster who planted the bomb in a mail pouch, but didn't reveal the name.

Two months after the South Bend News-Times story exposed the Rockne crash as a possible gangland bombing, the "City of Liverpool" — an Armstrong-Whitworth Argosy II passenger plane put out by the

British airline Imperial Airways — crashed near the Belgium city of Diksmuide. The deadliest crash in British civil aviation history at the time killed all 15 people on board.

Or did it?

Witnesses on the ground in northern Belgium saw the plane burst into flames in the sky before it lost altitude and plunged to the ground. Those same onlookers watched one passenger jump out of the aircraft without a parachute and free-fall to the Earth.

Crash investigators later identified the remains of the exiting passenger as Dr. Albert Voss, a German national who had worked as a dentist in the United Kingdom. Their investigation found that a fire had started in either the lavatory or the luggage area in the rear of the plane's cabin, possibly ignited by either a combustible substance lit accidentally by a passenger, crew member, or the natural occurrence of a vibration.

During the inquest into Dr. Voss's death, his estranged brother came forward and told jurors that the dentist and his niece had been on the flight together completely aware that they were under investigation by Scotland Yard for drug smuggling. Dr. Voss, according to his brother, had used the airlines to travel around Europe and buy anesthetics he sold on the side that provided a lucrative income in addition to his dental practice.

Prior to the flight, the brother noted, Dr. Voss had purchased airline accident insurance. He had planned to escape his pursuers by destroying the plane with incendiary materials available to him through his dental practice then bailing out in the pandemonium with all intentions of surviving. But an inquest into Voss's death showed that, other than a few minor burns, Voss's body — unlike the other 14 victims whose remains were retrieved

mangled beyond recognition — had otherwise been unharmed before he had exited the plane.

The inquest jury returned an "open verdict." Jurors concluded that while they believed Dr. Voss's death may not have been accidental, they didn't have concrete evidence to reach a definite decision. The brother's testimony, however, caused many to view the crash of the "City of Liverpool" as the first act of sabotage in commercial airline history.

Seven months later on Oct. 10, 1933, the fatal crash of a Boeing 247 airplane near Chesterton, Indiana hit too close to home to the Rockne crash for any bomb theorists to ignore.

United Airlines Flight 23 took off from Newark, New Jersey headed on a cross-country route toward Oakland, California with a first scheduled stop in Cleveland. With four passengers and three crew members aboard, the aircraft was on its way to its next stop in Chicago shortly after 9 p.m. when it exploded at an altitude of about 1,000 feet in mid-air.

Eyewitnesses on the ground heard the explosion and saw the plane plunge to the ground in flames. The plane exploded a second time on impact in a wooded area on the Jackson Township farm of landowner James Smiley. All four passengers and three crew members perished, including Alice Scribner, the first flight attendant in United Airlines history to be killed in a plane crash.

Findings from the debris left crash investigators stunned. The plane's toilet and baggage compartment had been obliterated into fragments. Metal shards pierced the inside of the toilet door only; the outside was completely devoid of metal traces. The plane's tail section had completely severed from the fuselage and was found a mile away, still intact.

Dr. Carl Davis from the Porter County

Coroner's office and investigators from the Crime Detection Laboratory at Northwestern University collectively concluded that the crash of United Airlines aircraft NC 13304 had been caused by a nitroglycerin-fueled bomb. Famed federal agent Melvin Purvis, who at the time headed the Chicago office of the United States Bureau of Investigation, offered a poignant description of the probe's result.

"Our investigation convinced me that the tragedy resulted from an explosion somewhere in the region of the baggage compartment in the rear of the aircraft," Purvis said. "Everything in front of the compartment was blown forward, everything behind blown backward, and things at the side outward... The gasoline tanks, instead of being blown out, were crushed in, showing there was no explosion in them."

A further look into the cause revealed that a packaged rifle had been retrieved from the wreckage. Investigators dismissed the gun as evidence when they learned the weapon had been carried aboard as baggage for a passenger returning home to Chicago from New York to attend an event at Chicago's North Shore Gun Club. With limited remains available after local souvenir hunters arrived at the crash site and made off with significant plane parts, investigators were certain that the cause was a bomb.

Why?

Some considered the possibility of a bomb being planted to hurt United Airlines in a labor dispute, but the company had a stellar reputation for working well with unions and its employees. The destination, Chicago, was rife with Mafia activity. Purvis, however, failed to develop any leads that implicated any mob links to the crash.

A motive for the bombing of United Flight 23 remained a mystery even after an elderly man named Howard Johnson — who had driven to the wreck site in his Ford Model T — came forward 66 years later and recounted something he had heard during an oral history project organized by the Westchester Public Library in northwest Indiana.

"It was all rather vague, but they said that someone got on the plane in Cleveland and had a suitcase and then they got off and no one saw them take the suitcase off," Johnson recalled in 1999. "So that's, no doubt, what happened. They just left the bomb on the plane."

The bombing of Flight 23 was said to be the first proven case of air sabotage in the history of commercial aviation. Considering the circumstances surrounding the Diksmuide crash a few months earlier, the incident over Chesterton, Indiana may have actually been the second known airliner bombing.

Then there was the Rockne crash two years earlier that shared several similarities: Witnesses claimed to have heard an explosion in the air. The tail was severed from the fuselage on Flight 23 and found on the ground about a mile away nearly intact; the wing that had separated from the fuselage on the Fokker F-10 was recovered more than a half-mile away from the Kansas wreckage site completely intact. In both cases, souvenir hunters made off with substantial pieces from the respective wreckages before investigators could arrive and collect significant plane parts that may have held key details regarding a definitive cause... or, a saboteur.

The two proven cases that occurred within months of each other two years later fuel the possibility that the crash of the Fokker F-10 that killed Knute Rockne and seven others on March 31, 1931 may have actually been the first act of airliner sabotage in United States aviation history.

"He literally got thrown out of that monastery ..."

62

GOD'S HANDFUL

Whatever dying words Jake Lingle whispered into the ear of the priest who cradled his last breath remained secret forever.

Father John Reynolds survived on his own terms. He wore the burden of his Bible-sworn testimony that created the untimely death of his beloved friend under his collar. Tell the truth. The whole truth. And nothing but the truth. Leave the consequences to God.

And always stay true to the sacramental seal of confessional.

A Chicago gangster might have put it this way: Never snitch on the confessor. Jake Lingle rests in eternal peace knowing that his dying words never passed Father Reynolds' mortal lips.

The rest of the story followed Father Reynolds like an extraordinary aura for the rest of his life. There was no sacramental seal to keep him from talking about the events that led to the crash that killed his friend Rockne to anyone who wished to listen. The truth may have been lost in the priest's brash nature, but it was Father Reynolds' fixed truth every time no matter how many years had piled up behind him.

"Yeah he did," said Father Richard Layton, a resident priest since 1969 at Our Lady of Guadalupe Abbey in Lafayette, Oregon, where Father Reynolds spent the final 24 years of his life. "The message I got was that he saw it, and he went over to the dying man... and supposedly heard his confession. He always believed that they were out to catch him, because he might have information through the confession. And then he just had an idea that somehow this was involved with (Knute Rockne) being killed in the plane accident.

"... he was very feisty. The story goes that when he was at Holy Trinity, he got into a fight with one of the other brothers ... The abbot said, 'You gotta go.'"

Father Richard Layton

"We didn't know whether to take it with a grain of salt or whatever, but he would tell the same story, pretty much in the same details. So, either he may have had an overactive imagination, but apparently most of the facts are there as far as his being there and the confession, and feeling rather unsafe."

Father Reynolds left Notre Dame in 1939. After entering the Holy Cross Order and joining the Trappists, a Catholic order of contemplative monks, he traveled to Kentucky in 1944, where he took residence at the Trappist Abbey Gethsemani and worked as a professor alongside noted writer Thomas Merton. The strong heads of Merton and Father Reynolds locked horns on more than one occasion during Father Reynolds' short stay at Gethsemani.

"Remote... he was a poet," is how Father Reynolds described Merton, who had been accepted into the monastery as a postulant by Gethsemani's Abbot, Frederic Dunne, and spent his time at Gethsemani writing journals and studying the complicated Cistercian sign language along with his daily work and worship routines.

"He tried to highbrow me, see, and I highbrowed him and he couldn't take it," Father Reynolds recalled of his relationship with the writer. "One time I was going through a door and he looked at me and he gritted his teeth at me. I looked at him and walked by."

Within a few months, Father Reynolds was shipped out of Gethsemani and sent west to Huntsville, Utah, to set up the Trappist Abbey of Our Lady of the Holy Trinity. His devotion to the priesthood was never questioned at Our Lady of the Holy Trinity, where he served as a one-man theological and philosophical faculty at the Trappist Abbey for the first four years.

"In those days," Father Reynolds remembered, "life was rugged and corn flakes frequent."

But Johnnie Reynolds remained a handful.

Father Reynolds never shed that angry little boy with the hair-trigger temper who grew up punching noses at the drop of a hat. Nor did Father Reynolds seem to care about putting the soul of Johnnie Reynolds behind him, a head-strong stubbornness that landed the holy man in several fights with fellow priests and monks over the years.

The last straw in Utah occurred in 1962. After 18 years, the spiritual and administrative leader of the Trappist Abbey of Our Lady of the Holy Trinity had had enough of Johnnie Reynolds.

"He literally got thrown out of that monastery," Father Layton recalled. "He was a feisty little guy, 5-foot-6, maybe 5-foot-5, he was very feisty. The story goes that when he was at Holy Trinity, he got into a fight with one of the other brothers... he got the guy in a half-nelson, in one of those knuckle sandwiches. That was enough: The abbot said, 'You gotta go.'

"So, we took him in here."

In 1962, Father Reynolds settled for the rest of his life at Our Lady of Guadalupe Abbey in Lafayette, Oregon. He converted to the Order of Cistercians of the Strict Observance and changed his name to Father Simon. Johnnie Reynolds, however, stayed the same talkative, joyously argumentative, cantankerous spirit that refused to leave his embattled youth in Bellows Falls.

"Everybody's hair shirt," is how one fellow Our Lady of Guadalupe monk described Father Reynolds.

"You want me to call him a curmudgeon?" Father Layton asked through a chuckle.

"One of the things he used to do, if you coughed in chapel, or if you were in choir and you coughed, he would cough back. I think he had an issue about sounds; certain sounds made him angry. So, if there was a guest in the guest chapel coughing, he would look out there and maybe cough back. He was a feisty little guy. He was in track ... he was very athletic in his younger years, so, he liked to pick a fight.

"One time," Father Layton recollected, "our Brother Fabian got after him because he was doing this — coughing after you cough — and he grabbed Father Simon and said, 'Stop that.'

"Simon said, 'You're gonna be excommunicated because you touched a priest.'"

Growing old while living among the wine vineyards of Oregon's serene wilderness mellowed Father Simon profoundly. He became accepted as the monastery's most "colorful" monk, and on June 16, 1982, his fellow monks at Guadalupe helped him celebrate the 60th anniversary of his

"Everybody's hair shirt ..."

ordination into the priesthood.

"He made it well here at Guadalupe," Father Layton said. "Because, any other place, they would've thrown him out, probably.

"But you know, in his last three months of life, he was dying. He turned extremely gentle, very gentle. We had a good time together. He was very nice, too. He had a soft spot, but he had that feisty attitude. Those three months before he died, those three months were very peaceful. I think death was on its way."

Father Simon's beard served as a form of personal restitution. Brother Fabian, Father Simon's chief antagonist at Guadalupe, wore a beard. Father Layton believed Father Simon grew his beard — a long, thick, bushy mass of hair that covered his face just like Brother

He was old, kinder, gentler, mellow as a lamb in the final weeks of his life ...

Fabian's — as an act of contrition.

"I always felt he was doing that in reparation," Father Layton said. "He would make up for things. He was the kind of guy; he would make amends by doing something to show that he had made a mistake. I think those last days he knew that the end was coming, and he just gave up the fight."

At the turn of 1986, Ron Karten, a reporter from Catholic Sentinel newspaper in Portland, Oregon, traveled to Our Lady of Guadalupe Abbey to interview Father Reynolds about his extraordinary life. When Karten arrived, he found a "very small, very old," Trappist monk wearing a black hooded robe, black-rimmed glasses, a long thick white beard, and a warm smile that greeted the writer with open arms.

Karten recorded the interview on a series of cassette tapes. The 91-year-old monk impressed Karten with a sharp mind, keen intellect, and a clear memory that recalled specific details of his life as if they had happened that morning.

"One of the most intelligent men I've ever encountered," Karten recalled.

It didn't take long for the interview to turn to that June 1930 day in Chicago when Father Reynolds witnessed the murder of Jake Lingle. During the interview, Father Reynolds recounted testifying at trial that Brothers "looked like" Lingle's killer, but refused to say outright that Brothers actually pulled the trigger. He made no mention of Lingle's dying confession, and he referred to Frankie Foster as "Frank Shepperd," one of the gangster's several aliases.

The conversation landed on the crash that killed Rockne. Father Reynolds didn't flinch from the same account he gave 52 years before to the two students hanging out in his rector's office at St. Edwards Hall — James Bacon and Kitty Gorman.

He was old, kinder, gentler, mellow as a lamb in the final weeks of his life, but Father Reynolds still held Johnnie Reynolds in his soul — the tough priest from Bellows Falls who once came face to face on the street with the real killer of Jake Lingle and his six mob goons. As he did that day outside the train station in Chicago, Father Reynolds chuckled out loud at the recollection of the notorious mobsters looking like children as they piled back into their car.

"I never feared death from those men," Father Reynolds maintained, "because you only die once, and you don't die until God calls you."

"Now, what happened with the plane?" Karten inquired.

"To the plane?" the priest asked. "They bombed it."

"That Rockne was on?"

"Yeah," Father Reynolds replied.

"Were you supposed to be on that plane?"

"No, no," he said. "It was going out to make a picture, see... But all of the newspaper headquarters were phoning me wanting to know if I was on the plane, see, and I told them I wasn't."

"But," Father Reynolds insisted, "that is the way they got even with Notre Dame."

"The mob rubbed out Knute Rockne because they let you testify?"

"Yeah, yup, absolutely, oh I am sure of that...oh, yeah..."

Father Reynolds paused.

"Isn't that some story?" he asked with a grin. "You like that story? I have plenty more."

His last night on Earth, Father Simon Reynolds penned a cryptic note that wound up pinned to the Our Lady of Guadalupe community bulletin board.

"Everybody is invited to my homecoming," the note read.

But Johnnie Reynolds wasn't about to go out without delivering one last act of defiance.

"We asked if he wanted to make Guadalupe his monastery of stability, but he refused," Father Layton said. "He wanted to remain as a monk of Holy Trinity, but some of that was in spite of the Abbot at that time, the Abbot of Holy Trinity. (Father Reynolds) would always insist that he was still a monk at Holy Trinity.

"At the end, the Abbot (at Guadalupe) asked if he wanted to be buried here, and he said, 'Yes,' so he kind of let go a lot of those grudges and resentments."

On the morning of January 28, 1986, Trappist Father John Simon Reynolds died at the age of 91. Later that day, the space shuttle Challenger exploded in mid-air 73 seconds after liftoff, killing five NASA astronauts and two payload specialists, including Christa McAuliffe, who would have been the first teacher in space.

It is highly doubtful Father Reynolds meant to go out in such ironic flare on the same day as the explosion of an aircraft like the tragedy that wore on his mind for the better part of his adult life. Perhaps it would be more fitting for the quiet end of Father Reynolds remarkable time on Earth to be remembered in the same compassionate breath as the words he penned in the conclusion of a paper dated August, 1972.

"To keep a mental balance, and my feet on solid ground, I feed the birds: wild birds (sparrows don't count; they are insolent). A bird writer writes, 'You will succeed well with birds if you are prepared to admit that, in some things at least, they are much smarter than you are.' Seems to me that fits humans, too."

The crown witness to one of Chicago's most infamous mob hits went to his grave as the lone constant in a whirlwind of theories, conjectures, questions and debates that to this day continues to surround the plane crash that killed Knute Rockne.

Say what you will about the holy man who put up his fists at the drop of a hat and once pummeled the head of a fellow priest locked in a half-nelson... the details of the extraordinary story Father Reynolds shared with James Bacon and Kitty Gorman at the age of 39 in 1934 stayed true to the same set of facts he told to Ron Karten 52 years later at the age of 91.

Father Reynolds rests among 38 graves in the back yard of the church on the grounds of Our Lady of Guadalupe Abbey. His unwavering testament that a bomb was planted on that plane meant for either him or his pal Rockne is etched in eternity.

"To keep a mental balance, and my feet on solid ground, I feed the birds ..."

SECTION 5
THE LEGACY

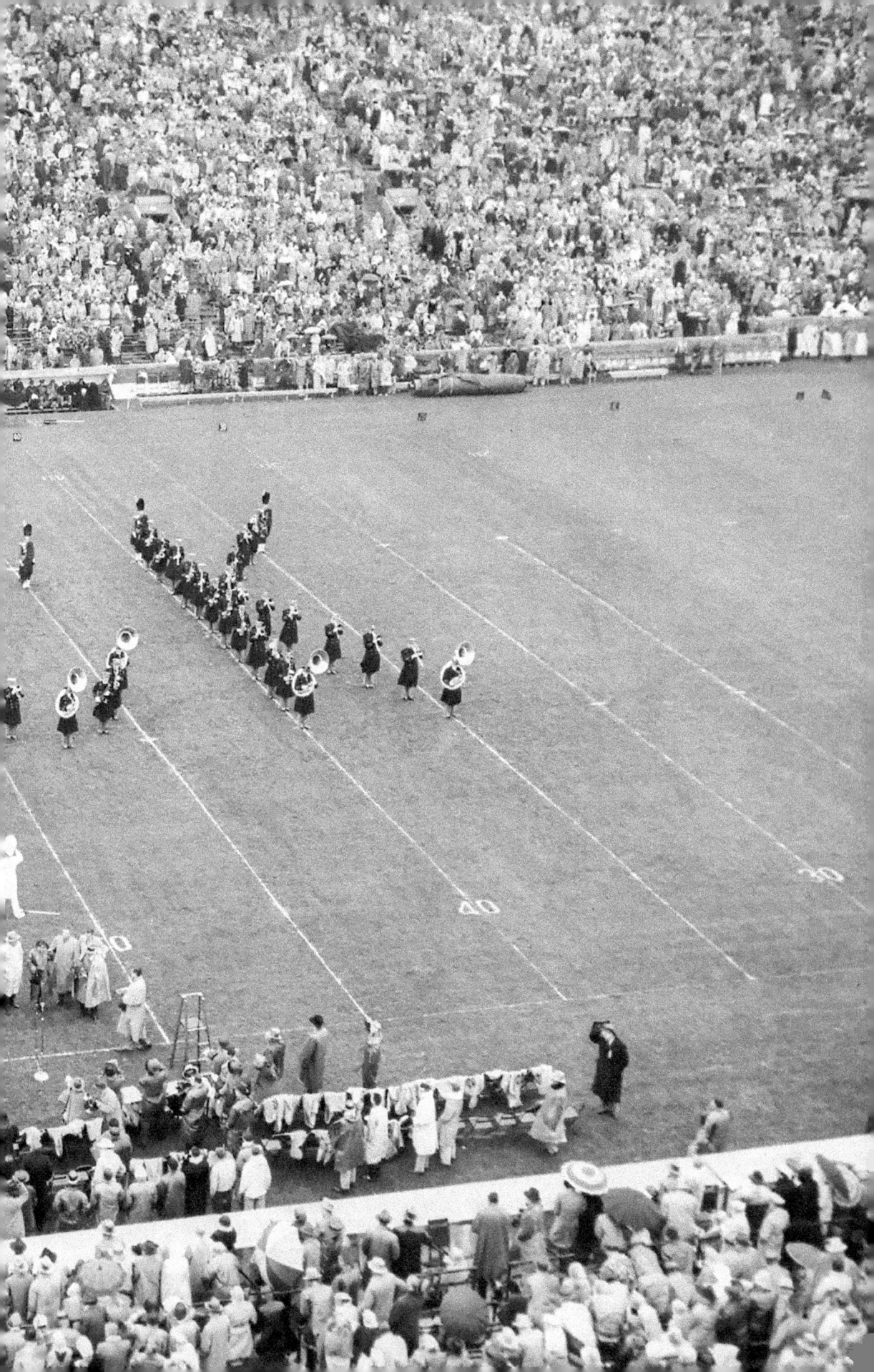

"No one ever asked me to pick the greatest football coach of all time, but if I were asked, I would unhesitatingly name Rockne ..." — Pop Warner writing in the Saturday Evening Post in 1934

63

HIS SPIRIT

Knute Rockne the man may have died on the morning of March 31, 1931, but it is impossible to kill a legend.

Step on the campus of the University of Notre Dame, and Rockne's presence is almost palpable. You can feel it as you walk the same paths that Rockne trod nearly a century ago. You enter Notre Dame Stadium, "The House That Rockne Built" and one of the true meccas of college football, and you can almost see it hovering in the sky on those sunny September Saturdays or those blue-gray October skies. If you are fortunate enough to be invited in, you can almost touch it in the locker room where he first commanded his "Ramblers."

Captured in bronze, the spirit of Knute Rockne still manages to emit an air of greatness that stands most prominently at the north gate of Notre Dame Stadium, the Rockne Gate as it's now called. During his legendary career, Rockne amassed a winning percentage of .881 — still unsurpassed by any coach of a major college football program nearly a century after his death. It's only fitting that a legend should be remembered for compiling the game's all-time winning percentage among college football's greatest coaches.

The statue captures Rockne — legs shoulder width. Hands on hips. Whistle on a chain around the neck. High-top football shoes fully laced to the top. It is at once a tribute and a relic, symbolic of time past when football's cherished and most recognizable forefather woke up the country's masses to a baby game hungry for maturation. With his head slightly cocked to the

... to this day, Rockne's .881 winning percentage remains the best of the top-tier coaches in college football history.

side, a gentle, fatherly grin greets all who stop to pay tribute as if to say, "Nice job, kid, now do it better tomorrow."

"I was trying to make him approachable," explained artist Jerry McKenna, who was born six years after Rockne died, but has made it his life's work sculpting Rockne's invincible spirit as if he had known the legend personally.

Rockne's expression is channeled through the sculptor's artistic vision in all nine of his pieces that stand at memorials across the country and around the world. Perhaps his most relevant location serves as a bookend to the time-honored path that runs out from under the Hesburgh Library's "Touchdown Jesus" mural, across the courtyard where Rockne's teams lined up on old Cartier Field, to the Rockne Gate.

"I wanted the face to reflect a man who is approachable, and who could hold your stare for a minute," McKenna said.

There are a number of coaches in the history of college football with far more wins than Rockne's 105. However, he only had 13 seasons at Notre Dame before his untimely death.

The winningest coach is John Gagliardi, who bests all challengers with an incredible 489 wins, 138 losses and 11 ties. It took Gagliardi 64 years, coaching at Carroll College in Helena, Montana, and St. John's University in Collegeville, Minnesota, to reach that height.

Eddie Robinson deserves his own category: 408 wins, 168 losses, 15 ties. The iconic head coach of Grambling State University turned his historic Black college into a college football landmark just as Rockne turned his historic Catholic institution into college football lore.

There's Penn State's Joe Paterno and the major college football reality of 401 wins, 135 losses and 3 ties. Amos Alonzo Stagg's 329 wins; Paul "Bear" Bryant's 325 victories; Pop Warner and his 318 wins; all top Rockne's total of 105 wins.

But to this day, Rockne's .881 winning percentage remains the best of the best of the top-tier coaches in college football history. In his brief tenure at Notre Dame from 1918 to 1930, Knute Rockne held the nation captive with 105 wins, 12 losses, five ties, five undefeated seasons without a tie, and three national championships.

And there was so much more.

From selling Notre Dame as a commercial football brand all across the country to redesigning the shape of the ball itself to fit more comfortably in the quarterback's passing hand, Rockne's imprint on the game itself remains firmly stamped on the mass audience that makes up modern-day American sports culture. The spirit of Rockne remains as strong as it is timeless.

"A lot of what he started here is what we, as coaches, try to carry on with tradition and excellence," said former Notre Dame All-American defensive back Todd Lyght, as he stood a few feet away from the Rockne statue following a youth football seminar at the stadium in June 2018.

"He is the genesis for everything Notre Dame football is today."

The indelible imprint Rockne left on Fighting Irish football barely scratches the surface of the influence his spirit still carries to an entire country. Often overlooked is the fact that in a nation reeling from the Great Depression, Rockne's teams provided a much-needed diversion.

His coaching legend spans every level of the game, and sports in general with all of its pom-poms, circumstance and glory. Rockne's indomitable spirit is still called on whenever a leader of athletes, corporate sales employees or military soldiers needs to serve up motivation. Anytime a coach or manager in any sport delivers a stirring locker room speech, the spirit of Rockne is conjured to inspire the troops just as Rockne so famously did in 1928 during halftime in the locker room at Yankee Stadium when the Irish were deadlocked in a scoreless battle with staunch rival Army.

That day, the stirring eloquence of Rockne spawned a blueprint for motivation. Believe in the actual happening or dismiss it as an illusion of hype created by Hollywood and perpetuated by cultural myth, but there isn't a coach in any sport who hasn't at one time or another conjured the Rockne spirit to:

"Win one for the Gipper ..."

Values in Footballs

Shure Winner Regulation Football

Regulation Size Genuine Pebbled Grain Cowhide Leather Football, furnished complete with pure gum bladder lace and lacing needle. Packed each in box.

No. 12R2. Per dozen........................ 6.75

Shure Winner

Regulation Size Football with valve. Made of selected genuine cowhide, pebbled grain—exceptional value. Heavy canvas lined. Complete with leather lace, lacing needle and fine quality rubber bladder. Packed each in box.

No. 12R19. Each........................ 1.50

Wilson

Mfg.
No. FG3

Dick Hanley Scholastic Football. An exceptionally good quality low priced ball—made of pebbled grain cowhide, canvas lined and valve inflated. Complete with stemless valve type bladder, laced ready for inflation.

No. 12R55. Each........................ 2.30

Mfg. No. 22RL.

Wilson Valve Football. New criss-cross rawhide laced. Made of selected pebbled grain cowhide, with our patented double lining feature, which holds the ball in shape. Complete with stemless bladder, and laced ready for inflation.

No. 12R48. Each........................ 3.68

Mfg.
No. RLF

Wilson Interscholastic Ready Laced Foot Ball. No lacing worries, as the ball is laced with a rawhide lace ready to inflate. No bladder stem to tie; inflates in a jiffy through a valve same as in an auto tire. Made of fine selected pebble grain cowhide with our patented double lining feature which holds ball in shape and prevents stretching. Regulation size and weight. Complete with stemless bladder and laced ready for inflation. Each in box.

No. 12R13. Each........................ 4.90

Mfg. No. KR

The Wilson-Rockne Double Laced, double lined Official Intercollegiate foot ball has become known as the perfect foot ball.

It's a livelier ball and holds its shape permanently because of the patented double lining. The double lacing double locks and permanently closes the lacing aperture and also insures a finer grip in passing.

The KR comes already laced, ready for instant inflation—through a valve just like an auto tire. Made of finest selected Gunnison pebble grain cowhide, sepecially tanned. Complete with seamless patented valve bladder. Each in box.

No. 12R37. Each........................ 8.50

"... the double lacing and double lining ... are the reasons why it is known as 'The Perfect Foot Ball.'"

64

SHAPING FOOTBALL

K nute Rockne did not invent the game of football.

American football traces its origins back to mid-19th century Britain and early versions of rugby and association football — both of which utilized a rounded, fat football kicked at a goal or over a line in an assortment of varieties.

College football had already achieved a level of supreme popularity throughout the United States by the turn of the century in 1900, largely due to the coaching innovations of Walter Camp, widely regarded as the "Father of American Football." Camp, head coach at Yale University and a Hopkins School graduate, instituted the Americanized game's first rules by introducing a line of scrimmage, downs, distance parameters, and the legalization of blocking.

If there were a Mount Rushmore for college football coaches, Rockne's visage would certainly be carved in stone alongside Camp, Glenn Scobey "Pop" Warner and Amos Alonzo Stagg — with Rockne being the most recognizable. The figure of Rockne in his trademark overcoat and tie, hat over a prematurely bald head and a wide flat-nosed boxer's mug remains the face of college football, transcending his era from 1918 to his final national championship season of 1930.

Like baseball's Babe Ruth, who during the same time period drove the game Abner Doubleday created into a primetime show of competition, the product Rockne put on the field was a spectacular display that sold tickets by the thousands, introduced college football to a national audience, and elevated Notre Dame to the college football stratosphere along with every school that played the Fighting Irish on any given Saturday afternoon.

485

Rockne may not have invented the game of football. But he was the first to breathe air into its shape — literally.

The first ball used in the game's infancy was round, but quickly reshaped into the semblance of a swollen watermelon made from a pig's bladder. In addition to bulky handling issues, one constant problem involved inflation, especially when the passing game was used more frequent during the second decade of the 1900s.

While Rockne coached Notre Dame football, his business interests included a football clothing line he designed and marketed through Wilson Sporting Goods. Rockne's clothing line carried the first football pants with pads sewn into a protective waistline.

In 1924, Wilson Sporting Goods introduced the Rockne Double-Lace football. Rockne had worked with Wilson to design the Wilson-Rockne Ball — a sleek pigskin leather model held together by thick cross-stitched lacing in the middle and a brand-new feature never before seen on a football: an air valve to regulate inflation.

"The Rockne Double-Lace method is an exclusive Wilson feature found only on Wilson-Rockne Official Footballs," Wilson announced in advertisements when the new ball was first introduced to the public. "The feature combined with the patented Wilson Double Lining and air-valve features place the Wilson-Rockne Ball in a class all by itself. It's the ultimate in a football. Perfectly shaped and keeps it shape longer than any ball made — the double lacing and double lining methods are the reasons why it is known as the 'The Perfect Foot Ball.'"

The modern football carries Rockne's handprint on the air valve. Why, if it weren't for Knute Rockne, today's fans may have never heard of "Deflategate."

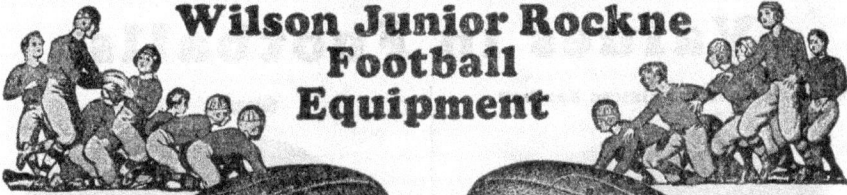

THE BEST OF SPORTING GOODS
N. SHURE CO., CHICAGO

351

Wilson Junior Rockne Football Equipment

Mfg. No. JR22

Junior Rockne Helmet. A real helmet which follows the general style of the higher priced numbers, made of special tanned "pig skin" strap leather, tan color, lined throughout with white felt, moulded crown reinforced with fibre; also six leather crown bands, equipped with inner web suspension crown, one-piece moulded ear and back of neck extension; forehead piece has soft leather sweat band and elastic adjustment. Each in box.
No. 12R43. Each........ 2.36

Mfg. No. JR20

Junior Rockne Laced Valve Type Football. Full regulation size, made of selected pebble grain cowhide, double canvas lined to hold its shape, complete with stemless valve type bladder; ready to inflate. Included with ball are full instructions for kicking and stencil for marking kicking guide lines. Each in box.
No. 12R42. Ea 1.62

Mfg. No. JR21

Junior Rockne Regulation Football. Full size, made of selected pebble grain cowhide, canvas lined, complete with bladder, rawhide lace and lacing needle. Included with ball are full instructions for kicking and stencil for marking kicking guide lines. Each in box.
No. 12R41. Ea. .98

All articles on this page attractively packed making them suitable for gifts.

Mfg. No. JR23

Junior Rockne Shoulder Pad, made of white felt covered with selected tan grain leather, moulded fibre shoulder caps, white felt lined, moulded fibre collar bone protector overlapping shoulder caps; round elastic under arms, laced front and back with Wilson "Adjusto" rapid lacer. Each in box.
No. 12R44. Each........ 1.96

Mfg. No. JR25

Junior Rockne Football Jersey. A real jersey in Junior sizes, made of a medium weight good quality pure worsted yarn; athletic cut, full length sleeves with turned cuffs; will be supplied in following colors: No. 4 orange with black sleeve stripes; scarlet with white sleeve stripes, and navy blue with No. 7 gold stripes. Football emblem included with each jersey, to be sewed on. Sizes, chest 26 to 36 in. State size and color wanted. Each in box.
No. 12R45. Each.......... 2.70

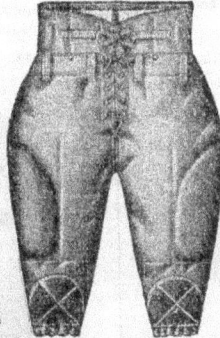

Mfg. No. JR24

Junior Rockne Football Pants. A real football pant built along the general lines of our higher priced pants with real protective features not usually found in a Junior size pants; made of heavy tan duck, white felt hip and kidney pads with flexible fibre reinforcement at top. One-piece curved fibre thigh guards fitted in special canvas pockets, well padded knee with leather patch. Sizes, waist 24 to 32 in. State size wanted.
No. 12R46. Per pair....... 3.28

Mfg. No. JR26

Junior Rockne Sweater, V-neck, slip-over style, made of a good quality medium weight worsted and wool yarn, shaker knit; will be supplied in the following colors: Black with No. 4 orange neck trim; scarlet with white neck trim, and navy blue with No. 7 gold neck trim. Football emblem included with each sweater, to be sewed on. Sizes, chest 26 to 36 in. State size and color wanted. Each in box.
No. 12R47. Each.......... 5.24

The genesis of the forward pass transported into the revelation set by Dorais and Rockne.

65

PERFECTING THE PASS

ontrary to popular football mythology, Knute Rockne did not create the forward pass. The concept of throwing a football spiral with an overhand motion was first drawn up in 1903 by two men — Howard R. "Bosey" Reiter of Wesleyan University, and Eddie Cochems, head coach at St. Louis University. Cochems' St. Louis University quarterback Bradbury Robinson completed the first legal forward pass in a game on Sept. 5, 1906, a 20-yarder to Jack Schneider that drew very little attention outside the stadium that day, and virtually no mention in the press.

A year later, the forward pass received its most notable public indoctrination with Pop Warner's revolutionary single-wing system — dubbed "the Carlisle Formation" — at Pennsylvania's Carlisle Indian Industrial School.

Carlisle featured the legendary Jim Thorpe, arguably the greatest athlete who ever graced a football field and the most powerful athletic force on any field, baseball diamond or running track in the world. Carlisle staggered opponents throughout the 1907 season by using the forward pass with such overwhelming success that one New York Herald sportswriter deemed Carlisle's passing dominance as "child's play ... any down and in any emergency, and it was seldom that they did not make something with it."

Warner's Carlisle Formation was also successful because the forward pass was such a new concept. Most teams were rendered helpless against the pass since opposing coaches had yet to design defenses to counteract even the most primitive passing schemes — most of which consisted

... Eddie Cochems, head coach at St. Louis University.

a summer job as a lifeguard on the beach — and both split-time working as waiters — at a summer resort at Cedar Point not far from Sandusky, Ohio

When the dishes were washed and packed away, Rockne and Dorais donned bathing suits and went swimming, always with a football in hand. Coming out of the water, the two would throw the football back and forth for an hour at a time. Day after day, workout after workout, in the water and on land, Dorais and Rockne relentlessly ran their own conceived passing drills. With Dorais passing, Rockne devised his own set of patterns. Sometimes he would run to a spot and turn around. Other times, Rockne ran a route without stopping as Dorais timed his pass in the air so that Rockne could run under it without breaking stride.

Those workout sessions not only elevated the forward pass to a new level, they gave birth to what is known in modern football as the "route tree."

Dorais-to-Rockne was the most sophisticated forward passing combination in all of football going into 1913. Later that year, Rockne and Dorais unleashed their newfound passing schemes on Army, shocking the college football powerhouse 35-13 in a game that drew national sports headlines. Dorais completed 14 of 17 passes for 243 yards, mostly to Rockne, and stamped the forward passing system with the timed running route as football's most lethal offensive weapon.

The genesis of the forward pass transported into the revelation set by Dorais and Rockne. Other teams were quick to follow, and the results would soon transpire with success in various parts of the country. But that was merely the beginning of the Rockne influence on intercollegiate football.

Advances in the forward-passing

of short pitches, shovel passes and primitive passing routes that involved the receiver running downfield a few yards to a spot, then waiting stationary for the ball to be thrown.

Knute Rockne and his best friend, speedy Notre Dame quarterback Gus Dorais, began practicing with each other privately during the summer of 1913 when Rockne was working

To
KNUTE ROCKNE
•••
In grateful memory of
the man whose standards of
fair play are an immortal
inspiration to the youth of
America; and whose many
contributions to the great
sport of football will never
be forgotten.
He developed the Forward
Pass on this strip of beach
at Cedar Point.

... at a summer resort at Cedar Point not far from Sandusky, Ohio.

movement arrived swiftly. The rules were changed to eliminate penalties for incompletions and throwing the ball over the center of the line, which opened the gates for the forward pass to become football's most exciting reason to buy a ticket.

The Dorais-to-Rockne game also served as a cornerstone in displaying the potency of the forward pass with an "open offense," prompting many coaches across the country to add passing plays designed with the running route to their playbooks.

Rockne served as a self-proclaimed "one-man merger" ... a literal jack of all trades unheard of in today's specialized world of major intercollegiate sports.

66

GOLD AND BLUEPRINTS

A s a coach, Rockne's innovative schemes laid strategic blueprints for the game that have been handed down and reshaped by coaches throughout the years. For instance, Rockne's 7-2-2 defensive structure was the early design for the way defensive coaches "stack the box" against a run-heavy team.

Rockne's "Notre Dame Box" offense — with the backfield lined up in a T-formation then quickly shifting into a single-wing box to the left or right of center just as the ball was snapped — arguably served as the game's first shift. Dubbed simply the "Notre Dame shift," Rockne's pre-snap shifting scheme proved so successful, it was banned by college rule-makers. Today, rules allow only one player at a time to be in motion before the snap; any additional pre-snap movement after the line is completely set draws a 5-yard penalty for a "false start."

Rockne was also the first coach to teach the "brush block," where an offensive blocker makes light contact with one opponent then continues downfield for secondary blocking. Another first — Rockne's strategy to break a team into smaller groups — became a precursor to platoon football.

His Notre Dame team was also the first to employ "shock troops," substitutes to give the starters a breather and soften up the opposition for a refreshed first team. Rockne strategically utilized second-string subs in the first and second quarters to wear down opposing teams' starters during the early part of game, then hit with first-teamers full force in the second half when the opposition's unrested starters were worn down. Today, the strategy of using "shock

493

troops" is not only prevalent in football, but also in basketball to get starters in foul trouble early, and to a smaller degree, relief pitchers in baseball.

Rockne was also the first coach to popularize coast-to-coast schedules. Once, Rockne chided a player for "having the nerve to travel 20,000 miles with Notre Dame and still flunk geography." He was also the first coach to carry the team's own local water supply on trips.

No football coach before Rockne thought enough to make spring practice drills the toughest, most grueling sessions of the year. Rockne was the first to organize practice sessions by breaking players down into small groups according to position rather than hold mass drills. He was also the first to activate otherwise inept substitutes for away games to use them as morale builders -- Rudy, anyone?

Rockne originally enrolled in college to be a doctor, and accumulated top-of-his-class grades in biology and chemistry — a subject he would specialize in and teach as a Notre Dame professor of chemistry from 1916 until 1922 when Rockne stepped away from the classroom to serve as full-time head football coach.

He knew his oxides as well as his pigskins, and possessed a brilliant knowledge of anatomy, a mindset that allowed the coach to double as a trainer since the school couldn't afford one. In turn, Rockne was the first coach or sports trainer to perform "heroic treatment" for sprained ankles by applying wet heat then making his player walk to reinforce blood flow to the injured ankle. In addition to head football coach and chemistry instructor, Rockne served as a self-proclaimed "one-man merger" as Notre Dame's graduate manager, athletic direction, track coach, treasurer of athletic funds, trainer, waiter, valet, a literal jack of all trades unheard of in today's specialized world of major intercollegiate sports.

"When Rockne first took charge of Notre Dame football, the team had no such financial resources as it has now," former sports and magazine editor John D. McCallum wrote in "We Remember Rockne," the book he co-penned in 1975 with former Rockne player Paul Castner. "He had to be coach, trainer, rubber, ticket-taker, baggage master and financial secretary. He did everything, and this included blowing up the footballs with which the boys played."

Rockne's broad intellect was unparalleled among football coaches during his time and thereafter. Unlike most who put the game above everything, education always took priority over football. Rockne's first question to any young man who applied to him to play football at Notre Dame was: "Do you want a college education?" He had no use for players who weren't good students and couldn't keep up with their classes. Holding to the idea that "a good student is a good athlete," Rockne always put brains at a premium.

But the nail Rockne forever hung his famous hat on was the same nail he first hammered during those summer workout sessions at Cedar Point with Dorais. Rockne coached the passing scheme he and Dorais had devised as players. Expanding a repertoire of patterns to fit into his pioneering offensive system was like nurturing, cultivating, and perfecting his child.

Today, there isn't a modern football team anywhere — pee wee, Pop Warner League, high school, college or professional — that doesn't prioritize the forward pass as an integral part of the offensive system. In the NFL, the best passing systems now utilize the timing route — a synchronized system of routes being run at the same time with the quarterback reading the defensive coverage and throwing the ball to what is anticipated will be an open spot on the field.

If the passing route schemes Rockne devised — first with Dorais as a college player, and later as mastermind of Notre Dame's shift offense — have one profound impact on the game, it's this: The running game grinds out yards on the ground and buys time off the clock — the forward pass sells tickets.

... and we're not gonna stop until we get across that goal line ...

67

THE GREAT MOTIVATOR

Knute Rockne was the antithesis of his own classic image.

A shy, self-effacing anomaly who sounded through a staccato-pitched stammer that heightened to a screech instead of a clamor, Rockne didn't even look the part of the greatest football coach in the land nor the game's most prodigious endorser.

He stood only 5-feet, 8 inches tall although some who knew him said he was shorter, perhaps the result of a pair of spindly legs that had been bowed and nearly crippled from severe phlebitis. A nose that had been crushed when he was a teen by either a baseball bat in a brawl or a foul tip off a bat while positioned as a catcher during a pickup sandlot game left Rockne with the flattened mug of a back-alley fighter. When he entered Notre Dame at the age of 21, Rockne had already started to go bald which made him look at least 10 years older all the way up to his death at 43.

"The first time I saw Rockne, he looked like a man far too old for college," Gus Dorais once said. "He was wearing blue cord pants, held up with white leather suspenders. He had on a light blue jersey with a black cap. He could have passed for a race track tout."

Rockne's sharp wit, keen intellect and engaging charm belied his appearance as a poor man's commoner. He took great pains trying to improve his physical appearance, spending hundreds of dollars on hair restoratives and consulting a plastic surgeon in Chicago about his nose. The coach outlined his struggles to refine his public speaking skills in an unfinished autobiography that was published in Collier's magazine under the title, "Knute Rockne, His Life and Legend."

497

But anyone who dared to call out Rockne's physical traits in public drew the coach's infamous wrath.

"He looks like an old, punched-up preliminary fighter who becomes door-tender in a speakeasy," wrote Westbrook Pegler, the one-time Chicago Tribune scribe who usually saved his poison pen for presidents from both parties, the tax system and corrupt labor unions. "He sits at a shadowy table in a corner near the door at night, recalling the time he fought Billy Papke in Peoria for $50. No one would ever suspect that Knute Rockne was a great football coach. He simply refuses to act or look the part."

A furious Rockne never spoke to Pegler again. Nevertheless, in the wake of Rockne's death, Pegler wrote: "I read that youth has no idols nowadays. But they had one at Notre Dame."

As a leader of young men, football never knew a more skillful field tactician, or a more powerful motivator. To this day Rockne's immortal speeches continue to stand over the test of time influencing every facet of life whenever a leader — from coaches, managers and military generals, to corporate CEOs — needs to inject a charge into the troops.

Rockne was not hesitant to stretch the truth to get his point across when the moment required an urgent spark. Former players readily recalled that Rockne said whatever he thought he had to say to ignite his team, whether he made up a story about his 6-year-old son being hospitalized or implying that Indiana's ferocious tackling style may have contributed to the death of George Gipp even though Gipp had succumbed to a strep throat infection compounded by the onset of pneumonia. Even Rockne's claim of being at Gipp's bedside to hear the dying words he would use eight years later during the famous "Win one for the Gipper" speech has provoked questions of truthfulness.

"They were all lies, blatant lies," recalled Jim Crowley, a member of Notre Dame's famed Four Horsemen backfield, speaking to a sports publication years after Rockne's death. "The Jesuits call it mental reservation, but he had it in abundance."

Perhaps 'exaggeration' warrants a more accurate description of Rockne's motivational tactics.

Little Billy Rockne had actually seen a doctor to remove a peanut stuck in his nose when Notre Dame traveled two days by train to play Georgia Tech in 1922, a powerhouse team that was heavily favored by 35 points against Rockne's Irish squad largely made up of first-year players. Rockne may have stretched the severity of his family situation a bit, but being a master motivator provided Rockne with the mental reservation to shift his fatherly concerns for his son into a general's charged attempt to light a fire under his underdog team.

"Rockne came into that dressing room before the game-time and he had a great number of telegrams in his right hand," Crowley recalled. "He said they were from all over the country. In his left hand held a lone wire. He said it was from his poor sick little boy, Billy, who was critically ill back in the hospital in South Bend. And then he read the wire. The lips began to tremble. A lump came to a throat. He says, 'I want Daddy's team to win.'"

Don Miller's recollection differed slightly than his Four Horsemen teammate Crowley's, but both shared the same reverent understanding of their beloved coach's method.

"I'll never forget the way he unfolded that one," Miller recounted in an interview years later. "Sort of hesitantly, and I'd have sworn his hands trembled a bit. It seemed he couldn't make up his mind whether he really wanted to read this

"...We're gonna go inside, we're gonna go outside, inside and outside, we're gonna get 'em on the run, boys. Once we get 'em on the run, we're gonna keep 'em on the run. And we're gonna go, go, go, go, go, go, and we're not gonna stop until we get across that goal line. This is the team; they say is good. But I think we're better than them. They can't lick us. Whaddya say, men..."

From Knute Rockne's "Todays the Day We're Going to Win, Men" locker room speech

---

one, but he did... 'It's just from my son, Billy,' Rock told us. 'Billy is ill and has been taken to the hospital.' He then read the telegram. It said, 'Please win this game for my daddy. It's very important to him.'"

Rockne's absolute truth that day paled in comparison to his plea for accomplishment. His son's presumed plight cut right to the jugular of his players' competitive souls.

"We all knew Billy, of course," Miller said. "He was Rock's little 4-year-old, a tow-headed kid who often came to watch us at practice, a great favorite of the players. Well, I'll tell you, it really got us.

"Rock didn't say another word, just put the telegram back in his pocket and walked out. We burst out after him onto the field, yelling and cursing our heads off.

"We tore that Georgia Tech team apart and beat 'em 13-3," Miller added. "They never had a chance."

And when the train carrying the victorious Irish football squad pulled into Union Station in South Bend the following Monday, the first one to beat the crowd and run up to his father "whooping and hollering" was Billy Rockne.

"You never saw a healthier kid in all your life," Crowley recalled. "He hadn't been in a hospital since the week he was born. But the guys on the team never considered they'd been

taken in by Rock. There wasn't even anything to forgive... and we'd find out over the couple of years that Rock would use any ploy he could think of to get the most out of us, whether it was at practice or in a game."

Rockne's truth was never challenged more than his narrative of the fabled George Gipp, although Hollywood, not Rockne, catapulted "... win one for the Gipper..." into eternity as the undisputed king of motivational speeches. Pat O'Brien as Rockne standing somberly at bedside leaning his ear into the dying words of Ronald Reagan as Gipp in the film "Knute Rockne: All-American" was the epitome of heart-wrenching drama when it was released to a national film audience in 1940, nearly a decade after Rockne's death.

The truth?

Had Rockne been anything less than the celebrated salesman he portrayed during his epic life, anything less than the savvy persuader who sold everything from Studebaker automobiles, to a line of sporting goods, to his own football teams on storming out of a locker room and destroying their opponents, Hollywood would never had wasted one cent to make a feature film on the life of Knute Rockne.

Where's that Hollywood bio-feature on Pop Warner or Tad Jones? And if Rockne hadn't been the charismatic superstar of his time who turned a few spirited words into Notre Dame legend every weekend for 13 consecutive autumns, the Gipper himself may have lost out on the immortality that launched his name into the eternal blueprint of every coach's most passionate call to arms.

Rockne's secret lay in his relentless pursuit of keeping his players tightly focused on their upcoming rival.

"The report that one time after he'd lost a ballgame, they rode the train someplace," recalled Don Hamilton, quarterback of the undefeated Notre Dame team in 1909 who served as an assistant coach in 1912 when Rockne was a player, during an interview shortly before his death in 1959. "He'd put up a photograph of each man's opponents in the sleeper so that that fellow could look at him last thing before he went to sleep, and first thing when he woke up in the morning."

Rockne's motivational magic was caste in his impeccable timing.

Gipp died in December 1920. Rockne, being a firm believer in holding his right words for the right time, let eight years go by before he pulled Gipp — his ace of spades — out of his motivation deck. Notre Dame was up against powerhouse Army on November 10, 1928, in Yankee Stadium. They had entered the game as heavy underdogs, but had battled Army to a scoreless tie in the first half. Rockne's men needed every volt of charge he could ignite before they took the field for what promised to be a brutal second half.

At halftime, the players huddled around Rockne in the locker room, sitting on old dusty blankets from World War I that covered a cold floor. Rockne lowered his head. There was a pause before he began speaking slowly in his familiar nasal staccato. None of the players had known Gipp personally, but every one of them knew his greatness. They listened in solemn silence as their great coach recounted what Gipp had said to him on his dying bed.

"I've got to go, Rock. It's all right, I'm not afraid. Sometime, Rock, when the team is up against it, when things are wrong and the breaks are beating the boys, tell them to go in there with all they've got and win just one for the Gipper. I don't know where I'll be then, Rock, but I'll know about it, and I'll be happy.

"The day before he died, George Gipp asked me to wait until the situation seemed hopeless," Rockne continued. His voice rose to a resounding alarm. "This is the day... and you are the team!"

Whether Rockne exaggerated the truth for his own motivational gain to light a charge into his Fighting Irish that day didn't matter. His players were transcended into a do-or-die call to battle in the name of Gipp.

"There was no one in the room that wasn't crying," assistant coach Ed Healey recalled years later. "There was a moment of silence, and then all of a sudden those players ran out of the dressing room and almost tore the hinges off the door. They were all ready to kill someone."

Army jumped out to a 6-0 lead in the second half, but fate never gave them a chance. Notre Dame scored two touchdowns and stymied a last-minute rally to beat the Cadets 12-6. When Jack Chevigny plunged over the goal line for a touchdown to tie the score at 6-6, the star running back jumped up in the end zone and shouted, "That's one for the Gipper!"

But as fate would have it, it was a reserve named Johnny "One-Play" O'Brien — a skinny hurdler on the track team who earned his nickname because he was normally used for only one play during a football game — who came off the bench and sealed the deal for the Irish. After O'Brien cradled a wobbly pass from halfback

Butch Niemiec on the 10-yard line and crossed the goal line for the winning touchdown, Chevigny screamed from the sidelines, "That's one for the Gipper too!"

"You could see a great big smile on his face," quarterback Frank Carideo recalled to an interviewer years later. "He was happy when things created during the week were used to perfection in the ballgame."

For Rockne, the only truth was winning.

VISITORS
NOTRE DAME
DOWNS   YARDS TO GAIN

	1ST	2ND	3RD	4TH	TOTAL

ROCKNE - MEANWELL COACHING CLASS
NOTRE DAME 1926

68

DISCIPLES

COACH OF COACHES

Two years after graduating from Notre Dame and a storied college football career as a member of the Four Horsemen, Harry Stuhldreher weighed his options between playing professional football and coaching in 1926.

His mentor offered some sage advice.

"If you plan to make a career of coaching, don't play," Knute Rockne told his former star quarterback. "If you are going into business, play and make the money as long as you can, and it's honest."

Coaching football was Rockne's business. Within three years, his national prominence had grown profoundly as the premiere coach in the country and his public acclaim had already reached new heights as a motivational speaker, so Rockne launched his first coaching school at Culver

Military Academy in Culver, Indiana.

The Rockne Coaching Schools quickly blossomed into a mandatory offseason learning session for hundreds of students across the country. Attendees paid $25 for the clinic, $25 for room and board, and they received two college credits in physical education to sit in on two weeks of classroom lectures and participate in hands-on drills taught by the greatest football coach in America.

Spanning nine years from 1922 until his death in 1931, Rockne took his summer clinics to 17 different schools throughout the United States: From William and Mary, Bucknell, and Washington & Lee in the East; to Southern Methodist in the South; from Wittenberg in Ohio, to Hastings in Nebraska; and West to Southern California and Oregon State. Rockne even landed across the Pacific in Hawaii for a series of clinics.

Occasionally, Rockne teamed with fellow coaching pal Pop Warner to conduct the Warner-Rockne Coaching School, which also encompassed basketball. Notre Dame basketball coach George Keogan headed the basketball segment of the schools before Rockne partnered with his friend W. E. "Doc" Meanwell, head basketball coach at the University of Wisconsin, to form the Rockne-Meanwell Schools in 1927.

The operation was one of Rockne's most lucrative financial endeavors. By 1927, the Rockne-Meanwell Schools cleared nearly $27,000 a year in profits, while Rockne's home clinic at Notre Dame brought in an additional $10,000 to $15,000 in annual revenues. Rockne's fee to speak at other coaching schools around the country was a flat $2,000.

But Rockne saved his personal best for those who played under his leadership at Notre Dame — four years of football tutelage that benefited his players greatly upon graduation. Colleges throughout the country openly sought players out of Notre Dame simply because they had played for Rockne. Irish players, in return, worked harder in practice and concentrated on learning everything they could from their master mentor with the full realization that they would be in high demand for a coaching job the minute they got their degree from Notre Dame.

Out of respect for the unparalleled football brilliance he handed down to all of his players at Notre Dame, Rockne was the first call for coaches and athletic directors from other schools seeking a graduating player who might be a potential coaching candidate.

After they were off and growing into their own coaching wings, Rockne made sure to stay in his pupils' lives and help them move up the coaching ladder. He spoke at their team banquets, lent advice on coaching and even personal family matters, and helped them acquire new coaching positions.

Rockne's recommendation launched Jim Crowley from assistant coach at the University of Georgia to the head coaching job at Michigan State. Rockne also had a hand in helping Elmer Layden land his first head coaching position at Duquesne, telling his former star Four Horseman, "They will give you full leeway — make sure you hire a couple of Notre Dame men to help you."

Rockne's one condition to former players he pushed into the coaching ranks, and to presidents of other universities, was simple: "Hire a couple of Notre Dame men." In return, Rockne's guys were the first to offer their mentor scouting reports of other teams.

It's why Rockne's coaching tree stands tallest and casts the widest shadow of legacy over the archives of college football to this day. In just 13 seasons as head coach of America's most relevant football team of the time, Rockne launched 50 proteges into head coaching careers, and more than 150 into college and high school programs as assistant coaches.

Nine — Hunk Anderson, Charlie Bachman, Harry Baujan, Gus Dorais, Frank Leahy, Slip Madigan, Jim Phelan, Buck Shaw and Frank Thomas — are enshrined as coaches in the College Football Hall of Fame. Four men under Rockne — Anderson, Shaw, Adam Walsh and Curly Lambeau — went on to coach in the NFL.

Adding more shadow under the legacy tree cultivated by the ultimate coaches' coach, the Notre Dame system was adopted by thousands of high school, college and professional instructors who attended the Rockne Coaching Schools.

Harry Stuhldreher took Rockne's advice to Villanova University, where he landed almost immediately after graduating from Notre Dame to serve as head coach from 1925 to 1935. The Four Horsemen's quarterback then coached the University of Wisconsin-Madison from 1936 to 1948. He retired after compiling a career coaching record of 110-87-15.

GUS DORAIS

• Played for Notre Dame (1910—1913), assistant for Notre Dame (1919), head coach for Gonzaga (1920—1924)

Dorais to Rockne...

In a parallel universe the two would be spoken in the same breath together, forever... Dorais and Rockne, like pass and catch.

Army didn't know what hit them on November 1, 1913. All game long Knute Rockne sprinted past Army's secondary defenders at full speed, and all game long Gus Dorais threw pass, after pass, after pass, and hit either Rockne, Joe Pliska or Charles Finegan in full stride, seemingly play after play after play.

Notre Dame unleashed the force of football future on Army that day. Dorais' passing statistics — 14 completions out of 17 throws for 243 yards and three touchdowns — may as well had been numbers he tossed out of an infinitesimal calculus theorem. Nobody before had ever seen such alien passing stats come out of a single game. By the time undefeated powerhouse Army realized they were on the helpless end of a 35-13 thrashing, Dorais to Rockne had given birth to the forward pass as a dynamic football system.

While Rockne possessed the cerebral vision to devise plays and schemes as a player and taught Dorais how to grip the football to be thrown far-

ther and more accurately during those famous 1913 summer workouts at Cedar Point, Gus Dorais rolled into Notre Dame from Chippewa Falls, Wisconsin, with a stunning set of physical skills facilitated by a slight 5-feet-7, 135-pound frame.

Rockne's renown would come later as a storied coach; Dorais was Notre Dame's undisputed star for three consecutive undefeated seasons that began his sophomore year in 1911 and ended after his senior season in 1913 with a record of 20-0-2 as a starting quarterback.

Versatility with a keen fundamental understanding of every position set Dorais apart from the college game's biggest stars at the time. In addition to quarterback, Dorais served as the team's punter, place kicker and punt returner, and he was a stellar defensive back. Lost in the spotlight of the unprecedented passing numbers Dorais put up against Army was an interception he picked off in the Notre Dame endzone deep in the game that ended an Army drive.

When Dorais was selected as a first-team All-American in 1913 by Walter Camp and the International News Service, he became the first consensus All-American in Notre Dame history. (Louis "Red" Salmon was named to Walter Camp's third-team All-American squad in 1903 to become Notre Dame's first official All-American player. When Dorais was selected to the 1913 All-American team by Walter Camp and the International News Service, he became Notre Dame's first "consensus" All-American named by two or more NCAA-sanctioned selection committees.)

Dorais to Rockne took the forward pass into professional football in 1915. Despite his feathery weight of 138 pounds, Dorais quickly entrenched himself as one of the pro game's most exciting stars, playing for the Massillon Tigers in 1915, 1918 and 1919, and the Fort Wayne Friars in 1916. During the 1915 season, Dorais and Rockne teamed up for perhaps pro football's first genuine passing combo in a season highlighted by two games against the Canton Bulldogs, which featured the player Rockne viewed as the greatest to ever put on a uniform — Jim Thorpe.

Dorais and Rockne played together into the pros, and they set out on the same coaching career path together. Dubuque College, a Catholic college in Dubuque, Iowa, was Dorais first coaching stop. As versatile in coaching as he was as a player, Dorais served as the school's coach for football, basketball and track, as well as athletic director, teacher, and chairman of commercial law.

Before leaving Dubuque for the U.S. Army in December 1917, Dorais compiled a 17-9-2 record as head football coach, including one undefeated season in 1916. His basketball teams won Hawkeye Conference championships in each of his three seasons at the helm.

Rockne and Dorais came together again in September 1919 when Rockne, who had been named Notre Dame head coach in 1918, hired Dorais as his assistant. Their coaching combination proved as lethal as their passing combination as they led the 1919 Notre Dame team to a perfect 9-0 record. Dorais also took over as head coach of Notre Dame's basketball and baseball teams.

In May 1920, the parallel football universe Dorais and Rockne had been residing in together for the better part of a decade split one-way west when Dorais was hired as athletic director at Gonzaga University in Spokane. While Rockne stayed put at Notre Dame until his death 11 years later, Dorais coached Gonzaga's football, basketball, baseball and track teams so successfully for five years, boosters helped raise his salary from $4,000 to $7,000 to keep him for a fifth season in 1924. Dorais guided the football team to an undefeated season in 1924 led on the field by Houston Stockton, the grandfather of future NBA Hall of Famer John Stockton.

When Dorais headed back to the Midwest in February 1925, the University of Detroit was launched onto the same level with Rockne's Notre Dame as one of the country's top tier of college football programs. Dorais served as the University of Detroit's athletic director and head football coach for 18 seasons until 1942, compiling a record of 113-48-7 playing against powerhouses such as Notre Dame, Army, Michigan

State and Arkansas, plus regular series against major Catholic colleges and universities that included Fordham, Boston College and Catholic University.

Like Rockne's teams, losses by Dorais' squads were scarce. Between October 1927 and November 1929, Dorais' University of Detroit teams went unbeaten during a winning stretch that lasted 22 games and included a perfect 9-0 season in 1928.

And like Rockne, Dorais had an innate knack for recruiting and coaching elite athletes, particularly players who could throw the ball. Among the finest football players who played under Dorais at the University of Detroit were Lloyd Brazil, an All-American halfback in 1928 and 1929 and a NCAA passing leader in 1928; and halfback Doug Nott, who was among the NCAA's passing leaders in 1933. As head coach of the college team for the fourth College All-Star Game at Soldier Field in Chicago in 1937, Dorais watched his quarterback Sammy Baugh lead the college stars to a 6-0 win over Curly Lambeau's Green Bay Packers — the first college All-Star team to beat the pros.

The pros called again in January 1943. Dorais left the University of Detroit to become head coach, general manager and part owner of the National Football League's Detroit Lions. The year before, the Lions recorded an abysmal 0-11 season. Dorais took over and the Lions immediately improved to 3-6-1. The following two years, Dorais put the Lions on the right path, leading them to second-place finishes two years in a row with records of 6-3-1 and 7-3. Small wonder that Dorais was credited by sportswriters with formulating "the best pass patterns in the NFL.

Things went south quickly, however. The Lions dipped drastically in 1946, finishing with a 1-10, nor did the team fare much better the following year with a 3-9 finish. Dorais had a fresh five-year contract he had signed prior to the 1947 season, but Lions owner Fred Mandel Jr. fired the Notre Dame legend, nonetheless.

Tragedy struck in July 1947 when Dorais' youngest son, David, drowned while swimming in Tecon Lake at the family's summer home in Otsego County, Michigan. Two years later, Dorais relocated to Wabash, Indiana, and purchased an automobile dealership with his son, William. His return to coaching as backfield coach for the Pittsburgh Steelers ended after only a few months when Dorais announced his retirement from football.

After becoming ill with a circulatory disorder, Dorais moved to the Detroit suburb of Southfield in 1953. Charles Emile "Gus" Dorais died January 3, 1954, at the age of 62, but his revolutionary overhand spiral throwing technique and his legacy as the "father of the forward pass" continues to be passed on to new football generations with the same immortal spirit as Rockne's motivational locker room speeches.

As long as there's a quarterback throwing a football to a receiver, there will be Dorais to Rockne.

STAN COFALL
• Played for Notre Dame (1914—1916), head coach for Wake Forest (1928)

Knute Rockne was an assistant football coach, one season removed from his final game as a Fighting Irish player when Stan Cofall arrived at Notre Dame in 1914.

Cofall burst onto Cartier Field with a blast. The halfback from Cleveland scored nine touchdowns and led the Fighting Irish with 82 points his first year. The following season in 1915, Cofall matched his Notre Dame inaugural by again scoring nine touchdowns, and again leading the team in points with 71. Cofall capped a brilliant Notre Dame career his senior season in 1916 when he scored 12 touchdowns and 84 points. Notre Dame's team captain was named to several All-American squads.

After graduating from Notre Dame in 1917, Cofall went back to Ohio and quickly landed with the professional Massillon Tigers football team, doubling as a player-coach alongside teammates Knute Rockne and Gus Dorais. He took a break from football in 1918 and 1919 to serve in World War I, then returned to his hometown of Cleveland and helped organize the Cleveland Indians football team.

When Cofall traveled to Canton, Ohio in 1920 to attend the first formal meetings of the American Football Association, (the future National Football League,) he was named the league's first vice president. The same year, Cofall played for the independent Union Club of Phoenixville, an independent team that featured several players from the Buffalo All-Americans.

Cofall later played for the Union Quakers of Philadelphia, and in 1922 he joined the Pottsville Maroons and became the team's star running back, helping the Maroons become the top team in the Pennsylvania coal region. In 1924, Cofall led the Maroons to the Anthracite League championship, a precursor for the Maroons to join the NFL the following year.

Cofall followed his playing career with coaching stints at various professional and college teams. He served as head football coach at Loyola College in Maryland from 1925 to 1927, and in 1928 he took over as head football coach at Wake Forest College, now Wake Forest University.

Cofall forever remains an indelible founding father of Cleveland sports. After settling in his hometown in 1935 and founding the Stanco Oil Company, a company that would later merge with the National Solvent Corporation, Cofall worked relentlessly to bring the Notre Dame-Navy football game to Cleveland in 1942, the same year he founded the Cleveland Touchdown Club. Cofall also served as chairman of the Cleveland Boxing Commission, and he became

director of liquor control for the State of Ohio.

Stanley Bingham Cofall died at his home in Peninsula, Ohio, on September 21, 1961, at the age of 68.

CHARLIE BACHMAN

• Played for Notre Dame (1914—1916), head coach for Kansas State (1920—1927), Florida (1928—1932), Michigan State (1933—1946)

Charlie Bachman was one of the coaching confidants Rockne called on in late spring of 1930 to help decide whether the Notre Dame coach was healthy enough to coach for one more season.

Like Rockne, Charles Bachman had arrived at Notre Dame from Chicago, where he had been a standout football and track athlete at Chicago's Englewood High School. At Notre Dame, Bachman played alongside Rockne in 1914, then was named an All-American at guard in 1916 during Rockne's first year as an Irish assistant coach.

After briefly setting the world record in the discus throw in 1917, Bachman spent the fall season as an assistant football coach at DePauw University. The following year, Bachman returned to the gridiron to play center for the U.S. Navy team at Great Lakes Naval Station, a team, that posted a 7-0-2 record, beating Navy, Illinois, Purdue, Mare Island Marine Base in the Rose Bowl, and tying

his former team, Notre Dame. Bachman's teammates at Great Lakes included future Chicago Bears legends Paddy Driscoll and George Halas.

At the age of 26 in 1919, Bachman took his first head coaching job at Northwestern University. He recruited a number of former players returning from World War I, but his team still was only able to win two games and lose seven.

The following season Bachman moved to Kansas State College to serve as head football coach. Over the next seven years, from 1920 to 1927, he proved that the losing record at Northwester was an aberration by posting a record of 33-23-9 at Kansas State.

Bachman moved south in 1928 when he took the head coaching job at the University of Florida in Gainesville. The Gators posted an 8-1 record in his first season, the best in Florida history at the time, and Bachman coached the school's first first-team All-American, end Dale Van Sickel, in 1929. Bachman stayed at Florida for five seasons, and posted an overall record of 27-18-3.

In spring of 1930, Bachman was on the receiving end of a letter from Rockne calling a meeting of the fabled coach's closest confidants to discuss whether he should continue coaching at Notre Dame for at least one more season while facing severe health issues. After consulting with Bachman and his other friends during that meeting, held on May 31, 1930, Rockne decided to continue coaching into the 1930 season, which would be his last.

Bachman left Florida in 1933 to become head football coach at Michigan State College in East Lansing. Under Bachman, Michigan State — which had lost to state rival Michigan for 18 years straight – defeated Michigan four consecutive seasons, from 1934 to 1937. While Bachman's Michigan State teams posted an overall record of 70-34-10, his Spartan teams were remembered for wearing gold and black uniforms instead of the school's official colors of green and white.

In 1953, Bachman took his final head coaching job at Hillsdale College in Hillsdale, Michigan. In one season, Bachman's team posted a record of 5-3-2.

Inducted into the University of Florida Athletic Hall of Fame in 1971 as an "honorary letter winner," and later into the College Football Hall of Fame in 1978, Charles Bachman died in Port Charlotte, Florida, in 1985, at the age of 93.

DUTCH BERGMAN

- **Played for Notre Dame (1915—1916; 1919), head coach for Catholic (1930—1940), Washington Redskins (1943)**

of 74-36-5 into the NFL for one season, coaching the Washington Redskins to a 6-3-1 mark in 1943 and leading them to the 1943 NFL Championship Game — a game they lost to the Chicago Bears, 41-21.

Arthur J. "Dutch" Bergman died August 18, 1972, at the age of 77. He was inducted into the Catholic University Hall of Fame in 1982.

Dutch Bergman played halfback at Notre Dame in 1915 and 1916, and under Rockne during his second year as head coach of Notre Dame in 1919.

Born in Peru, Indiana, Bergman left Notre Dame to become head coach at the New Mexico College of Agriculture and Mechanic Arts, now New Mexico State University, from 1920 to 1922.

In 1930, Bergman took over the head coaching helm at The Catholic University of America, a coaching stint that lasted 10 years. When Bergman left the school after his final season in 1940, his Catholic Cardinals had compiled a stellar record of 59-31-4, leaving him as the winningest varsity coach in Catholic University history.

Bergman took his career college coaching record

SLIP MADIGAN

- **Played for Notre Dame (1916—1917; 1919), head coach for Saint Mary's (1921—1939) Iowa (1943—1944)**

The only other coach who could have taken a team that had lost one game 127-0 and turn it into a national powerhouse was Knute Rockne himself.

Slip Madigan played center for Notre Dame in 1916 and 1917, when Rockne was an assistant, then again in 1919 during Rockne's second season as Fighting Irish' head coach. Upon graduating from Notre Dame, the native of Ottawa, Illinois took the football knowledge he learned at the hands of Rockne and headed west to the San Francisco Bay area.

It didn't take long for Madigan to land a head coaching job. Little St. Mary's, a small college on the fringes of Oakland better known as St. Mary's College, was badly in need of a Notre Dame football alum with Rockne pedigree to take over a floundering football team that was coming off an epic 127-0 thrashing by California in the final game of the 1920 season.

The new coach gutted the Galloping Gaels when he took over in 1921. Madigan replaced the old squad with 60 hand-picked recruits he brought into St. Mary's to play football. He taught his new team plays he picked up from Rockne's schemes as well as some fresh ones Madigan drew up from his own vision. Among Madigan's chalkboard innovations included the "forward fumble."

Like his mentor, Madigan proved to be a sil-

ver-tongued master motivator who cultivated the press as an ally. He used that friendship throughout the '20s and '30s to push tiny St. Mary's College — with an enrollment of 500 — into the national football spotlight traveling across the country, and even the Pacific Ocean, taking on all challengers with a squad that was every bit as skilled, tough and smart as Rockne's powerful Fighting Irish.

Under Madigan, the Galloping Gaels upset Pop Warner and Stanford, 16-0, in 1927 after Stanford had appeared in the Rose Bowl. In 1931, Madigan's Gaels knocked off another Rose Bowl team, Southern California, 13-7. When St. Mary's finally got a chance to play in a bowl game in 1938, they gashed Texas Tech, 20-13, in the Cotton Bowl. During Madigan's time at St. Mary's from 1921 through 1939, the Gaels were one of the country's top teams compiling a record of 117 wins, 45 losses, and 12 ties.

But it wasn't just the fact that Madigan — who also coached St. Mary's basketball and baseball teams — had taken a small West Coast school and turned its fledgling football squad into a national powerhouse playing in front of record crowds even though the school didn't have its own football stadium. It was the way he did it.

Madigan was flashy, flamboyant, and quick to offer a glib quote to any newspaper reporter or radio broadcaster who needed one, and the Gaels reflected his personality on and off the field. In one of Madigan's most celebrated public moments, the fun-loving coach took his team plus 150 fans on a cross-country train trip — tagged as "the world's longest bar" — to New York for a game against Fordham. When he arrived in New York, Madigan drummed up publicity for the game by throwing a party the night before and inviting everybody from sportswriters to Babe Ruth and New York Mayor Jimmy Walker.

St. Mary's was among the poorest schools in the country, yet Madigan was one of college football's highest paid coaches. Following that game against Fordham in 1936, nearly all the profits from the game (a total of $36,420) was handed to Madigan for back salary rather than to the school's creditors.

Madigan's flamboyant presence wore thin with St. Mary's administrators. Football had taken priority over academics during the 1930s, and Madigan's football recruits were mostly non-Catholic, thuggish, and largely viewed by the school's hierarchy as unfit for college. In 1939, star halfback Mike Klotovich was kicked out of the school for disciplinary reasons. By the end of the semester, 14 other football players were suspended from athletic competition because of poor grades.

When Madigan was summarily fired in March 1940, Brother Albert Rahill, president of St. Mary's College, insisted that Madigan was "an honorable man" who had not engaged in any financial dishonesty through-out his 19-year career at the school. But the St. Mary's president added that Madigan spent money too freely, and that toward the end of his tenure at St. Mary's, he seemed more concerned with his own business en-terprises than he did with his coaching obligations.

Students, however, did not take the firing of the popular Slip Madigan lightly. St. Mary's stu-dent body president told a reporter from the San Francisco Chronicle: "St. Mary's without Madigan would be like St. Mary's without the chapel."

Madigan returned to coaching in 1943 when he went to Iowa and took over as interim coach for fel-low Notre Dame football alum Eddie Anderson, who was serving in World War II. The war had depleted the rosters of most college football teams across the country, and Madigan was strapped with players of mediocre talent who were playing with physical con-ditions that exempted them from military service.

Despite an admirable coaching job that brought out some quality performances from the 1943 Hawkeyes, the team finished just 1-6-1. Still, Madigan was brought back for the 1944 season. The Hawkeyes finished 1-7 — the lone win being an inspired 27-6 victory over Nebraska — and Madigan retired for good after he spurned Iowa's offer to coach again in 1945.

Edward Patrick "Slip" Madigan moved back to California and spent the rest of his life managing various entrepreneurial interests. He died at his home in 1966, and is buried on the grounds of the school where he made his greatest mark, St. Mary's Cemetery in Oakland.

In 1974, Madigan was inducted into the Col-lege Football Hall of Fame as a coach.

HEARTLEY "HUNK" ANDERSON

**• Played for Notre Dame (1918—1921), head coach for
Notre Dame (1931—1933), NC State (1934-1936**

After Coach Rockne... there was Coach Anderson.

Born in Calumet, Michigan, on the Keweenaw Peninsula not far from the hometown of George Gipp, Hunk Anderson arrived at Notre Dame in 1918 and quickly earned a spot as a lineman on new-ly-named head coach Knute Rockne's first team.

At 5-feet, 11 inches tall and weighing a sol-id 170 pounds, Anderson played guard un-der Rockne from 1918 to 1921, a road-grader who blocked for Gipp right up to his legend-ary teammate's death in December 1920.

After graduating from Notre Dame, Anderson

started in 32 of 39 games he played professionally for the Cleveland Indians and Chicago Bears football teams. Anderson blocked for Gipp at Notre Dame... and he blocked for Red Grange with the Bears.

He was named to the National Football League 1920s All-Decade Team, and is one of only two players on the list that is not in the Pro Football Hall of Fame. Anderson was inducted into the College Football Hall of Fame as a player in 1974.

Anderson began his coaching career in 1928 as head football coach at Saint Louis University. Following the 1929 season, Anderson returned to Notre Dame to take a job as an assistant coach under Rockne. Upon Rockne's death, he served as head coach at Notre Dame for three seasons from 1931 to 1933, then moved to North Carolina State University where he coached from 1934

until stepping down in 1936 after compiling a career college football record of 34-34-4.

Anderson returned to the NFL in 1939 as an assistant coach for the Detroit Lions under Gus Henderson. Three years later, Anderson was named head coach of the Chicago Bears. In four seasons, from 1942 to 1945, Anderson guided the Bears to a 24-12 record, and won the 1943 NFL Championship.

Of Anderson's ability to pass on the knowledge behind the extraordinary skills that allowed him to block for two of football's greatest running backs of their day, Bears' iconic owner George Halas once said: "Whether at a collegiate or professional level, there never was a better line coach than Hunk Anderson."

Heartley "Hunk" Anderson died after a long respiratory illness in West Palm Beach, Florida on April 24, 1978. He was 79.

EDDIE ANDERSON

- **Played for Notre Dame (1919—1921), head coach for Iowa (1939—1949)**

Eddie Anderson followed Knute Rockne's footsteps on the gridiron and in the medical field.

A teammate of George Gipp's under Rockne from 1918 to 1921, the Mason City, Iowa, native was a consensus first-team All-American and captain

of the 1921 Notre Dame football team. In Anderson's final three seasons at Notre Dame, the Irish compiled a 28-1 record, with the only loss coming to Anderson's home-state school, Iowa, in 1921.

After graduating from Notre Dame, Anderson played professionally for the Rochester Jeffersons in the National Football League. He returned to Iowa to coach Columbia College in Dubuque to a 16-6-1 record from 1922 to 1924. The following year Anderson served as a player/coach for the professional Chicago Cardinals during the Chicago team's controversial 1925 championship season.

The same year, Anderson decided to follow the medical path Rockne had pondered upon his own graduation from Notre Dame and enrolled at Rush Medical College in Chicago. While studying to be a doctor, Anderson also coached basketball at DePaul University from 1925 to 1929, leading them to a four-year record of 25-21 before he took a job as head football coach at the College of the Holy Cross in Massachusetts.

In six years at Holy Cross from 1933 to 1938, Anderson guided his football teams to a record of 47-7-4, including two undefeated seasons in 1935 and 1937 — all while heading up the eye, ear, nose and throat clinic at Boston's Veterans Hospital.

Anderson returned home once again in 1939 when he was named head football coach at the University of Iowa. In true Rockne form, Anderson took a dismal football team that had finished 2-13-1 in two previous years and turned it around immediately by playing only the starters for significant amounts of time.

Of 85 players who showed up for spring practice, only 37 earned football letters under Anderson during his first season in 1939. Those starters, nicknamed the "Ironmen," powered one of Iowa's greatest teams in school history to a 6-1-1 record, led by 1939 Heisman Trophy winner, Nile Kinnick, and a first-year coach who was named national coach of the year by several organizations.

"It's doubtful if any coach in football history ever accomplished such an amazing renaissance as Eddie Anderson has worked at Iowa," sportswriter Jim Gallagher wrote in the Chicago Herald-American.

Before Anderson headed to the football field to coach the Iowa Hawkeyes in the afternoon, he spent mornings practicing medicine and studying urology under the head of urology at University of Iowa Hospital. He took a leave of absence from the school to serve in the U.S. Army Medical Corps during World War II, from 1943 to 1945. When Anderson returned in 1946, he was told that if he retired from coaching, he would be named successor to the head of urology.

As Rockne had turned down medical school at St. Louis to continue coaching football, Anderson said no to the University of Iowa Hospital's offer. He continued practicing medicine part-time, and returned to coach the Hawkeyes for a second stint that lasted three years until Holy Cross offered Anderson the opportunity to return, including another stint as head football coach.

Anderson spent 15 seasons at Holy Cross, from 1950 to 1964, and posted a record of 82-60-4. He resigned at Holy Cross in 1964 after compiling a career record of 201-128-15 in 39 seasons at four schools, the fourth coach in college football history to reach 200 wins.

Upon leaving Holy Cross, Anderson was named the chief of outpatient services at the Veterans Administration Medical Center in Rutland, Massachusetts. He also served a school for mentally-challenged children.

Eddie Anderson was inducted into the College Football Hall of Fame as a coach in 1971. He passed away of a heart attack at his home in Clearwater, Florida, in 1974, at the age of 73.

HARRY MEHRE

Photo: Harry Mehre: played for Notre Dame (1919—1921), head coach for Georgia (1928—1937), Ole Miss (1938—1945).

Harry Mehre is forever etched in newspaper print as one of the country's premiere sportswriters of his time.

"Auburn and Ole Miss are two teams that defense forgot, or else the Tigers and the Rebs just forget defense for the day, as they swapped touchdowns in the Gator Bowl's 26th annual classic," Mehre wrote in his column for the Atlanta Journal-Constitution following the 1971 Gator Bowl.

"Pat Sullivan and Archie Manning put on their show and were as good as advertised. Oh, yes, Auburn won, 35-28."

But in the fall of 1918, half-a-century before Harry Mehre covered that 1971 Gator Bowl in his column for the Atlanta Journal-Constitution, the dual-sport high school basketball and football star from Huntington, Indiana entered Notre Dame on a basketball scholarship.

Like the typical teenage Indiana boy at the turn of the 20th Century, Mehre grew up playing basketball. He attracted the attention of several colleges, including Notre Dame, as a basketball star at Huntington High School. Mehre also played football at the school — until his senior year when the sport was suspended following the death of a player.

Knute Rockne could spot a potential football player

in any sport. It didn't take long for the first-year head coach to notice the Irish basketball team's center — a solidly-built husky figure on the court who blended size and strength with swift mobility. Mehre took Rockne up on an invitation to come out for a football practice.

Because of his speed, Rockne at first positioned Mehre at fullback. But his size on top of shifty footwork skills he picked up on the basketball court made him an ideal fit for the offensive line in Rockne's "Notre Dame Box" offense, a variation of the single-wing system that opened up the passing game for quarterback (and Mehre's basketball teammate) Leonard "Pete" Bahan, and irrepressible running backs Dutch Bergman and George Gipp.

At center, Mehre backed starter Slip Madigan during his first season in 1919. And he caught up on his knowledge of football fundamentals by learning from the indomitable Madigan, and directly from Rockne, who handled both head- and offensive line-coaching duties.

"Big, heavy and fast..." is how the 1920 Notre Dame Football Review described Mehre's performance in 1919, a season that ended with the Irish undefeated at 9-0, yet tied for a national championship with Harvard's 9-0-1 squad in polls delivered by the National Championship Foundation and Parke H. Davis. "Harry Mehre played center like a regular whenever called upon during the season, and that was quite a few times... Mehre was a valuable asset to Rockne's section gang."

Mehre only got better in 1920. He stepped into the starting center position next to Buck Shaw and Hunk Anderson on an Irish offensive line that blocked for strong-armed quarterback John Mohardt and everybody's consensus All-American, George Gipp. Although Notre Dame finished undefeated at 9-0 for the second consecutive season and, again, was named national champions in one poll and shared the championship in another, tragedy struck when Gipp died.

By his senior season in 1921, Mehre was an All-American center who knew the intricacies of Rockne's dominant "Notre Dame Box" system inside and out. Like others who had graduated from Rockne's exclusive system, Mehre had colleges across the country lined up for his services with coaching offers. He landed his first coaching job at St. Thomas College in 1923, and doubled as a player/coach for the independent professional team, the Minneapolis Marines.

Mehre's Notre Dame pedigree drew the eye of Rockne's pal George "Kid" Woodruff, head coach at the University of Georgia. Woodruff had walked away impressed with Mehre after Notre Dame dominated Georgia rival Georgia Tech, 35-7, with the "Notre Dame Box" offensive system.

Woodruff not only hired Mehre as an assistant in 1924, he also brought in Mehre's Four-Horsemen teammate Jim Crowley. Three years later in 1927, Woodruff left Georgia to pursue private business. Mehre was named Georgia's head coach on Woodruff's recommendation.

For nearly a decade, Mehre led the Bulldogs to an overall record of 59-34-6. The most memorable game during Mehre's Georgia tenure was the first game played at the new Sanford Stadium on October 12, 1929, against the Yale Bulldogs. Georgia beat Yale, 15-0, in a game later billed as "one of the greatest football spectacles ever in the South." To this day the game is memorialized by Georgia loyalists as the most memorable day in Georgia's illustrious football history.

"Christopher Columbus discovered America on October 12, 1492," Mehre would later write in his column. "On October 12, 1929, 437 years later, Yale University came to Athens, Georgia and discovered Sanford Stadium."

Football wasn't the only sport Mehre would lead at Georgia. In 1932, he took the reins of the Bulldogs basketball squad in place of then-head coach Herman Stegeman. Mehre's leadership was instrumental in a 25-16 victory over hoops' powerhouse Kentucky — the first loss in legendary Coach Adolph Rupp's storied career at Kentucky.

Mehre left Georgia in 1938 and took the head football coaching job at the University of Mississippi. He got off to a flying start in the first game of his Ole Miss career when the Rebels beat the LSU Tigers, 20-7. Ole Miss also scored victories over LSU the following three seasons, the first time a Mississippi football

team won over the Tigers four consecutive years.

Mehre left Ole Miss at the end of 1945 after seven seasons. He had played for — and learned from — the best in Rockne. He had served as head coach of two major football schools and set a legendary bar of his own for future Bulldogs' and Rebels' coaches with an overall record of 98-60-7. And he had kept in constant touch with his mentor through personal letters that shared scouting reports on common opponents up until the day Rockne died.

By 1946, it was time for Mehre to start a new career away from the gridiron. He moved back to Georgia and started a private business in Atlanta. But it wasn't long before the former Bulldogs coach, whose colorful wit and acute football wisdom had been likened to Rockne, was summoned back into the sports world.

Like Rockne had spotted a promising football player moving effortlessly on the basketball court, Atlanta Journal-Constitution sports editor Ralph McGill knew a capable writer who could analyze the sport he had coached for readers. McGill hired Mehre as a columnist-analyst, and for the next 25 years the sports commentary of Harry Mehre served as a staple of game insight for Georgia football fans.

Mehre served up his best material through his regular feature, "The Football Review." The old ball coach was also a regular along with a panel of sportswriters on the "Sunday Show" hosted by Furman Bisher, the iconic sports editor of the Atlanta Journal-Constitution.

Recalled Jim Minter, former Atlanta Journal executive sports editor: "Coach Mehre could hit the nail on the head better than anybody."

Harry J. Mehre died at the age of 77 on September 27, 1978 in Atlanta, seven years after he had been inducted into the Georgia Sports Hall of Fame. Eight years after his death, Butts-Mehre Heritage Hall was christened on the University of Georgia campus in Athens to honor Mehre and the coach who followed him at Georgia, Wally Butts.

"The story of Harry Mehre is quite remarkable," wrote author and historian Mark Maxwell, who penned Mehre's biography, "From Notre Dame To Georgia: Harry Mehre, The Legend." "The most important thing to understand about Harry Mehre is there's never been one like him, and there never will be."

TOM LIEB

- **Played for Notre Dame (1919—1922), head coach for Loyola Los Angeles (1930—1938), Florida (1940—1945).**

When Knute Rockne was sidelined in a wheelchair with health issues during the 1929 season, one of Rockne's former players — a two-time All-American who had also won a bronze medal in the discus throw at the 1924 Paris Olympics — was handed the reins to lead Notre Dame in Rockne's place.

Tom Lieb earned his coaching stripes by leading the Irish to a 9-0 season and a national championship, the first of Notre Dame's back-to-back undefeated national championship seasons. The following year, with Rockne back at the helm, Lieb's success as an interim head coach of the nation's top college football team turned into a head coaching job at Loyola University in Los Angeles.

Born in Faribault, Minnesota, Lieb was a standout baseball, football, hockey, and track and field athlete in high school before he entered Notre Dame in 1918. Lieb earned a spot as a starting offensive tackle on Rockne's first Irish squad in 1919, then went on to letter in four sports and draw accolades as a two-time football All-American during a Notre Dame career that was cut short in 1922 when he broke his leg in a game against Purdue.

While Lieb pursued graduate studies at Notre Dame, he coached both the hockey and track and field teams, and served as an assistant line coach under Rockne's football team.

Lieb was also a two-time NCAA national champion in the discus in 1922 and 1923, and a national AAU open champion in 1923 and 1924. It was Lieb who introduced the modern spin delivery of the discus throw still used today, a pioneering technique he took into the 1924 Summer Olympics in Paris competing for the United States in the discus throw. Lieb took home a bronze medal from the 1924 Olympics. Several weeks later, he broke the discus world record with a throw of 156 feet and 2 ½ inches.

Lieb headed to Wisconsin after graduating from Notre Dame to coach linemen for the Badgers. In 1929, he returned to Notre Dame as an assistant line coach under Rockne, who spent most of the season recovering from a severe case of thrombophlebitis in the leg. Loyola came calling after the Irish championship season, and Lieb jumped at the opportunity to head west for his first head coaching position.

For eight years, Lieb worked diligently to build the Loyola Lions into a football powerhouse by forging an annual West Coast rivalry with Southern California. He was the kind of coach who had fun with his job, often posing with lion cubs in publicity photos while guiding his teams to a 47-33-4 record between 1930 and 1938. Lieb also coached Loyola's hockey Lions to four consecutive Pacific Coast Intercollegiate League titles on the power of a 38-3-2 record.

Lieb left Loyola in 1939 when his wife got sick. After she died, he moved back east and succeeded Josh Cody as head football coach at the University of Florida in Gainesville. Lieb doubled as the school's athletic director, but he fell short of the football success he had at Loyola. When a five-year tenure that showed a below-average 20-26-1 record came to an end in 1945, Florida did not renew Lieb's contract.

Alabama was Lieb's final coaching stop. He signed on as an assistant line coach working with an old friend, former Notre Dame teammate Frank Thomas, Alabama's head coach. Lieb also headed-up Alabama's track and field squad until he retired in 1951.

Following his retirement from Alabama, Lieb returned to Los Angeles where he found work as a public speaker.

Thomas John Lieb suffered a cardiac arrest and died on April 30, 1962 at the age of 62. He was inducted posthumously into the Loyola Marymount Hall of Fame in 1987.

BUCK SHAW

- **Played for Notre Dame (1919—1921), head coach for NC State (1924), Nevada (1925—1928), San Francisco 49ers (1946-1954), Philadelphia Eagles (1958- 1960).**

The "Silver Fox" was tall, slender and dignified, the sideline cut of a corporate board chairman rather than one of the greatest football coaches in collegiate and professional history.

In later years when his hair had turned silvery-white, Buck Shaw roamed the sidelines in dark sport jackets, white shirts with ties knotted tight, and he hawked the field through horn-rimmed glasses that were tinted green. Of his genteel coaching manner that was as polite as his suits, a former player under Shaw's championship tenure with the Philadelphia Eagles once said: "He's the first guy I ever played for who didn't curse his players."

Shaw may have carried his own refined verbal skills as a coach, but he got his tough-as-nails football disposition that opened holes for George Gipp from his mentor, Knute Rockne.

Born one of five children to cattle ranchers Tim and Margaret Shaw in Mitchellville, Iowa, Shaw moved with his family to Stuart, a town that had banned high school football in the wake of a player's death on the field, then re-established the sport during Shaw's senior year.

Shaw only had four games of high school football under his belt when he enrolled at Creighton University in Omaha, Nebraska, in 1918, and went out for the football team. Shaw's season ended after one game when he caught a severe case of the flu.

The following year, Shaw transferred to Notre Dame, but not to play football under Rockne, who was entering his second year as head coach. Shaw chose Notre Dame because of its track and field team. When Rockne laid eyes on the solid 6-foot, 175-pound track athlete, a spot opened up on the football team.

Rockne molded Shaw into a tenacious offensive lineman — first, at left tackle in 1919 and 1920, then moving to right tackle in 1920 and 1921. As well as steamrolling holes for George Gipp for two seasons, and finishing his Notre Dame playing career as an All-American selection by "Football World Magazine," Shaw booted 38 out of 39 extra points, (a school record that stood until 1976,) and is regarded as one of Notre Dame's all-time best place kickers.

Just before graduating in the spring of Shaw's senior year, Rockne presented him with two letters from schools in need of coaches: Auburn University in Alabama, and the University of Nevada in Reno. A friend suggested to Shaw that since rugby was the only game being played in Nevada, and that American football was virtually a new sport ready to be introduced, Shaw could cut his own path out west.

"It sounded like an interesting challenge," Shaw recalled later in a 1970 interview," so I took the Nevada job as line coach."

After four years at Nevada, Shaw tried to get out of football by taking a job at an oil firm. But his old Notre Dame teammate Clipper Smith pulled him back by persuading Shaw to come to Santa Clara University and work under Smith as an assistant coach.

During his first season in 1929, the stock market crashed: "I had a heck of a time getting on my feet," Shaw explained. Since Santa Clara could only afford to hire coaches on a part-time, seasonal basis, Shaw worked for Standard Oil and served as line coach at Santa Clara at the same time until 1936 when Smith resigned for a job at Villanova. When Shaw was named head coach to replace Smith, he resigned from his job at the oil company.

Shaw formed the Broncos into a powerhouse with the same immediacy Rockne molded his star lineman straight off the track field. During his first two seasons as head coach in 1936 and 1937, Santa Clara ran off a combined 18-1 record with back-to-back victories over LSU in the Sugar Bowls of 1937 and 1938.

Shaw may also be the first coach in major college football to get sick and "phone it in" — when he stayed home and coached the team to victory on the road over the telephone. When Santa Clara cut its football program in 1942 due to the war, Shaw remained at the school to help the Army's campus physical education program.

Coaching college players taught Shaw early-on that he was no Rockne when it came to over-the-top halftime speeches, a realization that served him respectfully when he coached professional teams later in his career. "When I discovered that I wasn't (Rockne), I dropped the histrionics," Shaw said during an interview. "Heaven help you if you try anything insincere on today's players."

Before World War II ended, the Morabito brothers of San Francisco began moving to ready the San Francisco 49ers to enter a new professional league, the All-America Football Conference (AAFC). The 49ers hired Shaw, along with his Santa Clara as-

sistant Al Ruffo, as the franchise's first head coach. The league finally got off the ground in 1946 after a delay. Shaw assumed the helm of the 49ers, and with left-handed quarterback Frankie Albert leading the way, Shaw's 49ers finished second to the Cleveland Browns four consecutive years (from 1946 to 1949) in the AAFC's Western Division. The following year, in 1950, the 49ers, the Browns and the Baltimore Colts merged with the NFL.

Shaw returned to the college ranks in 1956. He guided the Air Force Academy to a record of 6-2-1 in his first season, but the Falcons fell to a 3-6-1 finish in 1957. Shaw headed back to the pros in 1958 to take over a floundering Philadelphia Eagles team coming off a 4-8 season that was badly in need of Rockne himself to turn things around. When the Eagles lost their ninth game of the season to finish a miserable 2-9-1, Shaw locked the door and unleashed a verbal lashing on his players — many of whom had been out the night before carousing — that would have had his mentor running for cover.

"This has never happened to me before. It will never happen again," Shaw railed. "If you don't have any pride, I do. I'll be here again next year, but some you will not. We'll win if I have to use three teams — one coming, one going and one playing."

Just two years later, powered by the heroics of quarterback Norm Van Brocklin, Tommy McDonald, and one of the greatest two-way players to ever grace a football field, Chuck Bednarik, the Eagles beat Vince Lombardi's Green Bay Packers for the 1960 NFL championship. The chairman of the board had his greatest triumph as a football coach — and he subsequently retired.

"I wanted to get out while I was ahead," reasoned Shaw, who walked away from coaching at the age of 61 with a championship ring and the AP & UPI NFL Coach of the Year award.

Shaw headed back to California, where he landed a job at a paper products company in Menlo Park. In 1962, Santa Clara alum Sal Sanfilippo banded together with a group of former players, friends and fans of Shaw to form the Bronco Beach Foundation and begin a fund-raising effort to raise money to build a stadium at Santa Clara University in Shaw's honor.

On September 22, 1962, Santa Clara and UC

Davis lined up against each other to play the first football game at Buck Shaw Stadium.

Lawrence Timothy "Buck" Shaw died from cancer at the age of 77 on March 19, 1977. The Rockne protégé known as the "Silver Fox" is a member of the Iowa Sports Hall of Fame, the San Francisco Bay Area Sports Hall of Fame, the San Jose Sports Hall of Fame, and the Santa Clara University Hall of Fame.

At Notre Dame, Shaw's legacy rests forever alongside Rockne as a member of the all-time "Fighting Irish" football team.

FRANK THOMAS

• **Played for Notre Dame (1920—1922), head coach for Alabama (1931—1946)**

The common branch between Knute Rockne and Bear Bryant grew from Frank Thomas.

Born in Muncie, Indiana, the youngest of six children to immigrant parents from Wales who had arrived in the U.S. just six years earlier, Thomas grew up in East Chicago where he made a name for himself as an outstanding high school football and baseball player.

He skipped his senior year to get an early start at Kalamazoo College in Michigan. For two years, Thomas starred in both sports at Kalamazoo, and he caught the attention of former Notre Dame player and Rockne pal, Chipper Smith.

On the heels of Smith's repeated urgings, Rockne got his new quarterback admitted into Notre Dame in 1919. And Thomas got a new roommate — George Gipp.

Thomas and Gipp were best friends immediately. Like Thomas, Gipp was also an outstanding baseball player, and both played professional baseball in the off-season. Together at Notre Dame, they formed the most frightening backfield to date for any defensive opponent to encounter.

But Thomas' and Gipp's fast friendship ended too fast, tragically. In the middle of the 1920 season, Gipp suddenly came down with a severe throat infection. Within a few weeks on December 14, 1920, Gipp died from pneumonia. Thomas was devastated.

"I broke down and cried like a baby," Thomas said during an interview years later. "It was like losing a brother."

Thomas was Rockne's quarterback from 1920 to 1922, a span that saw Thomas and his Fighting Irish teammates compile a record of 27-2-1. Rockne was captivated by Thomas' skills; he praised his quarterback as "a fine field general" to sportswriters. Following one Thomas-led Notre Dame victory, Rockne reportedly told his assistants: "It's amazing the amount of football sense that Thomas kid has. He can't miss becoming a great coach someday."

Thanks to Rockne's personal reference, Thomas had his first assistant coaching job waiting in the wings at the University of Georgia when he graduated from Notre Dame in 1923. It would take only two years cutting his teeth as an assistant before Thomas landed his first head coaching position at the University of Chattanooga.

520

SECTION 5: THE LEGACY

Thomas turned Chattanooga into four seasons' worth of tough afternoons for opponents during the late 1920s. A four-year record of 26-9-2 captured the attention of the University of Alabama. When head coach Wallace Wade resigned in 1931 after establishing Alabama as a football powerhouse with three national championships, he hand-picked Thomas to take over a defending national championship team that was losing 10 of its 11 starters to graduation.

Few expectations were held out for the first-year coach with first-year starters going up against the toughest football teams the nation had to offer and a defending national championship target on Alabama's back. But Thomas's men picked up right where their predecessors left off by rolling off nine wins against only one loss and outscoring their opponents by a season-combined score of 370-57.

Thomas' Crimson Tide followed their initial season with eight wins and two losses in 1932. The next year, Alabama finished 7-1-1. Then, in 1934, Thomas's men steamrolled their way to an undefeated 10-0 season crowned by a win over Stanford in the Rose Bowl that sealed a national championship.

Among the players that helped Thomas win his first national championship as a head coach: Paul "Bear" Bryant. When Bryant graduated from Alabama in 1936, Thomas hired Bryant as an assistant and gave the future Alabama legend his first coaching job.

One of the premiere coaches in the country during an era that spanned from 1931 to 1946, Thomas guided Alabama to six bowl appearances, four of which were wins — the Rose Bowl in 1935 and 1946, the Cotton Bowl in 1942, and the Orange Bowl in 1943. However, Thomas was a heavy smoker who routinely smoked cigars on the sidelines while coaching. Health issues from heart and lung disease forced him to step down as head coach in 1946 after amassing a career record of 141-33-9.

Thomas was inducted into the College Football Hall of Fame as a coach in 1951. After leaving coaching in 1946, he stayed on at Alabama as the school's athletic director until 1952.

Thomas resigned from coaching with a career record of 141-33-9. He remained at Alabama as the school's athletic director until 1952; one year after Thomas had been inducted into the College Football Hall of Fame.

Frank William Thomas was only 55 years old when he died at Druid City Hospital in Tuscaloosa, Alabama, in 1954. Rockne's protégé was so beloved as an Alabama football legend, an illustrated book published later that year paid tribute to Thomas with his life story.

Today, the University of Alabama practice fields are named for Thomas and his 1946 successor, Harold Drew. And like his mentor, who has several statues erected in his memory, including the Rockne statue at the North Gate of Notre Dame Stadium, Thomas' bronzed likeness stands alongside the statues of Alabama's other national championship-winning coaches in the school's history — Wallace Wade, Gene Stallings, Nick Saban, and Thomas's protégé, Bear Bryant.

THE FOUR HORSEMEN

DON MILLER

• Played for Notre Dame (1922—1924), assistant for Georgia Tech (1925—1928), Ohio State (1929—1932).

Rockne's fastest Horseman had the law on his side.

Don Miller followed in the footsteps of four brothers when he left Defiance, Ohio, in 1920 and entered Notre Dame. One of his brothers, Harry "Red" Miller, had been a star halfback and team captain for the Fighting Irish whose heroics in Notre Dame's first victory over Michigan in 1909 were legendary.

Red Miller told Rockne about his speedy brother, who was running track his freshman year, and the third-year coach admitted that Miller "… surprised me when he came out for spring practice and with his fleetness and daring sized up as a halfback to cheer the heart of any coach."

The pen of Grantland Rice turned Don Miller, Elmer Layden, Jim Crowley and Harry Stuhldreher into the most storied backfield in college football history from 1922 to 1924. The lightning-fast Miller set school rushing records and, in 1923, was the lone member of the Four Horsemen to be selected to the first team All-America squad.

The following year, Layden, Crowley and Stuhldreher were all first-teamers while Miller was placed on the second team behind Illinois' Red Grange.

But Miller had other plans that stretched beyond football. After serving as president of the senior class, Miller graduated in 1925 with both a bachelor's and a law degree.

He couldn't outrun his legend as a member of the Four Horsemen on the football field, so Miller took a job as a backfield coach at Georgia Tech, a position he held from 1925 until 1928. In 1929, Miller moved to Columbus, Ohio when he landed a position as backfield coach at Ohio State University.

By 1932, Miller had had enough of football. He moved to Cleveland, and with the help of another brother, Ray T. Miller, the mayor of Cleveland and chairman of the local Democratic Party, pursued a law practice.

The fastest of the Four Horsemen went on to serve 12 years as the United States Attorney for Northern Ohio from 1941 to 1953. In 1965, Miller was appointed to the bench as a United States Bankruptcy Court judge, a federal seat he held until his retirement in 1977. He also spent a term as president of the Cuyahoga Bar Association.

The iconic Four Horseman spent the latter part of his life making frequent appearances as a speaker at football functions and Notre Dame alumni events.

The Honorable Don C. Miller died at Lakeside Hospital in Cleveland on July 28, 1979. He was 77 years old.

HARRY STUHLDREHER

- **Played for Notre Dame (1922—1924), head coach for Villanova (1925—1935), Wisconsin (1936—1948).**

The curly-locked kid was looking to get into Tiger Stadium in Massillon, Ohio, to see the Massillon Tigers professional football game when he spotted one of the team's stars, Knute Rockne, walking toward the entrance with a bag of gear in his hand.

"Carry yer bag, Mr. Rockne?" young Harry Stuhldreher asked.

Rockne handed his bag over to the star-struck fan on that fateful day in 1916. The sky may as well have thundered and lightning may as well have struck the Massillon ground with a bolt of football immortality. That fateful first meeting between Rockne and his future quarterback of the legendary Four Horsemen served up an omen for the first "Hail Mary" pass.

Stuhldreher grew up in Massillon, a football standout for both Massillon Washington High School and the Kiski School in Saltsburg, Pennsylvania. He graduated from the Kiski School in 1921, then headed to Notre Dame where he was a familiar face to Rockne.

Standing only 5-foot-7 and weighing a modest 150 pounds, the shifty German kid from Massillon could pass with uncanny accuracy, return punts, and block with the best of them. Most importantly

in Rockne's eyes, Stuhldreher possessed a strong, self-assured leadership characteristic that made him a natural fit to take over from graduating quarterback Frank Thomas and steer the helm of a four-man backfield that already featured three of the most jaw-dropping football talents in the country: Jim Crowley, Don Miller and Elmer Layden.

"Even as a freshman, Harry had the most promise of the Four Horsemen. He sounded the leader on the field," Rockne proclaimed. By the end of his sophomore season in 1922, Stuhldreher had been entrusted by his coach to call signals on the field.

From 1922 to 1924, Stuhldreher led the Four Horsemen and Notre Dame to 27 wins, two losses (both against Nebraska in front of record crowds), and one tie. They racked up 74 points in one game in a 74-0 win over Kalamazoo in 1923, and in 1924, Stuhldreher quarterbacked the Irish to an undefeated 10-0 season that finished with a 27-10 win over Stanford in the 1925 Rose Bowl — and a national championship.

Then there was the game against Georgia Tech in 1922, a gridiron battle that seemingly clawed for every yard. Late in the game with the Irish up 6-3 and the offense faced with fourth down, Stuhldreher was set to call the play in the huddle when offensive lineman Noble Kizer suggested "a Hail Mary prayer."

Stuhldreher promptly tossed a touchdown pass to give the Irish a 13-3 victory. After the game, Kizer loudly boasted, "That Hail Mary is the best play we've got."

Rockne's field general was destined to be a coach. Almost immediately upon graduation from Notre Dame in 1925, Stuhldreher walked into the position of head coach at Villanova University.

He also moonlighted as a player, and for six games in 1926 Stuhldreher re-teamed with fellow Four Horseman Elmer Layden on the Brooklyn Horsemen of the first American Football League. When the AFL's Horsemen merged with the Brooklyn Lions of the National Football League, the first AFL, Brooklyn's NFL franchise and Stuhldreher's playing career both came to an end.

Stuhldreher stayed at Villanova for 11 seasons and compiled a respectable 65-25-9 record. In 1936, Stuhldreher moved to Madison, Wisconsin to take over as head coach and athletic director at the University of Wisconsin-Madison.

Over a span of 13 seasons at Wisconsin, Stuhldreher guided the Badgers to a 45-62-6 mark. The highlight season of Stuhldreher's Wisconsin coaching career shined in 1942. Powered by All-Americans Elroy "Crazy Legs" Hirsch, Pat Harder and Dave Schreiner, Stuhldreher's Badgers finished 8-1-1, beat top-ranked Ohio State (coached by Massillon legend Paul Brown) 17-7, and ended the season ranked third in the Associated Press poll.

The lead Horseman had plenty to fall back on outside of football. Stuhldreher — whose wife Mary was a writer — penned two books, "Knute Rockne, Man Builder," published in 1931 not long after Rockne's death, and "Quarterback Play." He also wrote a short novel, "The Blocking Back," but it was "Knute Rockne, Man Builder" that was used as a significant reference for the film "Knute Rockne, All-American," that starred Pat O'Brien as Rockne and Ronald Reagan as George Gipp.

Stuhldreher left Wisconsin in 1948 with a career coaching record of 110-87-15. He moved to Pittsburgh and took a job at U.S. Steel in the company's industrial relations department. In 1958, Stuhldreher was elected to the College Football Hall of Fame.

Harry Augustus Stuhldreher remained in Pittsburgh until his death from acute pancreatitis on January 26, 1965. The quarterback of Notre Dame's legendary Four Horsemen was 63 years old.

JIM CROWLEY

• Played for Notre Dame (1922—1924), head coach for Michigan State (1928—1932), Fordham (1933—1941).

Droopy eyes got him tagged as the "Sleepy" member of Knute Rockne's most famous backfield, but Jim Crowley was wide awake when he lit up a dynamic three-year career running the ball as a member of Notre Dame's legendary "Four Horsemen."

Born in Chicago and raised in Green Bay where he starred at Green Bay East High School under coach Curly Lambeau, "Sleepy Jim" Crowley turned professional after graduating from Notre Dame in 1925 — both as a player and a coach.

Shortly after signing on as an assistant coach at the University of Georgia, Crowley hit the field as a halfback appearing in just three games for: first, the National Football League's Green Bay Packers, the Providence Steamrollers, and, finally, the Waterbury Blues.

Waterbury reunited Crowley with his fellow ex-Horsemen, Harry Stuhldreher, to field two of college football's most illustrious heroes to date against a team from Adams, Massachusetts. The Two Horsemen didn't disappoint: Crowley ran for three touchdowns and Stuhldreher booted two field goals and three extra points to power a 34-0 blowout.

Immediately after the game, Crowley picked up his check and walked away from the playing field.

He returned to Georgia on the sidelines, where he served as an assistant coach until 1929 when Crowley landed the job as head coach at Michigan State College, later known as Michigan State University. In four seasons, Crowley's Spartans launched their coach's epic coaching career with 22 wins, 8 losses and 3 ties.

Fordham University called in 1933. "Sleepy Jim" may have been a star of the offense as a player molded by perhaps the greatest offensive innovator in the history of the game, but as head coach at Fordham, Crowley built one of the top defensive teams in the country by 1936. A stout defensive line coached by Crowley's fellow Irish alum Frank Leahy became known as the "Seven Blocks of Granite," led by two-time All-American lineman and future Pro Football Hall of Famer Alex Wojciechowicz, and another future Pro Football Hall of Famer who would later share a Green Bay connection with Crowley — Vince Lombardi.

The first football game to be televised featured Crowley's Fordham Rams thrashing the Waynesburg Yellow Jackets, 34-7. His final two squads each went to bowl games: Fordham lost to Texas A&M, 13-12, in the 1941 Cotton Bowl Classic, then beat Missouri, 2-0, the following year in the 1942 Sugar Bowl.

Crowley left football to serve with the United States Navy in the South Pacific during World War II. In the Navy he still found time to coach the North Carolina Pre-Flight School "Cloudbusters" to a record of 8-2-1.

Following his discharge, Crowley returned to the States and agreed to become the first commissioner of the All-America Football Conference, a new professional league set to rival the National Football League.

He stepped down as commissioner at the end of the 1946 season to become part-owner of the AAFC's worst team, the Chicago Rockets. But Crowley's magic as a college head coach failed to rub off on the pros. The Rockets finished just 1-13 in 1947, and Crowley quit football for good just before the kickoff of the 1948 season.

Crowley moved to Pennsylvania and became an insurance salesman. In 1953, he took over as station manager and sports director of the independent television station WTVU in Scranton.

Two years later, Crowley was named chairman of the Pennsylvania State Athletic Commission, a position he maintained until 1963. After being named to the College Football Hall of Fame in 1966, Crowley was able to live the rest of his life cashing in on his legend as a highly sought-after speaker on the banquet and dinner circuits.

James Harold "Sleepy Jim" Crowley was the last living member of the Four Horsemen when he died in Scranton on January 15, 1986.

ELMER LAYDEN

• **Played for Notre Dame (1922—1924), head coach for Duquesne (1927—1933), Notre Dame (1934—1940)**

When you hear the "Star Spangled Banner" before a National Football League game, think of Elmer Layden.

Of all the players who emerged from Knute Rockne's indomitable football system at Notre Dame, it was the speedy 160-pound fullback who ran alongside Harry Stuhldreher, Jim Crowley and Don Miller as a member of the immortal Four Horsemen backfield that carried his fabled mentor's torch into Notre Dame coaching infamy.

Born in Davenport, Iowa, Layden's offensive accomplishments with the Four Horsemen earned him All-American honors his senior season in 1924 and overshadowed slick defensive skills Layden flashed on the other side of the ball. Most noteworthy were two interceptions Layden ran back for touchdowns in Notre Dame's 27-10 victory over Stanford in the 1925 Rose Bowl, his final collegiate game.

After graduating from Notre Dame, Layden played one season of professional football with a team made up of former college football stars. In one game, Layden was reunited with his fellow Notre Dame backfield icons by the Hartford Blues who paid $5,000 for the Four Horsemen to play against the Cleveland Bulldogs. Hartford not only lost money paying the quartet for their services, the team lost the game, 13-6.

Layden hung up his spikes in 1926 for a coaching job at Loras College in Dubuque, Iowa. The next year he moved to Pittsburgh to take over the coaching helm at Duquesne. In seven years at Duquesne, Layden's teams racked up a 48-16-6 record, and capped off the 1933 season by winning the Festival of Palms Bowl, the precursor to today's Orange Bowl.

The Festival of Palms bowl win on New Year's Day 1934 was Layden's final victory at Duquesne. Three years after Rockne was killed in a plane crash on March 31, 1931, Notre Dame brought Layden back to take on the dual role of head football coach and athletic director.

Layden helped to restore the Irish to college football prominence that had diminished in the three years after Rockne's death. Over the next seven years, Layden's teams won 47 games, lost 13 and tied 3 times, and the comeback rally to defeat Ohio State 18-13 in 1935 was viewed as one of the greatest wins in Notre Dame history. The Irish finished 8-1 in 1938, losing only to rival Southern California in the season finale which cost them a consensus national championship, but Layden's team was still named national champions by the Dickinson System.

Nobody mistook Layden's easygoing manner for Rockne's fiery presence. But like Rockne, Layden took it upon himself to serve as a goodwill ambassador for Notre Dame. One of Layden's most significant acts involved healing a decades-old rift between Notre Dame and Michigan. The two schools had not met on a football field since 1909, a year before Michigan had cancelled their scheduled game in 1910 and refused to play the Irish again.

Because of Layden's efforts as athletic director, Notre Dame and Michigan met again in 1942 and 1943, after Frank Leahy succeeded Layden as Notre Dame head coach. The 1943 game ended in a one-sided Irish thrashing of Michigan 35-12. Wolverine coach and athletic director Fritz Crisler was so upset over Leahy running up the score, Crisler refused to schedule the Irish again.

After taking over a Notre Dame football program that had suffered from sagging ticket sales since Rockne's death, Layden was appointed commissioner of the NFL in 1941 and left the Notre Dame athletic program with football ticket receipt totals that had nearly doubled since he took over.

Layden guided the NFL through the World War II years, a span that saw teams using many players with inferior professional football skills while the game's regulars were fighting in the war. Layden allowed some teams, most notably the Pittsburgh Steelers and the Philadelphia Eagles, to merge due to lack of manpower, and he once conducted an investigation into a betting scam without advising the owners.

Once the war was over, Commissioner Layden called on all of the league's teams to play "The Star Spangled Banner" before the kickoff. "The National Anthem should be as much a part of every game as the kickoff," Layden proclaimed. "We must not drop it simply because the war is over. We should never forget what it stands for."

Layden served as NFL commissioner until January 1946. He left the NFL and embarked on a successful business career, first as president of the Shipper Car Line Corporation in New York, and later in the railroad equipment business with the General American Transportation Corporation of Chicago.

The legendary Four Horseman was inducted as a charter member into the College Football Hall of Fame in 1951.

Elmer Francis Layden died June 30, 1973, at the age of 70.

NOBLE KIZER

• Played for Notre Dame (1922—1924), head coach for Purdue (1930—1936)

Noble "Nobe" Kizer was one of Rockne's vaunted "Seven Mules" blocking the way for the legendary "Four Horsemen."

Born in the Indiana countryside near LaPorte, Kizer came to Notre Dame in 1921 and by his sophomore year in 1922, he had earned the starting spot at right guard as part of the Fighting Irish's offensive line, the Seven Mules, blocking for Stuhldreher, Miller, Layden and Crowley during one of college football's most historic periods.

After graduating from Notre Dame, Kizer took a job as assistant coach at Purdue under another former Rockne protégé, James Phelan. When Phelan left Purdue for a heading coaching position at the University of Washington, Kizer inherited the reins as Purdue's head coach. During his six-year span at Purdue from 1930 to 1936, Kizer guided the Boilermakers to two Big Ten Conference championships and compiled an outstanding record of 42-13-3.

Kizer also served as Purdue's athletic director from 1933 until his death on June 13, 1940 as a result of a kidney ailment and high blood pressure. Noble Earl "Nobe" Kizer Sr. died at the age of 40 years old.

CHUCK COLLINS

**• Played for Notre Dame (1922—1924), head coach
for North Carolina (1926—1933)...**

Perhaps it was Knute Rockne's immortal influence that persuaded Chuck Collins to put off a law career and go into coaching football after he graduated with a degree in law from Notre Dame in 1925.

A native of Chicago, Collins played left end for Rockne from 1922 to 1924, one of the vaunted "Seven Mules" blocking for the legendary "Four Horsemen" on the Irish's undefeated national championship team in 1924.

Collins once explained his decision to sidestep law and go right into football: "At Notre Dame, I didn't even have a nickel for a cup of coffee. I went there on a basketball scholarship, but I couldn't even make the freshman team. After I graduated, I was able to make $5,000 for five months of coaching football."

Instead of joining the ranks of Clarence Darrow and William Jennings Bryant, Collins stayed the football course set by Rockne. His first job took him to Chattanooga to serve as assistant line coach. But it wasn't long before Rockne's former Mule landed the head coach's job at the University of North Carolina at Chapel Hill in 1926. Collins remained head coach of the Tar Heels from 1926 to 1933, and compiled a record of 38-31-9.

Collins left North Carolina — and football — in 1934. He took a position at National Carloading in Chicago, and settled into a career with a freight-forwarding firm that would vault the former Notre Dame football star to the position of company president in 1957. When Collins' company went through a merger in 1962, he stayed on as executive vice president of the Universal Carloading and Distributing Company until he retired in 1965.

Retirement wasn't exactly in the plan. At the age of 62, Collins passed the New Jersey bar examination. For the next 10 years Collins practiced law out of his office in Ridgewood, a village in northern New Jersey where he also served as village attorney from 1967 to 1970.

Charles C. Collins died in Ridgewood, N.J. on April 14, 1977. The Rockne protege forever renowned as one of Notre Dame's legendary Seven Mules was 73 years old.

JOE BACH

- **Played for Notre Dame (1923—1924), head coach for Duquesne (1934), Pittsburgh Pirates/Steelers (1935—1936; 1952—1953)**

blowing holes open for the Four Horsemen backfield as a member of one of college football's most prolific offensive lines ever, "The Seven Mules."

Ten years later, Bach was named head coach of the NFL's Pittsburgh Pirates, a team he would lead in 1935 to its best record to date with 4 wins and 8 losses, and the following year to the young franchise's first non-losing campaign with a record of 6-6.

Bach left Pittsburgh after the 1936 season and went back to coach in the college ranks. He returned to Pittsburgh in 1951 to coach the renamed Steelers, a team that had floundered for years running a single wing formation. Bach installed a T-formation offense similar to the one Rockne ran with the Seven Mules and the Four Horsemen at Notre Dame. Pittsburgh finished the 1952 season with 5 wins and 7 lessons, then followed up in 1953 with a record of 6-6.

But after three home losses to begin the pre-season in 1954, Bach resigned during training camp and left the team. Bach would move on to work as a state labor mediator while he continued his football career as a scout for the Steelers.

Moments after a banquet luncheon in his honor concluded in October 1966, Joseph Anthony Bach collapsed and died. He was 65.

He was one of Knute Rockne's famed "Seven Mules" who blocked the way for the legendary Four Horsemen, and in the end, Joe Bach took a page out of his mentor's playbook to turn his NFL team around.

As a senior on Notre Dame's 1924 national title team — the first Irish team to win a championship — Joe Bach played a magnificent role in the Irish's first and only Rose Bowl trip in January 1925,

REX ENRIGHT

• **Played for Notre Dame (1923—1925), head coach for South Carolina (1938—1942; 1946—1955).**

Rex Enright served as living proof as to how great Rockne's teams during the era of the Four Horsemen and the blocking Seven Mules.

Born in Rockford, Illinois, Enright entered Notre Dame in 1922, the year Rockne devised perhaps the Fighting Irish's most potent offensive lineup of his 13-year career as head coach — a starting backfield lineup that featured Harry Stuhldreher at quarterback, Jim Crowley at left halfback, Don Miller at right halfback, and Elmer Layden at fullback. Enright was the backup fullback behind Layden in 1922, then returned to the football team in 1925 to claim the starting fullback position.

Enright was also a standout basketball player who started all four seasons for the Notre Dame basketball team from 1922 to 1926. Upon graduation from Notre Dame, Enright returned to football and played professionally for the Green Bay Packers for two seasons.

A coaching career in both sports took Enright south during the early 1930s. He first took a job as assistant football coach at the University of North Carolina in Chapel Hill, then relocated to Georgia in 1931 where he doubled as head basketball coach and assistant football coach at the University of Georgia until 1938.

Enright left Georgia in 1938 to become head football coach and athletic director at the University of South Carolina, where he would eventually leave an indelible mark on the football history of the school, and what would be formed as the Atlantic Coach Conference.

Enright also coached the South Carolina basketball squad for two seasons before he joined the United States Navy in 1943. Sporting a rank of lieutenant, Enright served in the Navy working in the Navy's athletic program in the United States. After returning to South Carolina in 1946, Enright resumed his role as head football coach, and remained on the Gamecocks sidelines until 1955 when health issues forced him to resign.

Enright, who in 1953 was credited as being one of the "ring leaders" who helped in the formation of the Atlantic Coast Conference, stayed on as South Carolina's athletic director until 1960. Although his career record of 82-62 as basketball coach at South Carolina was far more impressive than his 64-69-7 mark as the school's head football coach, Enright left coaching as South Carolina's all-time winningest football coach until Steve Spurrier bested his mark in 2011.

Rex Edward Enright, who would be inducted into the South Carolina Athletic Hall of Fame, died April 6, 1960, as a result of peptic ulcers and a rheumatic heart. He was 59 years old.

FRANK LEAHY

• **Played for Notre Dame (1928—1930), head coach for Boston College (1939—1940), Notre Dame (1941—1943; 1946—1953).**

At the end of the 1930 season after Notre Dame had beaten Southern California in the final game to win their second consecutive national championship, Knute Rockne took an injured Irish lineman with him to Minneapolis "for company" when he checked into the Mayo Clinic.

Coach and student lay in adjoining hospital beds for two weeks talking football; Rockne was being treated for phlebitis in his leg, and the player had surgery to repair torn knee ligaments. During that time, Rockne mentioned to a friend that he wanted him to meet the player, a young offensive tackle named Frankie Leahy.

"The reason I want you to meet him," Rockne reasoned, "is that someday he will be recognized as the greatest football coach of all time."

Only Rockne stands in the way of his own prophecy: Today, nearly a century later, Rockne and Leahy rank No. 1 and No. 2 among Division I coaches with the highest all-time winning percentage in college football history. Born in O'Neill, Nebraska, it's only fitting that the coach with the second highest winning percentage in college football history grew up in the town of Winner, South Dakota, where he was a standout football player at Winner High School.

The friend replied by asking Rockne what was so exceptional about young Leahy. "That kid has the greatest football brain I have ever come in contact with," Rockne gushed. "He is just simply genius when it comes to planning ways and means of getting that ball across the goal line and smothering the play of the opponents. Take it from me, he is a super-strategist already."

If not for a knee injury that sidelined him for the final season of his Irish playing career, Leahy would have anchored the offensive line at left tackle for Rockne's last three teams, including the 1929 and 1930 championship squads. That injury turned out to be a fateful blessing for Leahy, who sat on the bench during games with Rockne and soaked up knowledge directly from the master that laid the foundation for a brilliant future coaching career.

Leahy graduated from Notre Dame in 1931. He immediately landed his first assistant coaching job at Georgetown. During a game against Notre Dame legend Jim Crowley's Michigan State team, Crowley was so impressed by Georgetown's line work under the rookie assistant, he recruited Leahy to join his staff at Michigan State in 1932.

Leahy's tenure at Michigan State lasted only one year. The following season, Crowley was hired to be the new head coach at Fordham, and Leahy followed Crowley to New York City to take on the task of Fordham's offensive line coach. From 1935 to 1937, Leahy's linemen were so dominant, they were tagged the "Seven Blocks of Granite" by the press. Included among the Seven of Blocks of Granite was a tough kid who would go on to become perhaps the NFL's greatest head coach — Vince Lombardi.

By 1939, Leahy moved on again, this time to take the helm of his own team at Boston College. In just two seasons, Leahy guided the Eagles to a 20-2 record, including an undefeated national championship season in 1940 that was capped with a victory in the 1941

Sugar Bowl. One of the players Leahy tried to recruit to Boston College was future beat author Jack Kerouac, a promising high school standout from Lowell, Massachusetts who wound up going to Columbia University.

In the wake of his undefeated championship season of 1940, Leahy turned down offers from three different schools, one of which would have set him up financially for life, to sign a new five-year contract and stay at Boston College. But a mere 24 hours after Leahy put his signature on a deal that would keep him with the Eagles for at least five more years, he got a call from his alma mater with an offer to return as Irish head coach.

Leahy jumped at the offer to coach the team his mentor had built, but Boston College wasn't about to tear up his contract before the ink of Leahy's signature had dried. Despite Leahy's pleas to the school's vice president, the mayor of Boston, and the governor of Massachusetts, he took his case in front of a press conference and announced: "Gentlemen, I've called you all here today to inform you that I recently received my release from my coaching contract. With the release went the good wishes and benediction of Boston College."

The South Bend Tribune called Leahy's announcement, "the biggest lie of his life." But as soon as Leahy had stepped away from the podium, a call came in from the vice president of Boston College. "Coach Leahy," the school's VP snarled, "you may go wherever you want, and whenever you want. Goodbye."

By the time Leahy returned to Notre Dame as head coach for the 1941 season, he had grown into his own man with his own methods and innovations. Any similarities between Leahy and Rockne were few and far between. Leahy, like Rockne, was a stubborn perfectionist who paid strict attention to every detail. And, like Rockne, Leahy won football games at an astounding rate with coaching innovations and strategies that nobody else in the college ranks came close to.

Among Leahy's most significant creations included the implementation of a double-quarterback formation, having his teams run from the stand-up position, optional blocking assignments for linemen on the same running play, and formulating a pass defense against Georgia Tech during the 1941 season that was used by most NFL teams at the time.

Leahy worked his men hard, but they held a profound respect for his authority and knowledge, and they appreciated his concern for their physical well-being. Using his own knee injury that sidelined him for Rockne's last season in 1930 as a barometer, Leahy was relentless in finding ways to safeguard his players from getting hurt.

Leahy left Notre Dame in 1944 to enter the U.S. Navy. For two years, Leahy served as lieutenant commander in charge of recreational programs for submarine crews. When he returned to South Bend in 1946, Notre Dame was the top-ranked team in the country. Leahy led the Irish on a 39-game winning streak that finally came to an end in 1950 with a loss to Purdue.

In addition to the national championship his Boston College Eagles claimed in 1940, Leahy's Notre Dame teams captured four national titles — 1943, 1946, 1947 and 1949 — an unprecedented run as head coach of his alma mater that earned him the nickname, "The Master."

Health problems began to creep in on October 24, 1953, when Leahy was stricken by a pancreatic attack. Although Notre Dame was, again, ranked as the best team in the country, ill-health forced Layden to step down as Irish head coach at the end of the 1953 season.

After leaving Notre Dame, Leahy spent his time giving football game previews on radio and television shows. He struck up a business friendship with financier Louis Wolfson, and in 1955 Leahy was elected vice president for trade relations for the marine construction and salvage firm, Merritt-Chapman & Scott Corporation.

Leahy returned to football in 1960 when he was named general manager of the Los Angeles Chargers during the inaugural season of the American Football League. Three years later, Leahy moved to Portland, Oregon when he landed a job as an executive in a vending machine company.

He was inducted into the National Football Foundation Hall of Fame in 1970.

Francis William Leahy, the coach who took the lessons he learned directly from Knute Rockne and forged a legendary career in his own right that to this day stands second only to his mentor in all-time winning percentage, died from congestive heart failure in Portland on June 21, 1973. He was 64 years old.

FRANK CARIDEO

• **Played for Notre Dame (1928—1930), head coach for Missouri (1932—1934)**

Knute Rockne himself called Frank Carideo "...the best quarterback ever."

Born in Mount Vernon, New York, Carideo played under Rockne at Notre Dame from 1928 to 1930 and led the Irish to a perfect 19-0 record over a two-year period as a starter.

A two-time All-American, Carideo was quarterback of the last Rockne-coached Notre Dame team in 1930, a team that went undefeated and secured Notre Dame's third national championship under Rockne with a crushing win over Southern California in December 1930.

After graduating from Notre Dame, Carideo followed in his mentor's footsteps at Purdue where he served as an assistant coach in 1931. Carideo left Purdue to take a coaching job at the University of Missouri from 1932 to 1934. Carideo's Missouri teams went 2-23-2 during his span.

He departed Missouri after three seasons to coach basketball at Mississippi State University from 1935 to 1939. Carideo returned to football as an assistant coach at Iowa from 1939 to 1942, as well as during the 1946 and 1949 seasons.

Francis F. Carideo died in Ocean Springs, Mississippi in 1992 at the age of 83.

69

CHANGING FLIGHT

In life, Knute Rockne charted the course for the game of football.

Rockne's death may have exerted an even more profound change on the nation and perhaps the world. When his plane crashed to the ground of a Kansas farm field at about 10:45 a.m. on March 31, 1931, Rockne's death forever altered aviation in the United States and future air travel around the globe for good.

The crash on March 31, 1931 forced the Aeronautics Branch of the Department of Commerce to become more transparent because Rockne was one of the victims.

For five years, following 1926 when Herbert Hoover installed the Department of Commerce as the regulating branch of the aviation industry, federal government investigations of air crashes had been kept confidential from the press and the public. Keeping federal crash investigations secret was meant to spur the growth of the blossoming aviation industry and sell the public on the safety of air travel, while airline companies colluded in efforts to keep crashes out of the public eye by removing wreckage from sites and destroying records to thwart investigations.

The public, however, clamored for information on the crash that killed Rockne. Media pressure, which had been mounting all across the country for five years to get access to federal crash investigations, swarmed over Bazaar, Kansas, like an intense storm cloud.

Because Knute Rockne was one of the victims, the Aeronautics Branch immediately sent a federal investigation team to a plane crash site for the first time. Because of Rockne, it would be the first time the Department of Commerce released its crash investigation findings to the media for public consumption.

Three years later in 1934, Congress passed the Air Commerce Act, which gave the Department of Commerce full authority to issue subpoenas and directions to make investigations public.

The crash that claimed the life of Rockne promptly grounded the wooden Fokker F-10 Trimotor plane and killed the Fokker airline as a viable company. More importantly, Rockne's death in a wooden-structured plane spelled the end of wooden aircraft flying in commercial aviation.

Airline manufacturers immediately began the move to replace wood with metal, and the all-metal Ford Trimotor and Boeing 247 airships seized the market. T&WA, frozen out of the Boeing market by rival companies, requested specifications for an all-new metal airliner from Douglas Aircraft. Within one year, Douglas developed the DC-1/2, which would eventually become the DC-3, the most successful and long-lasting airliner in commercial aviation history until it went out of service in the early 1990s.

Rockne's legacy is etched in the DC-3's metal foundation that turned air travel from an American adventure into a worldwide business.

As impressive as the DC-3's performance and safety factors were, even more startling were the drastic decreases in cost-per-seat mile, which made air travel not only safer, but more affordable and cost-effective. The 21-seat DC-3 became the first passenger airplane to make profits for airlines without the added funds provided by transporting mail. Well over 10,000 DC-3s would be manufactured in the U.S.A., with 2,000 more built in Russia and another 500 made in Japan. The DC-3 also flew in just about every Allied air operation of World War II, and served as a significant military air tool in both the Korean and Vietnam wars.

Granted, had the Rockne crash never happened and the legendary coach gone on to a long and unprecedented head coaching career at Notre Dame, the aviation industry would have progressed away from three-engine wooden airliners flying at 120 miles per hour. It's just that the development of the metal airliner would have been different, evidenced by the clunky, slow Junkers manufactured in the mid-1930s.

If not for the ambitious airline manufacturing market created by the Rockne crash, Douglas would not have built the DC-3, considered to this day to be the aviation industry's pioneering masterpiece. Perhaps worldwide air travel would have developed more slowly without the DC-3 and its passenger-friendly economy, safety and comfort. As well, there may have been slower acceptance of the high-performance military monoplanes and civil-service airplanes.

But Rockne did die in a plane crash.

And the aviation industry memorialized his incredible life by moving to right the wrongs of the airliner in which he was killed and to make aviation travel safer, technologically progressive, and more transparent for the public's consumption.

Section 5: The Legacy

The U.S. Navy memorialized Rockne in 1943 ...

70

IN MEMORIAL

In a message to Mrs. Rockne, President Herbert Hoover wrote: "I know that every American grieves with you. Mr. Rockne so contributed to a cleanness and high purpose and sportsmanship in athletics that his passing is a national loss."

Rockne's legacy lives in memorials across the country and around the globe — from his home in Norway to the continent of Australia — befitting not only a legendary football coach, but a true national treasure on the level of a president, a king, a fallen national hero.

Artist Jerry McKenna has no peer when it comes to sculpting memorial busts and statues of Knute Rockne. The Boerne, Texas-based sculptor, a 1962 graduate of Notre Dame, has crafted a total of 11 Rockne statues.

Among McKenna's prominent Rockne works include: the statue on the north end of Notre Dame Stadium; a statue of Rockne in downtown South Bend; the Rockne bust in the Notre Dame football team's locker room; a memorial statue in Rockne's birthplace of Voss, Norway; a statue in the town of Rockne, Texas; a bust at the Matfield Green travel plaza on the Kansas Turnpike eight miles from the crash site near Bazaar, Kansas; a bust at the Cottonwood Falls Museum in Cottonwood Falls, Kansas, the closest town to the crash; a bust in the Guglielmino Athletics Complex — "The Gug," — that houses the football practice locker rooms, coaches' offices and meeting rooms on the campus of Notre Dame; and, perhaps most appropriately, a bust in the office of current Notre Dame football coach Brian Kelly.

Capturing the expressive grin on Rockne's face on the statue outside Notre Dame Stadium

"I was a bit inhibited because I held him in such awe ..." — Jerry McKenna

is a testament to McKenna's spiritual kinship with the legendary coach.

"I gotta be honest..." McKenna says, pausing to collect his artistic perception of a muse so personally beloved, "all I want is to sculpt a masterpiece, and I fall short...

"Even though he's got very unique features, he's been very difficult to sculpt over the years. I've done hundreds of portrait busts, but I just find him very different to capture; it took a very long time to do the pieces. I was a bit inhibited because I held him in such awe. I just couldn't get over that, and I probably still haven't."

A marble and limestone memorial monument honoring Rockne and the five other passengers, pilot and co-pilot was erected at the site of the crash in Chase County, Kansas, a sprawling 1,539-acre plot of open pasture on the edge of the Flint Hills previously owned by the family estate of witness Easter Heathman. When the property was sold at auction for more than $4 million in February 2018, the auction company told the Kansas City Star that the Rockne memorial marked the land with "a little more character."

On March 29, 2019, two days before the 88th anniversary of the crash, the Rockne Memorial was officially dedicated at the Matfield Green travel plaza on the Kansas Turnpike. McKenna's bust of Rockne is the featured display at the newest memorial site located about eight miles north of the crash site.

In the wake of the crash in 1931, the children of Sacred Heart School in the small farming community of Hilbigville, Texas, were given the opportunity to choose a name for their town. The kids voted to rename the town, Rockne, to honor the fallen coach. On March 10, 1988, the town of Rockne opened its first post office and issued a commemorative, 22-cent Rockne stamp. On March 4, 2006, a life-size bust of Rockne was unveiled in the town.

In Allentown, Pennsylvania, the gymnasium inside Allentown Central Catholic High School is named Rockne Hall. The street next to the football field in Taylorville, Illinois., is called Knute Rockne Road. South Bend, and Stevensville, Michigan, where Rockne had a summer home, also have streets named after the legendary coach. A gas and food stop on the Indiana Toll Road not far from South Bend is called the Knute Rockne Travel Plaza.

Soon after his death, the Studebaker automobile company in South Bend began building the Rockne model automobile, a manufacturing project priced to sell in a low-cost market during the early years of the Great Depression.

Rockne also became the subject of various

... the most famous film tribute came in 1940 with the Warner Brothers release of "Knute Rockne, All American" ...

music and film releases that began shortly after the plane crash. In 1931, the year that Rockne died, composer Ferde Grofe, whose credits include the Grand Canyon Suite and Rip Van Winkle, penned a symphonic musical suite to honor Rockne.

Perhaps the most famous film tribute came in 1940 with the Warner Brothers release of "Knute Rockne, All American," starring actor Pat O'Brien who recreated the famous locker scene in which Rockne used the phrase, "win one for the Gipper." Young actor Ronald Reagan portrayed George Gipp in the film, and later used the phrase during one of his speeches after he had been elected president.

The 1944 film short, "I Am an American," also featured Rockne as a foreign-born American citizen. Most recently in 2008, a biographical musical of Rockne's life based on a play and mini-series penned by Buddy Farmer hit the stage at the Theatre at the Center in Munster, Indiana.

Rockne was enshrined as a charter member of the College Football Hall of Fame in 1951, as well as the Indiana Football Hall of Fame. He was also inducted posthumously into the Scandinavian-American Hall of Fame held during Norsk Horstfest. Rockne was also inducted into the Rose Bowl Hall of Fame in 2014.

The U.S. Navy memorialized Rockne in 1943 by naming a ship the SS Knute Rockne. Rockne's face was also featured on a stamp. In 1988, President Ronald Reagan appeared at No-

Built in 1939 ... "The Rock" still stands as one of the most complete recreational facilities on campus ...

tre Dame's Athletic & Convocation Center to give a speech and unveil the U.S. Postal Service's 22-cent Rockne commemorative postage stamp the same day it was released in Rockne, Texas.

The Knute Rockne Memorial Building also stands as a Notre Dame honorarium to Rockne. Built in 1939 with funding by donations from alumni and friends of the University, "The Rock" still stands as one of the most complete recreational facilities on campus for students, facility, staff, retirees and their families.

"The Rock" features a lower-level exercise room and weight room, a 25-yard swimming pool and warm-up pool with observation decks, racquetball and squash courts, plus lock-er rooms for men, women and families — a bustling facility for club sports, intramurals, fitness classes, aquatic instruction and life-saving classes. The upper level includes a gymnasium complete with two basketball courts.

The main lobby of "The Rock" stands as a true memorial to the legendary coach. Athletic trophies and mementos accumulated by Notre Dame teams under Rockne and his successors are displayed, as well as a bronze bust of Rockne that greets patrons and campus visitors. Students have turned the Rockne bust into a long-standing source of tradition by rubbing Rockne's nose for good luck.

... Students have turned the Rockne bust into a long-standing source of tradition ...

KNUTE ROCKNE
HEAD COACH
1918 — 1930
105 WINS, 12 LOSSES, 5 TIES
NATIONAL CHAMPIONS: 1924, 1929, 1930

... with the slightest grin of a football Mona Lisa ...

71

THE HOUSE THAT ROCKNE BUILT

His most magnificent and enduring legacy sits as the football centerpiece of the University of Notre Dame — Notre Dame Stadium.

By 1928, Notre Dame under Rockne had become such a national football powerhouse, a mediocre 5-4 season did little to dim net profits that soared to nearly $500,000. The team was getting way too popular to handle crowds that packed into the campus's smaller Cartier Field. A new stadium was in the planning stages; however, Holy Cross priests were dragging their feet on decisions that needed to be made to allocate money to build a new stadium.

Rockne grew increasingly frustrated with the delays, which were complicated by a variety of additional issues. Finally, chomping at the bit for a new stadium, yet armed with offers on the table from a handful of universities that promised richer annual salaries to coach their football teams and turn their schools into a national cash cow, Rockne submitted his resignation to the university's president, Father O'Donnell.

But Father O'Donnell knew that excess receipts from the 1928 season, plus projected receipts generated by playing all away games in 1929 on neutral fields, could adequately finance the construction of the new stadium without putting the university in debt. Father O'Donnell could

Notre Dame Stadium opened its gates on Oct. 4, 1930, holding a capacity of 59,075 people. That debut season, which ended with Rockne's Irish capturing their third and final national championship under his helm, would be the only season Knute Rockne coached football in the stadium he designed.

also offer a tempting caveat — allow Rockne input as to how he would like the new stadium to be designed.

Rockne was good to stay at Notre Dame and mold the new stadium in his own vision.

Working with Osborn Engineering of Cleveland, the firm that had designed both Yankee Stadium and Boston's Fenway Park, Rockne used the University of Michigan Stadium as a model. At a final cost of $750,000, the original Notre Dame Stadium was a smaller-scale version of Michigan Stadium, with space between the playing field and the stands cut to a minimum.

The main difference between the two was the location of the tunnel, which was opened on the north end of Notre Dame Stadium. Today, the Knute Rockne Gate where both Notre Dame players and the visiting team, plus the marching band and all cheerleaders enter for games, is marked by the iconic bronze Rockne statue.

Notre Dame Stadium opened its gates on Oct. 4, 1930, holding a capacity of 59,075 people. That debut season, which ended with Rockne's Irish capturing their third and final national championship under his helm, would be the only season Knute Rockne coached football in the stadium he designed.

Today, the original bowl of Rockne's view sits under the massive steel framework of two nine-story buildings added to the stadium as part of Notre Dame University's $400 million Campus Crossroads project. An additional six-story building is also being built on the stadium's south end. The field's natural grass was replaced by field turf in 2014. What began as a stadium that seated nearly 60,000 today boasts a capacity of 80,795.

While towering new construction, field turf, added press boxes and stadium suites overwhelm the view from the outside that once stood as a stark centerpiece of college football tradition in the massive surrounding parking lot, they have done little to diminish the old-school tradition of Notre Dame football.

The stadium sits at 2010 Moose Krause Circle. Statues of legendary Irish coaches greet fans entering each of the stadium gates: Dan Devine at Gate A; Ara Parseghian at Gate B; Frank Leahy at Gate C; Lou Holtz at Gate D — all Hall of Fame inductees, all having won at least one national championship at Notre Dame.

But there's only one Rockne Gate.

One "House That Rockne Built."

One statue with a cocked head to the side standing with the slightest grin of a football Mona Lisa that seems to encourage every passerby to make his next step just a little bit better than the last.

One life that shaped the football, perfected the forward pass, brainstormed the shifting offense, stacked the box on defense, took college teams coast to coast, forged lasting rivalries with reverence and respect, promoted Notre Dame as a national tradition, sold the game into a showtime of financial fortune... and won one for the Gipper.

Knute Rockne defined an era. He personified life in shoulder pads. In death, he dictated the future of aviation safety. There are countless memorials, tributes and lasting memories carried on into the afterlife by the people who knew him and the people who handed down their personal memories to their children, their grandchildren, and their grandchildren's children.

But to this day, and every day as long as there's life, just as there is only one football used in play during the game, there remains only one...

Knute Rockne — a man who became a legend.

... just as there is only one football used in play during the game, there remains only one ...

Epilogue

THE CHALKBOARD

"In a game of football, the chief thought of both teams is to get the ballcarrier across the goal line, as this means six points for the scoring team. The colorful part of football, therefore, is offense. You may talk about defense until you are blue in the face, though don't misunderstand me, defense has its part in the game. But the thrill, the big picture in football, is in offense."

Knute Rockne

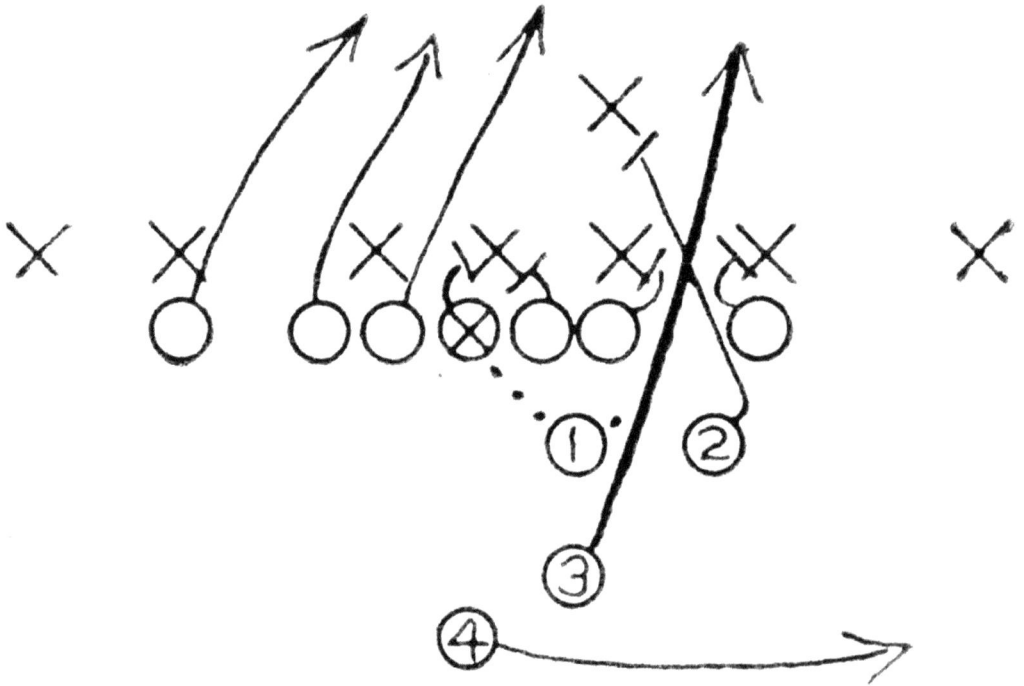

(DIAGRAM — BASIC PLAY)

10 PLAYS

These plays should work very successfully. It is well to remember that a successful offense is one that can gain ground against any defense, under any weather conditions.

BASIC PLAY: This play must be made to go as it is a basic play. Center passes ball to back 1, who hands it to back 3 for a quick plunge. Back 2 fakes one step to right and then drives through on the defensive linebacker. Back 4 fakes as though getting the ball from center and runs straight to right.

BASIC FORWARD PASS: Center passes ball to back 1, who fakes ball to back 3. Back 3 fakes a line plunge after which he continues down field and becomes possible pass receiver. Back 2 hits end and then goes out to right for a pass. Back 4 fakes as though getting ball from center and then blocks tackle. Back 1, after faking ball to back 3, runs back to the right and forward passes to one of three receivers.

CRISS-CROSS PASS: Back 4 gets the direct pass from the center, fakes off tackle, and gives the ball to back 1, after which he blocks. Back 1, after receiving the ball from back 4, fakes a reverse run. The ends criss-cross and the line, except for the right guard, block in the line. The right guard pulls out to the right and blocks. Back 3 blocks to the right, and back 2 blocks to the left. Back 4 then passes to either end.

FAKE LINE PASS: Back 4 receives the ball from center. Both ends block their tackles for two counts and then break for the open

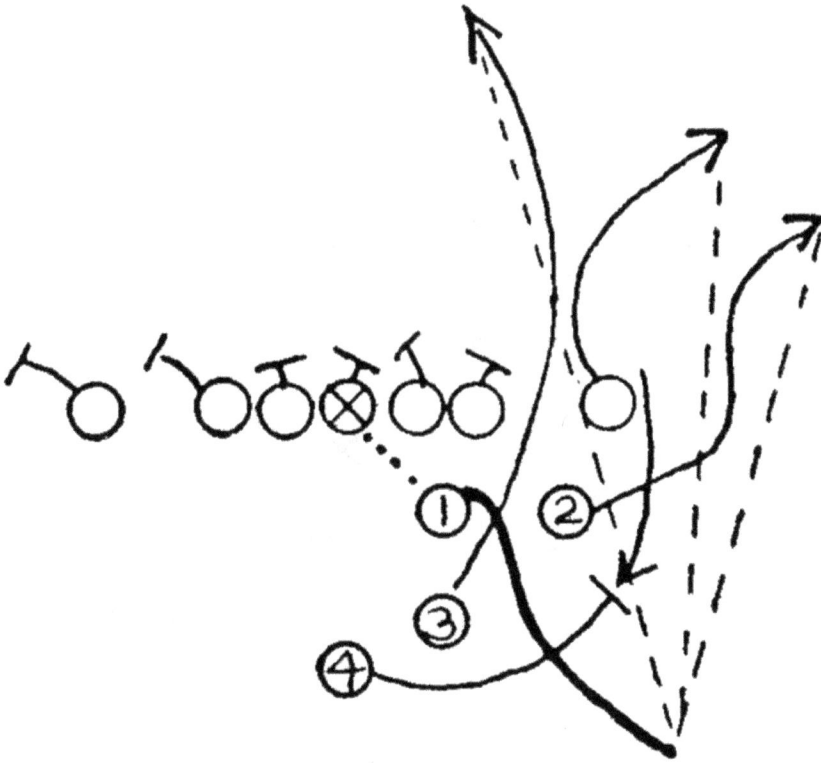

(DIAGRAM — BASIC FORWARD PASS)

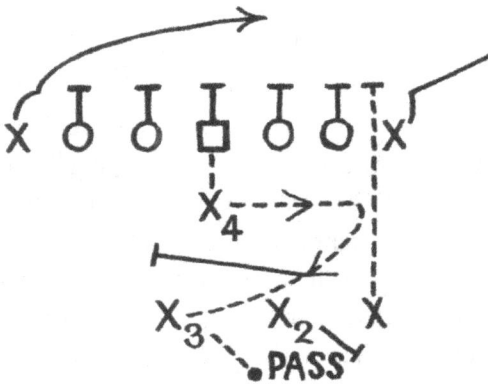

(DIAGRAM — FAKE LINE PASS)

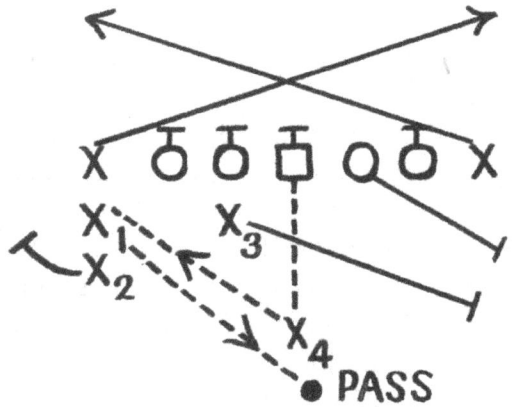

(DIAGRAM — CRISS-CROSS PASS)

(DIAGRAM — RUNNING PASS)

space. The line from tackle to tackle blocks, back 4 takes the ball and fakes it to back 1, faking a line buck. Back 4 then pivots around and tosses the ball to back 3, after which he blocks to the weak side. Back 2 will block to the strong side. Back 3 delays, then drops back a step and passes to either end.

RUNNING PASS: The center passes the ball to back 4. The right end goes down and out. The left end goes down a few yards and then comes across the field fast. The line from tackle to tackle will block. Back 1 fakes for the end, slips by, and goes out into the flat zone for a pass. Back 2 blocks the end and back 3 blocks the tackle. The passer fakes an off-tackle play for three steps, drops back, and passes to whomever of the three is clear. The right end and back 1 are in the same focus.

SCREEN PASS: The center passes the ball to back 4. The five center men charge down the field to take the secondary defense. The ends delay, then cut in short to catch a high lob pass. Backs 1, 2 and 3 block; back 4 takes one step back and passes to either end. The pass must be a short high lob, high enough so that it will not be blocked by in-charging line men.

DECOY PASS: Back 4 receives the ball from center and fakes a run. The right end goes down the field deep and slightly in towards the center. Back 3 goes down the field, fast and wide. Back 1 delays, then goes straight a few yards, then turns sharply across to the left. Back 2 blocks, back 4 then passes, generally to back 1.

END RUN: The center passes the ball to back 2. Back 2 then turns around to his left as

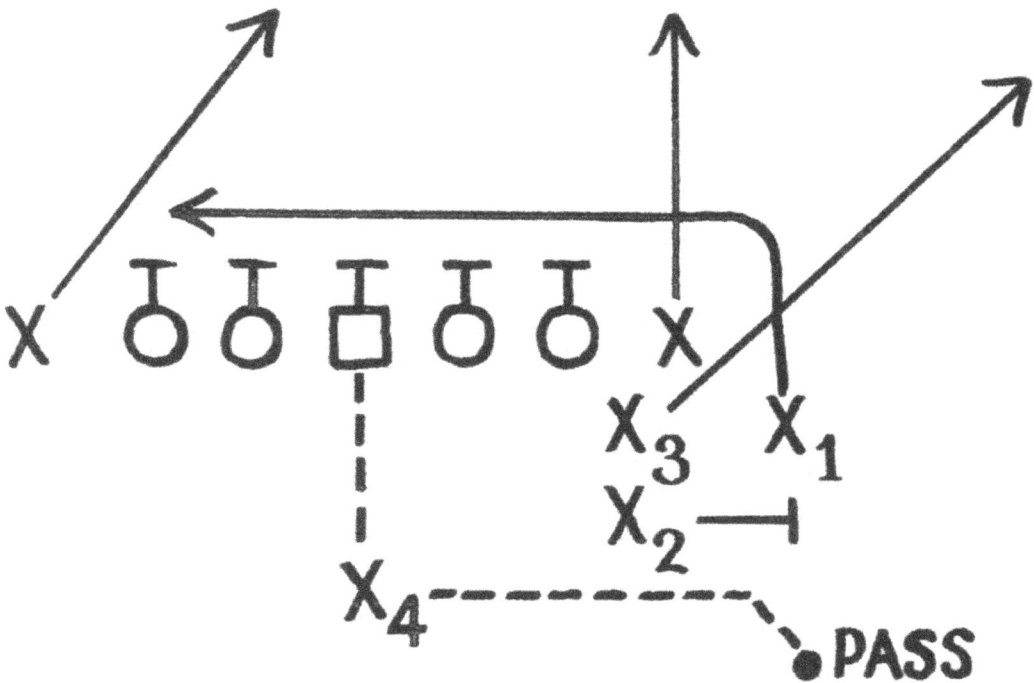

(DIAGRAM — DECOY PASS)

if to hand the ball to back 1 who is crossing to the right at his rear. There is a tendency because of this to cause the defense to wait, instead of charging full speed toward the area to be attacked. Back 2 follows back 1 around the end. Back 1 will block the first opponent to appear. Back 4 blocks the end. The right end boxes the defensive left tackle without aid. Speed is of the essence with this play. The right end boxes the defensive left tackle without any aid. The left guard, tackle and end break through the line to block down field.

BUCK INSIDE TACKLE: The spinning back 1 receives the ball from center. In this case, the same one who runs the opponents' left end also goes through the same motions as Play No. 14 when bucking straight ahead inside the defensive left tackle. Naturally,

you would think that back 1 was starting on another end run if this eleven had executed that play successfully earlier in the game when he received the snap from center and turned toward back 2. The defense would be convinced of this if back 2, as on the end run, again broke by to the rear of back 1 and started out around the end. Back 1 instead follows around the end, and he makes a complete turn and then drives straight ahead into the line inside the defensive left tackle. Back 4 in this instance helps his right end box this defensive tackle. Back 3 takes the defensive end. The play works because the fake to circle the end often draws the linebacker out of position to stop the plunge.

REVERSE: Plays do not run in the same direction. Now lined up on the left is the exact opposite to the right formation. This time the

555

ball is snapped to back 1 and he starts as if on an end run around his own left end. As he passes to back 2, he partly hides back 2 from the defense. He now hands the ball to back 2 who rushes to the right as though to flank the other end. Backs 3 and 4 go along with back 2 to make interference for him as do linemen 5 and 6. As the 2 interfering backs rush into the defensive left end driving him out toward that sideline, back 2 cuts in off the defensive left tackle preceded by linemen 5 and 6. It prevents the defense from shifting too much over to the long side of our formation, the side to which the bulk of the plays are run.

CHALKBOARD SUMMARY

1. Plays must not be over 30 in number.
2. Plays must all have following qualities:
   a. All plays including fakes must be strong plays in themselves; using deception alone is not enough.
   b) Be careful on all pass plays to see that ball is never thrown at dangerous angles.
   c) Play must fit in with a sequence of plays from the formation.
3. Formation must be one from which you can use any method of offense:
   a. Thrust.
   b. Flank.
   c. Kick.
   d. Forward pass.
4. Four kinds of formations are:
   a. Close — Quarterback handling ball, ends in close, backs in close. This formation stresses thrust plays.
   b. Open — Direct pass, ends flanking tackle, and backs a little wider apart; stresses flank plays.
   c. Punt formation — Man back ten yards should be triple threat; stresses kick.
   d. Spread — Ends and backs spread over a wide area, sometimes including the linemen; stresses forward pass plays.
5. Success of execution of good play depends on:
   a. Superiority of line charge and interference
   b. Fast starting and getting to point of attack fast.
   c. Timing.
   d. All assignments fulfilled by all eleven men.
6. Do not use offense which depends for success on fooling someone. Some trick plays are all right to keep a defense guessing, but that is all. Depend on deception, power and superiority in execution of fundamentals.
7. Timing and practice in remembering assignments can be perfected by dummy scrimmages.
8. Quick opening, wedge, and shoulder-to-shoulder turtle-back crawl should all be used so as to get versatility.
9. Shift plays should be fast enough so as not to permit defense either to shift fast enough to meet nor allow them to diagnose.
10. All plays should be covered or disguised as long as possible.
11. Do not use too many plays. A few plays well learned are better than too many not well learned.
12. Be sure to exhaust all the good possibilities of a formation. It is better to have only a few formations using all the possibilities than many formations with only a few plays off each.

Football Coach Knute Rockne runs the ball against a player who tries to tackle him at practice, circa 1920s.

Acknowledgements

JEFFREY G. HARRELL

T his book would not have been possible without the immeasurable contributions of time, resources and expertise generously gifted by an incredible group of people.

My huge debt of gratitude goes out to John Bybee, whose ceaseless supply of reference works, official documents and knowledge of aviation history guided me profoundly throughout the flight of this phenomenal story.

Jim Managan, Father John Reynolds' direct matriarchal descendant, graciously granted access to the cassette tapes of the last interview given by Father Reynolds. Because of Jim's generosity, this storyline is drawn directly from the tape-recorded voice of the only actual eyewitness to the Jake Lingle murder.

Blessings of appreciation to Father Richard Layton at Our Lady of Guadalupe Abbey, and to Ron Karten, for sharing candid and entertaining personal insights that make this book as much of a testament to Father Reynolds' mortal truth as it does to the football truth of Knute Rockne.

A warm heart extends to Jim "Augie" Augustine, a true blue-and-gold Notre Dame community institution, chief shopkeeper of Augie's Locker Room in South Bend, and provider of unrequited moral support on countless occasions, not to mention the actual historic newspapers photographed for this book.

I am proud to include Jerry McKenna's artistic insights into the brilliant memorials he has sculpted in Coach Rockne's image. Thank you, Jerry, for your art that will keep the spirit of Knute Rockne alive forever. Your presence lends an indelible majesty to this book.

Special thanks to Lesley Martin and Katie Levi at Chicago History Museum. They made tracking down rare, historical photographs a completely hassle-free, friendly exploration of Chicago.

Thank you, Craig Pinkus, for the legal consultation and the many years of friendship. Thanks also to Bill Jonas for the steady guidance, and for sticking as a buddy for too many years to admit now. To Dan Reutebuch, my lifelong Tippecanoe River brother, there aren't enough bro-hugs in the world to express my gratitude.

It was an honor to work with Kerry Temple and John Nagy at Notre Dame Magazine. The faith Kerry put in me to write THAT story and nail it down for the Notre Dame audience is too overwhelming for words. This book strives to meet the same high standards and dedication to integrity that graces Notre Dame Magazine under Kerry Temple's leadership.

All my love and appreciation to Hedy, my soul mate, my best friend. Without her unconditional support, I would have been lost in the wind instead of a writer on a mission to put out the greatest story that ever found my pen.

To Rochelle Day, Georges Toumayan, Richard Ryan and Dr. Len Clark, thank you for making one hell of a team.

Spiritual blessings go out to the memory of Dorothy Corson, "The Spirit of Notre Dame" herself who lit the first match on the Father Reynolds story in her online blog on March 31, 2003.

Lastly, to my dearly departed soul brother, Neil Raabe, the greatest Notre Dame football fan I'll ever know... bless you for siding up to Knute Rockne in heaven and talking him in to throwing me the greatest pass I've ever caught.

J.G.H., May 2020

FURTHER ACKNOWLEDGEMENTS

An extremely talented group of individuals also helped to make this book possible.

John Vincent "Jack" Rockne served as a profound inspiration to press forward with this project prior to his death in August 2008. Jack was always good company when it seemed that putting this book together wasn't possible. He answered every question and provided invaluable insight into his father, and he never ceased to encourage the early stages of this book.

The staff at Notre Dame Archives, especially archivist Charles Lamb, served as monumental navigators of the Archives' massive collection. Charles and Peter Ly were phenomenal sources of information. Rita Erskine was very generous in her guidance through Rare Books and Special Collections.

In addition to Notre Dame: Wabash College, Yale University, particularly Judith Schiff and Kristen McDonald at Yale University Library, and the United States Military Academy (Army) at West Point, were particularly helpful in providing historical resources.

ACKNOWLEDGEMENTS

Others who helped make this book possible include: Matt Spaulding, Emily Spaulding, Justin Loughran, Elizabeth Loughran, Cindy and Dennis Fines, Mike Malone, Henry Yee and Cavanaugh Hannan.

Sincerest indebtedness extends to Georges Toumayan, Rochelle Day, Richard T. Ryan and Dr. Len Clark. Their interminable loyalty to this project was nothing short of overwhelming.

About the Author

JEFFREY G. HARRELL was born to write and create music in Indianapolis, Indiana. The proud instigator of an award-winning newspaper career that took him from Fort Lauderdale to New York City, Jeff is a professional musician, songwriter, record producer, grilling aficionado, voyeur of the natural order, a lifetime subscriber to the human condition ... and a diehard fan of the Chicago Bears.

ABOUT THE CONTRIBUTORS

JOHN DAVENPORT is a longtime businessman whose office sits in the shadow of Notre Dame Stadium, the mecca that fuels his passion for Notre Dame football and devotion to the standards set by his idol, Knute Rockne. John is the father of two sons; Branden, an officer in the United States Navy, and Bradley. He lives in South Bend with his wife, Cathy.

ROCHELLE DAY has been in the journalism industry for more than 20 years, first as a reporter and, now, as a designer. When she's not plugging into her creative outlet on a computer, you'll find her utilizing it in the kitchen to make homemade bakes or with her two young sons who keep her constantly on her toes.

GEORGES TOUMAYAN is a freelance graphic designer and journalist with several years of marketing and PR experience working for non-profit institutions and museums. A graduate of the University of Notre Dame with a B.A. degree in graphic design and a M.A. degree in Journalism from the School of the Art Institute in Chicago, Georges loves all things digital media, reading unsolved mysteries, and has hiked the Alaskan wilderness with his camera photographing grizzly bears and other wildlife. He currently lives in South Bend.

Rockne of Ages

SOURCE INDEX

PROLOGUE

"Rockne of Notre Dame"
Delos W. Lovelace
G.P. Putnam's Sons
1931

Shake Down The Thunder: The Official Biography of Frank Leahy
Wells Twombley
Chilton Book Company; Radnor, Pennsylvania
1974

The New York Times — Oct. 30, 1929
"Rockne's Condition Pronounced Worse; Notre Dame Coach Must Forego Trips With Team
Perhaps for Rest of Season. Leg Injury Aggravated His Journey to Carnegie Tech Game in Defiance
of Physicians' Orders Causes Relapse."

The Tampa Daily News
"Rockne Sick And Weary After Record Grid Campaign" — **Dec. 11, 1930**
"Rockne Warned To Quit Strenuous Life" — **Dec. 23, 1930**

The Art of Manliness — **artofmanliness.com** — **June 26, 2008**
"Lessons in Manliness: Knute Rockne"

SECTIONS I, II, IV and V

Newspapers.com

Moberly Monitor — (Moberly, Missouri) — Wednesday, June 11, 1930
"Reward of $55,000 hangs today over the head of the man who murdered Alfred (Jake) Lingle"

St. Louis Star — June 26, 1930
"Jake Lingle Slain After Plan For Dog Track Near Loop Fell Through"
Harry T. Brundidge

The South Bend News-Times — Sept. 18, 1930
"Geisking Exonerated in Murder of Lingle"
United Press International

The New York Times — Dec. 8, 1930
"Notre Dame Fighting Irish ends the season undefeated"
"Notre Dame to repeat as National Champions after this game"

Des Moines Register — Jan. 8, 1931
"Lingle Slayer Is Identified"

Des Moines Register — Jan. 9, 1931
"Hide Lingle Murder Suspect"

St. Louis Star — Jan. 14, 1931
"Courageous Young Woman Took Important Part In Setting Trap For Leo Brothers at His Hideout"

Journal Gazette (Matoon, Ill.) — Friday January 16, 1931
"Lingle Plot Details Are Unearthed"

Chicago Tribune — March 25, 1931
"Trial of Leo Brothers: Calls 8 Witnesses; Rebuttal Today"
"Courtroom Jammed At Murder Trial"

St. Louis Post-Dispatch — March 25, 1931

"Alfred (Jake) Lingle

The Sedalia Democrat (Sedalia, Mo.) — Tuesday, March 31, 1931
"Death To Knute Rockne in Crash of Huge Plane"
"Plane Exploded in Mid-Air and Fell to Earth in Flames, Witnesses Said"

The Evening Independent (Massillon, Ohio) — Tuesday, March 31, 1931
"All Passengers On Air Express Perish In Fall: Witness Says Explosion Responsible for Plunge of Ship"

Argus-Leader — (Sioux Falls, S.D.) — Tuesday, March 31, 1931
"Rockne, 7 Others Die In Crash In Kansas"
"Rockne Jokes Before Taking Off Recalled"
"Rockne On Journey For Studebaker Co."
"One of Plane's Dead Persuaded By Coach"

The Coshocton Tribune (Coshocton, Ohio) — Tuesday, March 31, 1931
"Knute Rockne Killed In Crash"

The Daily Times (Davenport, Iowa) — Wednesday, April 1, 1931
"Hoover Leads Nation in Mourning Rockne"
"Fighting Spirit of Notre Dame is Crushed by Death"
"Funeral May Be Delayed Until April 8"

The Daily Times (Davenport, Iowa) — Thursday, April 2, 1931
"Weather And Human Element Blamed by Fokker For Crash"

Chicago Daily Tribune — Wednesday, April 1, 1931
"Thousands Will Pay Tribute to Football Chief"
"Defense Ends Testimony for Leo Brothers"

References & Credits

The Indianapolis News — Wednesday, April 1, 1931
"Thousands Mourn Passing of Rockne As Tributes Come From All Parts Of World"
"Coaches, Players Pay Tribute To Rockne As Coaching Genius"
"Rockne's Death Reveals His Many — Sided Career"

New York Daily News — Wednesday, April 1, 1931
"Knute Rockne And 7 Others Killed As Plane Crashes"
"Rockne Wire Gets To Wife After Crash"
"Tragedy Dazes All Notre Dame And South Bend"

The Boston Globe — Wednesday, April 1, 1931
"Mrs. Rockne On Her Way Home"
"Rockne's Sons Fight Against Their Grief"
"Leo Leary Tells About His Friend Rockne: Describes His Hold On Players, His Storytelling, And His Use of Psychology"
"Among The First To Identify Rockne"
"State Ends Lingle Case"
"Rockne Became Catholic in 1925"
"Rockne Had Said Death Might As Well Strike In Plane As Elsewhere"
"Refused at First to Believe Knute Had Been Killed"
"'Pop' Warner and 'Navy Bill' Ingram Told of Tragedy Upon Leaving Plane"
"Joked About Landings On Eve of Tragedy"

The Tampa Times (Tampa, Florida) — Wednesday, April 1, 1931
"Knute Rockne Death Crash Investigated: Coroner Would Learn Cause of Wreck of Air Liner"

Great Falls Tribune (Great Falls, Montana) — Thursday, April 2, 1931
"Cause of Tragic Airplane Crash Remains Mystery: Nearly Score of Witnesses Are Quizzed"

The Brownsville Herald (Brownsville, Texas) — Thursday, April 2, 1931
"Mystery today surrounded the disappearance of $55,000 which H.J. Christen, Chicago businessman, withdrew from his bank shortly before starting on the airplane journey..."

The Times (Munster, Indiana) — Friday, April 3, 1931
"Pay Respect To Rockne"

The Indianapolis Star — April 5, 1931
"Pilot Fry Buried"
"Widow Aided Through Crowd"

Kingsport Times (Kingsport, Tennessee) — Sunday, April 5, 1931
"Rockne Buried Among Branches of Old Council Oak"
"Rockne Eulogized"

Tallahassee Democrat (Tallahassee, Florida) — Sunday, Aprl 5, 1931
"Man of People"

Santa Ana Register (Santa Ana, California) — Friday, Jan. 6, 1933
"Claim Rockne Air Crash Due To Gangster's Bomb"

Washington Times (Washington D.C.) — Friday, Jan. 6, 1933
"Rockne Died Gangsters' Victim"

The Chillicothe Constitution-Tribune (Chillicothe, Missouri) — Friday, Jan. 6, 1933
"Claim A Bomb Caused Crash; Killed Rockne"

News-Record (Neenah, Wisconsin) — Friday, Jan. 6, 1933
"Rockne Plane Crash Due To Bomb, Claim"

Detroit Evening Times — Saturday, Jan. 7, 1933
"Bomb Killed Rockne, Put In Plane By Gang"
"Plot Bared by Secret Service: Timed Blast

Intended For Witness To Killing Whose Ticket Noted Coach Used"

The Kansas City Times — March 28, 1968
"Recalls Day Knute Rockne Died in Crash"

Journal American Aviation Historical Society
Fall/Winter 1983
"The Crash of the TWA Fokker F-10A" — by Mauno Salo

Chicago Tribune — Sunday, Sept. 18, 1994
"Aviation History on 2 Planes"

The Spirit of Notre Dame
Dorothy V. Corson
"Father Reynolds Life Story and His Friendship with Rockne"
Jim Managan

"Capone: The Life and World of Al Capone"
John Kobler
G.P. Putnam's Sons
1971

Tom and Kate Hickey Family History
"Rockne's Last Night in South Bend"
Tomandkatehickeyfamilyhistory.blogspot.com

The People v. Brothers 180 N.E. 442
Illinois Supreme Court Justice Norman L. Jones
Illinois Supreme Court — Feb. 19, 1932

My Al Capone Museum
"Jake Lingle"
myalcaponemuseum.com

American Hauntings
"Who Killed Jake Lingle"
americanhauntingsink.com

"Made In Hollywood"
James Bacon
1977

Father John Reynolds taped interview —

January 1986
By Ron Karten for Catholic Sentinel (Portland, Oregon)
Interview conducted at Our Lady of Guadalupe Abbey in Lafayette, Oregon,

Catholic Sentinel (Portland, Oregon) — Feb. 7, 1986
"Famed Trappist Dies at 91"
Ron Karten

"Who Killed Jake Lingle?"
American Hauntings — americanhauntingsink. com

Official Crash Investigation Report
Aeronautics Branch of the U.S. Department of Commerce
Filed: April 15, 1931

The Catholic Key Online
"Knute Rockne, Still Remembered After All These Years"
by Marty Denzer

Shake Down The Thunder: The Creation of Notre Dame Football
Murray Sperber
2002

"The One-Way Ride"
Walter Noble Burns
Doubleday, Doran & Company
1931

"Chicago Surrenders"
Edward Dean Sullivan
The Vanguard Press, New York
1930

Scarface Al and the Crime Crusaders: Chicago's Private War Against Capone
Dennis E. Hoffman
1993

"Salesman From The Sidelines — Being The Business Career of Knute K. Rockne"

McCready Huston
Ray Long & Richard Smith Inc.
1932

Goals — The Life of Knute Rockne
Hubert William Hurt
Murray Book Corporation, New York
1931

Knute Rockne: Football's Finest Fugitive
Coronet
November 1951

Knute Rockne Was Notre Dame's Master Motivator
Bob Carter
Sports Century Biography, Special to ESPN

The Game That Put The NFL's Reputation On The Line
Jan. 31, 1930
From: Smithsonian.com

Was Knute Rockne Killed By The Mob? Tracing The Origins Of One Of The Stranger Urban Legends In Sports
Deadspin
Jan. 7, 2013

Rockne of Notre Dame: The Making of a Football Legend
Ray Robinson
1999

UNCENSORED! TRUTH ABOUT ROCKNE'S STRANGE DEATH... Not a Broken Propeller, Not Ice on the Wing... At Last — Inside Story of the Fatal Crash
Graphics Arts, Corporation, Minneapolis, Minn.
May 1931

Aviation
May 1931

Tarpa Topics — TWA Active Retired Pilots Association
March 1998

Time
"On Rockne's Anniversary"
April 10, 1933

Kansas Climate Collection
"In March 1931"
Jan. 4, 2008

Topeka Capital-Journal — April 8, 2004
"Other fatal plane crash often forgotten"

Prairy Erth: A Day Map
"Regarding Fokker Niner-Niner-Easy"
William Least Heat-Moon
1991

Air & Space — Dec. 1991-Jan. 1992
"The Crash That Killed Knute Rockne"
Dominick A. Pisano

FBI Records — The Vault
"1933 Crash of United Airlines Trip 23 Boeing 247 NC13304"

The Vintage Airplane — January 1989
"The Forgotten Rockne Crash"
Lt. Col. Boardman C. Reed

Flying The Line
"The First Half Century of Airline Pilots Association"
George E. Hopkins

UND.com
"The Coach Maker"
Dr. Bernie Kish
Nov. 12, 2000

Wikipedia.com
Gus Dorais

York Daily Record — Sept. 17, 1975
"Gus Dorais To Be Honored"

Pro Football Archives
"Stan Cofall"

Encyclopedia of Cleveland History
"Stan Cofall"

Wikipedia.com
"Charlie Bachman"

National Football Foundation #Football Matters
"Charlie Bachman"

CatholicAthletics.com
"Former Coach Dutch Bergman Distinguished Himself In All Walks of Life"
Chris McManes
Dec. 14, 2002

The New York Times — Aug. 9, 1972
"Dutch Bergman, Ex-Coach of Washington Redskins"

St. Mary's College Magazine — March 11, 1940
"The Firing of Slip Madigan"

The Incredible Slip Madigan and the Flamboyant Coach Who Modernized Football
Dave Newhouse

Wikipedia.com
"Heartley (Hunk) Anderson"

The New York Times — May 26, 1978
"Hunk Anderson, Nicest Tough Guy"

Wikipedia.com
"Eddie Anderson"

The New York Times — April 29, 1974
"Dr. Eddie Anderson, Ex-Football Coach"

Life & Times — Aug. 2, 2009
"Dr. Edward N. Anderson"

Bull Dawg Illustrated
"Harry Mehre: From Notre Dame to Georgia"

Bull Dawg Illustrated — Nov. 15, 2017
"Watch Got Loran? Former Coach Harry Mehre"
Loran Smith

Harry Mehre: The Legend
Mark Maxwell

Athens Banner-Herald — Dec. 22, 2017
"Chronicling A Legend: UGA Sports Historian Publishes Book on Harry Mehre"
Red Denty

Wikipedia.com
"Tom Lieb"

Peoplepill.com
"Tom Lieb"

The New York Times — March 20, 1977
"Buck Shaw Dies at 77"

National Football Foundation #Football Matters
"Buck Shaw"

Wikipedia.com
"Frank Thomas"

Chicago Tribune — April 25, 2019
"Frank Thomas, Played for Knute Rockne and Coached Bear Bryant. Soon He'll Join the Indiana Football Hall of Fame"

Rollbamaroll.com — Nov. 18, 2009
"A Look Back at Frank Thomas"

The Desert Sun — Jan. 26, 1965
"Harry Stuhldreher, One of 4 Horsemen Dies"

The Hartford Blues Part I
Jim Hogrogian
1982

Goldenrankings.com
"A Season In Time: Notre Dame 1924"

Revolvy.com
"Harry Stuhldreher"

The New York Times — Jan. 16, 1986
"Jim Crowley, Final Member of Four Horsemen
Is Dead"

Los Angeles Times — Jan. 16, 1986
"Jim Crowley Dies at 83; He was the Last of the
Four Horsemen"

The New York Times — July 1, 1973
"Elmer Layden Dead"

Und.com
"Elmer Layden"

The New York Times — July 30, 1979
"Don Miller Dies at 77"

**Dave's History Corner blogspot — Nov. 11,
2015**
"Don Miller"

The New York Times — June 14 1940
"Noble Kizer Dies: A Football Leader"

Revolvy.com
"Noble Kizer"

The New York Times — April 15, 1977
"Chuck Collins, 73, Football End, Dead"

Steelersdepot.com — April 24, 2018
"Joe Bach Tries To Get Steelers Into Overdrive"
David Orochena

Wikipedia.com
"Joe Bach"

Dspace.ychistory
"South Carolina's Enright Is Dead"

Wikipedia.com
"Rex Enright"

The New York Times — June 22, 1973
"Frank Leahy, Notre Dame Coach Dead"

Ludington Daily News — Feb. 1, 1954
"Frank Leahy Resigns as Notre Dame Coach"

Chicago Tribune — March 22, 1922
"Ex-Notre Dame QB Carideo Dies"

National Italian American Sports Hall of Fame
Frank Carideo

SECTION III

The Chicago Sunday Tribune — Nov. 30, 1913
"Eckersall Finds Great Material For All
Western"

Los Angeles Evening Herald
"Irish Beat Trojans, 7-6." — **Nov. 26, 1927**
"Notre Dame Mentor In Tiff With Warner, " by
Davis J. Walsh — **Sept. 3, 1930**

The Denver Evening News — Sept. 24, 1928
"Rockne Prepares Irish For Traveling Schedule"

The Seattle Daily Times — Feb. 4, 1929
"Abolish Athletic Scholarships Plea Of Knute
Rockne, " by C. William Duncan

The Philadelphia Record — Nov. 8, 1929
"Knute Rockne Notre Dame Coach"

Collier's Magazine
The Halfback of Notre Dame" by John B.
Kennedy — **Nov. 19, 1927**
"Go In And Win" — **October 1928**
"From Norway To Notre Dame" — **Oct. 18,**

1930
"Beginning At Right End" — **Oct. 25, 1930**
"Fundamental Football" — **Oct. 27, 1930**
"The Four Horsemen" — **Nov. 1, 1930**

"Coaching Men" — **Nov. 15, 1930**
"Gipp The Great" — **Nov. 22, 1930**
"To Shift Or Not To Shift" — **Nov. 29, 1930**
"What Thrills A Coach" — **Dec. 6, 1930**

The Athletic Journal
"The Forward Pass" — **October 1923**
issue — **November 1924**
"The Shift Attack vs. The Set Formation" —
November 1925
"The Lateral Pass: Its Advantages Offensively"
— **September 1927**
"Pedagogy of "Football" — **Feb. 6, 1929**
"The Last Word! Knute Rockne On Football" —
February 1929

American Legion
"In His Own Words — If I Were A High School
Football Coach" — **Oct. 20, 1929**
"The New Football Is The Old Football" — **Oct.
27, 1929**
"Go In And Win" — **Oct. 28, 1929**
"The Hardest Coaching Job" — **Oct. 29, 1929**
"Spirit of Cooperation" — **November 1930**
"Rockne Story — Psychology" — **May 1932**
"Think Fast" — **May 1932**

Good Housekeeping
"Knute Rockne Jr." by Bonnie Rockne —
October 1932

American Boy

"What The New 1925 Football Rules Means"
— **Sept. 25, 1925**
"Football Pointers" — **September 1925**

Boy's Life
"Fundamental Football" — **October 1927**
"Before Shift — After Shift Diagram" —
October 1928
"Where Will You Play" — **October 1929**
"What Football Can Do For Me" — **October
1930**
"Football Offense — The Open Road For Boys"
— **October 1930**
"Coach of Coaches" — **October 1940**

Life
"Rockne At Luncheon Speech" by John Kieran
— **October 1928**
"The Comeback of Notre Dame" — **October
12, 1928**

Magazine World
"Football — A Man's Game" — **January 1930**

The Literary Digest
"What Of Football Without Knute Rockne?" —
April 11, 1931

The American Magazine
"Rockne Made Football What It Is Today" —
November 1929

A Football Classic
"The Life Of Knute Rockne" — **1931**

The Halfback of Notre Dame
John B. Kennedy

REFERENCES & CREDITS

Rockne of Ages
PHOTO INDEX

Sources: Notre Dame Archives; Getty Images; Chicago History Museum; University of Minnesota Library; Yale University Library; University of Nebraska Library; RMY; John Bybee; Jim Managan; The Rev. Richard Layton C.S.C.; Augie's Locker Room; John Davenport.

2, 3 — Notre Dame Marching Band performing during halftime of a game at Soldier Field, Chicago. Bagby Photo Studio, South Bend, Indiana; circa 1930.

AUTHOR'S INTRODUCTION

8 — (L to R) Lou Gehrig, Knute Rockne, Babe Ruth. Bettmann Collection/Getty Images, November 16, 1927.

PROLOGUE

12 — Knute Rockne spent most of the 1929 season being wheeled in and out of Notre Dame football games on a stretcher. International Newsreel, November 21, 1929

14 — The automobile Rockne coached practices from while sitting in the backseat shouting instructions over an "electric voice" public address system. Henry Miller News Picture Service, 1929.

17 — Knute Rockne golfing with Enoch Bagshaw in Seattle, Washington. International Newsreel, March 27, 1929.

SECTION 1 — THE HIT

20, 21 — The body of Alfred (Jack) Lingle lies in the passenger subway of the Illinois Central Railroad where he was murdered. NY Daily News Archive/Getty Images; June 9, 1930.

CHAPTER 1 — A TAIL ON JAKE LINGLE

22 — The Sherman Hotel near Randolph Street in downtown Chicago where Jake Lingle bought a cigar and a racing form on his way to the Randolph Street train station. Library of Congress/ Detroit Publishing Co.; circa 1930.

25 — Amos Alonzo Stagg and Knute Rockne watch the Ninth Annual Collegiate Track and Field Championships at Stagg Field at the University of Chicago. Wide World Photo, June 9, 1930.

CHAPTER 2 — PATH OF A MOB REPORTER

26 — Alfred "Jake" Lingle. City of Chicago, Cook County, circa 1920s.

28 — Law enforcement agent Edwin C. Arthur stands in the center of a collection of containers of moonshine taken during a South Side raid in Chicago, Illinois. Chicago Sun-Times/Chicago Daily News collection/Chicago History Museum/Getty Images; 1922.

29 — Chicago Police Chief William Russell. Chicago Sun-Times/Chicago Daily News collection/Chicago History Museum; circa 1929.

575

30 — Diamond studded belt buckle like the one given to close friends by Al Capone. Chicago Sun Times/Chicago Daily News Collection/Chicago History Museum; 1931.
31 — George "Bugs" Moran; circa 1920s. Davenport Collection.

CHAPTER 3 — KILLERS IN A SUBWAY
34 — The crowd gathered outside the Randolph Street train station following the murder of Jake Lingle. Chicago Sun-Times/Chicago Daily News Collection/Chicago History Museum, June 9, 1930.

CHAPTER 4 — FATHER REYNOLDS
38 — The Rev. Edward Reynolds, C.S.C. with nuns in Cherry Hill, New Jersey. Courtesy of Jim Managan; circa 1923.
40 — Johnnie Reynolds, center, with cousins from the Reynolds and Cray families in Bellows Falls, Vermont. Courtesy of Jim Managan; circa 1910.
41 — Father John Reynolds with his family in Bellows Falls, Vermont: (L to R) Mary Johns, Tommy Brennan, Mrs. Brennan, Mrs. Jay Cray, Father Reynolds and his Aunt Kate Reynolds. (Standing in front) Buddy, Marcella and Rosemary. Courtesy of Jim Managan; circa 1928.

CHAPTER 5 — AS GOD'S WITNESS
44 — Father John Reynolds minutes before he took the stand as the state's star witness in the murder trial of Leo Brothers. Emme & Cannon photo; March 27, 1931.
46, 47 — Pallbearers carry Jake Lingle's casket from the church past a color guard of Naval Reserves and American Legion members. N.E.A.; June 17, 1930.
50 — Al Capone going for a swim at his Palm Island home in Miami Beach. Photographer unknown/Public Domain; 1929.
53 — Robert Rutherford McCormick, publisher of the Chicago Tribune. Chicago History Museum; circa 1950.

CHAPTER 6 — MOB STEPS
54 — Jack "Jake" Zuta at the police station being interrogated by Chicago police. Chicago Police Department/Getty Images; circa June 1930.
56 — Bugs Moran-ally Joe Aiello and his gang pictured in front of a wall in a jail in Chicago. (L to R) Mika Bizarro, Joe Aiello, Joe Bubine, Nick Manzello and Joe Russio. Chicago Sun-Times/Chicago Daily News collection/Chicago History Museum; June 1930.
60 — Peter von Frantzius (front left), known as "The Armorer," surrounded in a Chicago Police Department

court on a warrant charging him with being an accessory before the fact in the murder of Jake Lingle. Mrs. von Frantzius stands front and center with her hand raised. Chicago History Museum; August 25, 1930.
61 — Frank Foster (rear seat right) covers his face from a photographer while being transported by police from Santa Fe, New Mexico back to Chicago to face preliminary charges in the murder of Jake Lingle. International Chicago; July 19, 1930.
62 — (L to R) Frank Foster; attorney Emmett Byrne; attorney Harold L. Levy, International Chicago; November 29, 1930.
63 — Miss Rose Huebsch, federal stenographer, supplied the ruse which led to the capture of Leo Brothers. ACME; January 8, 1931.
64 — Cook County District Attorney John Swanson (left), Patrick Roche (standing), and Chicago Tribune attorney Charles F. Rathbun (right) with Leo Brothers during a pretrial hearing at Cook County Courthouse. N.E.A.; January 13, 1931.
65 — Leo V. Brothers following his capture in Chicago. ACME, Chicago Bureau; January 8, 1931.
66 — Leo Brothers in court with arresting officer, Deputy Sheriff J. Hrody. CME Photo Chicago Bureau; January 1, 1931.

CHAPTER 7 — IN THE EYES OF CAPONE
70 — Alphonse "Al" Capone. Chicago Tribune; February 26, 1931.
72 — Martha's Midway Tavern & Dance Hall, Mishawaka, Indiana. Jeff Harrell, February 2020.
73 — Al Capone leaving court in Chicago during his 1931 trial for tax evasion. Chicago Sun-Times/Chicago Daily News collection/Chicago History Museum; November 16, 1931.
74 — Frank Foster Gang: (L to R) Marvin Hart, George Davis, Frank Foster, Frank Fisher, Herman Walters. International Newsreel; July 1, 1930.

CHAPTER 8 — A TICKET
76 — Knute Rockne plays solitaire soon after arriving back in Chicago following Notre Dame's 27-0 thrashing of Southern California. International Newsreel; December 15, 1930.
80 — Frank Carideo kicks a point-after-touchdown in Notre Dame's 27-0 win over Southern California. N.E.A.; December 13, 1930

References & Credits

SECTION 2 -- THE CRASH

CHAPTER 9 – DELAYED FLIGHT
82, 83 — Locals sift through the wreckage of the Fokker F-10 that crashed and killed Knute Rockne and seven others. N.E.A.; March 31, 1931
84 — The log cabin chapel on Notre Dame's campus, where Knute Rockne was baptized when he converted to Catholicism in 1925. Wide World Photo; February 26, 1936.
86 — Knute Rockne and his mother, Martha Rockne. International Chicago; circa March 1931
88, 89 — The severed wing, the only part of the Transcontinental & Westerner airliner that fell to the ground intact. N.E.A.; March 31, 1931.
92 — Investigators search through wreckage of a large chunk of the rear tail. N.E.A.; March 31, 1931.
93 — Front page of The Pittsburgh Press; March 31, 1931. Courtesy of Augie's Locker Room, South Bend, Indiana.
94 — (TOP) Front page of the Pittsburgh Sun-Telegraph; March 31, 1931. (BOTTOM) Front page of the Red Bluff (California) Daily News; March 31, 1931 Courtesy of Augie's Locker Room, South Bend, Indiana

CHAPTER 10 — IDENTIFICATIONS
96 — Knute Rockne in his office with his secretary, Ruth Faulkner. Bagby Photo Studio, South Bend; circa 1920s.
98 — Rockne's last telegraph to his wife. Western Union Image; March 31, 1931
99 — Knute and Bonnie Rockne. International Newsreel; January 1930
100 — Rockne's empty desk in the Athletic Department of Notre Dame. International Chicago; April 3, 1931.

CHAPTER 11 — GUILTY
102 — Leo Brothers with his mother, Mrs. Rose Jessen of St. Louis. ACME Photo Chicago Bureau; January 12, 1931.
104 — Otto Swoboda, witness in the trial of Leo Brothers. ACME Photo, March 26, 1931.
105 — (LEFT) Assistant State Attorney C. Wayland Brooks confers with defense attorney Louis Piquett prior to the opening of the trial of Leo Brothers. Associated Press; March 16, 1931. (RIGHT: Samuel Lederer, whose hobby as a criminal investigator landed him on the team of the Lingle murder investigation. ACME, January 8, 1931.

CHAPTER 12 — FUNERAL FOR AN ICON
108 — People gathered for Rockne's funeral outside Notre Dame's Basilica of the Sacred Heart. George Rinhart/Corbis/Getty Images; April 4, 1931.
110 — Father Michael Mulcaire, vice president of Notre Dame, stands between Knute Rockne's sons, Bill (left) and Knute Jr. (right) at the train station in Kansas City before Rockne's casket was transported back to South Bend. Dr. Michael Nigro (white hat) comforts Bill with a hand on the teen's shoulder. Heartley "Hunk" Anderson stands on the far right. ACME Photo; April 1, 1931.
111 — New York Mayor Jimmy Walker outside Rockne's South Bend home after paying final respects. ACME Photo, April 3, 1931.
112 — Rockne's daughter, Mary Jeanne, and youngest son Jackie, in a car traveling from Chicago to South Bend for their father's funeral. International Chicago, April 2, 1931
113 — Rockne's former players carry his casket from the hearse into his house on Wayne Street in South Bend. International Newsreel, April 3, 1931
114, 115 — Mourners gather graveside at Highland Cemetery in South Bend before Rockne's casket was lowered into the ground. George Rinhart/Corbis/Getty Images; April 4, 1931

CHAPTER 13 — PAYBACK
116 — Front page of the Detroit Evening Times; January 7, 1933. Courtesy of Augie's Locker Room, South Bend, Indiana.
119 — Ted Newberry police mugshot. Chicago Police Department; circa 1930.

CHAPTER 14 — MADE IN HOLLYWOOD
122 — Kitty Gorman; circa 1931. Davenport Collection
124 — James Bacon. Profile photo from "Made in Hollywood," 1977

SECTION 3--ROCKNE ON ROCKNE

126,127-- Knute Rockne at practice. Notre Dame Athletics; circa 1920s

THE BOY

CHAPTER 15 — STRAIGHT OUT OF NORWAY
130 — European immigrants on the deck of the SS Patricia arriving into New York Harbor on December 10, 1906. Documentary Photo Aids/Strangers at the Door by Ann

Indiana; circa 1920s.
190 — Players circle Rockne on the practice field. Bagby Photo Studio, South Bend, Indiana; circa 1920s.
192 — Knute Rockne addressing his players. Bettmann Collection/Getty Images; September 16, 1930.

CHAPTER 26 — PEDAGOGY
194 — Rockne explaining his point to an unidentified player at practice. Bagby Photo Studio, South Bend, Indiana; circa 1920s
196 — Edgar "Rip "Miller, one of Rocke's "Seven Mules" blocking for The Four Horsemen. Bagby Photo Studio, South Bend; circa 1922-1924
199 — Knute Rockne at practice at Cartier Field. H.C.Elmore, South Bend News Times; circa 1920s

CHAPTER 27 — PSYCHOLOGY
202 — Knute Rockne at practice. Bagby Photo Studio, South Bend; circa 1920s.
206-207 — Captain Knute Rockne leads the Irish football team onto Cartier Field to play against Ohio Northern on October 4, 1913. Notre Dame Athletics.
209 — Johnny Mohardt, circa 1919. PNDP Dome Yearbook 1920, page 214.
212, 213 — Coach Rockne surrounded by players. Bagby Photo Studio, South Bend, Indiana; circa 1920s.
214 — Students waiting in front of Hullie&Mike's in downtown South Bend. Bagby Photo Studio, South Bend, Indiana; circa 1917.
215 — Jack Cannon, circa 1929. Chicago Sun-Times/Chicago Daily News collection/Chicago History Museum.

CHAPTER 28 — DIFFERENT STROKES
218 — Pop Warner, coach of Temple University, during practice in Philadelphia. ACME News Pictures, Inc.; September 4, 1934.
220 — Princeton head coach Bill Roper instructing his men at practice. ACME News Pictures, Inc.; 1929.
221 — Dr. Clarence Spears, head coach University of Wisconsin. ACME News Pictures, Inc.; September 26, 1932.

CHAPTER 29 — THE NOTRE DAME SYSTEM
222 — Jesse Harper on his ranch near Ashland, Kansas. Associated Press Photo, April 25, 1931

CHAPTER 30 — SYSTEMS AND TACTICS
226-- Knute Rockne with Pathe Sound News and RCA

Photophone taping for his football practice films. Bagby Photo Studio, South Bend, Indiana; circa 1920s.
228 — Head Coach Harry Stuhldreher's Villanova football squad practicing an adaptation of the famous Notre Dame Shift. ACME News Pictures, March 28, 1928.

CHAPTER 31 — THE NOTRE DAME SHIFT
230 — Knute Rockne at the All-America Football Dinner in New York City flanked by two young artists representing two divergent views of the shift. Columbia Network promo photo; 1929.

CHAPTER 32 — THE OFFENSE
233 — Shift Diagram. Coaching: The Way of the Winner by Knute Rockne, 1928.
234 — A Notre Dame receiver catches a pass in scrimmage. Bagby Photo Studio, South Bend, Indiana; circa 1920s.
236 — Knute Rockne instructs a player. AP News Features Photo; circa 1920s.
238, 239 — Notre Dame football's first team practice under Heartly "Hunk" Anderson after Rockne's death. ACME News Pictures; September 17, 1931.
243 — Quarterback Gus Dorais. Notre Dame Athletics; 1913.
244 — Gus Dorais kicking a football. Notre Dame Athletics; 1913.
247 — A scrimmage game at Cartier Field. Bagby Photo Studio, South Bend, Indiana; circa 1920s.
248 — Football players in a huddle on Cartier Field; includes players Noble Kizer and Gus Strange. Notre Dame Sports Information; circa 1922-1924
250 — Posed action practice scene, center's view as he snaps the ball. Bagby Photo Studio, South Bend, Indiana; circa 1920s.
252 — Tom Yarr, center, Notre Dame. Wide World Photos; 1930.
255 — Joe Savoldi, circa 1928-1930. Bagby Photo Studio, South Bend, Indiana.
256 — Paul Castner, circa 1920-1922. Notre Dame Sports Information.
258 — Running back hitting the hole during practice. Bagby Photo Studio, South Bend, Indiana; circa 1930.
260 — Johnny Weibel, circa 1922-1924. Bagby Photo Studio, South Bend, Indiana.
262, 263 — Kickers during a Notre Dame practice. Bagby Photo Studio, South Bend; circa 1930.

References & Credits

354 — (L to R) Christy Walsh, Knute Rockne, Babe Ruth and Pop Warner visit at Yankee Stadium before Rockne and Warner sailed to Europe to attend the Olympic Games at Amsterdam, Holland. International Newsreel; July 19, 1928.
358 — Knute Rockne, February 27, 1928. Milwaukee Journal/Davenport Collection

CHAPTER 44 — NON-SCHOLARSHIP
362 — Notre Dame's Marchmont Schwartz tackles a Northwestern opponent, November 22, 1930. George Rinhart/Corbis/Getty Images; November 22, 1930.
367 — Stanford head coach Pop Warner with assistant Claude E. Thornhill watching Stanford vs. Minnesota at the University of Minnesota, October 14, 1930. University of Minnesota Library.

THE LEGENDS

374, 375 — Four Horsemen on horses: (L to R) Don Miller, Harry Stuhldreher, Jim Crowley and Elmer Layden. Bagby Photo Company; South Bend, Indiana; 1924.

CHAPTER 45 — THE FOUR HORSEMEN
376 — Grantland Rice, 1951. NBC Television Audience Promotion photo.
379 — Harry Stuhldreher, circa 1922-1924. Bagby Photo Company, South Bend, Indiana.
381 — James (Jim) Crowley, 1924. Bagby Photo Company, South Bend, Indiana
382 — Knute Rockne at practice with The Four Horsemen. Bagby Photo Company, South Bend, Indiana; circa 1924.
384 — Elmer Layden, circa 1922-1924. Bagby Photo Company, South Bend, Indiana.
386 — Don Miller, 1922. Notre Dame Athletics.
387 — (L to R) Don Miller, Harry Stuhldreher, Jim Crowley, Elmer Layden, at practice. Bagby Photo Company, South Bend, Indiana; circa 1922-1924.

CHAPTER 46 — FRANK CARIDEO
388 — Frank Carideo scores a touchdown in a football game vs. Penn State at Franklin Field in Philadelphia; November 3, 1928. Notre Dame Sports Information.
391 — The home where Knute Rockne lived at 1006 St. Vincent Street in South Bend. Cathy Davenport, 2019.
392-393 — Notre Dame backfield 1928: (L to R) Jack Chevigny, right halfback; Edmond Collins, fullback; John Neimiec, left halfback; and Frank Carideo, quarterback.

International Newsreel; 1928

CHAPTER 47 — GEORGE GIPP
394 — George Gipp, circa 1917-1920. Notre Dame Athletics.
397 — George Gipp preparing to pass to Eddie Anders, Notre Dame vs Nebraska, October 16, 1920. Bagby Photo Company, South Bend, Indiana.

CHAPTER 48 — PRIMED FOR GREATNESS
398 — George Gipp, circa 1918-1920. Bagby Photo Company, South Bend, Indiana.
400 — 1918 Notre Dame football team photo. Notre Dame Athletics; 1918.
401 — 1920 Notre Dame football team photo; Gipp is far left middle row, opposite Rockne on far right. Notre Dame Athletics; 1920.

CHAPTER 49 — TESTING THE BOUNDARIES
404 — George Gipp and Louis "Red "Salmon, the first All-American in Notre Dame history, on the sidelines at Cartier Field before Notre Dame vs. Purdue, November 6, 1920. Notre Dame Sports Information.

CHAPTER 50 — ULTIMATE GAMESMAN
408 — (L to R) John Mohardt, Chet Wynne, George Gipp. John Farr Collection; 1920.
411 — Chicago Tribune reporting George Gipp's death. Chicago Tribune, December 15, 1920.
413 — Death Takes Gipp After Hard Fight clip. Pittsburgh Post-Gazzette, December 15, 1920.

CHAPTER 51 — WIN ONE FOR THE GIPPER
414 — Jack Chevigny, circa 1926-1928. Associated Press.
416 — Jack Chevigny scores a touchdown in the third quarter to tie the game against Army at Yankee Stadium, New York, New York, November 10, 1928. Underwood Archives/Getty Images.
417 — Johnny "One Play "O'Brien, circa 1928-1930. Bagby Photo Co., South Bend, Indiana.
418 — Willie Heston, University of Michigan running back, 1902. ACME/Bentley Historical Library/Public Domain.
422 — Harold "Red "Grange, December 8, 1925. U.S. Library of Congress; December 8, 1925.

CHAPTER 53 — PARISIEN MELODRAMA
424 — Art Parisien, circa 1926. Bagby Photo Studio, South Bend, Indiana.

September 22, 1954.

CHAPTER 66 — GOLD AND BLUE PRINTS —
492-- Knute Rockne holding an Irish Terrier dog. Notre Dame Athletics; 1924.

CHAPTER 67 — THE GREAT MOTIVATOR
496 — Knute Rockne, circa 1930. Davenport Collection; circa 1930.

CHAPTER 68 — DISCIPLES
502, 503-- Rockne-Meanwell Coaching School participants in the Cartier Field stands. Bagby Photo Studio, South Bend, Indiana; 1926.

BIOGRAPHIES

506 — Gus Dorais with Bill "Bullet "Dudley of the Detroit Lions. Detroit Lions Press Photo; 1947.
508 — Stan Cofall, 1916 Notre Dame football team photo. Notre Dame Athletics; 1916.
509 — Charles Bachman, head coach, University of Florida. N.E.A.; December 5, 1929.
510—(TOP) Dutch Bergman, 1919 team photo. Notre Dame Athletics; 1919.
511 — Slip Madigan, circa 1935. Public Domain.
512 — Heartley "Hunk" Anderson, circa 1920s. Bagby Photo Company, South Bend, Indiana.
513 — Dr. Eddie Anderson, December 4, 1961. RSJ.
515 — Harry Mehre. University of Mississippi; May 23, 1967.
517 — Tom Lieb. Loyola University of Los Angeles; circa 1936.
518 — Buck Shaw. Associated Press, October 26, 1938.
520 — Frank Thomas. ACME; December 14, 1936.
522 — Don Miller. Associated Press; April 7, 1952.
523 — Harry Stuhldreher demonstrates a tackle during practice as head coach at Villanova. Villanova University; 1925.
524 — Jim Crowley. N.E.A., November 17, 1932.
526 — Elmer Layden. ACME; January 31, 1934.
527 — Noble Kizer, head coach, Purdue University. J.G. Allen, West Layette, Indiana/N.E.A.; December 6, 1932.
529 — Joe Bach, AP Wire Photo, 1950.
530 — Rex Enright. "Garnet & Black," University of South Carolina yearbook; 1939.
531 — Frank Leahy, 1949. The 1949 Dome, Notre Dame yearbook, p.215.

533 — Frank Carideo. Chicago Sun-Times/Chicago Daily News collection/Chicago History Museum; 1929.

CHAPTER 69 — CHANGING FLIGHT
534 — Knute Rockne standing by a Lockheed Vega monoplane in a hangar, Chicago, Illinois. Chicago Sun-Times/Chicago Daily News collection/Chicago History Museum/Getty Images); 1925.

CHAPTER 70 — IN MEMORIAL
538 — The U.S.S. Knute Rockne at the Kaiser Shipyards in San Francisco. Associated Press; May 6, 1943.
540 — Jerry McKenna and his wife, Gail, at the Rockne Memorial in Voss, Norway. Photo courtesy of Jerry McKenna
541 — Crowds flock to the premiere of "Knute Rockne, All-American" in downtown South Bend. Culver Pictures, Inc.; October 3-4, 1940.
542 — Elmer Layden, Notre Dame's Athletic Director, speaks at the opening ceremony for the school's new memorial fieldhouse dedicated to the memory of Knute Rockne. (SEATED L to R) Major John L. Griffith, Big Ten commissioner; Capt. William Wood, Army football coach: Arch Ward, Chicago Tribune sports editor; Chester McGrath, of St. Joseph, Michigan, a Notre Dame football teammate of Rockne. Associated Press Photo; June 3, 1939.
543 — (L) John MacCauley, Jr. and his brother, Mark, view a bronze sculpture of Knute Rockne in the Rockne Memorial. Davenport Collection; April 3, 1956

CHAPTER 71 — THE HOUSE THAT ROCKNE BUILT
544 — The Knute Rockne statue created by artist Jerry McKenna stands at the north gate of Notre Dame Stadium. Photo courtesy of Jerry McKenna
546, 547-- Overview shot of Notre Dame Stadium. Bagby Photo Studio, South Bend, Indiana; circa 1930.
549 — Knute Rockne's funeral prayer card portrait; April 4, 1931

EPILOGUE: THE CHALKBOARD

550, 551 — Heartley Anderson being instructed in play formations on the blackboard by Knute Rockne. International Chicago; circa 1930

584, 585 — Knute Rockne sitting on a bench. Paul Shideler, Indianapolis News/Indianapolis Star Archives; circa 1920s.

www.ingramcontent.com/pod-product-compliance
Lightning Source LLC
Chambersburg PA
CBHW050401110426
42812CB00006BA/1769